Airframe Album
20

The Heinkel He 177

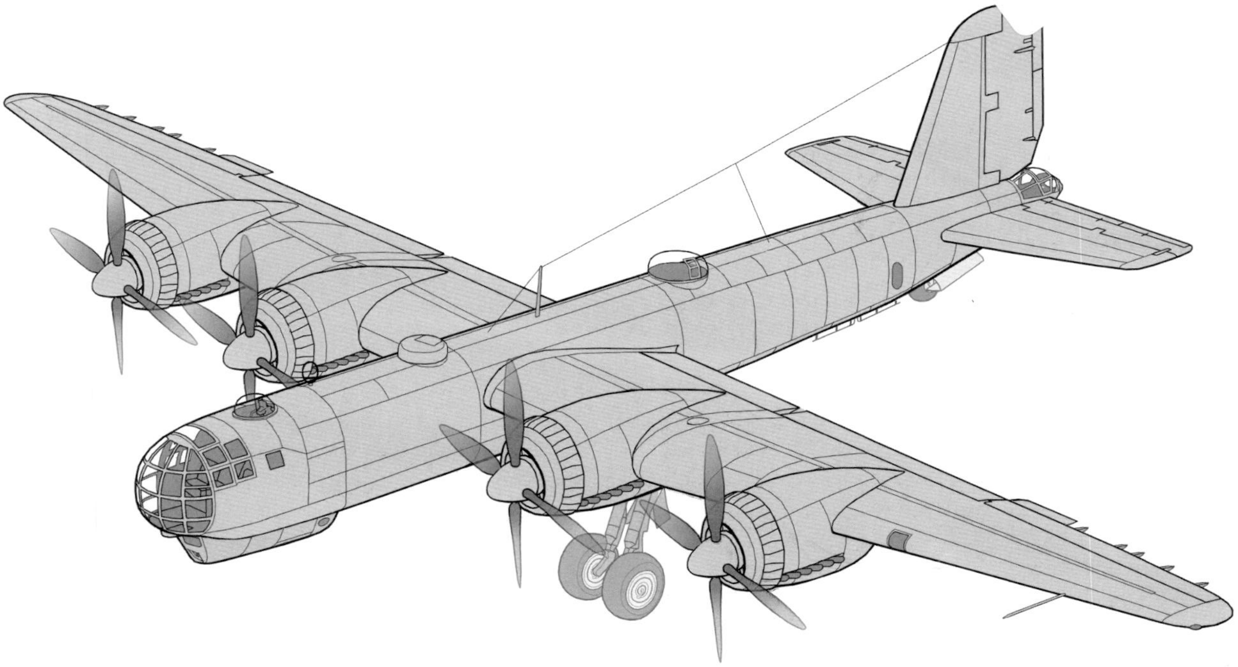

Sections

Airframe Album No.20
The Heinkel He 177 Greif
A Detailed Guide to the Luftwaffe's Troubled Strategic Bomber
by Richard A. Franks

First published in 2024 by Valiant Wings Publishing Ltd
Unit 3, Glenmore Business Park, Stanley Road, Bedford
MK42 0XY
+44 (0)1234 413843
enquiries.vwp@gmail.com
www.valiant-wings.co.uk
valiantwingspublishing

ISBN: 978-1-912932-38-2

Acknowledgements
The author would like to give a word of thanks to Libor Jekl for his excellent model build and Richard J. Caruana, Wojciech Sankowski and Arkadiusz Wróbel for their superb artwork.

Note
There are many different ways of writing aircraft designation, however for consistency throughout this title we have used one system (He 177 V1 and He 177A-1 etc.)

Cover
The cover artwork has been specially commissioned for this title ©Arkadiusz Wróbel 2024.

Please note, whilst we are always happy to hear from readers, we are not in a position to enter into discussion (in person, in writing or via electronic mail) with any individual, nor to undertake or supply research/supporting material relating to this, or any of our other titles. Our apologies for this, but it is inevitable if we are to meet our production schedule each year, and all sources (excluding those from private collections) are listed in the bibliography.

He 177A-5s under construction at Flugzeugwerke Eger, Cheb, Czechoslovakia

The He 177A-02, DL+AQ, in flight

AGO . . . . *Aktien Gesellschaft Otto Flugzeugwerke* GmbH
Aufklärer . . . . Reconnaissance aircraft
Aufklaringsgruppe (AGr) . . . . Reconnaissance Group
BFW . . . . *Bayerische Flugzeugwerke*
BMW . . . . *Bayerische Motorenwerke* GmbH
BK . . . . *Bordkanone* (on-board cannon)
DB . . . . Daimler-Benz
DFS . . . . *Deutsche Forschungssanstalt für Segelflug* (German Research Institute for Sailplanes)
Dipl. Ing. . . . . *Diplom Ingeneur* (Master of Science)
DVS . . . . *Deutsche Versuchsanstalt für Luftfahrt* (German Aviation Experimental Establishment)
EKdo . . . . *Errpobungs-Kommando* (Test detachment)
E-Stelle . . . . *Erprobungsstelle* (Test establishment)
Erprobungsgruppe (ErpG) . . . . *Erprobungsgruppe* (Test/evaluation Group)
ETC . . . . *Elektrische Trägervorrichtung für cylinder bomben* (Electrically operated carriers for cylindrical bombs)
FA . . . . *Fensteueranlage* (Remote Control System)
FDL 131 . . . . *Fernetätige Drehkafette 131* (Remote Control Moving Mount 131)
Feldwebel (Fw.) . . . . Sergeant (Sgt) (RAF)
Fernaufklärungsgruppe . . . . Long-range Reconnaissance Group
F/Off . . . . Flying Officer (RAF)
Flak . . . . *Fliegerabwehrkanone* (anti-aircraft cannon)
Flt Lt . . . . Flight Lieutenant (RAF)
Funkgerät (FuG) . . . . Radio or radar equipment
Generalluftzeugmeister . . . . Director-General of Luftwaffe Equipment
GM-1 . . . . Nitrous Oxide injection system
Geschwader . . . . Squadron
Grp Capt. . . . . Group Capitan (RAF)
Gruppe . . . . Group
Hauptmann (Hptm.) . . . . Flight Lieutenant (RAF) or Captain (USAAF)
Jagdgeschwader (JG) . . . . Fighter Wing
JUMO . . . . *Junkers Motorenbau*
kg. . . . . Kilogram (= 2.20462lb)
km/h . . . . Kilometres per hour (= 0.621mph)
Kampfgeschwader (KG) . . . . Bomber Wing
KW . . . . Kilowatt (= 1.341hp)
Lt. . . . . Litre (= 0.22 Imperial Gallons)
m . . . . Metre (3ft 3 3/8in)
MG . . . . *Machinengewehr* (machine-gun up to 20mm calibre)
MK . . . . *Machinenkanone* (cannon over 20mm calibre)
Nachtjagdgeschwader (NJG) . . Night-fighter Wing
NII VVS . . . . *Nauchno-Issledovatel'skij Institut Voyenno-vozdooshnykh Sily* (Russian Air Force Scientific Test Institute)
Oberfeldwebel (Obfw.) . . . . Flight Sergeant (RAF)
Oberst . . . . Group Captain (RAF), Colonel (USAAF)
Oberstleutnant (Oberstlt.) . . . . Wing Commander (RAF)
OKL . . . . *Oberkommando der Luftwaffe* (Luftwaffe High Command)
PaK . . . . *Panzerabwehrkanone* (anti-tank cannon)
PS . . . . *Pferdestarkes* (Metric Horsepower)
Pz. . . . . *Panzerjägerstaffeln* (Anti-tank Squadron)
RAE . . . . Royal Aircraft Establishment
Rb . . . . *Reihenbildner* aerial reconnaissance camera
Revi (*Reflexvisier*) . . . . Reflector gunsight
RLM . . . . *Reichsluftfahrtministerium* (Reich Air Ministry)
rpg . . . . Rounds per gun
rpm . . . . Revolutions per minute
Rüstsatz . . . . Field conversion pack
SC . . . . *Sprengbombe-Cilindirsch* (Explosive bomb – cylindrical) GP bombs
SD . . . . *Sprengbombe-Dickwandig* (Explosive bomb thick walls) fragmentation bomb
Slachtgruppe (Sch.G) . . . . Close-support (ground-attack) group
Staffel . . . . Equal to Squadron in RAF
Stammkenzeichen . . . . Primary identification (code letters)
TsAGI . . . . *Tsentral'niy Aero-Gidrodinamicheskiy Institut* (Central Aerodynamic and Hydrodynamic Research Institute VVS [Russian Air Force])
Technisches Amt . . . . Technical Department of the RLM
Versuchs or Versuchsmuster . . . . Research or test aircraft (V-series)
Waffenträger . . . . Weapons Carrier
Werknummer (W/Nr.) . . . . Works (construction) number
W/Gr. . . . . *Werfer-Granate* (Rocket-propeller mortar)
Wg Cdr . . . . Wing Commander(RAF)
Zerstörer . . . . Heavy fighter (Destroyer)
Zerstörergeschwader . . . . (ZG) Heavy fighter wing
ZFR . . . . *Zielfernrohr* – Telescopic gunsight

Preface

The story behind the Heinkel He 177 is inexorably linked to one man, General Walther Wever, who became the Commander of the *Reichsluftfahrtministerium* (RLM) on the 1st September 1933. He advocated, as early as 1934, the development of a strategic bomber to allow attacks on the Soviet Union's factories in the Ural Mountain area. However, the Luftwaffe was envisaged to support the *Wehrmacht* as they rapidly moved forward in 'Blitzkrieg' (Lighting War), so such a bomber was unnecessary when any future war would be a quick and decisive one. When Wever became the Chief of Staff of the Luftwaffe shortly after its creation on the 26th February 1935 he continually pressed for such a strategic bomber and this was finally recognised by the RLM, when they released a new specification for the *Langstrecken-Grossbomber* (long-range, heavy bomber) during the summer of 1935. The so-called 'Urals Bomber' specification was issued to two aircraft manufacturers, Dornier and Junkers*.

On the 3rd June 1936 a discussion took place in the office of the Chief of the *Technische Amt* in the RLM, General R. Lucht (presiding), with Dr Kruckel, Dr Bohm (both LC II/I), Dr Sachse and Count Westarp (both LC II/2) plus four other Luftwaffe engineering officers and representatives of the Nazi German aircraft industry (Richard Vogt of Blohm & Voss, Eichler and Meschkat of Heinkel, Frierish Nikolaus of Henschel, Ernst Zindel of Junkers & Robert Lusser of Messerschmitt) all present to tentatively discuss the requirements for such a new strategic bomber. This aircraft was to have a take-off weight of 27,000kg, a range of 5,000km, a bomb load of 2,000kg, and a speed of 500km/h at 5,500m. The service ceiling was to be at least 6,000m, with a maximum of 10,000m and it was to have a crew of three or four and possess good defensive armament. The type would also have to be able to approach its target in a medium dive. Power was to be via four engines, either Daimler-Benz DB601 (V12), Junkers Jumo 206 (six-cylinder diesel), Jumo 211 (V12), BMW 139 or Bramo 329 (14-cylinder, air-cooled, radials) or Argus AS 412 (24-cylinder, liquid-cooled).

Just over a year after the conference, which gave the RLM due time to consider the possible concepts that could be submitted to meet the new requirements, on the 2nd June 1937 Ernst Heinkel A.G. at Rostock-Marienehe received the new 'Bomber A' specification. Only Heinkel was given the specification, as the RLM hoped to pressurise the firm into concentrating its work on developing bombers. At Heinkel, the overall design was supervised by technical director and chief of development, *Dipl. Ing.* Heinrich Hertel with Siegfried and Walter Günter responsible for detail design and Schwarzler responsible for manufacturing engineering. The new design, designated Project 1041 on the 16th October 1936, was submitted to the RLM within a few months and a development contract was issued on the 2nd June 1937, so work on a mock-up began. On the 22nd June Heinkel issued a production schedule, with the first mock-up due for inspection on the 1st July 1937, the mock-up finalised on the 1st August 1937, the first prototype cleared for flight testing on the 1st June 1938, the first prototype delivered on the 1st September 1938 and the first pre-production airframe delivered on the 1st October 1939. The mock-up was actually first inspected by the LC II department of the RLM *Technische Amt* on the 6th August 1937 at Rostock-Marienehe, but a number of problems were highlighted. After a series of modifications to correct the problems, the mock-up was viewed again on the 5th November 1937 and approved on the 11th, with authorisation was given to build the prototype, which was now given the RLM designated '8-177' or 'He 177'.

For the era, the new specification was asking a great deal as the resulting bomber would have been able to outrun any in-service fighter and out-perform, by a considerable margin, any bomber (the *Schnellbomber* concept). To attempt to meet the requirements of the specification, Heinkel would have to adopt a number of untried features, something that would cost the resulting design dearly. To achieve the required performance, the type would have to use two engines of 1,490kw and at this time in Germany, there was no such engine. To overcome this therefore, Heinkel planned to use two of the new 'coupled' Daimler-Benz DB606 engines, which linked two DB601 12-cylinder, 60° inverted-V engines to drive the propeller through a connecting gear train and clutch assembly and each developed over 2,600PS (1,912kw) on take-off. Initially Günter intended to dispense with the bulk and drag of coolant radiators and run the new DB606s using a surface-evaporation cooling system. The

The Dornier Do 19 V1, D-AGAI, W/No.701 was Dornier's four-engine response in the mid-1930s

engine already ran very hot, so the pressurised coolant could reach 110°C (230°F) before steam began to form, after which this super-heated water was ducted away and de-pressurised and it was only at this point that steam formed. The resulting water was returned to the motor while the steam was sent via pipes through the wings, thus being cooled by the airflow so that, as water, it could also be returned to the engines. The system was pioneered with the Heinkel He 119 high-speed reconnaissance aircraft and was also tested on a He 100 fighter, where it performed quite well, but even before design was being finalised on the He 177, it was obvious that the system would never cope with the heat generated by the DB606, so its use was abandoned in favour of more conventional coolant radiators with their associated drag. To keep the new design as aerodynamically clean as possible, it was also intended to adopt three remote-controlled (from the cockpit) gun barbettes, combined with a conventional tail turret for defence. Whilst such barbettes offered less weight and an operator that could be in the most favourable position, in the late 1930s the technology was simply not developed enough for it to be adopted, so once again the He 177 design had to revert to conventional manned turrets with all their attendant weight and drag.

Not long after the evaporation cooling system was dropped Ernst Udet indicated that the He 177 might not be needed at all, because any conflict Nazi Germany envisaged at this time would only have involved Poland and Czechoslovakia, so the Luftwaffe only needed a medium bomber with a small range and bomb load. He went on to say that work on the He 177 would continue on a research basis, or for potential use by the Navy, but that it had to be capable of a dive, or it wouldn't stand a chance. Heinkel replied that an aircraft as big as the He 177 can't be a dive bomber, to which Udet replied that the He 177 was in practice a twin-engine bomber and the Ju 88 was a twin-engine bomber that could dive, so why couldn't the He 177! At this time dive-bombing was far more accurate than conventional bombing and Ernst Udet was a big fan of it, having seen its potential proven by the US Navy, but to make the He 177 capable of a dive at 60° put much strain on the airframe, so it had to be strengthened, which once again imposed a great weight penalty. All of these factors meant that the design now had to carry more fuel to be able to meet the original specifications range requirements, plus it would do so at a much-reduced speed. Extra fuel tanks had to therefore be installed in the wings, meaning that the wings also had to be strengthened to do this, which added yet more weight. Such was the overall increase in weight that the undercarriage had to be re-designed to cope, going from conventional single oleo strut units to a twin strut unit, with each oleo leg retracting into the wing inboard or outboard of it. The extra weight also resulted in the K 14 winch catapult system being considered between September 1940 and February 1941, to propel this heavily laden bomber into the air. In the end though this was never used or even tested by the type

The Munich Crisis in September 1938 highlighted the fact that Nazi Germany might well be involved in a war with the UK, so on the 19th October 1938, Jeschonnek asked Göring to authorise the production of as many He 177s as possible, so that at least five *Geschwaders* could be equipped by the autumn of 1942. In December 1938 an order was placed

The Ju 89 was Junker's response to the four-engine bomber requirement

for six He 177 prototypes. By this stage Heinkel had serious misgivings about the engine installation and asked if the second prototype could be fitted with four separate Jumo 211 engines, but this was vetoed by Udet, as he was fixated on the type being capable of a dive and four-engine bombers could not be dive bombers. Design work on the four-engine Jumo 211 did commence as the He 179, but this too was stopped by Udet on the 12th September 1939.

In January 1939 a construction description for the He 177 was issued and on the 24th February the order for prototypes was doubled from six to twelve. This was followed on the 6th July 1939 by an order for twenty pre-production aircraft. Once the revised mock-up had been examined during August 1939, the initial order for prototypes was reduced from twelve to eight, whilst that for pre-production airframes was increased from twenty to thirty. In November 1939 after the He 177 prototype was examined by Udet and Milch an order was issued that a monthly production rate of 120 He 177s was to be achieved by the middle of 1940 and the Heinkel factories at Oranienburg and the Weserflug plant at Bremen were assigned to the programme.

**This resulted in the Dornier Do 19 and Junkers Ju 89, with the former first flying on the 28th October 1936, some four months after the death of Wever in a He 70 during a flight from Dresden to Berlin (the aileron gust locks had not been removed), while the Ju 89 V1 first flew on the 11th April 1937. With the death of Wever the whole four-engine 'Urals bomber' concept died, with the RLM officially cancelling the programme on the 29th April 1937. The Do 19 was later converted to a transporter, whilst the other two being built were scrapped. The Ju 89 V1 and V2 were also converted to transports and operated for a short time with the Luftwaffe, while the V3 (which was to have been powered by DB600 engines) was never completed.*

The Prototypes

Despite all the problems and delays the He 177 V1 (CB+RP) took to the air for the first time on the morning of the 20th November 1939 (some sources state 19th) from Rechlin test centre (some sources state Rostock-Marienehe) with *Dipl. Ing.* Carl Franke, who had been seconded from Rechlin's E-2 Flight for the task, at the controls. This first flight only lasted for twenty minutes (some sources state twelve), as vibrations in the propeller shafts and engine overheating (the motors reached 1200°C) were encountered, so the forced reduction in power resulted in the prototype having to descend and land. A second flight was undertaken the next day, but it only lasted fourteen minutes. Although these first flights were short, valuable data was collected and whilst the take-off and general handling were good, considerable flutter was noticed with the elevators. Complains about the stability of the type also resulted in the vertical fin and rudder later being increased in area by 20%. The V1 undertook seven flights between the 6th and 18th December, with *Dipl. Ing.* Hans Friedrich Rickert from the E2 (airframes) section at Rechlin at the controls. The He 177 V1 was officially purchased by the RLM on the 27th February 1940 for 1,357,000 Reich Marks, the order being signed by *Generaloberst* Ernst Udet. Flight testing continued at Rechlin, where this helped to deal with such problems as propeller shaft vibrations, but there was still an alarming level of engine overheating. The V1 was finally lost on the 26th April 1940, when it burnt out after crash-landing at Rechlin, the cause being the destruction of one of the propellers.

The He 177 V2's (CB+RQ) first known flight is recorded as the 21st April 1940, although it probably actually flew for the first time some weeks earlier. It and the V3 (D-AGIG), which flew for the first time shortly after the V2, all had a reduced crew of four (the V1 had five) and had an additional second bomb bay fitted ahead of the single rear one seen on the V1, which increased the loaded weight to 24,130kg when the V1 was 23,920kg. It was on the 27th June 1940 the V2 undertook its first test dive, but during the dive it developed severe control flutter and broke up in mid-air over the Baltic Sea, near Graal-Müritz, due to malfunction of propeller pitch control (*Dipl. Ing.* Fritijof Urinus and his crew of three were killed – some sources wrongly list this as the V4). The loss of the V2 meant that the fin/rudder of the next three prototypes were all subjected to increases in the surface area in the hope of curing the type's stability problems.

The Fowler flaps added to the wings are very prominent in this head-on shot of the V1 coming in to land

We have found no period overall images of the He 177 V1 in initial form, this does show the expensively glazed nose region with crew access in the top

The V3 was odd in that it was allocated a civil registration, D-AGIG, which was probably because it was initially going to be tested by Lufthansa. The start of the war however meant that it was assigned to engine development at Rechlin in early February 1940, but was lost when it crashed near Gehlsdorf whilst being flown by *Dipl. Ing.* Hans-Friedrich Rickert due to inadequate balancing of the rudder (some sources state faulty trimming) causing failure of the tail surfaces during diving trials on the 24th April 1940. All the crew, including *Dipl. Ing.* Rickert, were killed.

Essentially similar to the V3, the V4 had the revised tail plus the elevators were also increased in size by 20%, the tailplane span was increased from 8.0m to 9.5m and the whole tail assembly was moved 500mm aft. It had the bulge around the bomb bay eliminated and a third bomb bay was added. It also had increased fuel tankage, raising weight to 24,820kg. Before it went to Rechlin it had limited armament installed, comprising an MG 15 in the upper nose, front and rear of the ventral gondola and in the tail position. It was used for inclined flight tests and it was planned to fit it with ejector seats for the crew, but they were never installed (many sources claim they were, but period accounts from test crews confirm this was not the case and it is also doubtful the large braking parachute some claim was fitted actually was). It was lost in a crash-landing at Rostock-Marienehe due to engine failure on the 8th June 1941.

The V5 (PM+OD) was generally similar to V4 but it was 150kg heavier. Period images seem to indicate that it was

Many published sources state this is the V1, but this is the V2, CBV+RQ seen prior to being painted out on the ramp at Heinkel's factory with He 111s visible in the background

Although poor, this is the only confirmed image of the V3 (D-AGIG, W/Nr.0003) known to exists and it shows it at Rostock-Marienehe during trials

(partially) armed, with what looks like an MG 15 in the nose glazing and another in the tail position (the ventral gondola had no armament and the dorsal cupola also lacked a gun). Some sources claim that at some stage it was fitted with improved (DB606A-1 (port) and B-1 (starboard)) engines. It did carry out a few shallow dives, but it was lost during simulated low-level attacks in March 1941, when both engines burst into flames and the V5 hit the ground and exploded.

The He 177 suffered throughout its life from engine fires, the causes of which were numerous. The first was the lubricating oil which was of poor quality and this often led to the connecting rod bearings seizing, which resulted in the con-rods snapping, then puncturing the crankcase, with the remaining oil spilling out onto the red-hot exhausts. The engine throttle also had to be handled gently, because if it was moved too abruptly, this would cause the fuel-injectors to leak neat fuel into the bottom of the engine bay, which would usually end up on those hot exhausts again, resulting in fire. Trials to overcome the problems with the engines were problematic, as *Dipl. Ing.* Walter Baist, who was responsible for engine installation and performance testing, lacked any airframes to work with until the V8 was allocated to him, along with a pre-production A-02 (DL+AQ). After completion of trials with the A-02 in early 1942 *Dipl. Ing.* Baist recommended the lengthening of the engine mounts by 10cm to provide better routing of pipework and easier access. The fuel and oil lines needed to be relocated in each nacelle to lessen the chance of fire as well as giving better access for inspection and maintenance. A firewall was needed ahead of the main spar, as close as possible to each engine and the oil tank was to be relocated so as not to be punctured by a disintegrating engine. Finally, the exhaust system needed to be completely redesigned to eliminate the common centre manifold and to better distribute and control the engine heat in each cowling. All of these changes would have caused considerable delay on the production lines and the RLM wanted the type as soon as possible, so they initially only agreed to the relocation of the oil tank. Once in service, the need to operate the type at night would result in service personnel requesting exhaust flame dampers, so their fitment allowed the final point to be undertaken with the exhaust system revised as a whole. The lengthened engine mounts would only come about from the A-3 production variant.

Again, this is the only period image that exists showing the complete V4 and it apparently shows it with limited armament fitted prior to tests at Rechlin

Although of poor quality, this is once again the only image that exists of the V5 PM+OD

A rather grainy still from a film showing the He 177 V6, BC+BP, coming in to land at Rostock-Marienehe

A well-known photo of the He 177 V7, SF+TB, in flight

The He 177 V6 (BC+BP) was similar to the V5 and was the first to use pre-production series Daimler-Benz DB606 engines driving four-blade propellers, with a DB606A-0 on the starboard side rotating counter-clockwise and a DB606B-0 on the port rotating clockwise, so they rotated away from each other at the top of the propeller arc. The airframe was structurally strengthened and the nose was revised, with fewer glazed panels, but was still not the same layout as the production version. It was initially unarmed, but the ventral gondola was of a revised size/shape, with less glazing and a flat clear panel in the front. It is said that it was the first to have a bulged bomb bay, raising the loaded weight from 24,000kg to 28,070kg and it was also used to test bomb release mechanisms at E-Stelle Rechlin in February 1941. It was later fitted with pre-production DB606A-1 (port) and B-1 (starboard) engines and flexible armament comprising MG FF cannon in a modified gondola under the nose (known as *Kanzelform 2* – [cabin type 2]), MG 15 in an Ikaria ball-mount in the nose (A1-*Stand*), MG 131 in the forward dorsal position (B1-*Stand*), MG 151 in an Ikaria ball-mount in the rear of ventral gondola (C1-*Stand*) and MG 131 in the tail (*Heckstand*) prior to operational evaluation. The tail gunner's position was later partially armour-plated and this airframe also tested a two-section bulged bomb bay along with the V8 (some sources state the V6 and V7 were fitted with two-section bomb bays). It was later transferred to *Erprobungsstaffel 177* and also tested by IV.(Erg)/KG 40 at Lechfeld (other sources state Bordeaux-Marignac), but crash-landed on the 28th June 1943 and was never flown again.

The V7 (SF+TB) was similar to V6 but was 18cm shorter. It had the capacity to carry an MG 131 in the nose glazing, but this was not fitted, while there was a MG FF in front of the ventral gondola (A2-*Stand*), MG 131 in the rear of the ventral gondola (C1-*Stand*), MG 131 in the manually-operated dorsal turret above the cockpit (B1-*Stand*) and MG 131 in the tail position (*Heckstand*). It undertook armament trials at E-Stelle Tarnewitz then was operationally evaluated by IV/KG 40 at Orleans, France, although its ultimate fate is unknown.

The V8 (SF+TC) was the last airframe to be built from the outset as a pure prototype and was basically similar to the V7. It was used to test changes in the undercarriage system and although surviving period images do not show any actual armament fitted*, it had the capacity to carry the following armament: 1x MG 131 in a manually-operated dorsal turret aft of the cockpit (B1-*Stand*); 1x MG 15 in an Ikaria ball-mount in the aft ventral position (C2-*Stand*) and 1x MG 131 in the tail (*Heckstand*). Whilst a real turret was not fitted a mock-up (aerodynamic shape only) of the aft turret was installed in the dorsal spine. The wings had shortened Fowler flaps and the engines featured enlarged engine cowlings and radiators. The four-blade propellers had blades that were much narrower that had previously been the case, this was probably because it was used to test various propeller blade types (metal, wood and Elecktron alloy). It was also used to test cooling equipment and flaps and was later fitted with de-icers in the wing leading edges.

It soon became apparent that the He 177 was too big to use as a dive-bomber. The pilot had to reduce his speed right back before he could force the nose down and almost as soon as the dive began, the recovery had to be implemented. Even with the airframe specially strengthened to withstand the stress of a dive, it was all too easy to over stress the airframe on pull-out. Thankfully by the time this shortfall was apparent, the need to use the type as a dive-bomber had passed and the new *Lotfe Bobenvisier* (tachometric bomb-sight) then entering service, promised far greater horizontal bombing accuracy. The V8, like all the prototypes, had dive brakes installed in the wings, but when it returned to Rostock after trials, these were removed.

**Some sources claim it had an MG 131 in the A1-Stand and MG 15s in the B1-Stand, C2-Stand and Heckstand, but all surviving images show it without armament fitted*

The last He 177 prototype the V8, SF+TC, photographed possibly while with Erprobungsstaffel 177 at Rechlin

The first pre-production airframe was the He 177A-01, WNr.0016, DL+AP, seen here on the ground at Heinkel's factory

Pre-production (test airframes)

The evolution of the He 177 involved eight true *Versuch* (prototype) airframes, as already recounted, plus a batch of twenty A-0 pre-production airframes that were built purely for test and research work. These were all allocated identity numbers '1' to '20', which we list as 'A-01' to 'A-020' to differentiate them from the true pre-production A-0 series that followed. To go through the individual history and features of each would be rather time consuming, plus all that data is included in Chapter 2, so we will just restrict our recount here to each airframe's W/Nr., *Stammkenzeichen*, first flight (if known) and ultimate fate (again, if known). The A-01, W/Nr.177 000 0016, DL+AP, 7th February 1941 was similar to He 177 V8 and was destroyed in fire at Marienehe on the 8th July 1941 after it collided with a Ju 52 whilst taxiing. The A-02, W/Nr.177 000 0017, DL+AQ, 5th May 1941 was the same as the A-01 except for revised armament and it was destroyed after a crash-landing in May 1942, the crew managed to escape before the aircraft exploded. The A-03, W/Nr.177 0000 0018, DL+AR was the same as the A-02 but had a MG FF cannon in the lower nose (A2-*Stand*) and its ultimate fate is unknown. The A-04 was also the V26 (W/Nr.177 000 0019, GA+QM) and was the same as the A-03 and was used for trials with the remotely-controlled defensive armament at E-Stelle Tarnewitz (other state Lärz) from October 1941. It was later used for testing the carriage of aerial torpedoes and modified by Lufthansa at Berlin-Staaken to carry two LT 5 torpedoes under the forward fuselage and one under each wing. Its ultimate fate is also unknown. The A-05, W/Nr.177 000 0020, GA+QN was the same as the A-03 but it had a further enlarged fin and rudder, with a more curved top and lengthened engine mountings. It tested split ailerons in 1942 and whilst some list this as the V9, that was converted from the A-08. It crashed and was destroyed at Priepert 13th June 1942 after a con-rod failed in one engine. The A-06 (W/Nr.177 000 0021, GA+QO, 21st October 1941) is a mystery as no data survives about airframe. Some sources list this as the V10, but that was converted from the A-09. The A-07 (W/Nr.177 000 0022, GA+QP) was the same as the A-03 except it was fitted with Daimler-Benz DB610 (coupled DB605s) engines. It was delivered to *Erprobungsstaffel 177* at Rechlin for evaluation but received 90% damaged there on the 10th February 1942 (some sources state 70% damage on the 11th February) after it caught fire during static testing of the heating system when the fuel was jettisoned. Some sources list this as the V11, but that was converted from the A-10. The A-08 (W/Nr.177 000 0023, GA+QQ, 6th February 1942) was also the same as the A-03 and initially it was intended to test the new pressurised cockpit, but this was never fitted. It did however have a new control system and split ailerons. Later the A-08 became the V9 when it was fitted with a horizontal tailplane that had separate fin/rudder units on each side combined with a longer fuselage [length not clarified in period documents] and K12 auto-pilot. Later still it was rebuilt to become

Probably one of the better-known pre-production machines was the He 177A-02, DL+AQ, seen here in one of a number of images taken at the time that highlights the rectangular fin fitted to the first nineteen pre-production airframes

The He 177A-03, DP+AR, taxies in after a test flight

In this starboard side shot of the He 177A-04, WNr.0019, GA+QM, you can clearly see the ailerons and landing flaps moved aft on their rails

the He 177 V102. The A-09 (W/Nr.177 000 0024, GA+QR, 5th February 1942) was the V10 and it was fitted with a pressurised cockpit (2.75m longer than original cockpit/nose) intended for the He 274 programme. It crash-landed on the 20th February 1943 and even though repaired all testing was abandoned from 3rd November 1943, so that by the 2nd May 1944 it was listed to be cannibalised for spares, but by 28th June 1944 it was with Heinkel for training purposes, so its ultimate fate is unknown. The A-010 (W/Nr.177 000 0025, GA+QS) acted as the V11 and also had the pressurised cockpit and associated 2.75m longer nose. It was used to test the K4 camera installation intended for the He 177A-2. As with the A-09, all testing was abandoned from 3rd November 1943 and on the 2nd May 1944 it was grounded due to staff shortages, but its ultimate fate is unknown. The A-011 (W/Nr.177 0000 0026, GA+QT) was apparently the same as He 177A-03, but as no images exist we cannot be 100% sure. It crashed and caught fire (probably due to fuel leak) in the Müritzsee region on the 18th February 1942 (all crew killed). The A-012 (W/Nr.177 0000 0027, GA+QU, 7th November 1941) is like the A-011 in that no images survive. It was issued to *Erprobungsstaffel 177* and two reports of its loss exist, one states it was 60% damaged on the 12th June 1942 at Rechlin due to elevator failure in a shallow dive, while the other states it was badly damaged at Fassberg on the 14th October 1942? The A-013 (W/Nr.177 0000 0028, GA+QV) also has no surviving images. It was issued to *Erprobungsstaffel 177* and lost when the wing broke off after too fast a pull-out from a dive was initiated over the Plauer lake near Rechlin on the 16th July 1942. The A-014 (W/Nr.177 000 0029, GA+QW) has only a single period image extant and it seems it was based on the A-03 but was fitted with narrow-chord four-blade propellers and lacked any armament (this may have been added later). It went to *Erprobungsstaffel 177* and was 80% damaged on take-off from Rechlin 4th July 1942, so we presume it was scrapped thereafter. The A-015 (W/Nr.177 0000 0030, GA+QX) acted as the V18 and once again only a single close-up image exists. As the V18 this was the second pattern aircraft (after A-1/U1 GI+BR) fitted with heavy armament of two Mk 101 30mm cannon in revised/deep chin position with rear access hatch. These had canvas covers at the base of each cannon, which may indicate these had limited movement? The A-016 (W/Nr.177 0000 0031, GA+QY) is completely unknown as no records or period images survive. The A-017 (W/Nr.177 0000 0032, GA+QZ) is another airframe for which no period images exist. Records

No images survive of the He 177A-05 to A-07, this shot shows the A-08 acting as the V9 with Erprobungsstaffel 177 at Rechlin-Lärz in February 1942

There are no surviving images of the A-09 to A-013, this one claims to be the He 177A-014, WNr.0029, GA+QW

show it was issued *Erprobungsstaffel 177*, but no other data survives. Nothing is also known about the A-018 (W/Nr.177 0000 0033), while the only thing known about the A-019 (W/Nr.177 0000 0034) is that it was destroyed at E-stelle Tarnewitz due to oil loss. This test airframe pre-production series is rounded out by the A-020 (W/Nr.177 0000 0035), but again there are no surviving images of this airframe and all that is known is that it was issued to *Erprobungsstaffel 177* and crashed on the 16th April 1942.

Pre-Production A-0 Series

The true pre-production batch intended for service evaluation and use comprised two batches; W/Nrs.2001 to 2015 built by Heinkel at Oranienburg and W/Nrs.5001 to 5005 built by Arado at Brandenburg. A number of these pre-production airframes were also used for trials and allocated V-series (*Versuch*) numbers, so it gets a bit complicated (see Chapter 2). By the end of 1942, 170 major and 1,395 minor modifications had been applied to the He 177. Series production had already been accelerated, so such changes led to unacceptable delays, however Ernst Udet stepped in and ordered all licence production was to cease and Heinkel's Rostock-Marienehe plant was only to make five per month throughout the period. This was a turn-around by Udet, who had initially thought testing could continue whilst the type was accepted into frontline service. The three month period allowed the modifications to catch up with production, however all hope of this ended with Udet's suicide on the 17th November 1941, after which *Major* Peterson was put in control and he ordered the He 177 back into series production without having let the required modifications catch up (all of them had to be added whilst each airframe was on the production line, seriously delaying their completion). The RLM then set-up a special deputy position for the development of the He 177 and Col. Ing. Platz, who had been the chief designer for Fokker during WWI took the role. He refused to accept the need to build the type with four separate engines for better performance at altitude and to give better range, plus the removal of the need for dive bombing as unnecessary, as Heinkel had requested. However, that is all he achieved, because for some reason he was then replaced by Prof Dr Heinrich Hertel and he complained to Heinkel about the design of the engine installation, which, in fact was his design originally anyway! He proposed that Heinkel's design team visit Junkers and see how they were installing DB 610 engines in the Ju 288 (albeit that was another design that would go nowhere). In his reports to Vorwald however, he stated that if the engine installation could be cleaned up, production could resume to reach 110 per month by April 1944.

There are few confirmed A-0 in-service images, this one claims to show E8-HK with 2./KG 50

Often listed as being the V18 (GA+QX), this close-up in fact shows the MK 101 cannon in the nose of the A-015 with the canvas covers around the base due to the armament not being fixed, but having limited movement; no images survive of the A-016 to A-020

A-Series Production

The first production variant, the He 177A-1, was built in a number of batches (W/Nrs. 332101 to 332142 by Heinkel, with W/Nrs.135006 to 135025 and 15151 to 15280 by Arado at Brandenburg-Neuendorf), with a number also being allocated V-series numbers for various trials. The type could be operated as a short, medium or long-range bomber, it had a crew of five and all featured the enlarged rounded style fin and rudder first used by the He 177A-05. Whilst some sources state the dive brakes were removed, all period service, operating and parts manual show them still in place. The variant used Daimler-Benz DB606A-1/B-1 engines driving narrow-chord, four-blade VDM metal propellers. Its bomb load comprised six Type 2000 XIIIB racks internally for bombs up to 2,000kg. Armament comprised a MG 81 (manually-controlled) in the upper nose (A1-*Stand*), MG FF cannon in the lower front nose/ventral gondola for use against ground targets (A2-*Stand*), although some later had this changed to a

MG 131. It was originally intended to have a WL 131 (manually-controlled) in the ventral position (C2-*Stand*), but this was changed to a MG 81Z (remotely-controlled) with 1,000 rounds before production started. A remotely-controlled barbette with a single MG 131 was located in the forward dorsal position (B1-*Stand*) with a manually-controlled, electrically powered DL 131 turret in the B2-*Stand* (this was deleted from the initial production, but reinstated from the 61st airframe. It was originally intended to have a MG 151 (manually-controlled) in the tail (*Heckstand*), but this was replaced by an MG 131 before production. The radio and location equipment comprised FuG 10 and FuG 16 radios, PeilG 2a direction finder and FuBl.1 (blind approach) system.

Although the special experimental squadron, *Erprobungsstaffel 177* was formed at Rechlin-Lärz to prepare the type for operational sorties and *Kampfgeschwader* 40 (initially as 10. (*Erhänzungs*)/KG 40 and later 15./KG 40) and I./FKG 50, all attempting to bring the type into operational service, the He 177A-1 was pronounced unfit for operational use in late 1942 and all were returned to Germany for use in second-line role. Here they were used to convert and train crews and few A-1s saw any frontline action. By September 1942 serious questions were being asked about the He 177 programme as a whole, with *Generalstabsing* Rudolf Lucht (General responsible for Air Equipment) stating that Heinkel had failed to deal with the question of the type's structural strength and Göring saying that the whole idea of tandem engines was ridiculous and that the type did not have to dive! The RLM decided that the problem lay with the Heinkel technical bureau and therefore, in November 1942, *Dipl. Ing*, Heinrich Hertel returned to Heinkel (he had left and moved to Junkers after having a differing opinion to Ernst Heinkel as to how the revised specifications for the He 177 should be met) as an RLM deputy with the power to reorganise the development of the type. Little changed though, the mind-set in the RLM and Luftwaffe still saw the type as a dive bomber and did little to change or improve it. All production of the A-1 therefore ceased in October 1942 in favour of the A-3 series.

The He 177A-2 series never got into production. It was intended as a special long-range reconnaissance version fitted with a pressurised cockpit, GM-1 nitrous oxide power-boost system for the engines and two or three large cameras in the bomb bay. The initial range requirement of 5,800km was to be increased to 9,500km with the use of in-flight refuelling and it was intended to make a limited production run of 40 such aircraft, but in the end, none were ever built He 177A-1s W/Nr 5215 (VE+UQ), W/Nr 5161 (GI+BV), W/Nr 5210 (VE+UJ), W/Nr 5211 (VE+UK) and W/Nr 5212 (VE+UL) were all used by *Versuchsstelle für Höhenflüge* (Experiment Establishment for High-Altitude Flights) in temporary support

He 177A-1s of Erprobungsstaffel 177 photographed at Rechlin-Lärz

of this proposed reconnaissance version.

The He 177A-3 was the first variant to be built in any great number, with W/Nrs. 332143 to 332252, 332351 to 332410, 332471 to 332519, 332536 to 332555 and 332610 to 332629 built by Heinkel at Oranienburg and W/Nrs. 535351 to 535375, 535436 to 535460, 535531 to 535575, 535670 to 535699, 535726 to 535760 and 535846 to 535870 built by Arado at Brandenburg-Neuendorf. The first fifteen had Daimler-Benz DB 606A/B engines, whilst from the 16th airframe, Daimler-Benz DB 610A/B engines were used. These engines were mounted 20cm further forward of the main spar and had enlarged cowlings and radiators in an attempt to deal with the overheating. The fuselage was also lengthened to 22.0m with a 1.60m extension aft of the wing root trailing edge to improve stability. The DL 131 (manually-controlled, electrically powered) turret in the aft dorsal position (B2-*Stand*), which had originally been deleted from the initial A-1 production, but reinstated from the 61st airframe, was updated from one to two MG 131s. In January 1943 *Dipl. Ing*. Hertel ordered a detailed investigation into the engine problems and the engine test section at Estelle Rechlin identified fifty-six different potential sources of engine fires. When one He 177 was modified to include all the recommendations it completed all remaining testing without a problem. Whilst the RLM by this stage were already setting in motion plans to scrap the He 177, the Technical Office was sure that at last all the problems with the type's engines had been sorted, so the actual termination order was never issued. Production of the A-3 series gives the first link to the use of slave labour by Heinkel, when Herr Hayn, Heinkel's director, made request to obtain prisoners for this purpose on the 16th October 1942. *Reichsführer-SS* Heinrich Himmler further endorsed this in a letter to *SS-Brigadeführer* Hermann Fegelein on the 10th March 1944 that confirmed the use of 6,000 (increased to 8,000) prisoners at Heinkel's Orianienburg factory building the He 177.

The He 177A-4 was to have been a high-altitude bomber, derived from the He 177A-3 and fitted with a pressurised cockpit, crew of three and armament comprising, MG 131 (A1-*Stand*), twin MG 131 (B1-*Stand*), MG 131 (C2-*Stand*),

A He 177A-3, ND+SS, acting as the V24 with flame dampers in early 1943 at Rostock-Marienehe where it was used to test the DB 610 engines and de-icing equipment

The remains of a He 177A-5 after an unsuccessful belly-landing

MG 131 or MG 151 (*Heckstand*). Some sources list the type as having had four separate engines, but it was derived from the A-3 and retained that type's tandem engines. In the end none were built thought, although the pressurisation system led via the He 177H project to the He 274.

The He 177A-5 was the next major production variant and it was also the last. It came about really because of Admiral Donitz's repeated demands for aircraft that could be used for attacks on Allied shipping in place of the stop-gap Focke-Wulf Fw 200. The first A-5 left the Heinkel factory in February 1943 and W/Nrs. 550001 to 550006, 550031 to 550090, 550117 to 550175 and 550191 to 550200 were built by Heinkel at Oranienburg, while W/Nrs. 550202 to 550266 and 550316 to 550333 were built by Arado at Brandenburg/Neueundorf. The type used two DB610 engines, which were coupled Daimler-Benz DB605s, the wing featured shortened Fowler flaps and the ailerons no longer dropped with the flaps. It has a redesigned undercarriage with shortened oleo legs and the wings were strengthened to allow the carriage of heavier external loads outboard of the engines such as the LT 5 torpedo, Fritz-X and Hs 293. Whilst the type still suffered from many of the problems seen in previous variants, the need for it was such that the A-5 was issued to a variety of frontline units.

The He 177A-6 was a proposed high-altitude bomber project derived from He 177A-5. It had a longer fuselage, pressurised cockpit with revisions to the forward fuselage and glazing. Armament comprised MG 1311 (A2-*Stand*), two MG 131s in FBL 131 turret (B1-*Stand*), two manually-operated MG 131s (C1-*Stand*) and two MG 131s in HL 131Z turret (*Heckstand*). Its bombload would be one SC250 bomb on the external fuselage rack and two SC500s in the rear bomb bay. In the end though the series was never but into production as it was cancelled in favour of the A-7 (some sources state it was cancelled in favour of the He 177B).

The final A-series sub-variant was the He 177A-7, which in its original form was to be like the A-5 but have standard wings and a fuselage lengthened to 23.915m (some sources state 22.915m, but period diagrams confirm 23.915m). It would have had two MG 131 in a remotely-controlled turret in the front of the ventral gondola (A2-*Stand*), combined with an MG 81Z in the rear (C1-*Stand*). Alternatively, it could have two MG 151s in a remotely-controlled turret in the front of the ventral gondola (A2-*Stand*), combined with an MG 131 in a remotely-controlled barbette on the fuselage underside, aft of the gondola. The remaining armament would have been two MG 151s in the B1-*Stand*, two manually-operated MG 131Zs in the rear of the gondola (C1-*Stand*) and a HL 131V turret with four MG 131s in the tail (*Heckstand*). As well as an internal bomb load the type was also to have the capacity to carry one SC2500 bomb on the external fuselage rack. In its revised form the A-7 would have been basically similar to the initial design but with an entirely new cockpit/nose with extensively glazed upper and front sections. It would have had a longer wing span of 35.0m [some sources state 36.0m] for the DB610-powered version and 36.5m [some sources state 31.64m] for the DB613-powered version. It was initially intended to have four separate engines (BMW 801E, BMW 803 or DB 613), but in the end two DB610A/B engines were chosen. Armament would have been a Drehlafette FDL 131Z in lower A2-*Stand*, two FDL 151Zs as the B1-*Stand* and a Walzenlafette WL 131Z as the C2-*Stand*. The bombload would have been one SC2500 bomb on the external fuselage rack and two SC500s in the rear bomb bay.

Two undercarriage options exist in period documents, the first remained as standard, whilst the second had a new double-wheeled unit each side that retracted backwards into the engine nacelle. Some sources state that ten (maybe less) were converted from existing airframes, while others state that none were ever completed before the He 177 programme was abandoned in the summer of 1944. The example listed as an A-7 and captured by American forces at the end of the war (W/Nr.550256), was actually an A-5 and period images

Although confirmed images of A-7s are rare, this one claims to show one converted from A-5 WNr.550316, note the FuG 200 mounts, MG 151-20 in chin position and squarer canopy side windows. It was captured in damaged condition by US forces in mid-1944

confirm it retained all the features of the A-5 series, without any of those proposed for the A-7. There is also another account that states the 'third' built was stripped of armour and armament with additional fuel cells added in the wings and fuselage, so that it could fly non-stop to Japan over Siberia at high altitude, as the VVS lacked any fighters able to reach it. Japan had a non-aggression pact with Russia, so insisted that it fly over Persia and India, which was too far, so the flight never took place and the airframe was captured by American forces in 1945; there is no other evidence to support this story though. The whole He 177A-7 programme was abandoned in the summer of 1944.

The He 177A-8, A-9 and A-10 became the He 177B-5, B-6 and B-7 respectively.

The He 177A – Frontline Service

As has already been mentioned a special experimental squadron, *Erprobungsstaffel 177* was formed at Rechlin-Lärz under the command of *Hptm.* Rudolf Mons on the 1st February 1942, with a view to preparing the He 177A-1 for operational sorties. By August eight He 177s had been delivered to the unit, but there were only four crews available. Whilst *Erprobungsstaffel 177* was to undertake development work on the operational use of the type, it was intended to have the He 177 introduced into actual operational service by *Kampfgeschwader* 40 (KG 40). The first two (the V6 and V7) were accepted by 10. (*Erhänzungs* – training and replacement) *Staffel* of KG 40, who passed their Fw 200s to 11 *Staffel* and started to equip with the He 177 at Lechfeld, and later at Orléans-Bricy from January 1942. On the 20th May 1942, 10.(Erg)/KG 40 was redesignated 15./KG 40, with its small number of He 177s intending to start operations as a *Fernkampfstaffel* (long-range bomber squadron), but in June it formed the basis of a new unit, I./FKG 50 (first *Gruppe* of *Fernkampfgeschwader* 50 – long-range bomber wing 50) commanded by *Maj.* Kurt Schede. The unit received its first He 177A-1s that month, with a few specially modified with dual-controls arriving in August. They lost their first aircraft, W/Nr.5161 on the 2nd September, although the crew (including Schede as pilot) all escaped. Such was the level of problems with the He 177 that Schede refused to take responsibility for sending the type into action in early 1942. Nevertheless, in mid-November a third *Staffel* was added to I./FKG 50, followed by the training and replacement 4th *Staffel* at the end of that month. By early December the *Gruppe* had a strength of thirty-three aircraft, although only ten were serviceable, with twenty-seven crews.

The second operational unit to receive the He 177 was 1 *Staffel* of KG 40, when it transferred from Trondheim-Vaernes in Norway to Fassberg on the 8th September 1942. Five He 177A-0s were delivered on the 29th of the month, so that crew familiarisation and training could start. On the 10th October the technical personnel of the unit started to receive training and seven He 177A-1s were delivered throughout the month. At the beginning of December, 1. and 3./KG 40 sent a number of their Focke-Wulf Fw 200s (between ten and eighteen, the exact number is unknown) to Berlin-Staaken, where they formed the basis of a special transport unit (KGrzbV 200) under the command of *Maj.* Hans-Jürgen Williers. This unit moved to Stalino to assist in the air-supply of the Sixth Army in Stalingrad and a number of 1./KG 40's He 177s received the *Rüstzustand A* modification to carry supply containers, but the problems experienced by I./FKG 50 operating the He 177 from Saporoshje-Süd (see elsewhere) stopped them from being sent to Russia. During the next three months KG 40 underwent bomb-aiming and gunnery training with the He 177, but lost its first aircraft (W/Nr.5269) on the 23th January 1943 due to engine failure. On the 1st February 1943, 2 *Staffel* transferred from Trondhiem to Fassberg, intending to also convert from the Fw 200 to the He 177, but on the 6th, continual problems with the He 177 led to 1./KG 40 being grounded. Those parts of 1. and 2./KG 40 that were still trying to convert to the He 177 remained at Fassberg and on the 3rd February 1943 a third *Gruppe*, I./KG 4 moved from Köningsberg-Gutenfeld to Lechfeld to convert to the He 177, but the continuing problems with the type led the RLM to block all training from the 7th February until at least May 1943. Regardless of the ban, plans were put in motion in March 1943 to create the newly formed 8./KG 40 operating the He 177. It was therefore not until mid-May 1943 that I./KG 4 received its first He 177s and instructor crews from I./FKG 50, while the first five He 177A-1s were delivered to 2./KG 40 on the 26th May. By the 1st July I./KG 40 had eleven He 177A-1s on charge alongside Fw 200s and 8./KG 40 began to undertake its first training flights with the He 177. By August I./FKG 50 had fourteen He 177A-1s and two He 177A-3s. 4.(Erg)/FKG 50, which retrained the pilots of I./KG 4, was re-designated 17./KG 40 and moved from Brandenburg-Briest to Burg, near Magdeburg. At the same time, I./FKG 50 was augmented with flight instructors from the FFS C schools and re-designated II./KG 40 (the existing II./KG 40 was in turn re-designated

The first unit to fly the He 177 was Erprobungstaffel 177 and here you can see He 177A-1, WNr.5215, VE+UQ operated by them as it crosses the Müritz river, close to Rechlin

He 177A-5s of 4./KG40 at Bordeaux-Mérignac airfield in 1944

V./KG 2) and when this charge was officially ratified on the 25th October the unit moved to Bordeaux-Merignac on the French Atlantic coast for operations against Allied shipping with the He 177A-3. The situation was somewhat complicated by the fact that on the 24th October I./KG 4 and I./KG 100 were ordered to exchange designations with 10.(Erg)/KG 4, which had operated as the training replacement unit for I. *Gruppe*. They therefore passed their He 177s to I./KG 100, but shortly afterwards, 2./KG 40 exchanged identity with 8./KG 40, with the former reverting to the Fw 200 due to plans for re-equipping III./KG 40 with the He 177 being abandoned. By the end of November 1943, the *Gruppe Stab* and two *Staffeln* of KG 40 had thirty-one He 177A-3s (3./KG 40 at Trondheim-Vaernes continued to operate the Fw 200).

On the 20th September 1943, 8./KG 100 transferred to Schwäbisch Hall to convert from the Dornier Do 217 to the He 177. Twenty-one (one A-0, seven A-2s and thirteen A-3s) He 177s were assigned to the unit, but most were discovered to be in need of major overhauls plus others were at Burg, where they had been left outside without protection. As a result, on the 1st December 1943, the unit moved to Fassberg, but most of the servicing equipment remained at Schwäbisch Hall and Burg. A combination of flooding during the winter months combined with a lack of fuel for the tractors to tow the aircraft to dispersals meant that training proceeded slowly. In November 1943, 4./KG 100 also began to convert to the He 177 at Leck, then moved to Aalborg in Denmark towards the end of February 1944. This unit received the He 177A-5 and it was W/Nr.550003 that was to be the first of this sub-variant to be lost when it crashed during transfer to Aalborg on the 22nd February. On the 17th March 4./KG 100 was joined by 5./KG 100, who had transferred from Toulouse and they began to re-equip with the He 177A-5. On the 1st June 1944, 6./KG 100, which had remained operational with the Do 217 at Toulouse-Blagnac, swapped designations with 8./KG 100 so that all of II. *Gruppe* was now equipped with the He 177. A second training and replacement unit was established in January 1944 when 10. and 12.(Erg)/KG 100 converted from the Do 217 to the He 177. See the Operation *Steinbock* section elsewhere for details of KG 100s operations against London.

The He 177A-3 in the Mediterranean

With II./KG 40s move to Bordeaux-Merignac at the end of October 1943, the unit started to operate the He 177A-3 against Allied shipping under the command of *Maj*. Rudolf Mons, the previous commander of *Erprobungsstaffel 177*. The workload was further complicated by the need for the crews to familiarise themselves with the new radio-guided Hen-

He 177A-3, 6N+SK, 'Susi' of 2./KG100 at Rheine in the spring of 1944

Crews congregate around a He 177A-5 of 4./KG 40 at Bordeaux-Mérignac prior to a mission

schel Hs 293 glide-bomb, three of which the He 177 could carry, although it is unlikely many ever undertook operational sorties with both the fuselage and wing racks carrying this weapon. The observer in the He 177 used his control stick to move the control surfaces of the bomb during both the powered and glide stages with the help of the flare in the tail of the Hs 293 to help him sight it with the target. The Hs 293 had a 500kg warhead and reached a maximum powered speed of 595km/h in twelve seconds, but its impact velocity was only 725km/h, which meant it did not have much penetrative capacity, so it was therefore mainly used against merchant ships and lightly-armoured warships. The first operational sortie by KG 40 with the He 177 took place on the afternoon of the 21st November 1943, when *Maj.* Rudolf Mons leading twenty-five aircraft against the convoy SL139.MKS30 some 675km, north-east of Cape Finistere, Spain. Low cloud and the fact that many of the He 177s missed the main convoy, resulted in the force concentrating on two straggling merchantmen, *Marsa* and *Delius*. Whilst four He 177s released their Hs 293s against *Marsa*, none of them hit the target due to good defensive manoeuvres by the ship's Captain. A short while after the initial attack a fifth He 177 managed to hit the *Marsa* on the port side in the engine room. The damage was such that the vessel could not be saved, so an escort vessel came alongside and took off all surviving crew. The *Delius* suffered similar attacks and was also hit once, but it managed to make port under her own steam. The He 177s attacking the convoy did not just have the anti-aircraft fire of the vessels to contend with because P/O A. Wilson of No.224 Squadron in a Liberator decided that his role to ensure the safety of the convoy extended to air-to-air combat, so he engaged the Heinkels, causing damage to two before returning to patrol over the convoy. Whilst the *Marsa* had been lost II./KG 40 had failed to damage even one of the vessels within the main body of the convoy and the Hs 293 had proven to be a very difficult weapon to use effectively and aim accurately. The sortie resulted in one aircraft crashing some 48km from base (reasons unknown), one was lost without trace during the attack, one ran out of fuel on the way home and its crew had to take to their parachutes, one crash-landed on return and received 45% damage, with four more returning with varying degrees of damage. *Hptm.* Nuss claimed two ships sunk, so he was most likely the pilot who made the successful attack that sunk the *Marsa* and the other that damaged the *Delius*. These were small achievements for the loss of some many aircraft, plus the sortie had proved that the He 177 still had many technical problems. On the 26th November, twenty-one He 177s of II./KG 40 attacked convoy KMF 26 off Cape Bougie on the Algerian coast. As the He 177s attacked they were met by fierce anti-aircraft fire as well as fighters in the form of Supermarine Spitfires from GC 1/7, Bell P-39 Airacobras from the 350th Fighter Group and Bristol Beaufighters of No.153 Squadron. In the battle that followed six He 177s were shot down including those of *Major* Mons and *Hptm.* Nuss, while they managed a single Hs 293 hit on the troop-carrying liner *Rohna*, which sank. Sadly, the approach of night combined with a heavy swell led to over a thousand American troops being lost. When II./KG 40 got back to base though the weather made it unusable and two more aircraft were wrecked trying to land. In just two sorties, II./KG 40 had lost twelve aircraft, had one seriously damaged and eight crews were dead. With *Major* Mons dead, *Hptm.* Dochtermann assumed command of II./KG 40 and as Allied defences over the convoys had proven far too costly for the unit to consider more daylight operations, it switched to night attacks. For the remainder of 1943, II./KG 40 continued to attack Allied convoys as they passed through the Mediterranean and even by using flares dropped on the far side of a convoy to silhouette the ships, successes with the Hs 293 were few. See the 'Anzio' section for details of He 177/Hs 293 operations in response to these landings.

He 177A-3 on the Eastern Front

The first A-3s were delivered to I./FKG 50 (first *Gruppe* of *Fernkampfgeschwader* 50 – long-range bomber wing 50) at Bradenburg-Briest in late 1942, having previously used twenty-eight A-1s since June. These were transferred to Saporoshje-Süd [others list as *Zaporozhye-Süd*] (200km west of Stalino in the Ukraine) between the 13th and 15th January 1943 in a desperate attempt to use them in the transport role to support the Nazi German 6th Army at Stalingrad. Each of the unit's seven serviceable aircraft was fitted with the supply-dropping modification (*Rüstzustand A*) and hurried into use under the command of *Maj.* Schede, who was appointed *Luftwaffe Transport Führer Saporoshje*. The first sortie was flown on the 13th January 1943 but the aircraft, E8+FK

He 177A-1s of I./FKG 50 prepare for a mission at Zaporozhye-Süd

crashed landing due to a fuel pump failure. Another aircraft, E8+FH was lost on the 16th, when it crashed in flames near Poljakowa and W/Nr5242 was destroyed at Saporoshje-Süd the next day. A third aircraft, W/Nr.5241 was lost on the 20th, when its tail collapsed on landing at Kirovograd aircraft. On the 22nd the last available airfield within the Stalingrad pocket was captured, so from then on, the He 177 reverted to the bomber role in support of the ground forces. Three aircraft were lost on the 27th January, a fourth was damaged on the 28th, and a fifth the next day. The He 177 had proven to be poor in the transport role, as its bomb bay was poorly suited for carrying supplies and it only had a useful load of eight 250kg containers (1,120kg of food). When Stalingrad fell in February 1943 the He 177s returned to Bradenburg-Briest, after which the unit continued training on the type and its specialist role of launching Hs 293 anti-shipping missiles.

Operation Steinbock

Reichsmarschall Göring sent a signal to this *Luftflotte* commanders in the west and to *Generalmajor* Peltz, his Chief of Staff for bombers, in December 1943 to increase attacks on the UK, specifically targeting cities, industrial centres and ports. The units involved in this operation were widely dispersed on airfields from Brittany to Germany, so as not to be visible to Allied aerial reconnaissance and were only brought together a few hours before a raid was to take place. Two He 177s units were involved in Operation *Steinbock* (the astrological sign 'Capricorn', although some sources call this 'Ibex'), the first *Gruppe* of KG 40 and the third *Staffel* of KG 100 (some sources state I./KG 100), operating from airfields in Rheine, west of Osnabrück and Château-dun north-west of Orleans. The first attack (Operation *Mars*) took place on the night of the 21st-22nd January 1944, with the bombers forming two

He 177A-3, 6N+SK, 'Susi' of 2./KG100 at Rheine in the spring of 1944 during Operation Stenbock

He 177A-3, 6N+HK, 'Helga' of I./KG100 (others state I./ KG 40) at Châteaudun being bombed up before a raid

waves, about six (some sources state eight) hours apart. It was during this first raid that F/O H. Kemp (some sources state Keep) and Flt Sgt J. Maidment of No.151 Squadron brought down the first He 177 on British soil. The aircraft (W/Nr.5747, F8+HH) from I./KG 40 crashed near Haslemere, Surrey, with two of the six crew killed and the remainder taken prisoners. The first wave landed back at Châteaudun, while the second returned to Rheine and W/Nr.5471 was apparently lost over London, whilst W/Nrs.5745 and 5730 (both A-3s) were damaged during emergency landings and W/Nr.2198 from 3./KG 4 was lost south-east of Dieppe as it returned home. The raid was a failure and although over 243,000kg of bombs had been dropped, less than 32,500kg had hit the target. Hitler, on hearing of the mission and the He 177s performance, stated that it was "the worst junk ever to have been manufactured".

The raids continued though, with the next on the night of the 29th-30th January comprising 285 aircraft including those of I./KG 40 and 3./KG 100 against London (with only a 23% success rate). Both units operated from Rheines for the mission and afterwards I./KG 40 was withdrawn to Fassberg, where it joined 2./KG 40 in training with the He 177A-5 with the Hs 293 for anti-shipping missions. On the 3rd-4th February, 240 aircraft including those from 3./KG 100 operating from Rheine attacked London. From the 4th to the 13th February the second *Staffel* of KG 100 (2./KG 100) moved from Lechfeld to join 3./KG 100, moving their aircraft between Rheine, Château-dun and Rennes in Brittany in readiness for sorties that did not take place. After this point both units were based together at Rheine for Operation *Steinbock* sorties. The next raid on London took place on the night of the 12th-13th February, with thirteen He 177s taking part, although some had to return to base because of overheating engines (probably down to poor maintenance). One aircraft had to jettison its bomb load over the Zuider Zee (now the Ijssel Meer) and one may have been shot down by night-fighters. On the night of the 18th-19th February, 200 aircraft including those from I./KG 100 attacked London and during the 19th I./KG 100 moved from Rennes to Châteaudun, then on to Rheine on the 20th. Another raid took place on London on the night of the 20th-21st February with some 200 aircraft including those from I./KG100, while during the day on the 21st I./KG 100 moved from Rheine to Châteaudun, then on the night of the 20th-21st fourteen He 177s took part in a 200+ aircraft attack on London. On the night of the 23rd-24th February He 177s from Châteaudun took place in a 160-aircraft raid on London, with W/Nr.2227 (5J+QL of 3./KG 100 crashing at Wolseley, near Yoxford, Suffolk (three crew were reported missing, one was killed and the other injured). The next sortie on the night of the 24th-25th February was a 170-aircraft raid on London, although only six He 177s from I./KG 100 took part and one (W/Nr.2222) was intercepted and shot down by a Mosquito at Lamberhurst near Tunbridge, Kent. The final raid of February was on the night of the 28th February-1st March, with He 177s from I./KG 100 taking part and no losses being reported. From March the raids shifted to focus on Bristol and Hull, with just four against London that month and the final Operation *Steinbock* raid, and the last large-scale attack on the British capital in WWII took place on the night of the 18th-19th April with about 125 aircraft, only five of which were He 177s. By the end of April 1944 the raids on Britain petered out, as the units involved were now having to prepare themselves for an imminent invasion on mainland Europe.

Bomber Destroyer

In June 1943 it was proposed to mount thirty-three WGr.21 (210mm) rocket launcher tubes in the fuselage of the He 177 in three rows of eleven, inclined forward and slightly to starboard at 60°. The weapons could be fired all at once, or in two groups at roughly quarter of a second intervals or singly. By late 1943, five He 177A-1s were with the *Kampstaffel* of *Erprobungskommando* 25, which had been set up in April 1945 to develop weapons for use against heavy bomber formations. Modification of the He 177A-1s was undertaken at Diepholz and Quakenbrück, but on the 21st February 1944 three of them were severely damaged during a strafing attack on Diepholz. One of the two remaining aircraft was used for trials with the weapons during the 23rd to 25th March 1944 at the Tarnewitz ranges and they proved to be quite accurate (mainly due to the longer launch tubes in comparison with those used by the Ju 88/Bf 110 etc.). It was demonstrated to members of the General der Jagdflieger and the KdE on the 11th April 1944, with the planned conversion of four aircraft due by the 15th June 1944. The *Kampstaffel* of *Erprobungskommando* 25 was transferred to Udetfeld for training on the 21st June 1944, but lost another He 177A-1 on the 27th of the month. The Allied invasions meant that by this date there was a serious need for fighter pilots in the Luftwaffe, so the unit was disbanded and most of its pilots went to the newly formed JGr 10, so that the WGr.21 was never used by the He 177 against Allied bomber formations.

Anzio

With the Allied advance North into Italy halted at the Gothic Line between Naples and Rome, 36,000 Allied troops and 3,000 vehicles were landed at Anzio and Nettuno, south of Rome on the 22nd January 1944. The Luftwaffe attempted to stop supplies reaching the beachheads by using Hs 293-carrying He 177s of II./KG 40 and Do 217s of II and III./KG 100. The first operation was undertaken on the 23rd January by seven He 177s from Bordeaux-Merignac against shipping off the Nettuno beachhead. Low cloud on route forced two aircraft to fly low and get shot down by Beaufighters on route, while the remaining aircraft did reach the target area, but had little success. On the 24th, eleven Hs 293-equipped He 177s were joined by Do 217s from II./KG 100 in another attack against Nettuno. During the next three operations against Nettuno, II./KG 40 lost eight He 177s, whilst only managing to sink a 3,000 ton freighter and the destroyer HMS Janus (originally only claimed as damaged) and damage another destroyer, HMS Jervis. Once the landings were over, II./KG 40 returned to night harassment raids in the Mediterranean and II./KG 100 transferred to Aalborg-West in March 1944 to re-equip with the He 177, while at the end of May, 6 and 8./KG 100 exchanged designations, which meant that II *Gruppe* was now entirely equipped with the He 177.

Eastern Front

Plans to use the He 177 in its true role as a strategic bomber in Russia had been proposed as early as the autumn of 1943. It was not until late 1943 that anything happened, when the *Geschwader Stab* and I and II./KG 1 handed over their Ju 88s to KG 54 and KG 76. By the middle of November 1943 both *Gruppen* had transferred back to Germany. I./KG 1 moved to Brandis, near Leipzig, while the *Stab* and II./KG 1 moved to Burg near Magdeburg so that they could all start converting to the He 177. It was hoped to have the first He 177s delivered on the 25th November, but such were delays in He 177 production that everyone from I. *Gruppe* was told to go on leave on the 6th December and not to return before the 6th January 1944. On their return they began to learn about the He 177, although the first actual airframe was not delivered to Brandis until the 12th February and by the beginning of March I./KG 1 still only had nine aircraft and all of them were worn out, having been previously used by I./KG 100, II./KG 1 or FKG 50. I./KG 1 had originally supposed to have received twenty He 177A-1s, but eleven did not arrive because they were unserviceable, so Ju 88s were substituted, arriving between the 1st February and the 12th March. The choice was not liked by the crews, who felt the He 111 would have been a better option. In February 1944 the He 177A-3 was released for training and on the 1st March crews started to undertake training with the type with IV.(Erg)/KG 1 based at Neuburg. In March the first new A-1s and A-3s were delivered to I./KG 1 and by April the *Gruppe* had eighteen, but only two were serviceable and this was mainly down to a chronic shortage of equipment for servicing and repairing the type. Thirty brand-new He 177A-3s were delivered to I./KG 1 in March, although five were diverted to IV. *Gruppe*, which had been training its crews on He 111s and Ju 88s at Neuburg because none of the He 177s it had received were serviceable. On the 25th April I./KG 1 had twenty-two He 177A-3s, but only six were serviceable. A third *Gruppe* was added to KG 1 by re-designating I./KG 100 at Fassberg on the 31st May 1944 and

A He 177A-3 and A-5 of I./KG 100 visit Munich-Riem on route to the Eastern Front

shortly afterwards the *Geschwader* received one-hundred new He 177A-3s directly from the Arado factory at Küpper bei Sagan. As a result, in June 1944, the unit moved to operational airfields in East Prussia, centring around Prowehren and Seerappen. The *Geschwader* comprised ninety He 177s making it the most-powerful, long-range force on either side on the Eastern Front. The unit went into action as soon as it arrived, attacking Russian supply and troop concentrations, but it did not attack strategic targets that were easily within its range because the Nazi German ground-forces needed as much support as it could before the Russian's summer offensive began. With the unit operating the He 177 at high altitude in daylight, loses were light, as the VVS was equipped mainly with fighters designed for use at low-level and the pilots had a healthy respect for the He 177s defensive armament. The unit also operated at night, but once again all targets were purely tactical ones near to the frontline in support of the ground forces. Engine fires with the He 177 were now far less common, as various modifications had been incorporated plus the two main causes, over-rough use of the throttles and holding too high a power setting for too long, were both well known and all crews were advised of the dangers. The Russian summer offensive started on the 23rd June 1944 and the Nazi German ground forces were quickly overwhelmed, with Russian armour penetrating deep into the rear. In desperation Göring directly ordered Obstlt Horst von Riesen the *Kommodore* of KG 1 to use He 177s in low-level ground-attack sorties against the Russian armour. A pair of He 177s was sent, one to give covering fire for the other, but most pairs got split up and some ten aircraft were lost on that first day, mainly to Russian fighters that were patrolling above the battlefield. A lack of fuel forced the *Geschwader* to cease operations on the 28th July 1944 and return to Brandis, where the He 177s were put into storage.

Allied Landings

On the 6th June 1944, Allied forces launched the long-awaited liberation of Europe and to counter this He 177s of I./KG 40 at Orléans and II./KG 40 at Bordeaux were out in force. Allied night fighters were also operating and during the night of the 6th-7th June 1944 No.456 Squadron alone claimed four He 177s (W/Nrs.550206 of 1./KG 40, 550197 and 550204 of 2./KG 40 and 550117 of 5./KG 40) as they attempted to reach the Allied beachhead. Towards midnight on the 7th June two more He 177s were claimed by Mosquitos of No.604 Squadron and early on the 8th, three more were shot down by No.456 Squadron. Operations continued and whilst claims were made for sinking four merchant ships, two destroyers and another destroyer and cruiser set on fire, Allied records only show that the destroyer HMS Boadicea was sunk off Portland whilst escorting a convoy from Milford Haven, with only twelve of her 138 crew surviving. The continual operations over the beachheads by I. and II./KG 40 were annoying so B-24 Liberators of the US 8th AF attacked Châteaudun and Orléans-Bricy on the 10th and 14th June and so on the 18th, I./KG 40 moved to Toulouse-Blagnac. This did not deter the 8th AF, who bombed that airfield and nearby Toulouse-Francazal a week later. Attempts by Fliegerkorps IX to hit the Allied forces had been intense, but the effects were very limited, so in the ten days after the initial landings, just five ships were sunk as a direct result of air attacks. Attention therefore turned from attacking shipping to dropping mines in the main shipping lanes. In the following weeks over 3,000 mines were dropped and by the end of June these had sunk nine warships and seventeen auxiliary vessels and merchantmen. These numbers were nothing in comparison with a massive Allied armada that had been amassed, so in early July 1944 I./KG withdrew to Celle for the training and replacement of crews. The ten crews that remained were transferred to II./KG 40 at Bordeaux-Merignac. This *Gruppe* had undertaken six operations up to the 5th July 1944 and in that time the sunk 67,000 tons of merchant shipping and a 5,700 ton warship. The situation in France deteriorated though, so the remnants of I and II./KG 40 moved to Norway in late July 1944, with the former going to Tronheim-Vaernes and the latter to Gardemoen.

Few operations took place from Norway and in October 1944 eight He 177s were blown up and the remains of I./KG 40 was withdrawn to Neuburg am Donau, while II./KG 40 went to Parchi. Shortly afterwards both were ordered to begin converting to the Me 262 jet fighter-bomber, with I./KG 40 being re-designated I./(KG(J) 40 in November 1944. Plans were made in December 1944 for II./KG 40 to convert to the Arado Ar 234 jet bomber, but these were abandoned in February 1945 and both *Gruppe* were disbanded. What remained of the training and replacement unit, IV.(Erg)/KG 40 at Lechfeld had already disbanded on the 11th July 1944.

Other Units

The *Wetterkundungstaffel* (*Wekusta*) 2 (meteorological reconnaissance squadron) of the OKL, based at Mont de Marsan on the French Atlantic coast in July 1944, also operated the He 177. It later moved to Burg bei Magdeburg and had some seventeen He 177s on strength.

Four *Flugzeugführerschulen* (pilot training schools) operated obsolete He 177A-1s, many of which had been trans-

He 177A-1s used for training by FFS(B) 16 at Burg bei Magdeburg

ferred from defunct units such as I./FKG 50, along with some He 177A-3s and He 177A-5s. These training schools comprised FFS B15 at Bourges to the south of Orléans, France, FFS B16 at Burg bei Magdeburg, FFS A/B 31 in the Dresden region and FFS C 5 at Brandenburg-Briest.

On the 12th July 1944 the remaining aircraft from the *Ergänzungsgruppen* of KG 1, KG 40 and KG 100 joined to form *Ergänzungs-Kampfgruppe* He 177 at Neuburg am Donau. This unit was made up of the *Stab* formed from the *Stab* of IV.(Erg)/KG 1, the 1st *Staffel* formed from 10./KG 1 and 10./KG 40, the 2nd *Staffel* formed from 11./KG 40, the 3rd *Staffel* formed from 12./KG 100 and a 4th *(Kehl)Staffel*. Almost as soon as it formed the order was issued to cease all He 177 operations due to fuel shortages, but the *Gruppe* remained in a dormant state until it was re-designated IV.(Erg)/KG(J) 40 in October 1944, with the intention of converting the crews to fly the Me 262. In the end this proved impossible due to shortages of the Me 262 and the unit was finally disbanded on the 22nd January 1945.

The End – Part 1

From May 1944 Allied bombing operations had been concentrating on the Nazi German oil industry, so by August, aviation fuel production was down by some 90% to that of May. The Luftwaffe had no option but to drastically reduce flying and as a result all heavy bombers were immediately grounded. Shortly afterwards, production of the He 177 also ceased, as the war situation was such that there was no need for heavy bombers. The crews of KG 1 flew their bombers back to bases in Germany, where these aircraft spent the rest of their days parked out in the open, often alongside brand-newly built aircraft, where they became the target of ground-strafing Allied pilots during the last few months of WWII. I./KG 100 had transferred to Fassberg in May 1944, where it was re-designated III./KG 1 at the end of the month. Training by IV.(Erg)/KG 100 halted in May 1944 due to the fuel shortages and the *Gruppe* was finally disbanded on the 7th September 1944 at Giebelstadt. At this point the only unit operating the He 177 in the west was II./KG 100. This unit had not moved forward in response to the invasion and remained at Aalborg-West in Denmark but few sorties were ever undertaken after the invasion, due to the shortage of fuel.

Operation Bergund

The idea of using the He 177 against the Russian armament industry had already been considered, but on the 6th November 1944, Göring ordered that ten He 177s from II./KG 100 remain operational at Fassberg to undertake attacks on the Russian hydroelectric facilities at Rybinsk, Uglich and Volkhovstroi under Operation *Bergund* (Burgundy). The aircraft were to carry BM 1000F *Sommerballon* (Summer Balloon) bombs and the whole operation was under the command of KG 200. The BM 1000F was designed to be dropped into water upstream of a hydroelectric facility and be carried by the current into the turbine grate, where it is hoped it would explode, thus destroying the turbine with the resulting pressure wave. As plans for the operation went ahead though it was soon realised that fuel for the operation was not available, so Operation *Eisenhammer* (Iron Hammer) was proposed instead. This operation used *Mistel* composite aircraft, to be released against the electric powerplants in the Moscow/Upper Volga region. The 7th January 1945 plan would see the operation taking place during subsequent moonlit periods in February and March, with Obstlt Werner Baumbach's KG 200 in control. The targets were designated as the hydroelectric facilities at Rybinsk and Uglich along with the steam power stations at Aleksin, Balakhna, Dzerzhinsk, Gorkiy, Kashira, Komsomolsk, Shatura, Stalinogorsk (Novomoskovsk) and Yaroslavl. Although II./KG 100 was disbanded on the 20th February 1945, its aircraft were kept serviceable for possible use in Operation *Eisenhammer*, however, the final blow was dealt on the 10th April 1945 when eighteen *Mistel* composites were destroyed on the ground at Rechlin-Lärz after a US Eighth Air Force attack and on the 14th April 1945 the orders were finally given to abandon Operation *Eisenhammer*, with the aircraft being used for attacks against rivers over the Oder. The *Versuchs-kommando* of KG 200, which had formed from Lehr- und *Erprobungskommando* 36 in December 1944 did use its He 177s to launch Hs 293s against bridges over the Oder, but with little success.

The End – Part 2

Operations by the He 177 in December marked the end of its career and today most people see the type as a failure, sighting its poor engines and tendency to burst into flames with little provocation. The truth is far more complex though and whilst over 1,000 He 177s were built, less than 200 ever saw combat and the type had no direct effect on the war in any way. Its failure was caused by official sources constantly changing the requirements, coupled with the fact that when the initial specification was created, its demands were way outside anything that the aircraft manufacturers in Germany could possible achieve. This resulted in the use of novel approaches to overcome some of the obstacles raised in the specification and as nearly all of these were new and untested, it is not surprising that they were problematic or failed completely. In hindsight the easiest option was to make the type a true four-engine bomber, but the Luftwaffe was only ever seen as an offensive tool to support the *Wehrmacht*, and the need for strategic bombers was only realised by those in power when it was far too late. Had the four-engine He 177B/He 277 ever gone into production instead of the He 177, then it may have been a whole different story, as it is, the He 177 will probably always go down as the *Reichsfeuerzeug* ('Reich's lighter')!

The Four-Engine Greif

As early as mid-1939 Prof. Ernst Heinkel had proposed a He 177 fitted with four separate engines as the He 179, but this was abandoned in September 1939 with all future attempts to get the project restarted, being rejected. However, after the conference at Obersalzburg on the 27th June 1943, when Hitler demanded development of a bomber capable of attacking London by day or night at an altitude that made them impervious to Allied fighters, Heinkel once again but forward the idea of a four-engine He 177 to meet this need. Designed the He 177B, instructions were given to proceed with it immediately. The first prototype was the He 177 V101 (W/Nr.525550, NE+OD), which was rebuilt from a He 177A-3. It first flew on the 20th December 1943 from Zwölfaxing with Gotthold Peter at the controls. It had four DB603A engines in new cowlings with annular radiators, each driving a three-blade propeller. The second prototype

The He 274 V1 as the AAS 01A at Orléans-Bricy after completion in 1945

neath each wing. Conversion work was slow, but on the 22nd November, Heinkel offered to produce a *Mistel* prototype at the Eger factory, stating that a second could be available in fifteen days. Work on the He 162 *Volksjäger* was a priority at this stage however, so work on the He 177 *Mistel* got continually delayed, although a first flight date of the 1st February 1945 was mooted. By the end of 1944 it was obvious that fuel shortages combined with a lack of suitable airfields made the use of the He 177 *Mistel* against Russian power stations (it's intended target) impossible, so Carl Frydag suggested that the whole project be cancelled, but this was rejected. Finally, on the 27th January 1945, *Dipl. Ing*. Francke issued an order that the He 177 *Mistel* project should be cancelled completely and none of the prototypes were ever completed before the war ended. Another *Mistel* composite using the He 177 was considered before the end of the war, this used the Me 328 parasite fighter as the control aircraft, but this got no further than the drawing board.

He 274

Back in early 1941 Heinkel had proposed a high-altitude development of the He 177A-4, which was designated the He 177H. The type was to be powered by two DB610 engines, have a span of 36.0m and a length of 22.0m. As work continued on the project it was soon realised that the type would need a wing of a much higher aspect ratio than could not be achieved with simple spar extension, as the existing single spar was already exhibiting flexing problems. Heinkel therefore proposed to the RLM an entirely new two-spar wing combined with the He 177H fuselage. It was also suggested to combine this with Heinkel-Hirth 9-2291 exhaust-driven turbo-superchargers (some sources state the V1 was fitted with DVL-designed TK 11 turbosuperchargers and it was only the V2 that used the 9-2291?) . The use of such superchargers could only be achieved with conventional twelve-cylinder engines, so it was proposed that the new design (designated He 274 by the RLM in December 1941)

The A.A.S.01A with the SO-M1 (mock-up of the Sud-Quest SO 4000) mounted on its back

The AAS 01A shortly before its maiden flight at Orléans-Bricy on the 27th December 1945

be powered by four separate DB 603A engines. Fitment of the new wing, four separate engines and turbo-superchargers also necessitated the use of a twin fin and rudder units to achieve sufficient lateral stability.

The He 274 was to have a pressurised cockpit, so to test this the He 177 V10 (ex-He 177A-09, W/Nr. 177 000 0024, GA+QR) was fitted with the 2.75m longer cockpit cabin, which remained unpressurised under 2,500m, but above which the turbo-superchargers came into action to maintain the desired pressure. The V10 first flew in this configuration on the 5th February 1942, piloted by Gotthold Peter, but crash-landed on the 20th February 1943 and all testing was abandoned on the 3rd November 1943. By the 2nd May 1944 it was listed as being cannibalised for spares, but by 28th June 1944 it was with Heinkel for training purposes, although its ultimate fate is unknown.

Development of the whole He 274 programme was handed over to the Société Anonyme des Usines Farman (SAUF) based in Paris, France on the 13th July 1942. Whilst the hand-over was slow, the order for a mock-up was placed on the 15th September 1942. The original He 274 concept had had a 22.450m fuselage, standard wing, tail and undercarriage assemblies and a crew of five, but by the time the mock-up was ordered the design had been modified to gave a 44.25m span (two-spar construction) and a 22.28m fuselage, the twin fin/rudder assemblies and the undercarriage was modified to be two main legs with twin wheels that retracted back into enlarged nacelles. Full transfer of the He 274 programme was completed on the 20th February 1943 and on the 21st July two prototypes and four pre-production airframes were ordered, all to be built at the company's plant at Suresnes. As work continued the crew number was revised to four with the addition of a navigator/bomb aimer and a radio operator seated behind the pilot, the former was to operate the dorsal FDL 131Z gun barbette (sighted via the cupola above the rear of the cockpit), while the latter would operate the ventral FDL 131Z barbette. The fuselage was also lengthened with a 1.52m extension (23.80m total) being added in the rear section to improve directional and longitudinal stability. About 250 French draughtsmen spent about 964,000 hours working on the He 274 before the Suresnes facility was liberated by Allied troops. The first prototype, which was being prepared for flight just prior to this, had three of the engines, which were separately crated at the time, damaged by the German personal with explosive charges before leaving the factory and taking all the drawings with them.

With the liberation of Paris in August 1944 work on the He 274 resumed with *Ateliers Aéronautiques de Suresnes* (AAS) [SAUF nationalised]. Little damage had been caused to the V1 by the explosives and the three engines were quickly replaced with new ones discovered at another factory. The He 274 V1 was re-designated the AAS.01A and it flew for the first time in December 1945 from Orléans-Bricy. By this stage AAS had been absorbed by Société Nationale de Construction Aéronautiques du Sud-Quest (SNCASO) but continued testing took place from Bretigny-sur-Orge, mainly to do with cockpit pressurisation, then the type was allocated as the carrier aircraft for testing piloted mock-ups of new jet bombers, the SO.M-1 (a mock-up of the SO.4000) and the NC.271 (mock-up of the NC.270). The He 274 V2's history has been a little confused in all account thus far, but recent published data in France confirm that the V2 was completed and first flew on the 22nd December 1947, before later joining the A.A.S.01A as a carrier aircraft. The AAS.01A and A.A.S.01B were grounded at the end of 1952 and finally scrapped at Marseilles-Istres in late 1955 (some sources state late 1953, but a British magazine published an article in 1954 that stated that the dismantled two airframes were still at Istres at that stage; they also listed the overall colour as 'dark red-brown', but this is more likely to have been weathered French Khaki).

He 277

The whole concept of the four-engine He 177B series was further developed by Heinkel as a private venture in February 1943 designated the He 277. Whilst it still used the twin-spar wing and four separate engines of the He 177B, the fuselage was modified with an enlarged bomb bay (maximum capacity of 5,600kg) and it had a new extensively glazed cockpit, twin fin and rudder units and the twin-wheel undercarriage of the He 274. The type had heavy defensive armament of two remotely-controlled 20mm MG 151s in the *Fernbedienbare Drehlafette* FDL 151Z turret under the nose (A2-*Stand*), two 20mm MG 151s in a remotely-controlled *Fernbedienbare Drehlafette* FDL 151Z turret on the (forward) dorsal spine (B1-*Stand*), two 20mm MG 151s in a manually-operated *Hydraulische Drehlafette* HDL 151Z turret on (rear) dorsal spine (B2-*Stand*), two 20mm MG 151s in a *Fernbedienbare Drehlafette* FDL 151Z barbette under fuselage, aft of the bomb bay (C2-*Stand*) and four 13mm MG 131s in a *Hecklafette* HL 131V manned tail turret (*Heckstand*), although a HL 151Z turret with twin remotely-controlled MG 151 20mm cannon was also an option in this location. Two versions were proposed, the He 277A with 40m span, 23m fuselage, 5,200km range and 2,000kg bomb load and the He 277B with 33m span of

He 177A-5/R6 TS439 at Farnborough in 1945, with H.P. Manx, Blenheim, He 177, Firefly, Spitfire and Argus visible in the background

Outside the flight hangar at Farnborough in 1945 in the company of a Firefly, Mosquito and two Spitfires, this angle of TS439 allows you to see the *'Prise de Guerre'* text on the fuselage side as well as the way the demarcation curves down to the wings and tail

the He 177A-7 and 21.8m fuselage with a maximum speed of 550km/h and a range of 4,300km. Four different engine types were proposed, the BMW 801E radial, Daimler-Benz DB603E or G and Junkers Jumo 213A or 222. The latter was a twenty-four-cylinder engine that was hoped would at last give sufficient performance, but although tested in a few Ju 288s, the type was never reliable enough for full production and adoption in service. No real He 277 prototypes were ever completed before the war ended, although the He 177 V102 tested the twin rudder/fin assembly and the He 177 V104 was fitted with the four-gun rear turret intended for the type.

Foreign Evaluation

The He 177 was never operated by any other nation other than Nazi Germany, however examples were captured by Allied forces after the war, so we thought we would list their subsequent evaluation and fate.

United Kingdom (evaluation)

Allied forces had wanted to obtain a He 177 for some time prior to the summer of 1944 and on the 2nd September a team from the SOE (Special Operations Executive), supported by British and American paratroops and led by G.R. Starr, DSO, MC undertook a raid on the *Ateliers Industriel de l'Air* (AIA) overhaul facility at Toulouse-Blagnac. Shortly afterwards the RAE at Farnborough received notification that two intact He 177s had been captured, so Group Captain A. F. Hands, the CO and a team flew to Toulouse-Blagnac in a Lockheed Hudson escorted by two Bristol Beaufighters.

On arriving at Toulouse-Blagnac they found He 177A-5, W/Nr.550062, F8+AP (KM+UK) that had been used by II./KG 40 (some sources state 6./KG 40) ready for transfer. French national insignia was applied with invasion stripes applied around the wings and fuselage to reduce the risk of 'friendly fire' on the flight back to Farnborough. The aircraft was flown by Wg Cdr R.J. Falk, the RAE's chief test pilot and arrived at Farnborough after a 2hr and 45min flight on the 10th September 1944. Once in the UK, RAF roundels were applied along with the serial number TS439 and a large prototype 'P' marking on each side of the fuselage (applied by 20th September). The first flight test was undertaken by Sqn Ldr A. F. Martindale, on the 20th September with numerous other pilots flying the type in the coming weeks (including Capt. E. M. Brown). A total of twenty flights were conducted by the RAE, totalling 19 hours, 35 minutes, concluding on the 20th February 1945, when it was ferried to A&AEE Boscombe Down and handed over to the Americans. The engines were not sent with the aircraft though (one of its DB610 engines was damaged on the last flight, and the Americans already had replacements) and these ended up in a scrapyard in Aylesbury, where in 1973 one was acquired and still remains part of the Science Museum's Large Object Store at Wroughton, Wiltshire. Another example of the DB610, with sectioned front radiator cowling, is displayed at the RAF Museum, Cosford, Shropshire and the Deutsches Museum and Luftfahrt Technisches Museum, Rechlin have examples on display, while the Auto- und Technikmuseum at Sinsheim has an incomplete example.

The forward fuselage of He 177A-5, W/Nr.550062 can just be made out (arrowed) in store at Park Ridge, Illinois in the late 1940s

He 177A-5 (late production), W/Nr.550256 with Indian nose art and 'Hunter' name photographed at Bovington in 1945

United States of America (evaluation)

The second He 177 captured by the SOE (He 177A-5 W/Nr.550256 GP+RZ, although some wrongly list this as an A-7 it was a late production A-5) at Toulouse-Blagnac was overhauled and handed to Col. H. E. Watson who test flew it on the 28th November 1944, then ferried it to Villacoublay. There American radio equipment was installed and the aircraft serviced by the 10th Depot Repair Squadron. Flown from Villacoublay to RAE Farnborough by Sqn Ldr Randrup on the 14th January 1945, it was then flown to

Starboard side of the nose of He 177A-5, W/Nr.550256 at Bovington

He 177A-5, W/Nr.550256 at Bovington in 1945

Bovington by Lt Col R. J. Koster on the 19th January. On the 2nd February an order was issued to ferry the aircraft to Wright Field. In support of this the aircraft made flights from Bovington the next day totalling 2 hours 30 minutes. It was flown by Lt Col. R.J. Koster to Paris-Orly on the 9th February 1945, as the first leg of its intended delivery flight, but experienced engine problems and remained at Paris-Orly while an engine change took place. On the 28th February the aircraft attempted to leave Paris-Orly on route to the USA but a tyre burst on take-off and the aircraft was damaged beyond repair (the fuselage was broken in two) in the resulting ground-loop (this was caused by the synthetic tyres 'setting' out of shape due to the aircraft sitting in one position whilst the engine was replaced and this caused too much stress on take-off) and it was subsequently scrapped.

The loss of this airframe led to the other example captured by the SOE (W/Nr.550062) and tested by the RAE being handed over to the Americans, after it made its last flight to A&AEE Boscombe Down in February 1945. It was dismantled and shipped to USA without engines, arriving at Freeman Field it was allocated Foreign Evaluation code FE-2100 (later became T2-2100). It was fitted with new engines, which the American's had, but it was probably never flown in USA before it was crated for storage on the 16th May 1946. It was sent to No.803 Special Depot at Park Ridge, Illinois for museum storage on the 4th October 1946. The depot, using the assembly hangars build by Douglas, lost this storage facility with the onset of the Korean War in 1950 and as many airframes as possible were dispersed to museums or put out in store in the desert. It seems that W/Nr.550062 was not one of the lucky ones and anecdotal rumours are that it was buried on site, which today is part of O'Hare International Airport. It is interesting to note that the National Air & Space Museum have a complete DB610 in their collection that is in a set of He 177 cowlings, so maybe this came off of FE-2100 or were one of the spares acquired for it?

Specifications

Please note that there is much confusion with regard the various specifications for the He 177 series in both period German and British/American documents and post-war published material. We have tried to sort it all out, but where there is conflict, we have listed all options, so you can make your own minds up.

Engine
- He 177 V1 – Two 2,600hp Daimler-Benz DB606 V5 and V6 twenty-four-cylinder (coupled twelve-cylinder, 60° inverted-vee), liquid-cooled engines
- He 177A-1 – Two 2,600hp Daimler-Benz DB606A/b twenty-four-cylinder (coupled twelve-cylinder, 60° inverted-vee), liquid-cooled engines
- He 177A-3 – Two 2,975hp Daimler-Benz DB610 twenty-four-cylinder (coupled twelve-cylinder, 60° inverted-vee), liquid-cooled engines
- He 177A-5 – Two 2,975hp Daimler-Benz DB610 twenty-four-cylinder (coupled twelve-cylinder, 60° inverted-vee), liquid-cooled engines
- He 177A-0 & A-1 – Two 2,600hp Daimler-Benz DB606A/B twenty-four-cylinder (coupled twelve-cylinder, 60° inverted-vee), liquid-cooled engines
- He 177A-3 – Two 2,975hp Daimler-Benz DB610 twenty-four-cylinder (coupled twelve-cylinder, 60° inverted-vee), liquid-cooled engines
- He 177A-5 – Two 2,975hp Daimler-Benz DB610 twenty-four-cylinder (coupled twelve-cylinder, 60° inverted-vee), liquid-cooled engines
- He 177B-5 (Stage I) – Four 1,750hp Daimler-Benz DB603, twelve-cylinder, 60° inverted-vee, liquid-cooled engines
- He 277 V1 (AAS 01A) – Four 1,750hp Daimler-Benz DB603A-2, twelve-cylinder, 60° inverted-vee, liquid-cooled engines with Hirth 9-2881 turbo-superchargers

Span
- He 177V1, A-0 & A-0, A-3, A-5 & A-6 – 31.44m
- He 177B (Stage I) – 31.44m
- He 177A-7 – 36m
- He 277 V1 (AAS 01A) – 44.25m
- He 274 with DB603 – 44.1m
- He 274 with DB603G or BMW 801 – 40.0m
- He 277A – 40.00m

Length
- He 177 V1 – 20.58m
- He 177A-0 – 20.58m (some list as 21.58m, but this is probably a typo)
- He 177A-1 – 20.40m
- He 177A-3 – 22.00m
- He 177A-5 – 22.00m
- He 177A-6 – 22.92m
- He 177A-7 – 22.92m
- He 177B-5 (Stage I) – 22.45m
- He 274 V1 (AAS 01A) – 23.80m
- He 274 with DB603 – 19.84m
- He 277A – 23.00m

Height (tail up)
- He 177 V1, A-0, A-1 & A-3 – 6.67m
- He 177A-5 – 6.39m
- He 177A-6 – 6.39m
- He 177A-7 – 6.39m
- He 177B (Stage I) – 5.50m
- He 274 V1 – 5.50m
- He 274 with DB603 – 5.58m
- He 277A – 5.60m

Weight
- He 177 V1
  Empty – 13,720kg
  Loaded – 23,920kg
- He 177A-0
  Empty – 17,000kg
  Loaded – 31,000kg (some state 30,000kg)

- He 177A-1
  Empty – 16,300kg (some state 16,500kg)
  Loaded – 31,000kg (some state 30,300kg)
- He 177A-3
  Empty – 16,800kg [A-3/R5 18,410kg]
  Loaded – 31,000kg (some state 29,800kg) [A-3/R5 29,890kg]
- He 177A-5
  Empty – 16,800kg (A-5/R7 17,000kg)
  Loaded – 32,000kg
- He 177A-6
  Empty – 16,800kg (A-6/R2 16,900kg)
  Loaded – 32,000kg [A-6/R2 32,600kg]
- He 177A-7
  Empty – 18,100kg
  Loaded – 34,600kg
- He 177B-5 (Stage I) – *estimated*
  Empty – 19,115kg
  Loaded – 33,500kg
- He 274 V1 (AAS 01A)
  Empty – 21,300kg
  Loaded – 36,010kg
  Maximum Loaded – 38,010kg
- He 274 with DB603s – *estimated*
  Empty – 21,020kg
  Loaded – 36,050kg
- He 274 with DB603Gs or BMW 801 – *estimated*
  Empty – 25,790kg
  Loaded – 42,000kg
- He 277A – *estimated*
  Empty – 28,620kg
  Loaded – 55,000kg

Performance
- He 177 V1
  Maximum Speed – 460km/h @ 6,000m
- He 177A-0
  Maximum Speed – 440km/h @ sea level & 510-515km/h @ 4,000m
- He 177A-1
  Maximum Speed – 420km/h @ sea level & 500km/h @ 5,500m (some state 5,000m)
- He 177A-3
  Maximum Speed – 480km/h
- He 177A-5
  Maximum Speed – 488km/h
- He 177A-6
  Maximum Speed – 520km/h [A-6/R2 535 km/h]
- He 177A-7
  Maximum Speed – 540km/h
- He 177B-5 (Stage I) – *estimated*
  Maximum Speed – 440km/h @ sea level & 540km/h @ 6,300m
- He 274 V1 (AAS 01A)
  Maximum Speed – 430km/h @ sea level, 490km/h @ 3,000m and 580km/h @ 11,000m
- He 274 with DB603s – *estimated*
  Maximum Speed – 585km/h @ 6,000m
- He 274 with DB603Gs – *estimated*
  Maximum Speed – 535km/h @ 6,000m
- He 274 with BMW 801s – *estimated*
  Maximum Speed – 555km/h @ 6,000m
- He 277A – *estimated*
  Maximum Speed – 495km/h @ sea level & 575km/h @ 5,600m

Service Ceiling
- He 177 V1 – 7,000m
- He 177A-0 – 6,900m (some state 10,000m)
- He 177A-1 – 6,900m
- He 177A-3 – 10,000m
- He 177A-5 – 8,000m [A-5/R7 15,200m]
- He 177A-6 – 15,000m
- He 177A-7 – 16,000m
- He 274 V1 (AAS 01A) – 14,300m (absolute)
- He 274 with DB 603s – 14,300m – *estimated*
- He 274 with DB 603Gs or BMW 801s – 9,200m (absolute ceiling) – *estimated*

Range
- He 177 V1 – 5,000km
- He 177A-0 – 4,800km
- He 177A-1 – 4,500km at 6,000m (some state 5,600km)
- He 177A-3 – 5,600km at 6,000m [A-3/R5 5,800km]
- He 177A-5 – 6,000km
- He 177A-6 – 5,800km
- He 177A-7 – 7,200km
- He 177B-5 (Stage I) – 3,850km – *estimated*
- He 274 V1 (AAS 01A) – 2,850km @ 5,700m, 3,440km @ 11,000m or 4,250km @ 11,000m (maximum range)
- He 274 with DB 603s – 4,000km – *estimated*
- He 274 with DB 603Gs or BMW 801s – 5,300km – *estimated*

Armament
- He 177A-0 – One 7.9mm MG 81I in upper nose (A1-*Stand*); One 20mm MG FF cannon in lower nose (A2-*Stand*); Two 13mm MG 131 machine-guns in remotely-controlled barbette in forward dorsal spine (B1-*Stand*); One 13mm MG 131 machine-gun in manually operated HL 131 turret in aft dorsal spine (B2-*Stand*); One MG 81Z machine-gun in the rear ventral gondola (C1-*Stand*); One 13mm MG 131 machine-gun in the tail turret (*Heckstand*)
- He 177A-0 – One 7.9mm MG 81I in upper nose (A1-*Stand*); One 20mm MG FF cannon in lower nose (A2-*Stand*); Two 13mm MG 131 machine-guns in remotely-controlled barbette in forward dorsal spine (B1-*Stand*); No B2-*Stand*; One 13mm MG 131 machine-gun in the rear ventral gondola (C1-*Stand*); One 13mm MG 131 machine-gun in the tail turret (*Heckstand*)
- He 177A-3 – One MG 81I in upper nose (A1-*Stand*); One 20mm MG FF cannon (A-3/R1 or two 20mm MG 151 (A-3/R2) in lower nose (A2-*Stand*); Two 13mm MG 131 machine-guns in remotely-controlled barbette in forward dorsal spine (B1-*Stand*); One 13mm MG 131 machine-gun in manually operated HL 131 turret in aft dorsal spine (B2-*Stand*); One 13mm MG 131 machine-gun in the rear ventral gondola (C1-*Stand*); One 13mm MG 131 machine-gun (A-3/R1) or one 20mm MG 151/20 (A-3/R2 & A-3/R5) in the tail turret (*Heckstand*)
- He 177A-5 – One MG 81I in upper nose (A1-*Stand*); One 20mm MG 151 in lower nose (A2-*Stand*); Two 13mm MG 131 machine-guns in remotely-controlled barbette in forward dorsal spine (B1-*Stand*); One 13mm MG 131 machine-gun in the rear ventral gondola (C1-*Stand*); One 20mm MG 151/20 in the tail turret (*Heckstand*)
- He 177A-6 – One MG 81I in upper nose (A1-*Stand*) – none in A-6/R2; One 20mm MG 151 (A-6/R1) or 13m MG 131Z (A-6/R2) in lower nose (A2-*Stand*); Two 13mm MG 131 machine-guns (A-6/R1) or one 20mm MG 151 cannon in FDL 151Z (A-6/R2) in remotely-controlled barbette in forward dorsal spine (B1-*Stand*); One 13mm MG 131 machine-gun in manually operated HL 131 turret in aft dorsal spine (B2-*Stand*); Two 13mm MG 131 machine-guns (A-6/R1) or four 13mm MG 131s in HL 131V turret (A-6/R2) in the tail position (*Heckstand*)
- He 177A-7 – One MG 81I in upper nose (A1-*Stand*); Two 13mm MG 131 in lower nose (A2-*Stand*); Two 20mm MG 151 cannon in remotely-controlled barbette in forward dorsal spine (B1-*Stand*); No B2-*Stand*; Four 13mm MG 131s in HL 131V turret in the tail position (*Heckstand*)
- He 177B-5 (Stage I) proposed – Two 13mm MG 131 machine-guns in the lower part of the nose (A2-*Stand*); Two 20mm MG 131 machine-guns in remotely-controlled FDL 131/2A barbette in forward dorsal spine (B1-*Stand*); One 13mm MG 131 in manually-operated turret in aft dorsal spine (B2-*Stand*); One 13mm MG 131 machine-gun in the rear of the ventral gondola (C2-*Stand*); Four 13mm MG 131s in HL 131V turret in the tail position (*Heckstand*)
- He 274 proposed – Two 13mm MG 131 machine-guns in the nose (A1-*Stand*); Two 20mm MG 131 machine-guns in remotely-controlled FDL 131/2A barbette in forward dorsal spine (B1-*Stand*); Two 13mm MG 131 machine-guns in remotely-controlled FDL 131Z ventral barbette (C2-*Stand*)
- He 277A planned – Two 20mm MG 151/20 cannon in the lower nose (A2-*Stand*); Two 20mm MG 151/20 cannon in the FDL 151Z barbette in the forward dorsal spine (B1-*Stand*); Two 20mm MG 151/20 cannon in the FDL 151Z barbette in the aft dorsal spine (B2-*Stand*); Two 20mm MG 151/20 cannon in the FDL 151Z barbette in the ventral position (C1-*Stand*); Four 13mm MG 131 machine-guns in an HL 131V manually-operated tail turret (*Heckstand*)

Ordnance
- He 177A-0 & A-1 – Internal bomb load of a minimum of 800kg and a maximum of 2,200kg
- He 177A-3 – Internal bomb load of a minimum of 800kg and a maximum of 2,200kg (A-3/R1) or 2,500kg (A-3/R2 & A-3/R5)
- He 177A-5 – Internal bomb load of a minimum of 2,200kg and a maximum of 2,800kg
- He 177A-6 – Internal bomb load of a minimum of 2,200kg and a maximum of 3,500kg
- He 177A-7 – Internal bomb load of a minimum of 2,200kg and a maximum of 4,200kg
- He 177B-5 (Stage I) proposed – Internal bomb load of sixteen SC 50, four SC250 or two SC500 general-purpose bombs, plus external bomb load of two LMA III parachute sea mines, two LT950 torpedoes, three Henschel Hs 293 or Fritz-X radio-guided bombs
- He 274 proposed – Internal bomb load of 4,000kb in two bays
- He 277A planned – Internal bomb load of a maximum of 5,600kg comprising two SC1800 and two SC100 bombs, plus external bomb load of two SC2500 bombs, Hs 293/Hs 294 or Fritz X radio-guided bombs

Electrical Equipment
- He 177A-5 – FuG X (HF transmitter/receiver in the 6-12 MHz range); *Peilgerät* 6 (HF direction-finder linked to FuG X); FuG 17Z (VHF communications and direction-finding equipment in the 42.3 to 47.9 MHz range); FuB1 2 (blind-approach); FuG 101A (radio altimeter); FuG 25 (IFF); FuG 200 *Hohentweil* (air-to-surface vessel radar, only fitted in anti-shipping role); FuG 203 (radio-control equipment for Hs 293 glide bombs operating on eighteen frequencies in the 48 to 50 MHz range

Note: Please note that as the He 177 was built and tested using metric measurements we have refrained from offering Imperial conversions in the above data.

Technical Description

What follows is an extensive selection of images and diagrams that will help you understand the physical nature of the Heinkel He 177. With no complete or even partial airframe existing, we have had to base this section entirely on period images and diagrams.

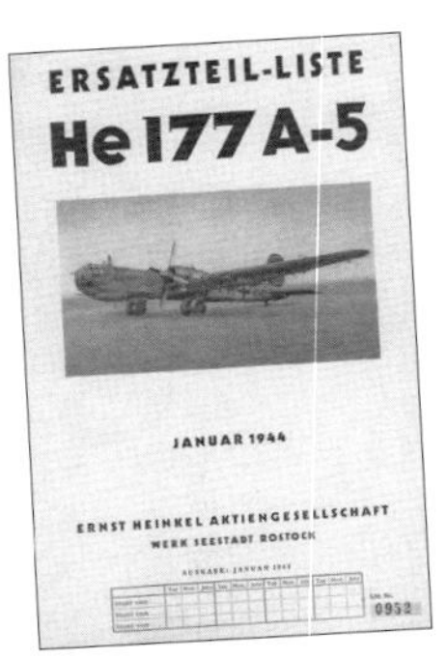

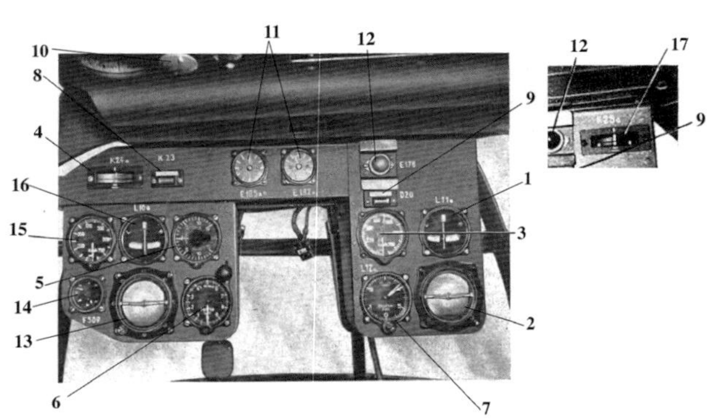

This is the pilot's instrument panel in the He 177A-0

1. Turn & bank indicator
2. Artificial horizon
3. Airspeed indicator
4. Course indicator
5. Variometer
6. Fine and coarse altimeters
7. Contact altimeter
8. Course control indicators
9. Pitot tube indicator
10. Emergency pull button for heading control
11. Position indicator for propellers
12. Pitot tube heater warning lamp
13. Horizon
14. Flap indicator
15. Airspeed indicator
16. Turn & bank indicator
17. Course pointer (only shown in certain images in the A-0 manual)

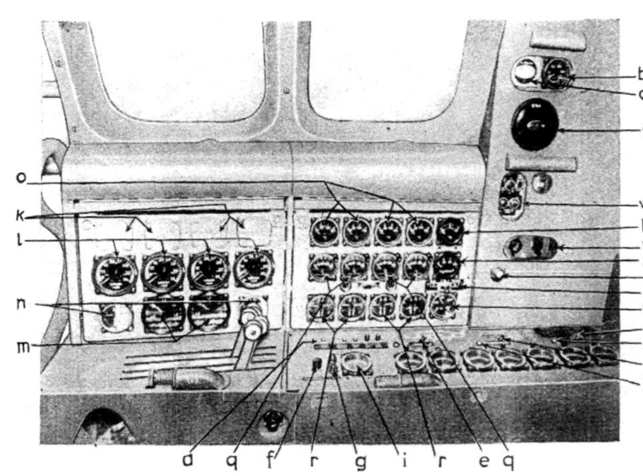

This shows the equipment on the starboard side of the cockpit in the He 177A-0

a. O_2 monitor
b. O_2 pressure indicator
c. Bosch horn
d. Automatic switch for fuel level/ remaining level warning, supply measuring system, feed pumps and pump main switch
e. Switch for wing fuel container and fuselage fuel container
f. Push button for horn shutdown
g. Fuel level/remaining level warning lamps
h. Indicator for fuel tank pumps
i. Fuel tank content indicator
k. Fuel consumption meter (not yet installed)
i. Speedometer
m. Boost pressure gauge
n. Transmission oil pressure gauge
o. Temperature meter for coolant
p. Outdoor air temperature meter
q. Temperature gauge for engine oil inlet and outlet
r. Oil and fuel pressure gauges – see oil pressure gauge for pressure accumulator
t. Selector switch for the pressure gauges of the hydraulic oil pumps and pressure gauges for hydraulic oil pumps
v. Junction box for intercom
w. Switch for smoking devices (e.g. RATO)
x. Override push button switch

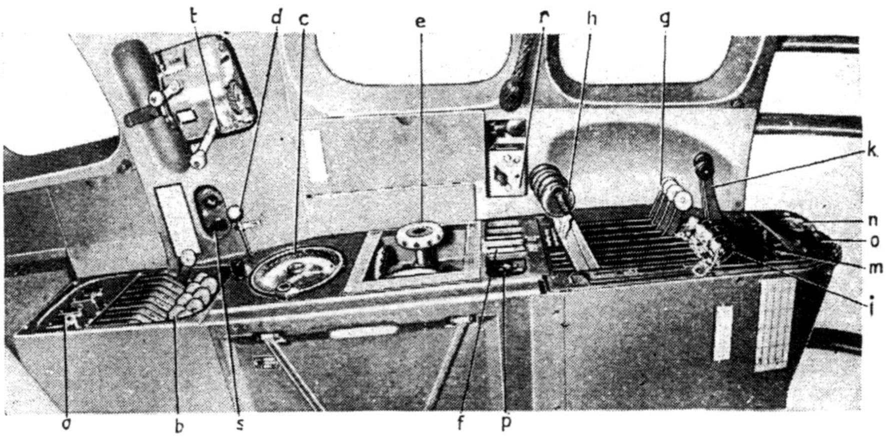

This shows the equipment on the port side console of the cockpit in the He 177A-0

a. Starter switches and push buttons for injection valves
b. Lever for engine shutdown, spark plug cleaning, oil filter cleaning and fluid nose de-icing
c. Radio direction finding device
d. Hand pump for starting fuel
e. Trim drives
f. Switches for Fowler flaps and landing gear
g. Lever for engine clutches
h. Throttle lever (2 levers with thumb switch for propeller adjustment)
i. Ignition switch
k. Firecock shifter
m. Warning lamps for landing gear and Fowler flaps (twelve-lamp device)
n. O_2 monitor
o. O_2 pressure indicator
p. Switch (dive brake trim)
r. Control unit for FuG 25
s. Junction box for intercom
t. Remote control device for target flight receiver

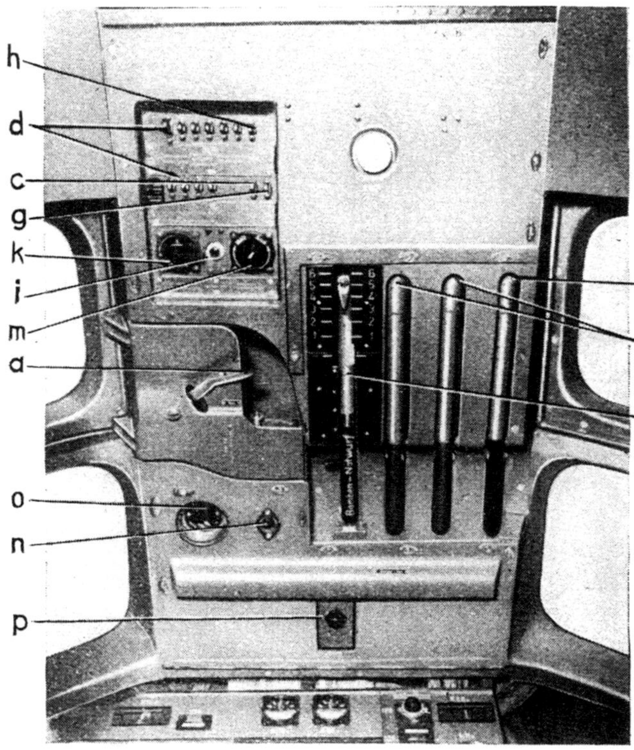

This is the instrument panel built into the overhead panel in the canopy and again comes from the He 177A-0 manual

a. Release lever for Stuvi storage
b. Emergency bomb release lever
c. Propeller de-icing switch
d. Switch for lighting
e. Fuel quick start lever
f. Lever for bomb release
g. Switch-off for rear parking heater
h. Pitot tube heater switch
i. Switches for signalling systems
k. Skin switch for three-axis control (not connected)
m. Blackout for device lights
n. Power off switch
o. Switch for heating
p. Remote control device for FuG 16

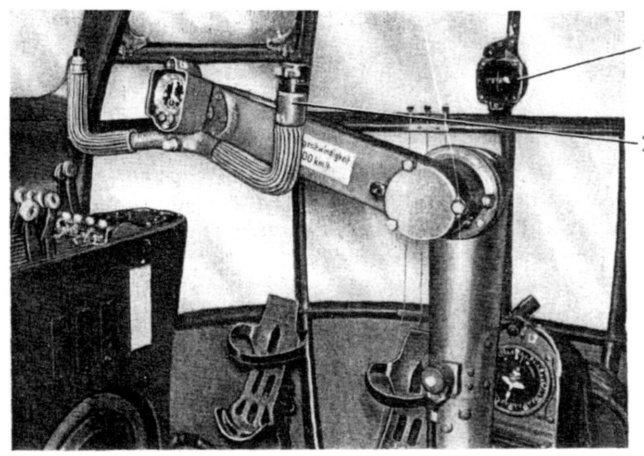

This shows the main compass (1) and Direction Indicator on the control column (2) in the cockpit of the A-0

This shows the main distribution panel on the starboard side in the rear of the cockpit in the A-0

a. Auto switch
b. Volt and ammeter
c. O_2 monitor
d. O_2 pressure indicator
e. Main power switch

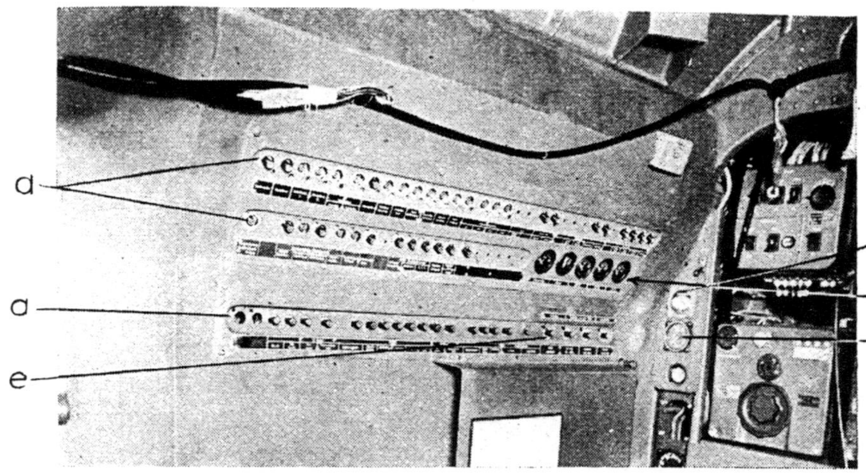

These are the additional devices alongside the control column in the A-0

1. Pilot's slave compass
2. Distance course indicator
3. Direction indicator

This is the trim drive in the port side console of the A-0

1. Dive switch

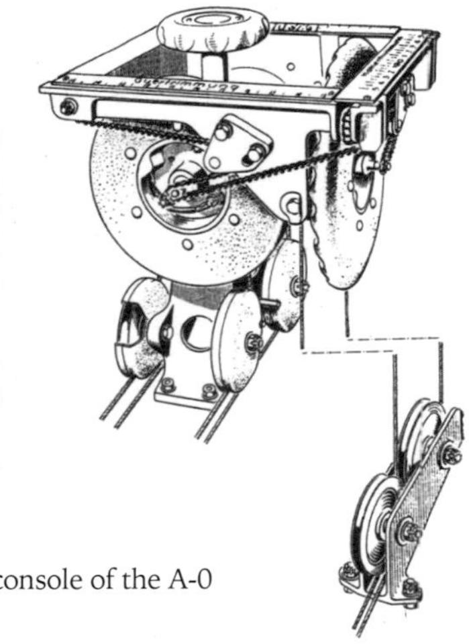

This is the control ('encoder') panel (relating to bomb release) built into the pedestal at the front of the starboard side console of the A-0

1. Wind speed
2. Height correction
3. Own speed

These are the controls at the rear of the starboard side console in the A-0

a. Automatic switch for outboard connection
b. Switching crank for emergency fuel delivery
c. Hand pump for emergency oil operation
d. Switch for oil and water cooler thermostats
e. Loading switch for opening the bomb hatches while stationary
f. Emergency cable for chassis
G. Switch for emergency operation of the oil pressure system

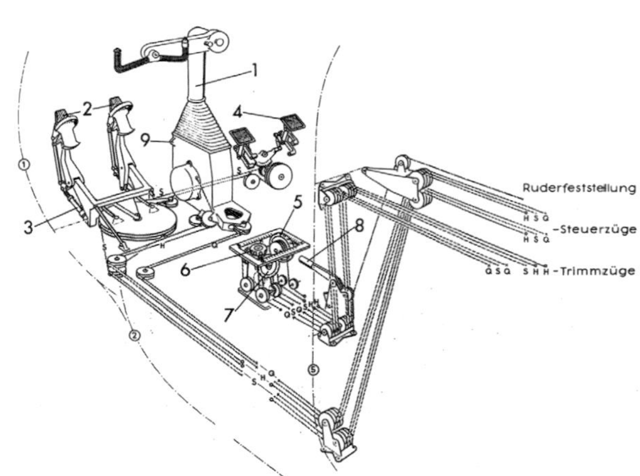

This diagram gives an overview of the controls in the A-0 cockpit, but also applies to all other A-series sub-variants

1. Control column with Steierhorn (height control and transverse control)
2. Rudder, main controls
3. Oil brake valves
4. Rudder, auxiliary control
5. Height trim handwheel
6. Side trim handwheel
7. Cross trim hand wheel
8. Rudder locking lever
9. Connection for sighting turret

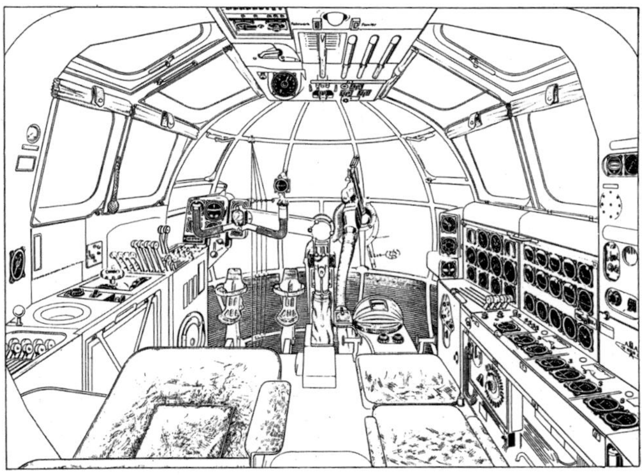

This diagram gives an overview of the cockpit interior of the He 177A-1

The pilot's instrument panel in the He 177A-1 went from the overhead version in the He 177A-0, to this one mounted on the front of the port side console

1. Airspeed indicator
2. Fine-Coarse altimeter
3. Course indicator
4. Artificial horizon
5. Variometer
6. Indicator for Straurohr heating
7. Lever for pivoting part of the driver's panel for navigation
8. Pilot's slave compass
9. Radio navigation display device
10. Pivoting part of the driver's equipment panel
11. Emergency compass

This is the equipment on the port side console in the He 177A-1 (below)

1. Starter switches and push buttons for injection valves
2. Lever for engine shutdown, plug and lubricant filter cleaning and surface de-icing
3. Hand pump for starting fuel
4. Starting fuel pressure indicator
5. Trim drives
6. Connection for self-understanding
7. Switch (trim-dive brake)
8. Throttle lever
9. Ignition switch
10. Engine clutch lever
11. Fire cock control lever
12. Eleven lamp device
13. O_2 monitor and pressure indicator
14. FuG 25
15. Speed selector lever (not connected)

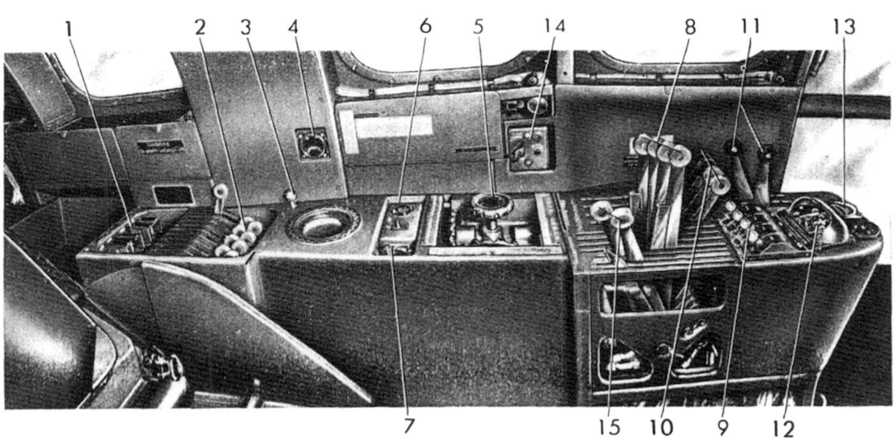

This is a close-up of the controls in the rear of the port side console in the He 177A-1 that were marked as items '1' and '2' in the image below

1. Engine stop control lever
2. Control lever for wing de-icing
3. Operating lever for lubricant filter cleaning
4. Control lever for plug cleaning
5. Starter switch
6. Push buttons for starting fuel

This shows the ignition switches at the front of the port side console in the A-1

1. Ignition switch
2. Ignition switch connection

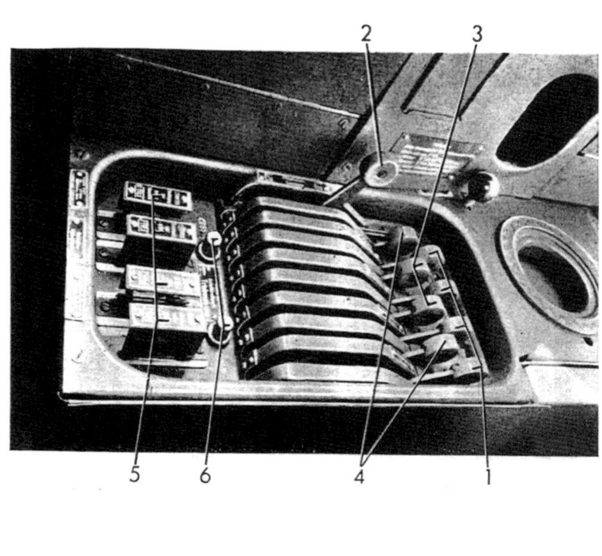

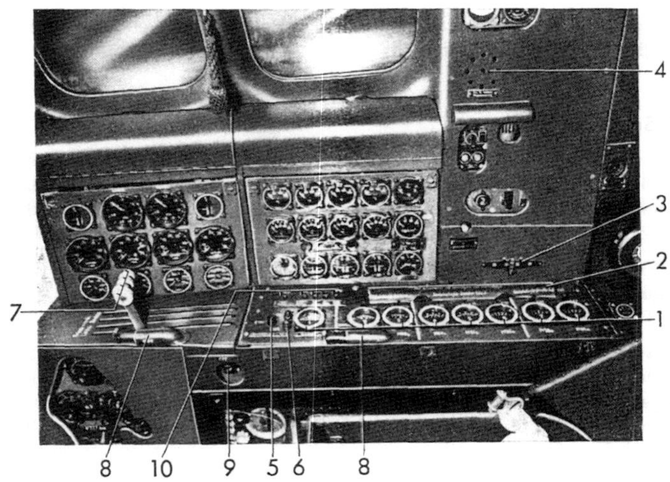

These two images cover some of the equipment in the side console and on the sidewall of the starboard side of the A-1

Right operating table
1. Fuel Gauges
2. Cover plate
3. Fuel tankage plate
4. Bosch horn
5. Horn shutdown
6. Warning lights
7. Throttle lever
8. Device light
9. Device light switches
10. Pump auto switch

Partial view of the right operating table
1. Fuel gauges for removable containers
2. Fuel gauges for containers in the centre wing section
3. Fuel gauges for fuselage containers
4. Fuel gauges for containers in the centre wing section
5. Full warning light
6. Remaining level warning lamp
7. Pressure gauge for emergency delivery
8. Crank drive for emergency delivery changeover valve

This shows the UV lights on the port side of the cockpit in the A-1
1. UV lights
2. Cladding panels
3. UV ballasts

This image covers the remainder of the equipment in the side console and on the sidewall of the starboard side of the A-1

1. Fuel gauges
2. Warning lights
3. Horn shutdown
4. Device light
5. Device light switch
6. Cover plate for hand switch
7. Fuel tankage plate
8. Bosch horn
9. Pump auto switch
10. Throttle lever
11. Pressure indicators for lubricant and fuel
12. Lubricant temperature indicator
13. Coolant temperature indicator
14. Transmission oil pressure gauge
15. Tachometer
16. Boost pressure gauge
17. Consumption meter
18. Outdoor air temperature indicator
19. Pressure indicators for hydraulic pumps
20. Oil pressure accumulator pressure indicator
22. Hydraulic pump toggle switches
23. Switch box for smoking devices
24. ADb box
25. Pressure accumulator switch

This is the additional instrument panel at the front of the side console on the starboard side of the A-1
1. Altitude compensated airspeed indicator
2. Variometer
3. Turn indicator

This is the overhead console in the A-1, which is only slightly changed from that in the A-0
1. Hand lever for quick release

This is a close-up of the switchgear in the rear/left quarter of the overhead console in the A-1
1. Toggle switch
2. Blackout switch
3. Push button switch

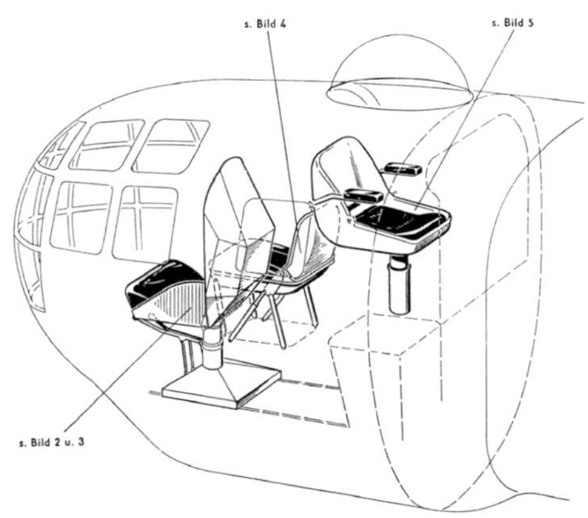

This is an overall diagram of the seating in the cockpit of the A-1

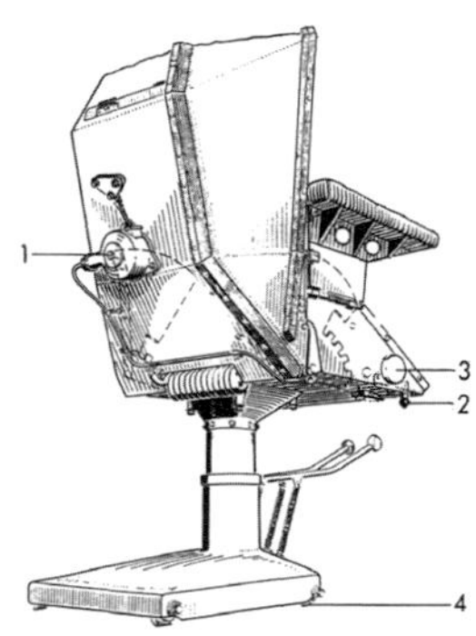

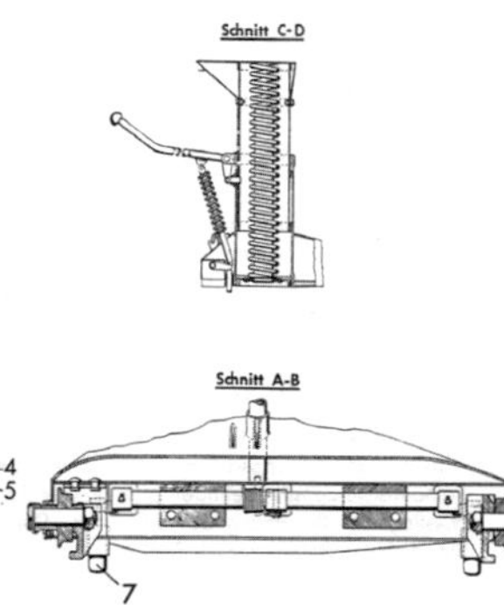

There are two illustrations of the pilot's seat in the A-1 manual, one from the front (right) and one from the back (left) – The upper section of the armour on the image on the left is truncated

Pilot's seat from the front
1. Armrest
2. Seat pan
3. Seat carriage
4. Lever for longitudinal adjustment
5. Height adjustment lever
6. Locking holes for height adjustment
7. Detents for longitudinal adjustment

Pilot's seat from the rear
1. Shoulder strap adjustment device
2. Lever for shoulder strap adjustment
3. Backrest adjustment lever
4. Seat brackets

These three images show the bombardier's seat in the A-1, A-3 & A-5 in the upright (middle) and extended (left) positions, as well as what is behind/below it (right)

Bombardier seat attachment
1. Connecting pipe
2. Footpeg linkage

Bombardier seat
1. Seat pan
2. Telescopic strut
3. Notch for setting the cushion
4. Bowden cable

Bombardier's seat as a cushion
1. Footrest
2. Upholstery

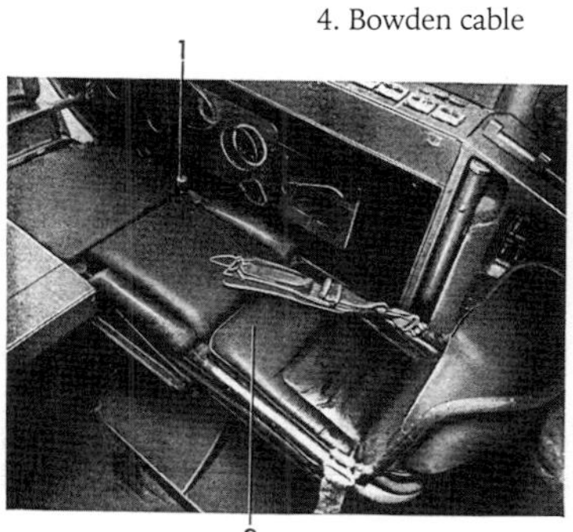

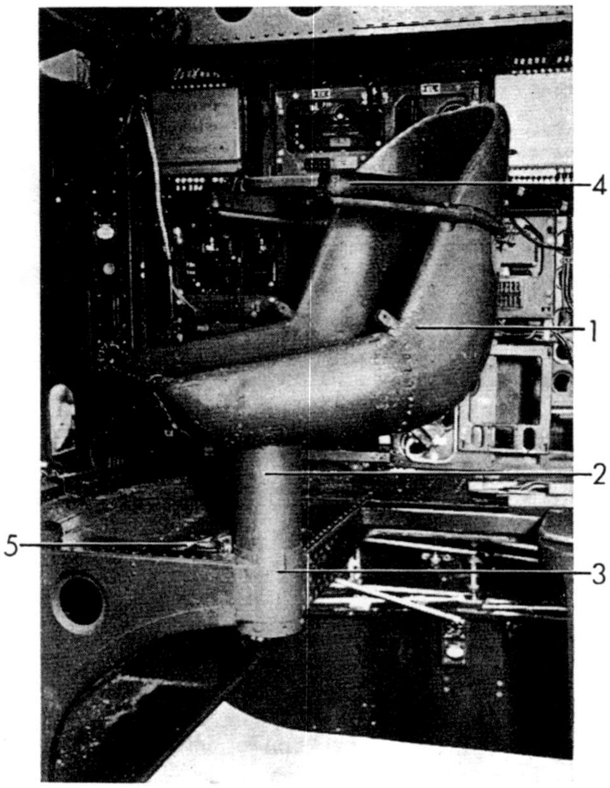

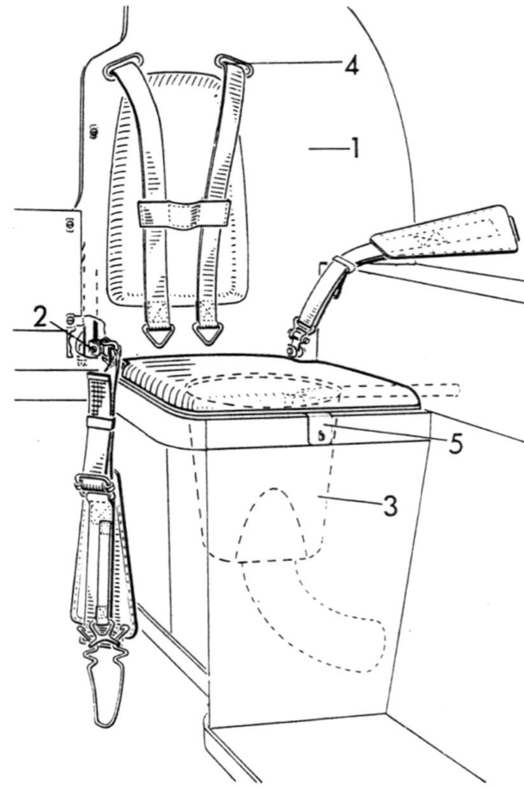

This is the seat for the B-*Stand* gunner in the A-1

1. Seat pan
2. Seat base
3. Storage
4. Armrest
5. Footrest

This is the seat for the C-*Stand* gunner, which also doubles as the toilet for the crew

1. Cover wall
2. Waist belt attachment
3. Toilet
4. Slots for shoulder strap
5. Lid closure

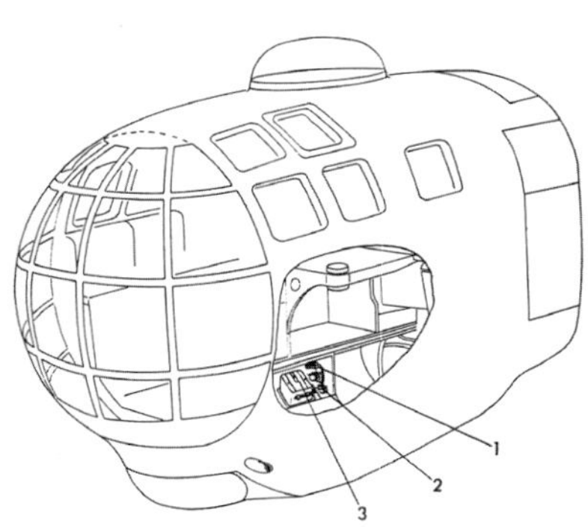

These diagrams and images show the location of the flare pistol (right), as well as its access from the outside (top, left) and cockpit interior (bottom, left)

Installation sketch of the flare gun with flare cartridge box (right)
1. Flare gun
2. Flare gun holder
3. Flare cartridge box

Flare gun and flare box seen from the inside of the cockpit (upper left)
1. Flare gun
2. Hammer
3. Trigger
4. Locking lever
5. Handle
6. Barrel
7. Bracket for flare gun
8. Clamp screw for bracket
9. Flare cartridge box
10. Lid to the cartridge box
11. Strap with snap to lid
12. Operating lever for engaging or disengaging the insert

Flare gun and flare box in the cockpit with panelling (lower left)
1. Fairing panel
2. Quick release

This is the additional equipment in front of the control column in the A-1
1. Pilot's slave compass
2. Distance course indicator

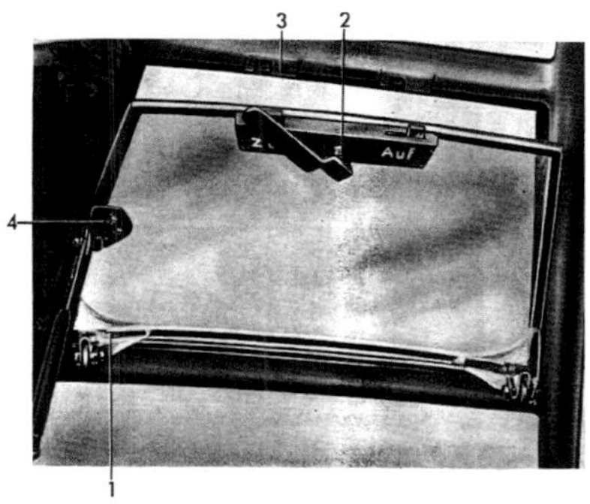

This shows the hinged window in the upper port side of the canopy in the A-1, it is presumed the A-0 also had this, but there is no such diagram in that variant's handbook

1. Bearing piece
2. Bolt lock
3. Locking piece
4. Bracket

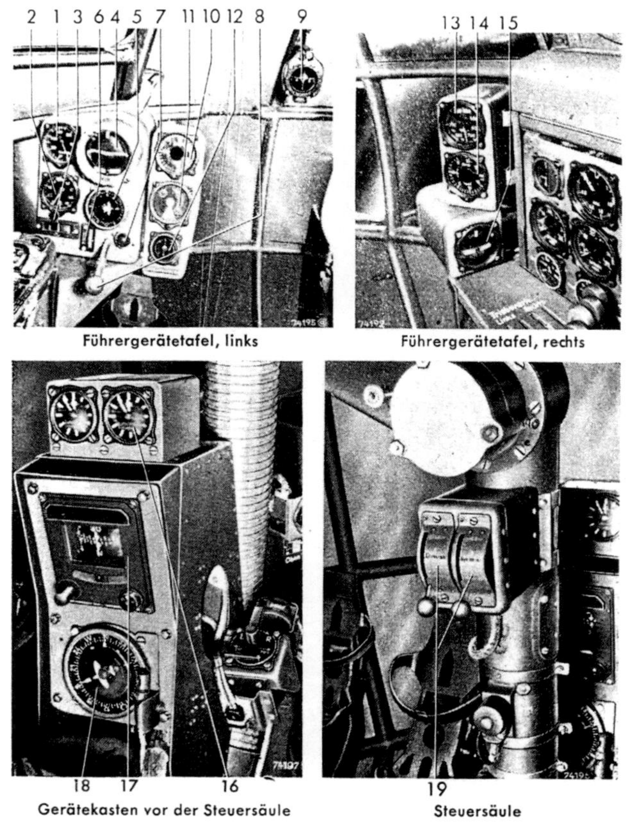

These four images show the arrangement of flight controls and navigation equipment in the cockpit of the A-3

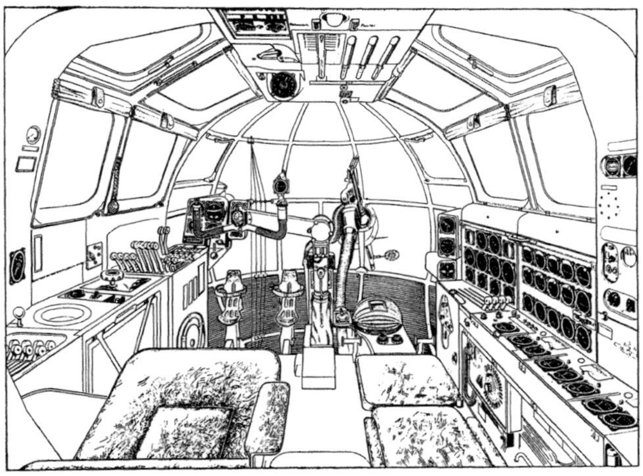

This is an overview of the cockpit interior taken from the He 177A-3 handbook

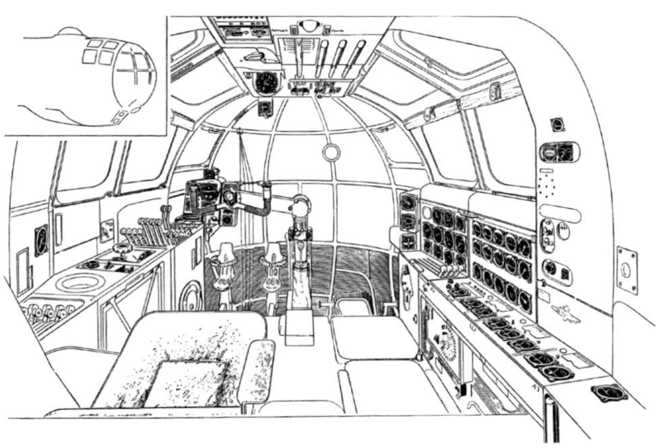

This is another overview of the cockpit interior taken from the He 177A-3 parts manual and as you can see, it is slightly different

Pilot's device panel, left (top left)
Pilot's device panel, right (top right)
Equipment box in front of the control column (bottom left)
Control column (bottom right)

1. Airspeed indicator
2, Fine-Coarse Altimeter
3. Course pointer
5. Pilot's slave compass
6. Indicator for pitot tube heating
8. Handle for pivoting board
9. Emergency compass
10. Variometer
11. Homing indicator
12. Altitude compensated airspeed indicator
13. Variometers
14. Turn & bank indicator
15. Position indicator for propellers
16. Direction indicator
17. Pilot's Patin compass
18. Adjustment switch for propellers

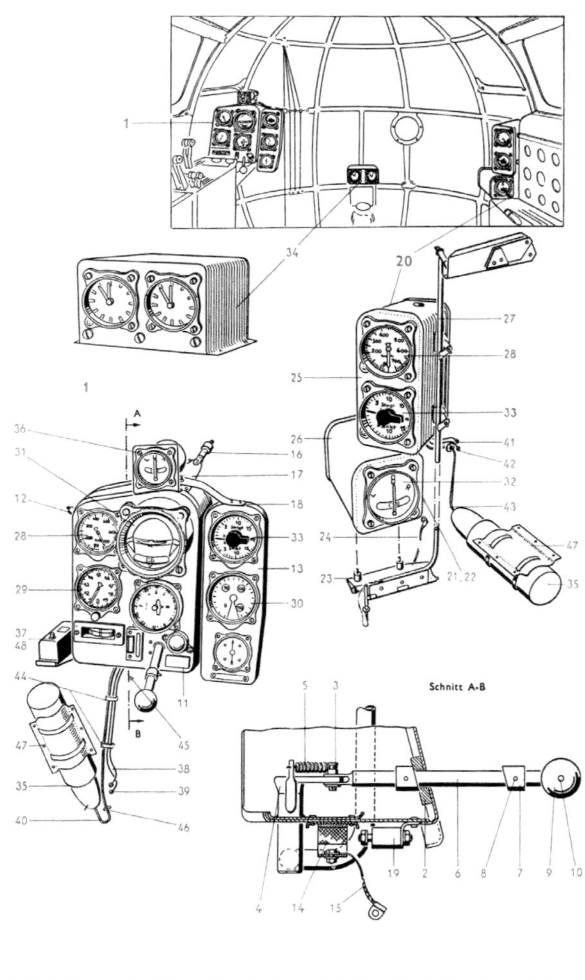

There are no images of the main instrument panel etc. from the He 177A-3 handbook, there are these diagrams in the parts manual though, even if they lack notation

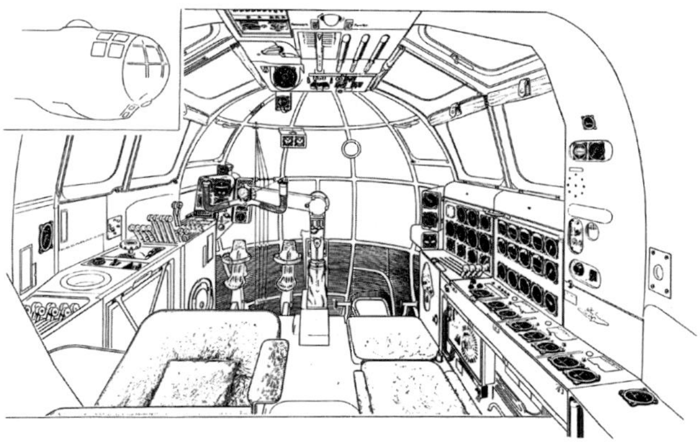

This is an overview of the cockpit interior taken from the He 177A-5 parts manual. Note how the lower sections of the nose glazing are painted over

This is the port side of the cockpit interior of a He 177A-5

Not the best quality, but this is the starboard sidewall and side console in TS439, the He 177A-5 captured and tested at Farnborough

A nice shot of the control column, rudder pedals etc in He 177A-5, TS439

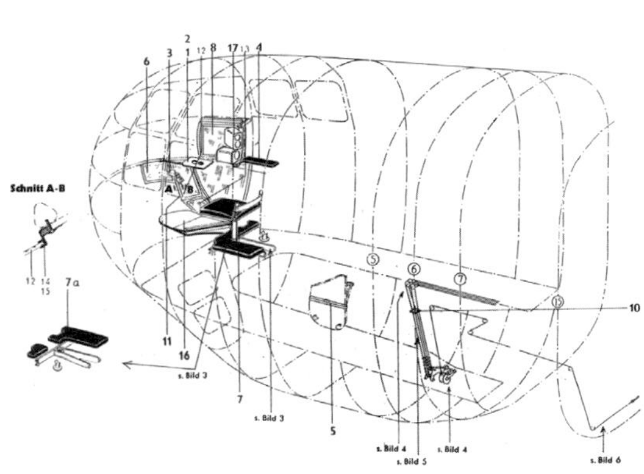

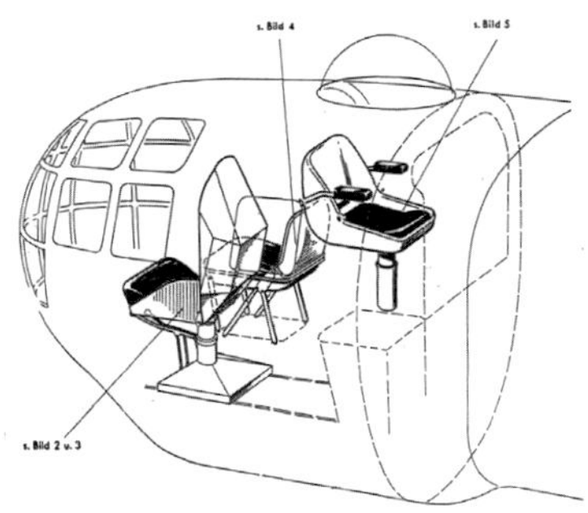

These two diagrams from the He 177A-5 parts manual, show the front-gunner and bombardier's seat on the left, and an overall view of all crew seats on the right

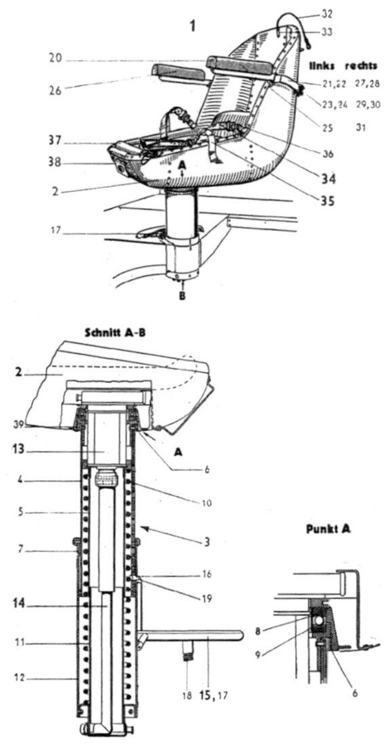

This diagram shows the B-*Stand* gunner's seat and comes from the He 177A-5 parts manual

This image from the He 177A-1 manual, showing the He 177A-03, W/Nr.0018, DL+AR with an MG FF in the lower gondola A2-*Stand* and a single machine-gun in the original style mount for the A1-*Stand*

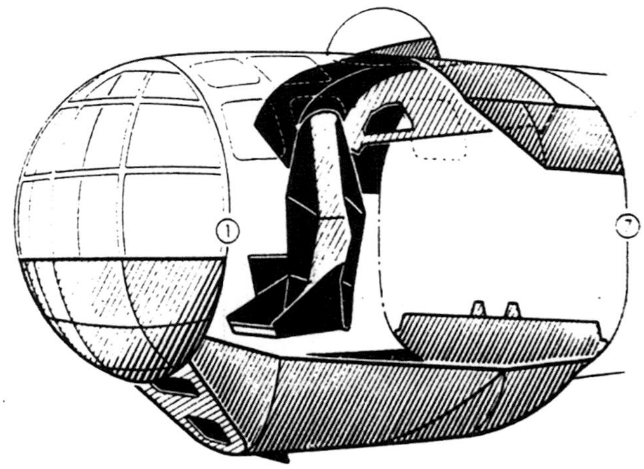

This diagram, from the A-1 manual, shows the armour plating installed in the cockpit region from Frame 1 through to 7 and this applies to all A-series sub-variants

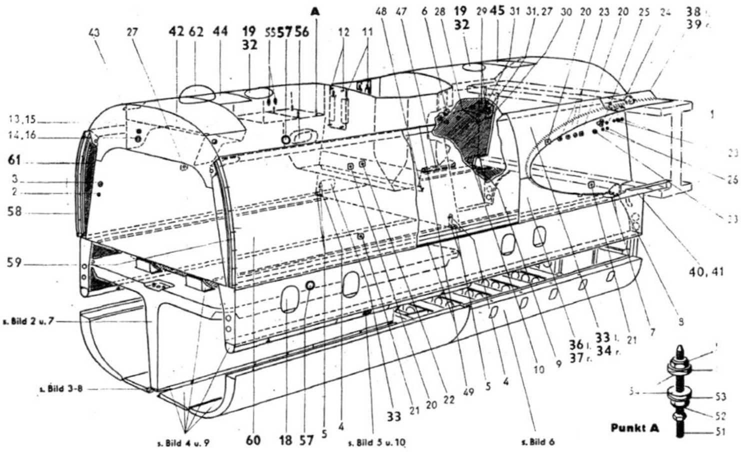

This shows the forward fuselage region aft of the cockpit and ahead of the wing root from the A-5 parts manual. It is basically the same as the A-3, but has things like the little clear blister ('62') offset to starboard on the dorsal spine

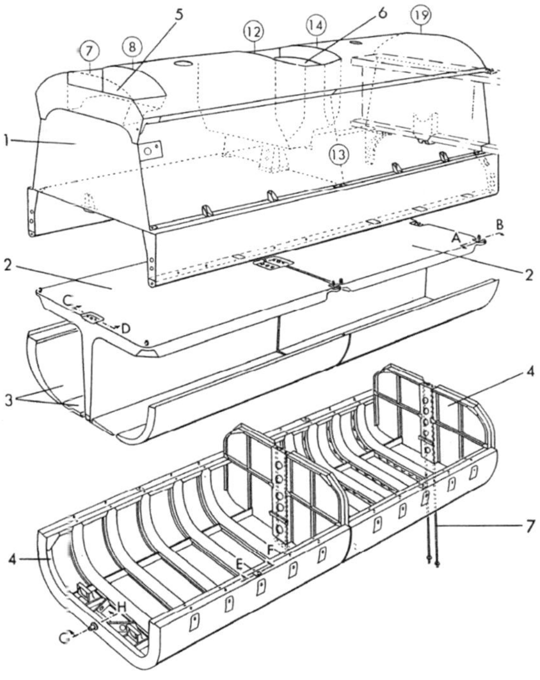

This diagram from the A-3 manual deal with the forward fuselage region aft of the cockpit and ahead of the wing root

1. Front part of the fuselage
2. Bomb carrier
3. Bomb doors
4. Container carrier
5. Opening for the hydraulic oil container
6. Opening for the remote-controlled B-*Stand*
7. Rod bolts

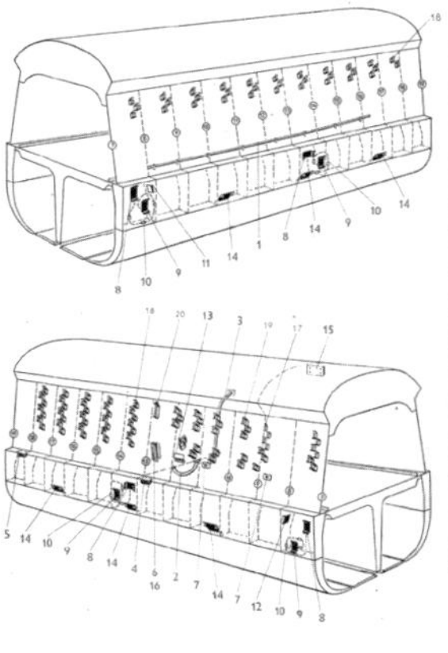

The two diagrams on the left are from the A-3 manual and deal with the tunnels in either side of the forward fuselage region aft of the cockpit, while the image on the right shows wrecked A-3 'Edith' of 2./KG 100 with the covers off the tunnel, allowing you to see the control linkage, fuel/air/hydraulic lines etc. that ran within them

This close-up of the nose of an He 177A-3/R2 of FFS(B) 16 shows the way in which the lower regions of the nose cupola were often painted over. You can also see the double balloon cable cutters attached one above the other around the nose and down the fuselage sides

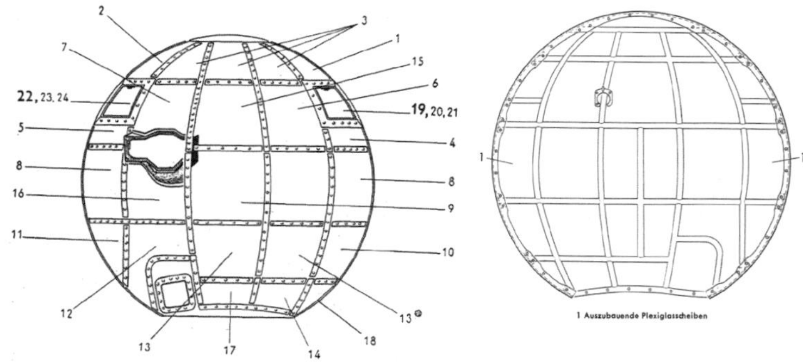

Here you can see the evolution of the nose cupola, the diagram on the right is from the A-1 manual and shows the cupola viewed from the inside looking out, while the diagram on the right is from the A-5 parts manual and shows the cupola viewed from the outside, looking in

These two close-ups from period image show the clear nose glazings on the right, whilst on the left you can see the lower ones painted over. Note the two narrow vertical panels in the port side, with screens inside, this seems only to occur late-war, but can be found on both A-3s and A-5s

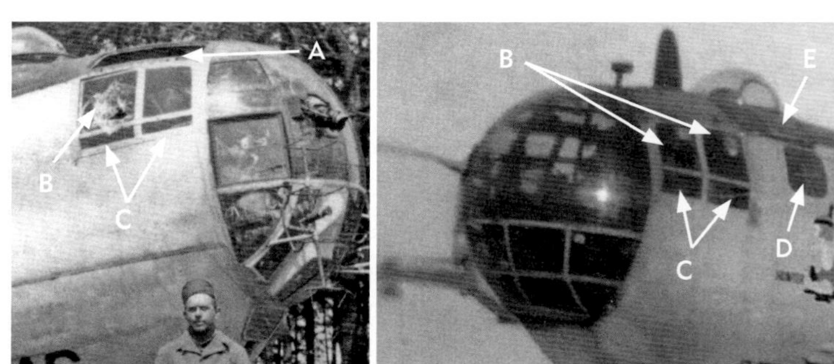

The last two production batches of the A-5 series had revisions to the windows on either side of the nose, with the upper one being made into a single unit [A], where it had previously been two, then the lower ones were made larger (deeper) [B] with a narrow pair added below [C]. The clear panel below the sighting cupola on the port side was also increased in size [D], moved and a second one added above it [E], as seen in these two images of a wrecked example on the right (W/Nr.550316) and the example captured by British forces and passed to the Americans (W/Nr.550256) on the left

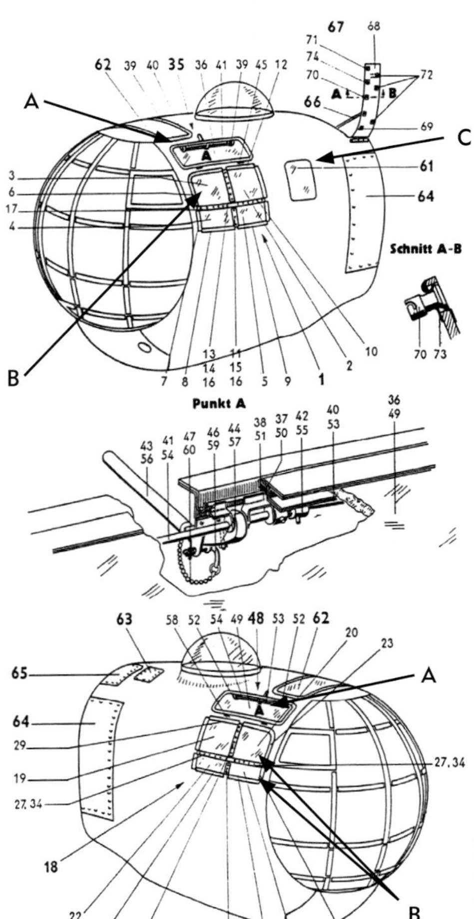

Here is the diagram from the A-5 parts manual showing the revised upper [A] and lower [B] windows, but still showing a single one [C] below the sighting cupola

These three images show the forward fuselage of the He 274 V2 (A.A.S.01B) on the right during assembly in July 1945 [note fuselage of V1 in background] and in the middle, while the image on the left show the He 274 V1 (A.A.S.01A) prior to test flying. The revised forward fuselage, cupola and glazing, as seen in these images, all seem to point to the type being intended to be pressurised

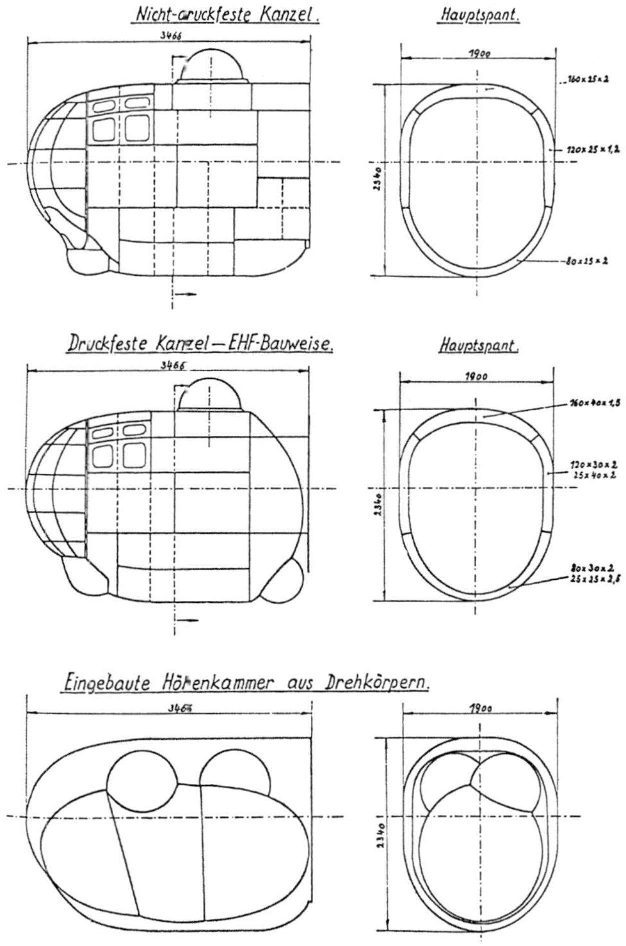

These diagrams show the various pressurised cockpits planned for the He 177H/He 274 series
Non-pressure-resistant cockpit (top)
Pressure-resistant cockpit – EHF-Baiweise (middle)
Built-in height chamber on rotating bodies (bottom)

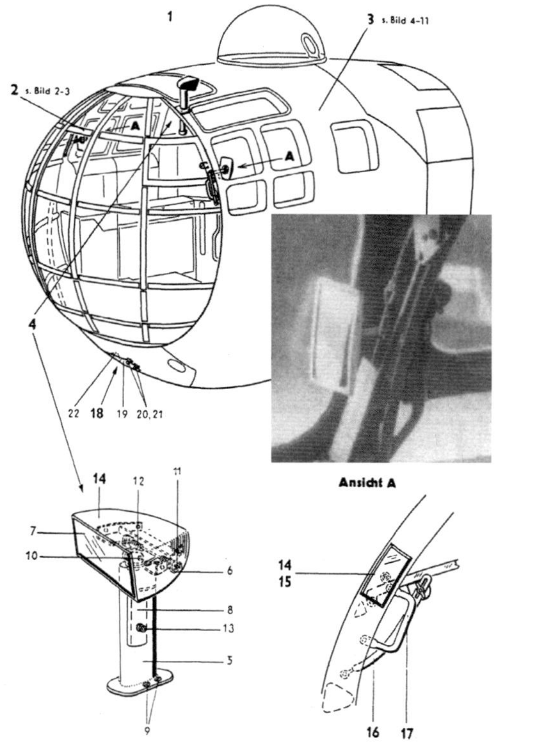

This diagram comes from the A-5 parts manual, but you will find interior and exterior rearview mirrors on A-3s and even some A-1s. The inset is a close-up from a period image taken inside an A-5, just to show you what that mirror looks like in more detail

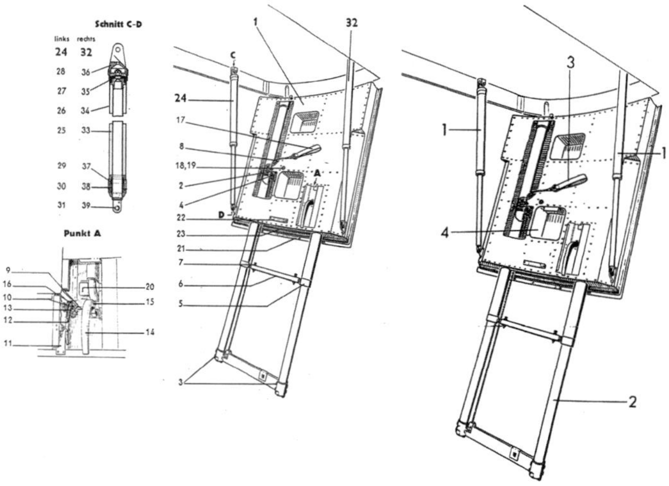

The crew access hatch in the ventral gondola remained the same throughout A-series production. These two identical diagrams, from the A-1 (right) and A-5 (left) manuals confirm this

1. Telescopic strut
2. Entry ladder
3. Pull-in rope for ladder
4. Recess

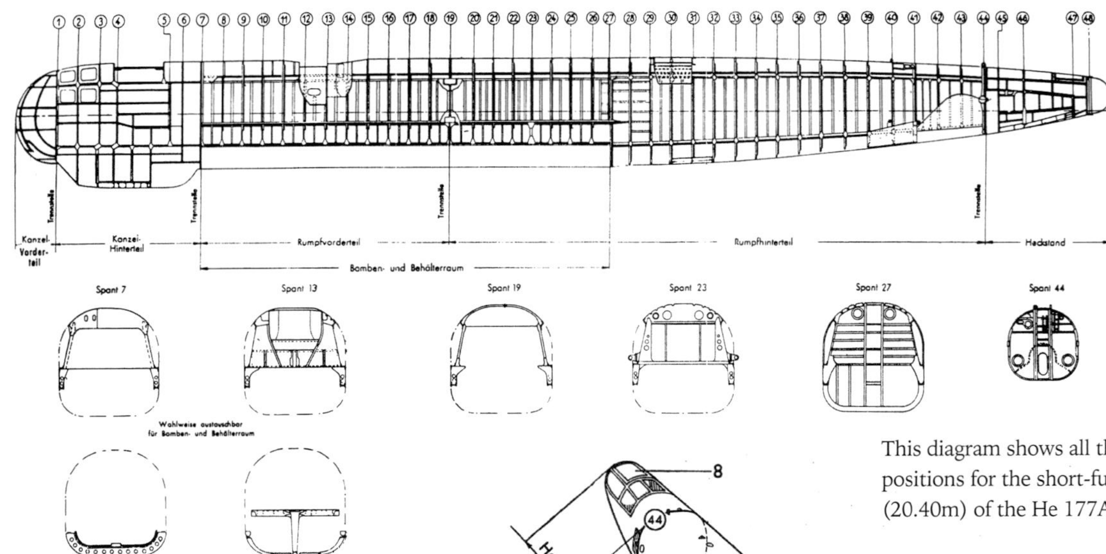

This diagram shows all the frame positions for the short-fuselage (20.40m) of the He 177A-1

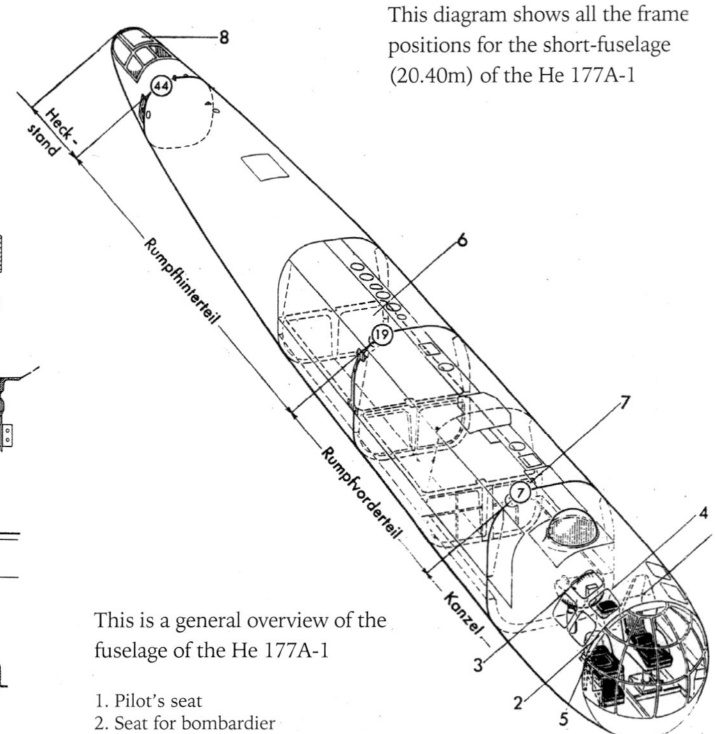

This is a general overview of the fuselage of the He 177A-1

1. Pilot's seat
2. Seat for bombardier
3. Seat for B-stand gunner
4. Seat for C-stand gunner
5. Entry hatch for cockpit
6. Bomb carrier
7. Container carrier
8. Access hatch for rear gunner's position

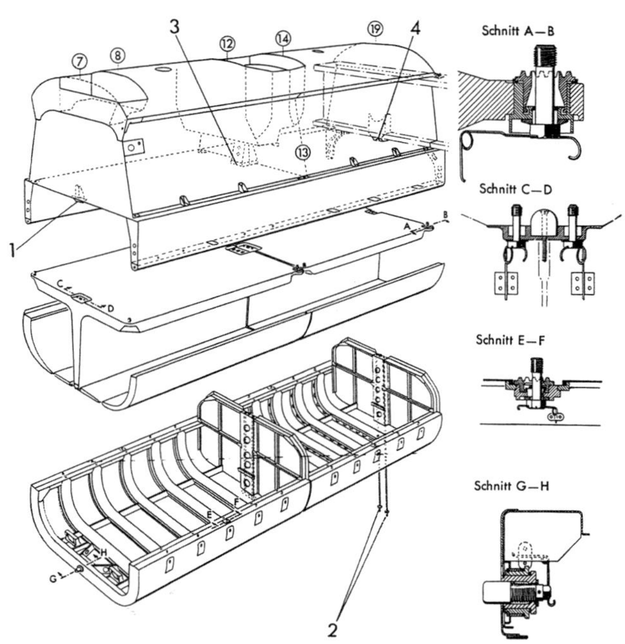

This shows the mid-fuselage section and bomb bay from frames 7 through to 19 of the He 177A-1

1. Fitting on the frame 7
2. Rod bolts
3. Fitting on frame 13
4. Fitting on the spar of the wing centre section

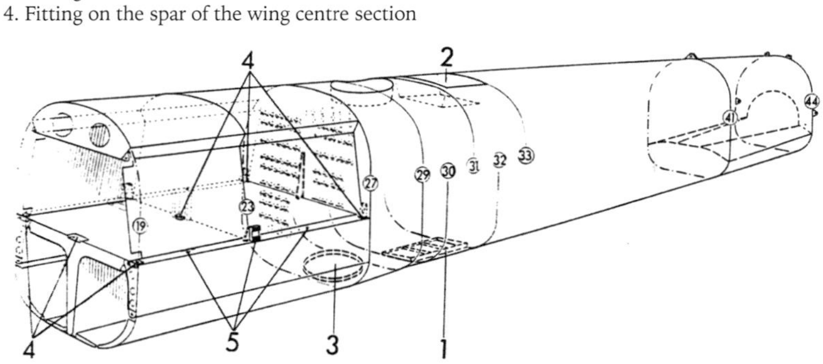

This shows the rear fuselage section from frames 19 through to 44 of the He 177A-1

1. Entrance flap
2. Container for inflatable boat
3. C-weapon range
4. Connection fittings
5. Cable connections

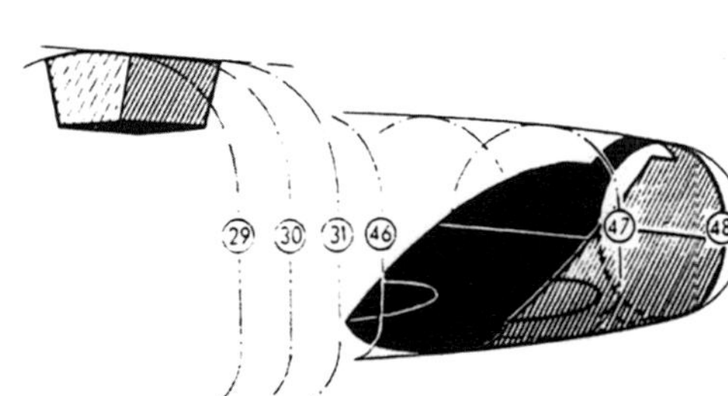

This shows the armour plating added in the rear fuselage of the He 177 and applies to all A-series variants

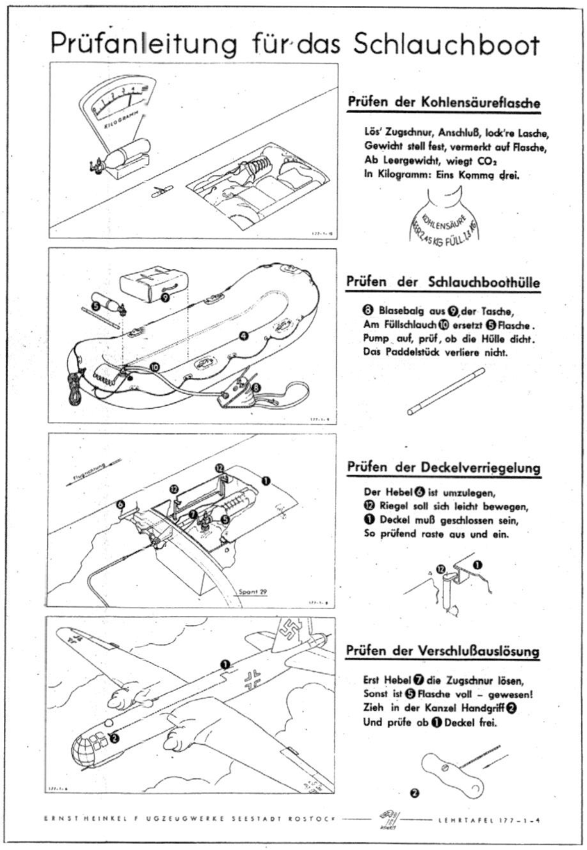

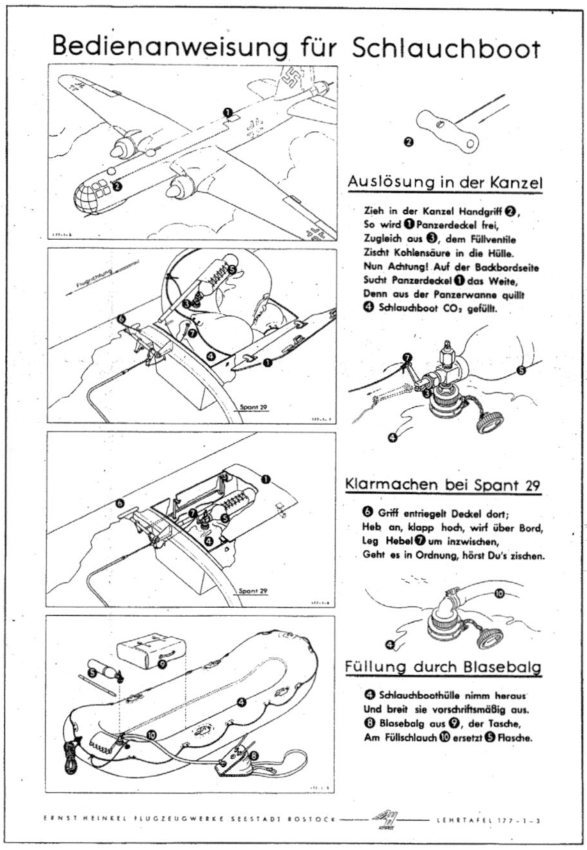

These three diagrams show the testing and loading procedures for the dinghy located in the dorsal spine of the He 177 between Frames 31 and 33

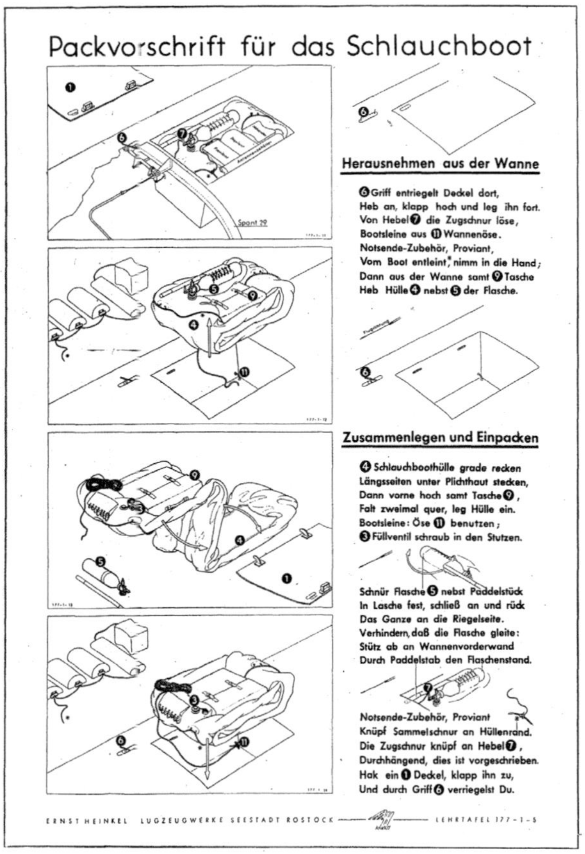

This is a general overview of the fuselage of the He 177A-3, but once again it is not 100% accurate as it still shows 44 frames to the back of the rear turret, which is the 20.40m (short) fuselage of the A-1, the diagram has just been changed with regard the shape of the *Heckstand* and the addition of the B2-*Stand* turret

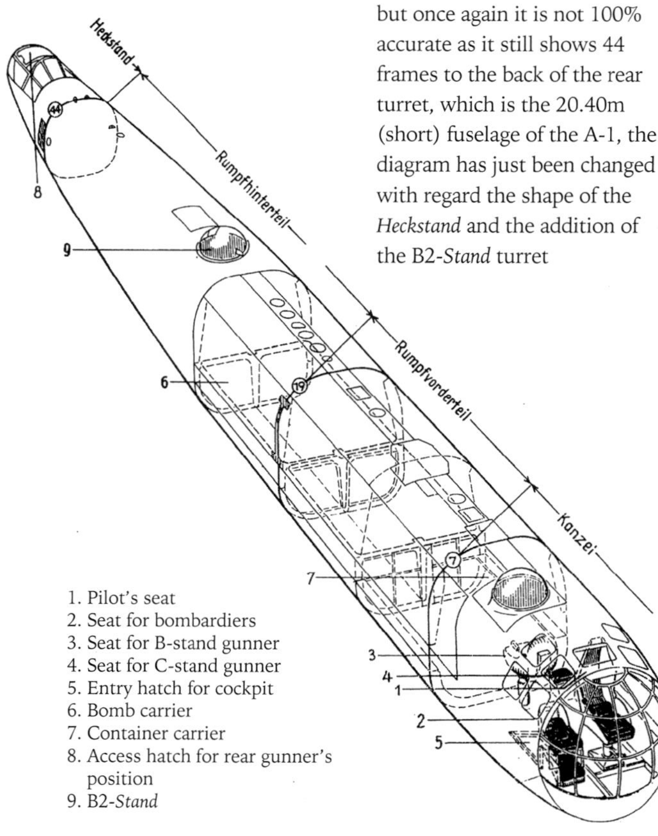

1. Pilot's seat
2. Seat for bombardiers
3. Seat for B-stand gunner
4. Seat for C-stand gunner
5. Entry hatch for cockpit
6. Bomb carrier
7. Container carrier
8. Access hatch for rear gunner's position
9. B2-*Stand*

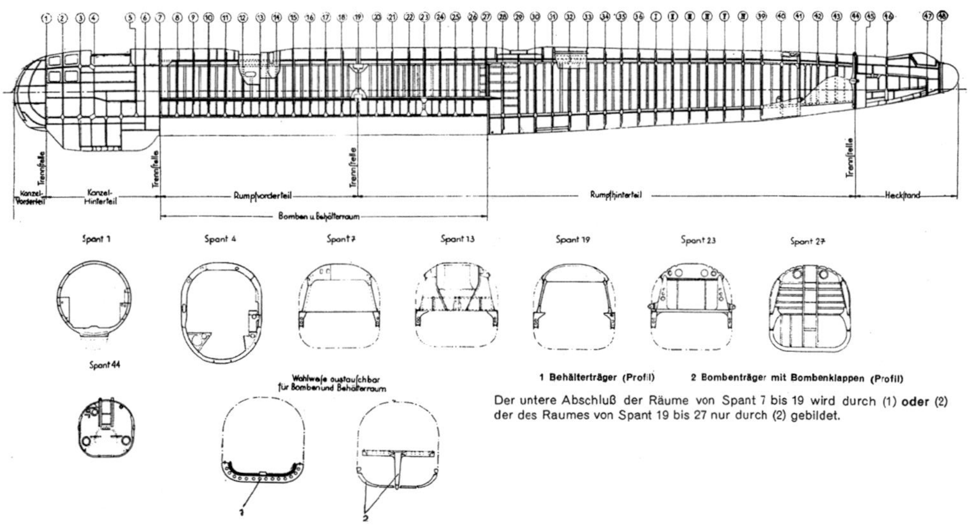

This diagram comes from the A-3 handbook and is supposed to therefore shows all the frame positions for the longer (22.00m) fuselage of the He 177A-3, however it only shows a total of 48 frames, but the longer fuselage had 51, the additional three accounted for the 1.60m increase and these were inserted at Frame 27 – you always have to be very careful of diagrams, even in period documents, as they are often not 100% accurate!

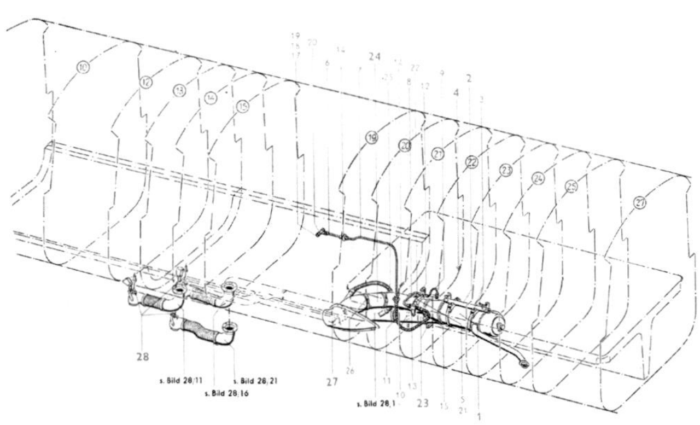

This diagram from the He 177A-3 parts manual shows the intake on the port fuselage side and heater, fitted in the upper section of the rear bomb bay aft of Frame 19. This was in relation to the bomb racks that could be fitted under the front bomb bay for the carriage of Fritz X, Hs 293 etc. (see the ordnance part of the Armament section elsewhere in this chapter)

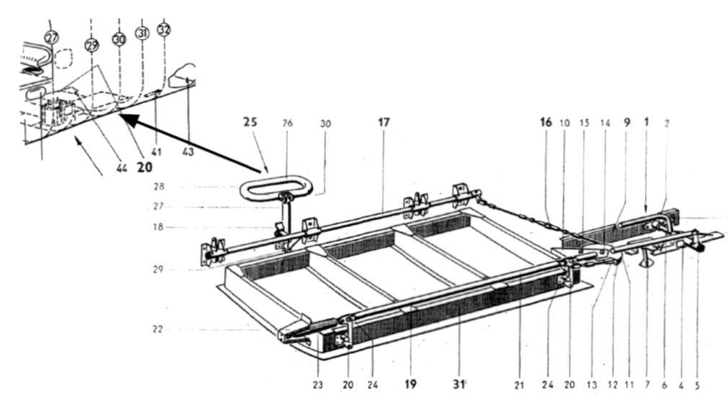

This shows access hatch built into the rear fuselage underside and is only found in the He 177A-5 parts manual. The location of the hatch is shown in the inset at top left (arrowed)

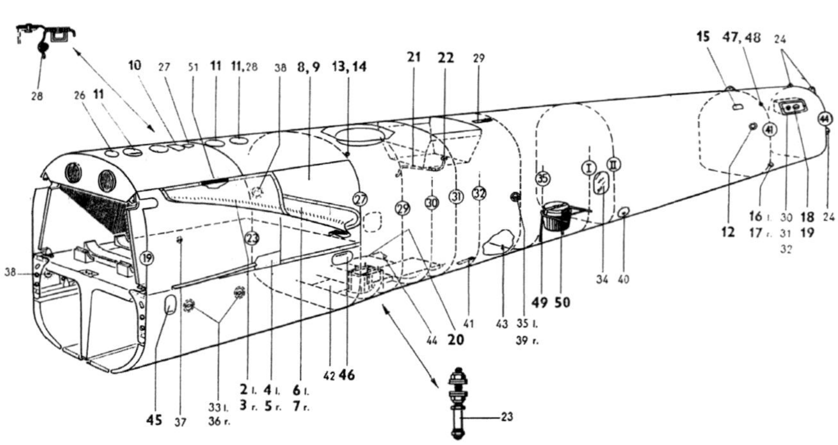

This diagram comes from the A-5 parts manual and apparently shows the rear fuselage section (the mid-section remained as per the A-1), however it ends with the bulkhead behind the rear gunner's position being noted as '44', when with the 22.00m fuselage of the A-3 and A-5 it would have been Frame 49 at that point – another example of only certain aspects of some diagrams being updated

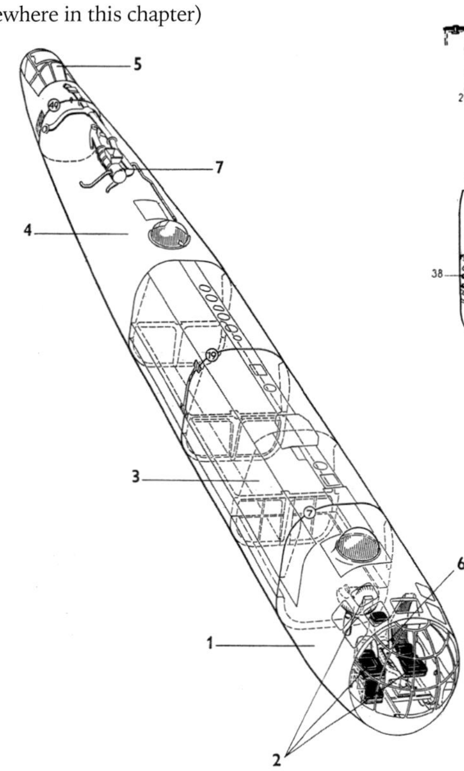

This is a general overview of the fuselage of the He 177A-5, this time it correctly shows the 22.00m version with Frame 49 (not 44) now at the back of the *Heckstand*. Also note the heater for the tailplane leading edges ('7')

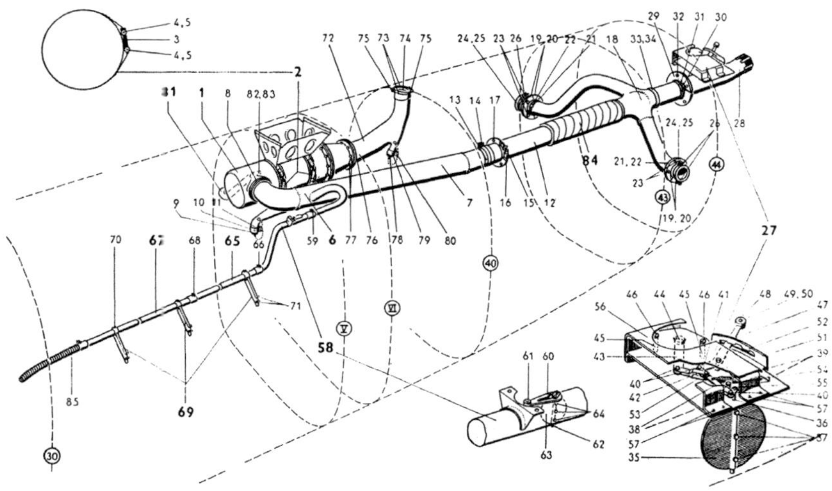

This is the heater unit ('2') in the upper rear fuselage and this diagram comes from the He 177A-5 parts manual, the pipes fed to the rear gunner and to the de-icing duct for the leading edge of each horizontal tailplane

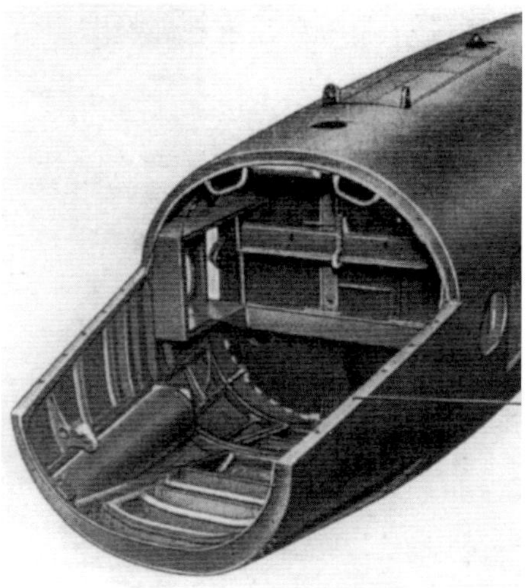

Regardless of the variant, this period image from the manual shows the construction of the rear gunner's (*Heckstand*) position

This period image inside the rear fuselage of captured He 177A-5, W/Nr.55006, shows the hot air ducts running along either side, plus the heater unit in the roof

Another period image inside the rear fuselage, looking aft, of captured He 177A-5, W/Nr.55006, showing the seat for the B2-*Stand* gunner at the top and the oxygen bottles on the right and rear

These two images show the He 274 V1 (A.A.S.01A) during assembly in October 1944, while in the one on the left you can also see the forward fuselage of the V2 on the left

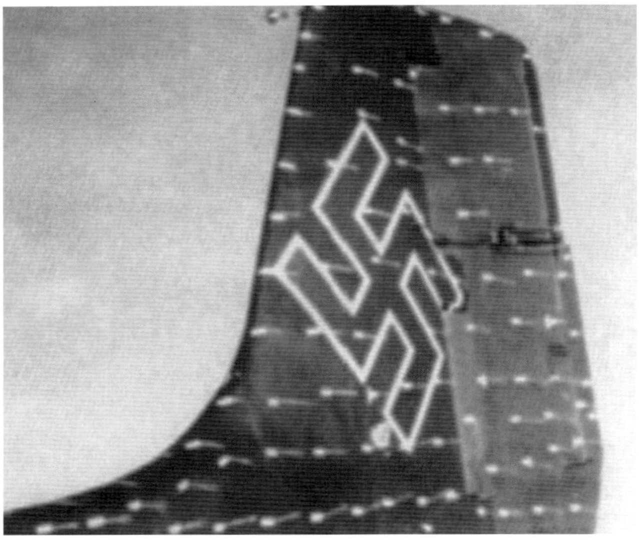

The first vertical fin/rudder used by the V1 was this one, with the extension at the front. It was not liked and quickly changed. The dots are wool tufts used to determine airflow, as obviously problems were already being experienced

There are no period images of the V3 or V4 to prove the style of fin/rudder installed, these five however show the V5 (top right), V6 (top middle) and V7 (top left), which all have the same fin/rudder as seen in detail in the two lower images of the V8 – mass balance weight inset at top, inset hinge half-way down and step at bottom of rudder

This is the fin/rudder of the V2, on the right is the remains of this prototype being hoisted out of the Baltic Sea, whilst on the left you can see the intact tail, with the shorter, rounded top and single inset mass balance weight (as per the second version used by the V1)

The A-01 (left) and A-02 (right) plus the A-03 and A-04 all retained the same fin/rudder as the V5 through V8

This is the second and third versions of vertical fin/rudder fitted to the V1, the one on the right is the second version, which was squarer than that used originally, while the middle and far left image show the final version, which was actually taller, more rounded at the top and back and with the inset hinges

The fin/rudder changes made after the A-04 as seen in these two period images with the A-04 fin/rudder on the left and the A-05 on the right, which is higher and more rounded. This remained the layout/shape of the fin/rudder throughout A-series production

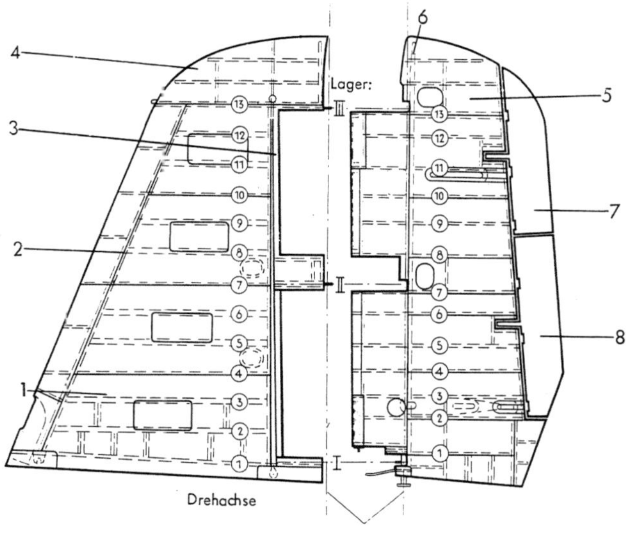

This is an overview of the production fin/rudder and comes from the He 177A-1 manual

1. Vertical fin
2. Nose spar
3. Main spar
4. End cap
5. Rudder
6. Rudder spar
7. Trim tab
8. Relief rudder

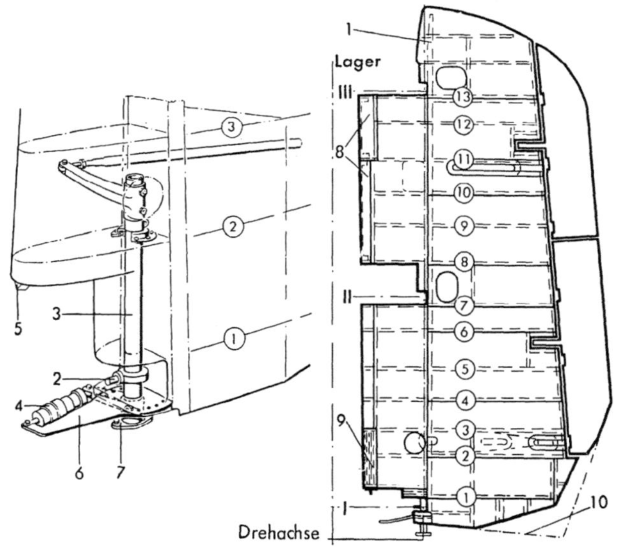

This shows how the rudder is operated and applies to all production A-series variants

1. Rudder spar
2. Bearing journal (bearing I)
3. Drive shaft for relief rudder
4. Spring body (component of the control unit)
5. Locating lug
6. Drive lever
7. Flange
8. Upper balance weights
9. Lower balance weight
10. Outline of the older design rudder

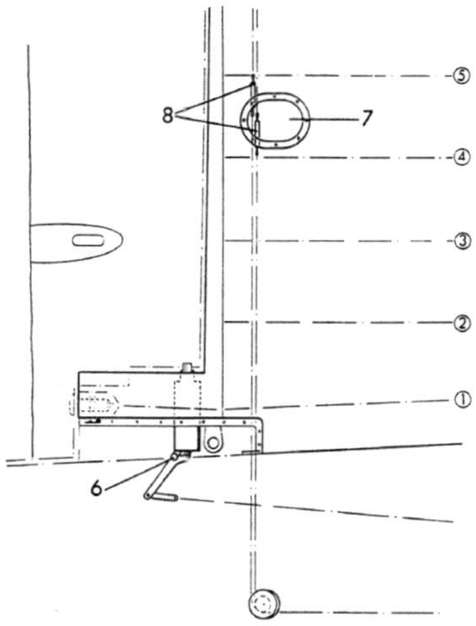

Details of the vertical fin, viewed from the starboard side

6. Rider locking lever bolt
7. Access cover
8. Control lines for trim rudder drive

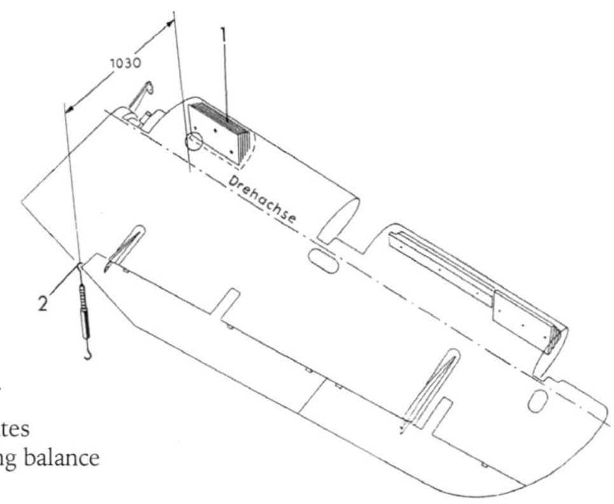

Details of the rudder

1. Replaceable steel plates
2. Connecting the spring balance

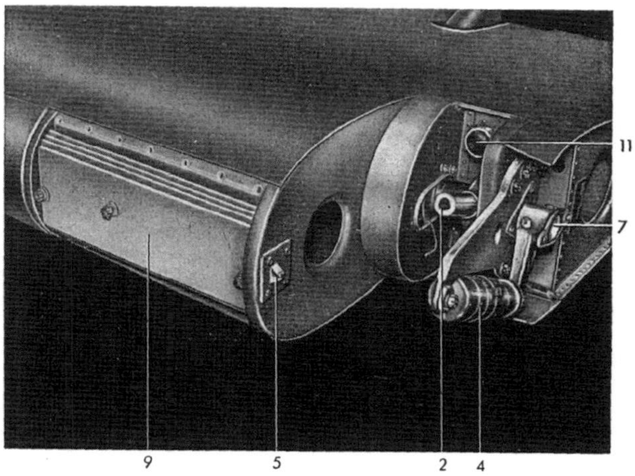

This shows the rudder bearing I and balance weight in more detail and applies to all A-series variants

2. Rudder peg
4. Spring body
5. Locating lug
7. Flange with drive pipe
9. Plate weight
11. Rubber stop

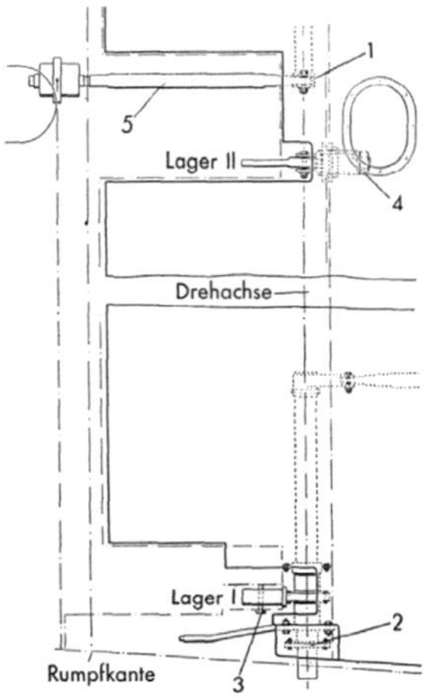

This shows how the rudder is removed, but thus serves to highlight the hinges etc.

1. Connecting the trim spindle
2. Drive shaft flange
3. Bearing plug screw I
4. Screwing the bearing holder II
5. Trim spindle

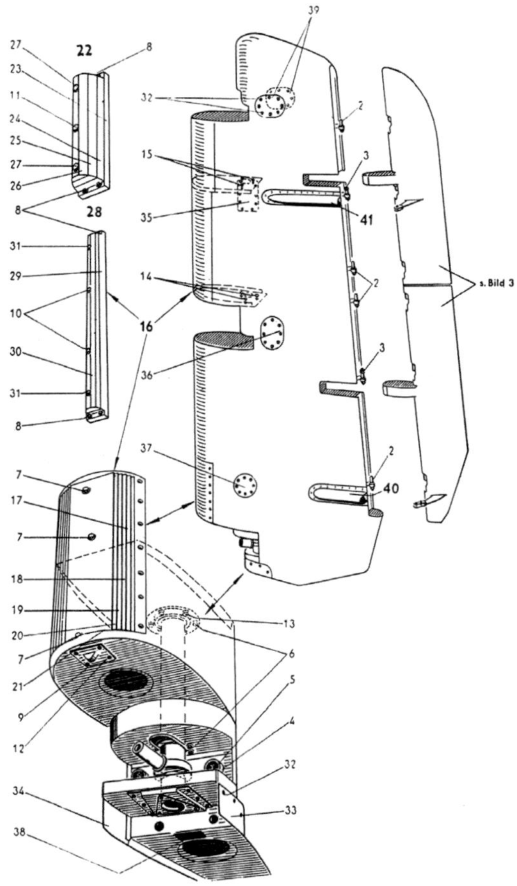

The components of the rudder and comes from the He 177A-5 parts manual, but applies to all production A-series variants

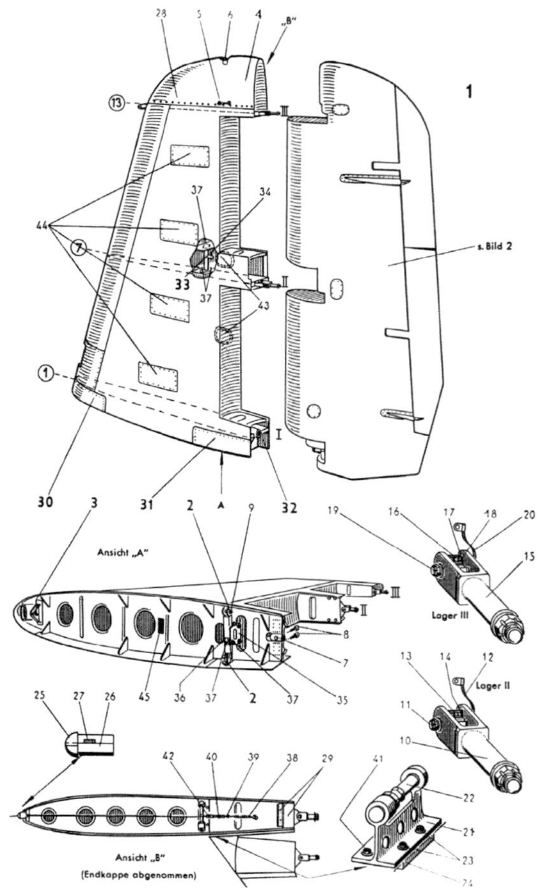

The components of the rudder and vertical fin and once again comes from the He 177A-5 parts manual, but applies to all variants

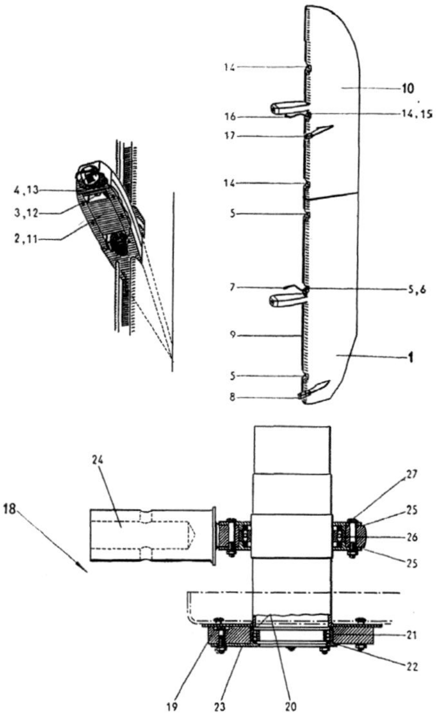

This shows the components of the rudder trim tab and applies to all production A-series variants

Let's end this section with a nice overall view of the fin and rudder on He 177A-5, W/ Nr.550062, shown on arrival at Farnborough after capture in France

Note: The only real change that occurred with the early prototypes, was that the elevators from the V4 onwards were 20% larger than those used by the V1, V2 and V3. Sadly, no period images exist of sufficient quality or detail to show this.

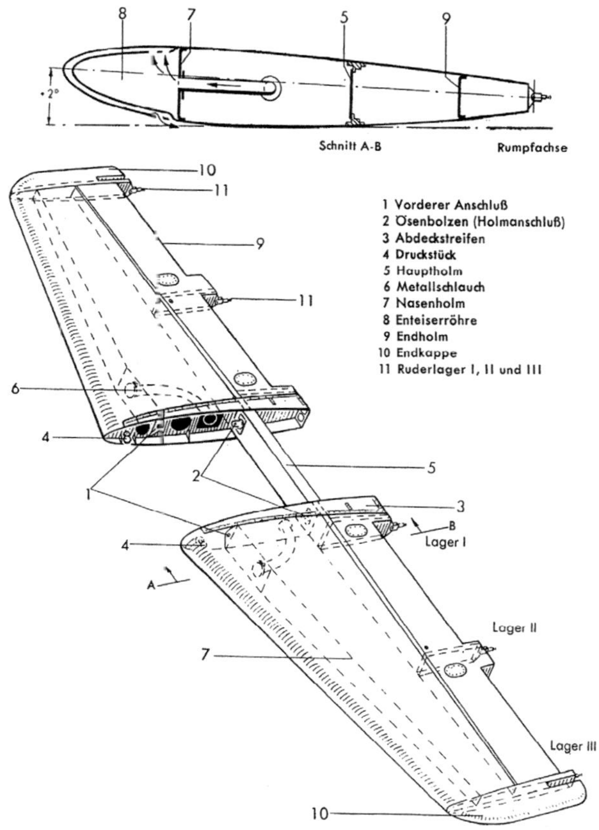

This same diagram of the horizontal tailplane is used in all (A-1, A-3 and A-5) manuals. The image at the top shows how the hot air from the heater in the roof inside the rear fuselage is fed into the leading edge portion entering in the middle/back, going up to the top, circulating around the leading edge and venting at the bottom, to clear ice

Adjustment of the horizontal tailplane was achieved via an adjusting spindle (2) below the spar (1) inside the tailwheel bay

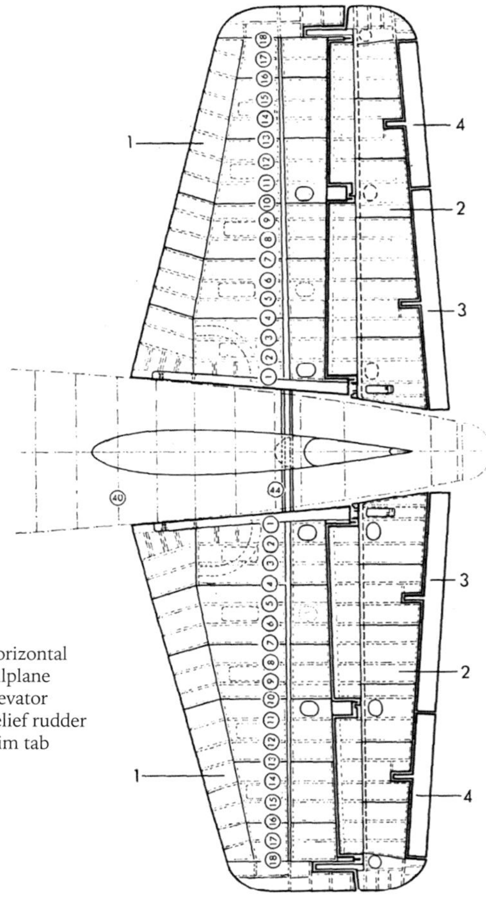

1. Horizontal tailplane
2. Elevator
3. Relief rudder
4. Trim tab

From the V4 the horizontal tailplane and elevators remained the same throughout He 177A-series production. This diagram from the He 177A-3 handbook shows the overall construction and rib positions

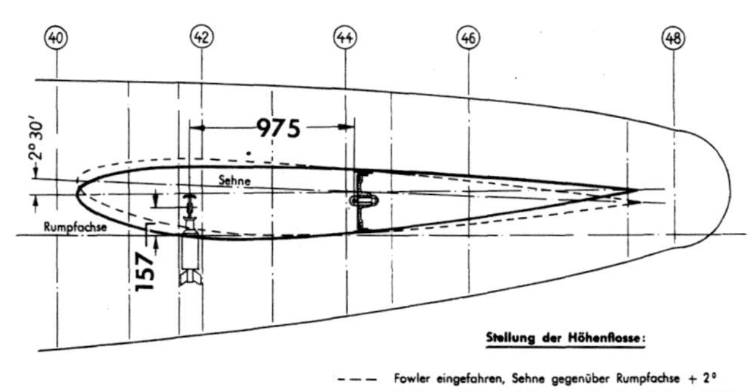

The horizontal tailplane could be adjusted through 2° 30', as seen in this diagram – this shows the short 20.40m fuselage (with 48 frames, instead of the 51 of the longer 22.00m fuselage, as this diagram comes from the A-0 handbook)

Horizontal stabilizer adjustment
(Hull axis is marked by levelling rivets)
Extend skewers. Namely:
Spoke I, II and IV 900mm +/- 3
Spoke VI 590mm +/- 3
Spoke VIII 445mm +/- 2
Spoke IX 367mm +/- 2
Set stops M1 for extension according to these dimensions.
The positions of the extension stops on skewers II, V and VII are inevitable
Position of the horizontal stabilizer:
Fowler (flaps) retracted, chord given over trunk axis +2°
Fowler (flaps) extended, chord given to trunk axis -0° 30'

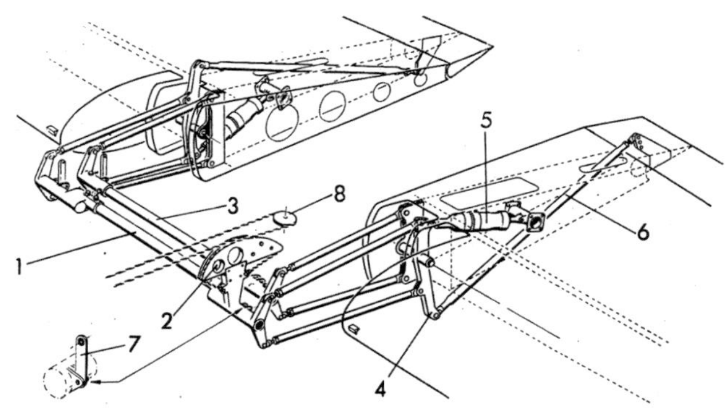

This shows how the elevators and inboard trim tabs were operated, which remained the same throughout A-series production

1. Elevator drive shaft
2. Control line segment
3. Clutch shaft
4. Elevator drive lever
5. Spring body
6. Bumper to relief rudder
7. Suspension in the fuselage
8. Pulley

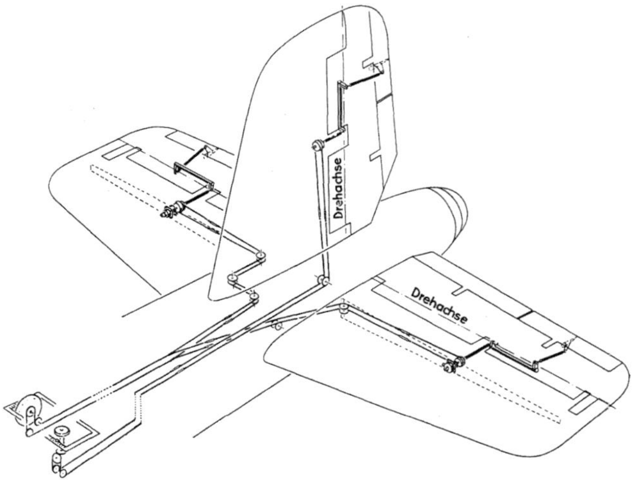

This diagram from the A-0 manual shows how the upper rudder and outer elevator trim tabs were operated and it also applies to the A-1, A-3 and A-5 series

Not shown in any of the handbooks or parts manual, this close-up of captured He 177A-5, TS439, does allow you to see the aerodynamic fairing over the linkage for the inboard trim tab, something that was obviously added without this ever being noted in the official publications. Also note the double linkage tube inside, when the manual only shows as a single tube

The balance weight size/ position for the elevators changed between the A-1 (left) and A-3 (right)

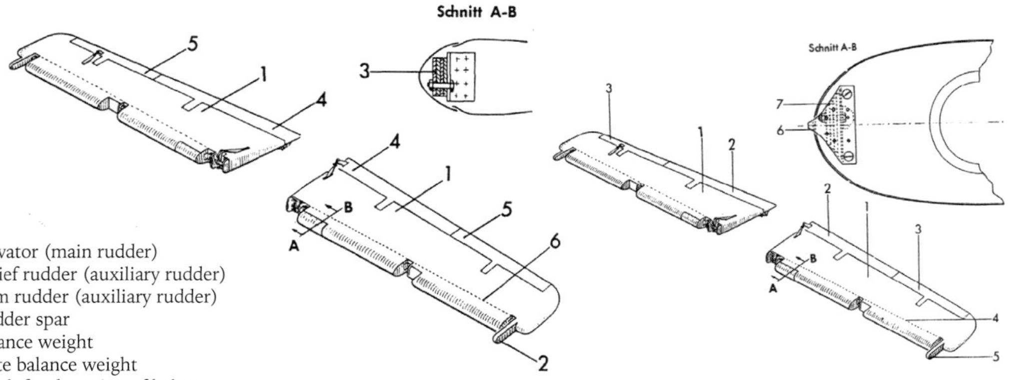

Left
1. Elevator
2. Balance weight
3. Plate balance weight
4. Relief rudder
5. Trim tab
6. Rudder spar

Right
1. Elevator (main rudder)
2. Relief rudder (auxiliary rudder)
2. Trim rudder (auxiliary rudder)
4. Rudder spar
5. Balance weight
6. Plate balance weight
7. Tooth for detection of balance weight

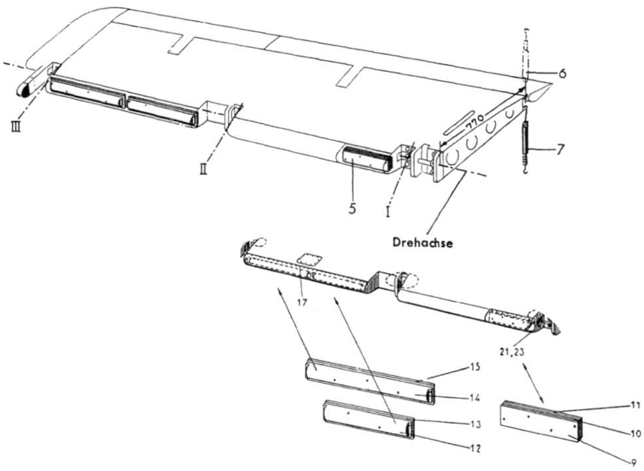

Balancing the elevator as a whole in addition to the balance weight for trim fitted out towards the tip, was achieved via steel plates inboard ('5') and shaped weights ('12' to '15') outboard of the middle hinge as seen in the main (upper left) diagram and highlighted in the inset image, bottom right

5. Removable steel plates
6. Exclusion of the spring balance for the preliminary adjustment (see point 5)
7. Exclusion of the spring balance for the final adjustment (see points 7 and 8)

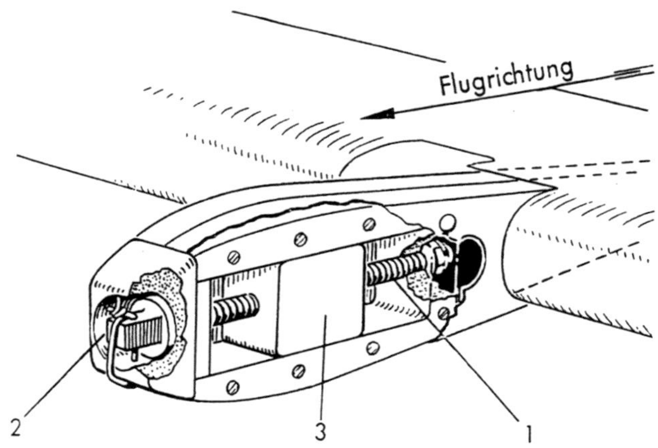

The elevator mass balance weight for trim was situated out at the tip and was adjusted by moving the weight inside the fairing forward or back on the screw-thread, as shown in this diagram

1. Spindle screw
2. Recess for the spindle head
3. Balance weight

Overall view of the elevators, deflected down, on the captured He 177A-5, TS439 at Farnborough in 1945

This close-up period images shows the horizontal tailplanes, fin/rudder endplates and rear fuselage/tail cone of the He 274 V1 (A.A.S.01A) during final assembly in October 1944

Few good clear/large images exist of the twin fin arrangement used by the He 274 and intended for some He 177B and all He 277 variants. These three close-ups of the He 274 V1 give you an idea of the layout of the endplate fin/rudder assemblies as well as the steep angle of the horizontal tailplanes

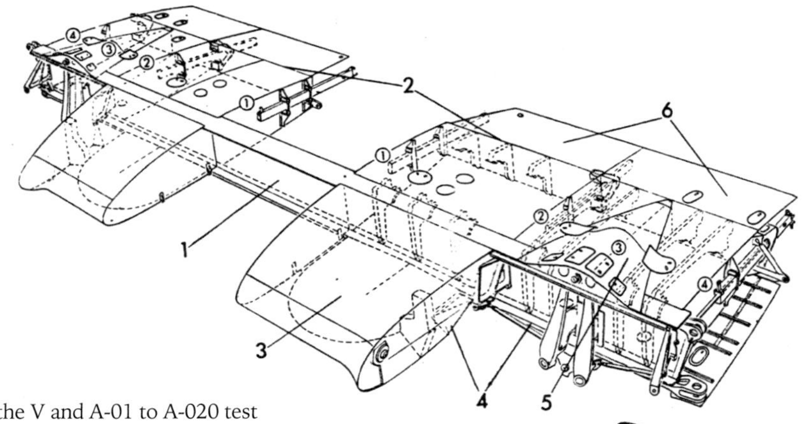

Wing centre section (top)
1. Main spar
2, End spar
3. Nose box
4. Engine cut-out
5. Hood drain, top
6. End boxes inside

Wing outer part (bottom)
1. Main spar
2. Nose spar
3. Ribs
4. End spar
5. Deck opening in lower skin
6. End cap
7. Fowler flap rails
8. Spit storage
9. Lid, top
10. Landing gear door, bottom
11. Gap cladding
12. Aileron balance weight
13. End boxes, outside

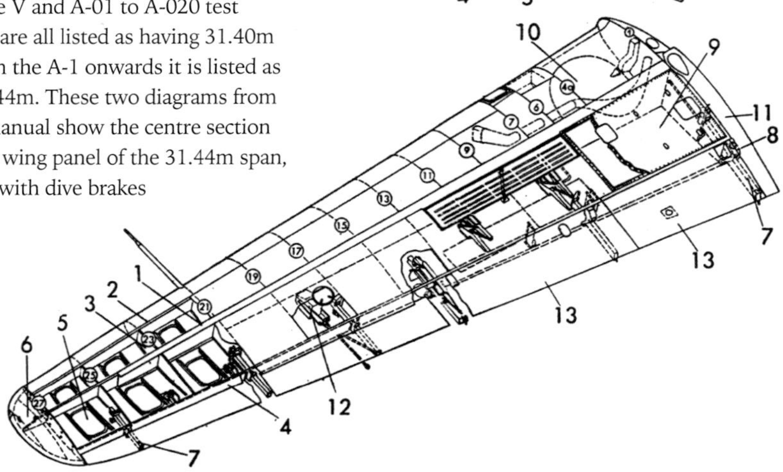

Whilst the V and A-01 to A-020 test airframes are all listed as having 31.40m span, from the A-1 onwards it is listed as being 31.44m. These two diagrams from the A-1 manual show the centre section and outer wing panel of the 31.44m span, complete with dive brakes

This shows the landing light in the leading edge of the port wing from the front

1. Fixing screws 'B'
2. Landing light disc hinge 'S'
3. Cable junction box

This shows the landing light in the leading edge of the port wing from the back

1. Mirror back
2. Fluted nut

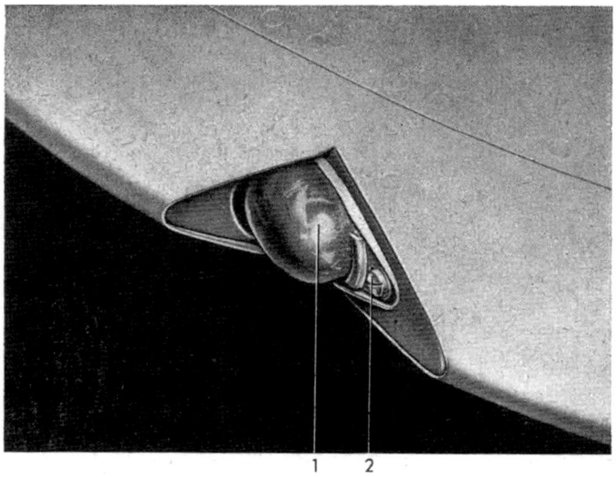

All variants had an inset light at each wing tip

1. Cover tray
2. Fixing screw

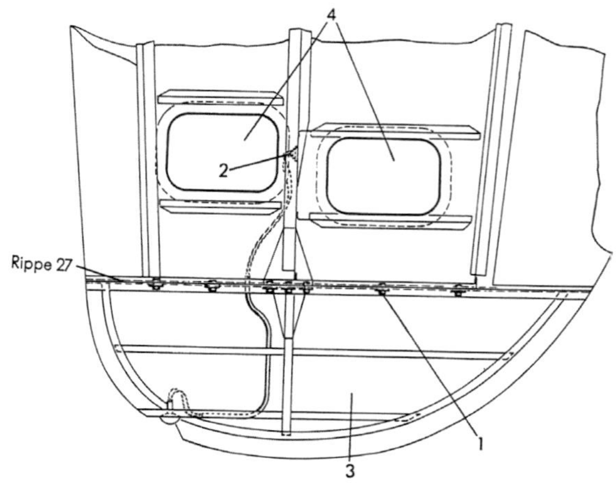

This shows the separate wing tip and comes from the He 177A-1 manual, although it also applies to the A-0, A-3 and A-5

1. Mounting screws
2. Eltrical Plug
3. End cap
4. Lid openings on the underside

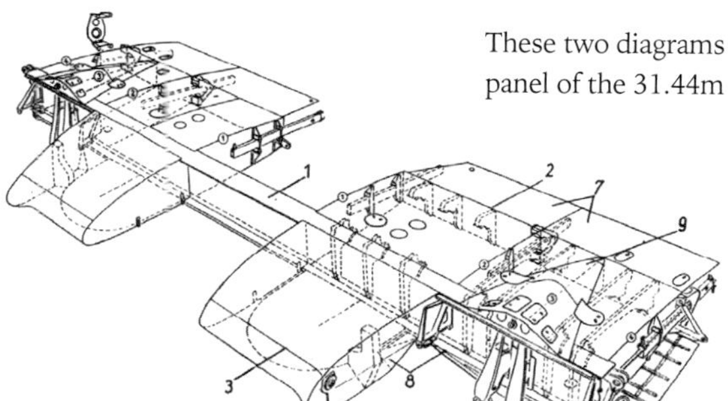

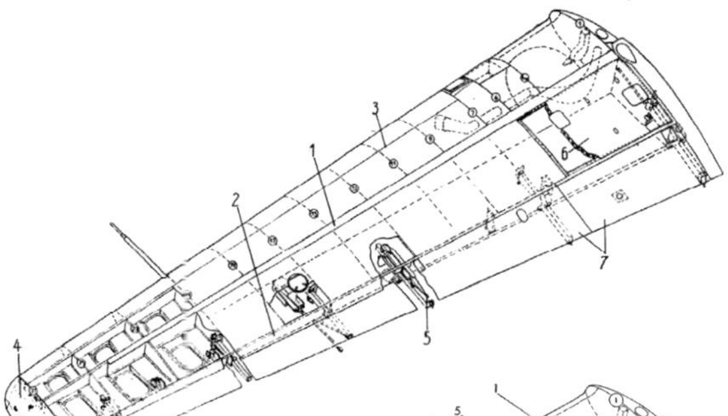

These two diagrams from the A-3 manual show the centre section and outer wing panel of the 31.44m span, the latter now lacking any dive brakes

Wing center section
Wing outer part
1. Main spar
2. End spar
3. Nose spar
4. End cap
5. Fowler flap rails
6. Lid, top
7. End boxes
8. Engine cut-out
9. Hood drain

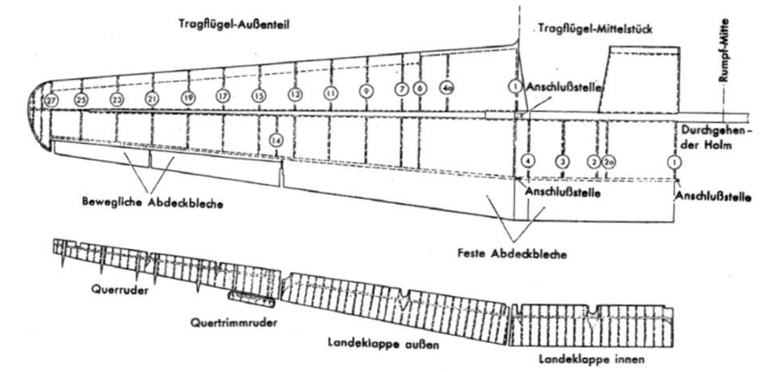

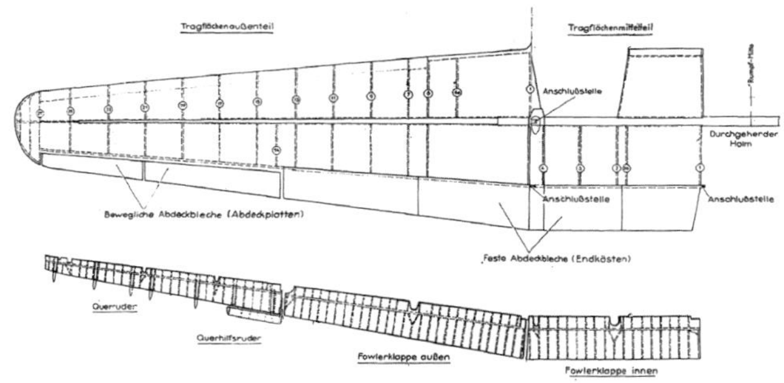

Until the longer spans of the A-7, B-series etc. came along, the span remained unchanged at 31.44m, these two diagrams show the wing of the A-1 (top) and A-3 (bottom), along with the aileron and landing flaps for each

Wing outer part
Wing center piece
Connection point
Continuous spar
Fixed cover plates (end boxes)
Movable cover plates (cover plates)
Aileron
Aileron trim rudder
Landing flap outside (or Fowler flap, outside)
Landing flap inside (or Fowler flap inside)

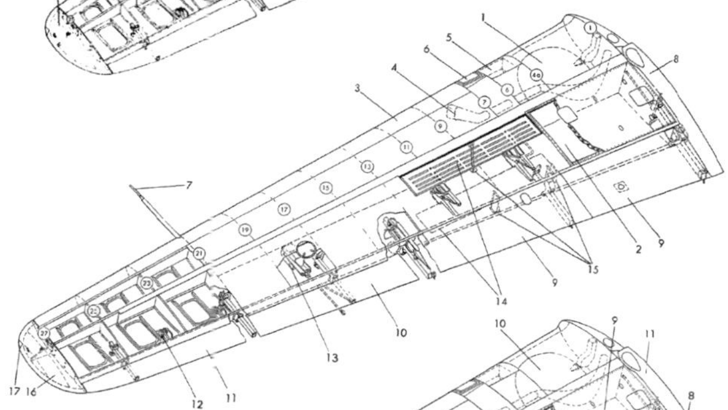

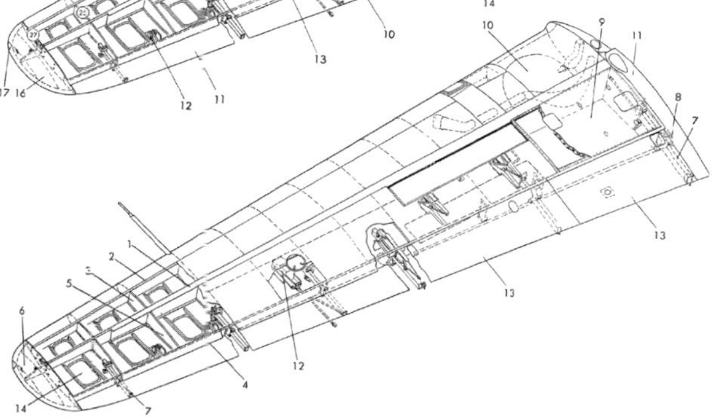

There are two diagrams of the outer wing panel in the He 177A-3 manual and whilst one has the dive brakes (upper) the other one (lower) only lacks them because that diagram deals with the exterior panels. Dive brakes were removed at some point during A-3 production, with older airframes having them removed retrospectively

Top
1. Gear compartment
2. Fuel bag container room
3. Nose box (cut-out with de-icer tube)
4. Warm air supply
5. Lubricant cooler
6. Landing light (left on y)
7. Pitot tube (left only)
8. Gap cladding
9. End boxes
10. Cover plate, inside
11. Cover plate, external
12. Cover plate balancer
13. Aileron balance
14. Airbrakes
15. Smoking device hanging points
16. End flap, removable
17. Side marker light

Bottom
1. Main spar
2. Nose box with nose bar
3. Nasal rib
4. End spar
5. End rib
6. End cap
7. Fowler's skewer
8. Spit storage
9. Lid (for fuel bag container)
10. Landing gear door, bottom
11. Gap cladding
12. Aileron balance weight
13. End boxes, outside
14. Lid opening in lower panelling

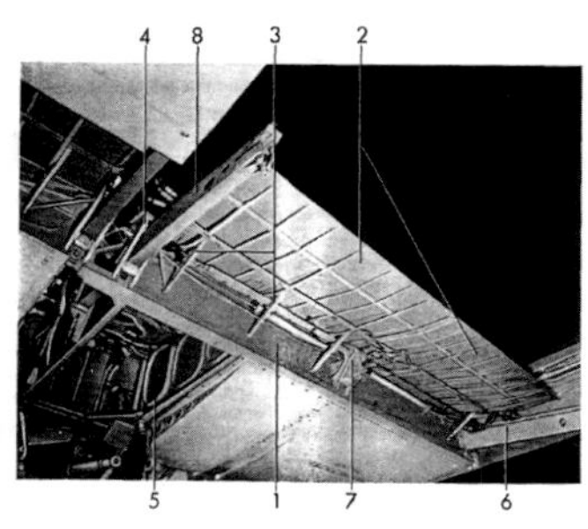

These two diagrams show the built-in end spar and end box for the He 177A-1 on the right and the He 177A-3 on the left

Right
1. End spar
2. End boxes
3. Detachable support struts
4. Spit storage
5. End rib 3
6. Fowler flap rail I
7. Fowler flap rail II retracted
8. Fowler flap rail III

Left
1. End spar
2. End boxes, inside
3. Detachable support struts
4. Spit storage
5. Fowler flaps rail III
6. Armour-plate for aileron power control

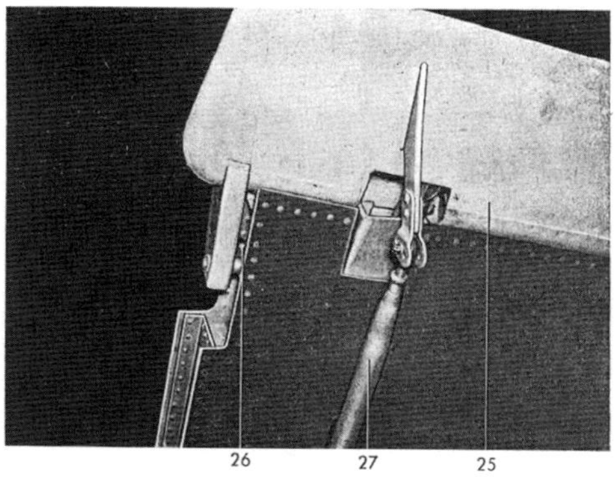

This image from the He 177A-3 handbook shows the attachment of the aileron and linkage to the trim tab on the starboard side (underside view)

25. Trim tab, right
26. Toothed segment
27. Actuating tube

Here is the port aileron without the cover plate in position

1. Bumper for balance weight
2. Drive lever

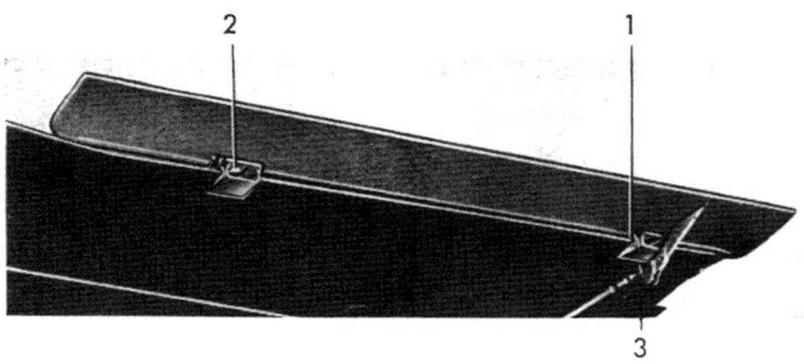

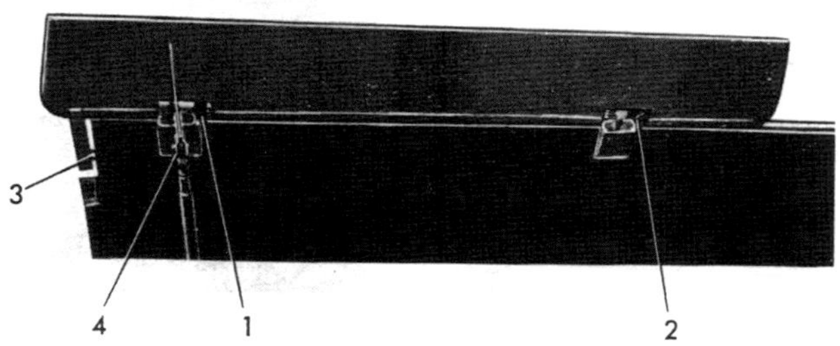

These two images show the port aileron trim tab (under view) at the top and the starboard aileron trim tab, fixed (under view) at the bottom

Top
1. Bearing I
2. Bearing II
3. Bumper connection

Bottom
1. Bearing I
2. Bearing II
3. Toothed segment
4. Strut connection

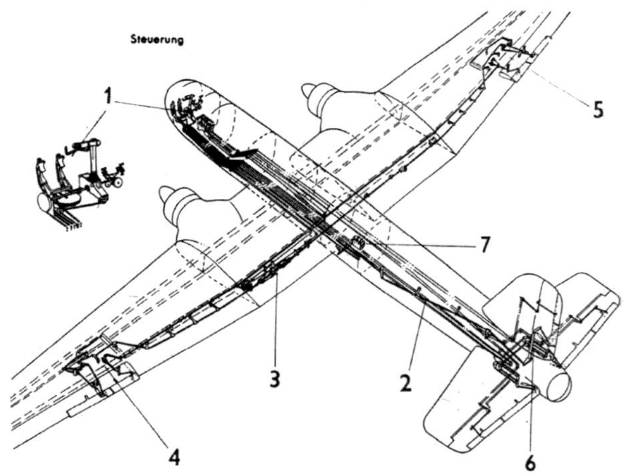

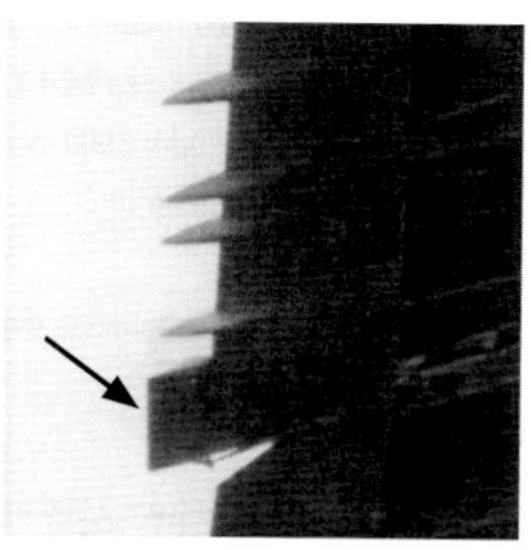

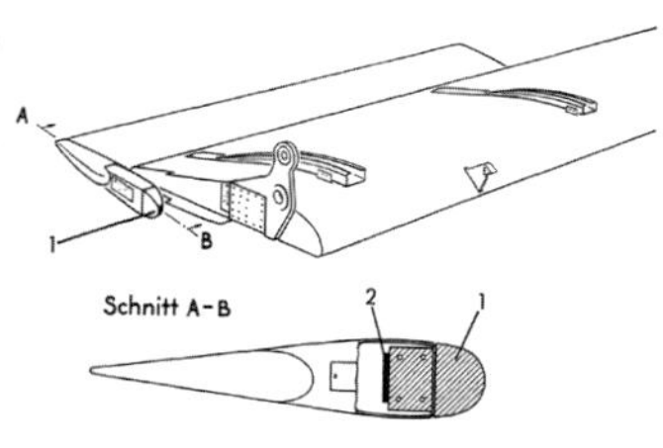

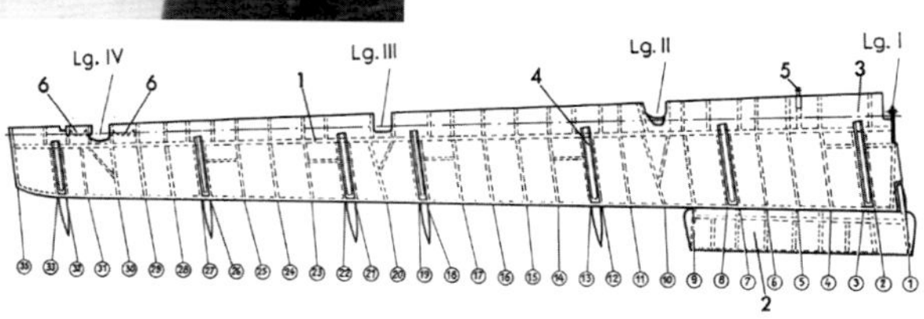

The starboard aileron of the He 177A-0, A-1 and A-3 had a trim tab that extended aft of the trailing edge as depicted in the diagram on the top right and the close-up of the He 177A-04 on the top left (arrowed), while the diagram at the bottom shows the ribs etc. within the aileron

1. Balance weight
2. Additional weight

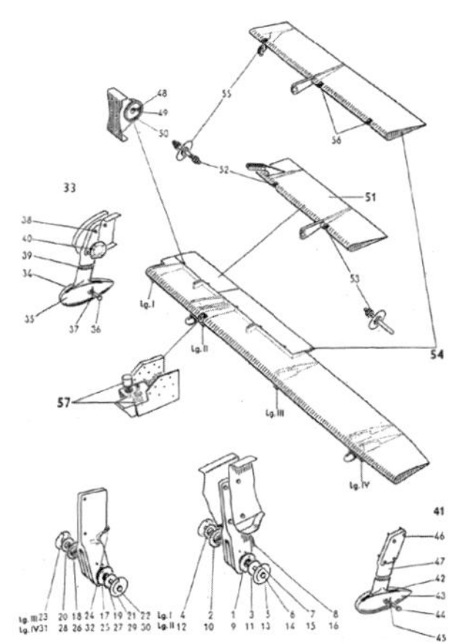

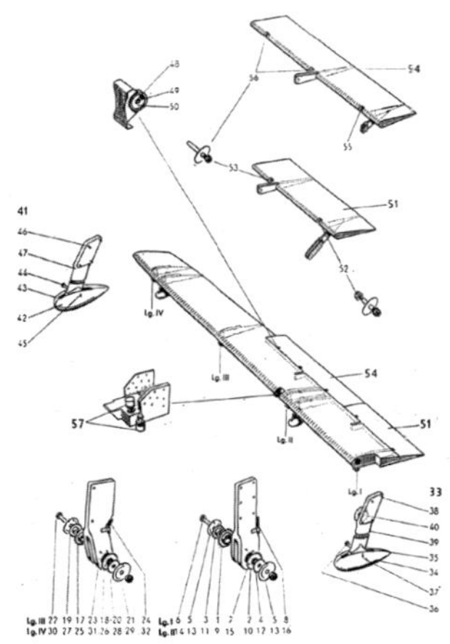

The He 177A-5 dispensed with the split aileron/flap arrangement plus it also adopted two trim tabs on each aileron, as depicted in the upper diagram, whilst the lower two show all the components of each aileron along with their trim tabs, linkage and mass balance weights because the aileron no longer used a weight inboard of the trailing edge as had been the case with the A-0, A-1 and A-3

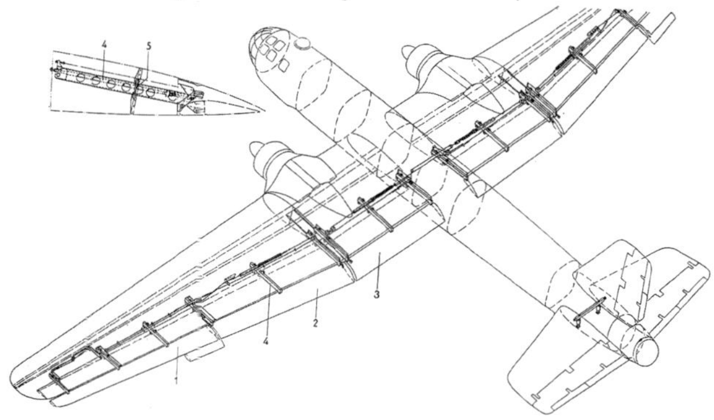

These two images show the overall layout of the Fowler flaps, in the dropped position at the top, with an overview of how the flaps were linked in the bottom image – both come from the He 177A-3 handbook, but also appear in the A-0 and A-1 handbooks as well

Fowler flaps inside and outside (extended)
1. Fowler flap, inside
2. Fowler flap, outside
3. Rubber plugs

Overview of the Fowler drive
1. Aileron
2. External Fowler valve
3. Inner Fowler flap
4. Fowler flap rails
5. Roller guide for the flap rails

The Fowler flaps ran in rails to allow them to move back and down when dropped, as seen here in this diagram for the outboard rail of the inner section and inboard rail of the outer mid (in the A-0, A-1 and A-3) or outer (in the A-5) section
1. Bearing III with drive lever, flap inside
2. Bearing I with drive lever, flap outside

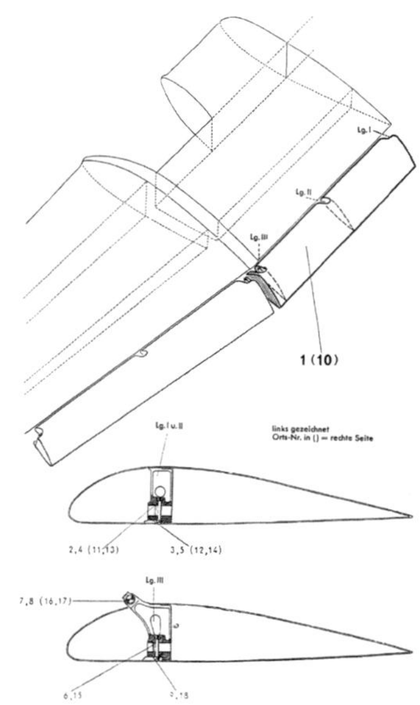

The Fowler flaps remained the same throughout A-series production, this diagram comes from the He 177A-5 parts manual

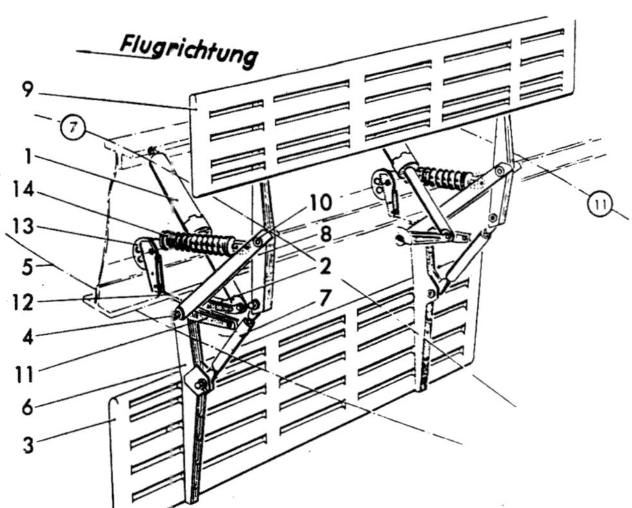

The A-0, A-1 and A-3 series all had dive brakes fitted above and below the wings, although the latter had these removed at some unspecified stage in production (with older machines probably having them removed retrospectively). This diagram give an overview of the installation

1. Hydraulic cylinder
2. Drive lever
3. Brake caliper, bottom
4. Support bracket
5. Surface outer edge
6. Lower lever arm
7. Adjustment strut
8. Upper lever arm
9. Brake flap, top
10. Pivot point
11. Lever
12. Tension wire
13. Pulley
14. Return springs

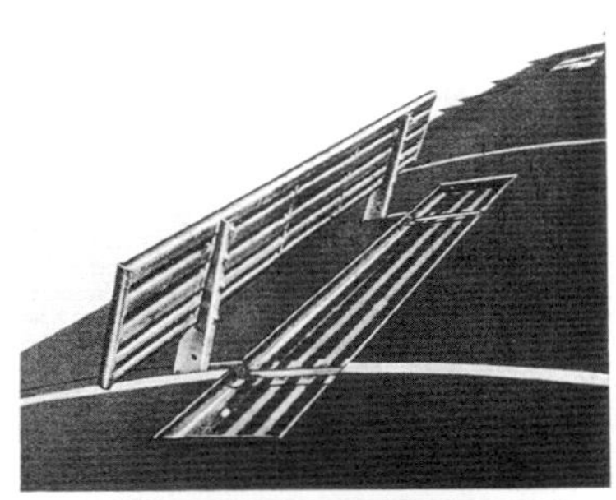

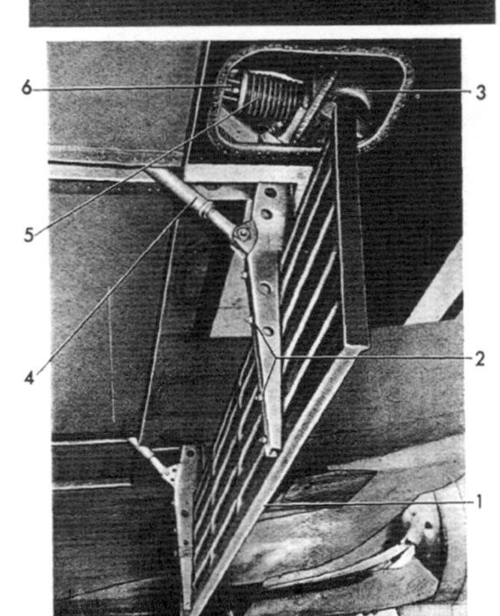

These two diagrams show the dive brake extended above (top) and below (bottom) the wing

1. Brake flap
2. Mounting screws
3. Handlock
4. Adjustment strut
5. Spring pack
6. Inner tension nut

All of the V-series prototypes used prototype, pre-production or production versions of the Daimler-Benz DB 606 as seen here, which was a coupled pair of DB 603s

In service, the A-0, A-1, A-3 and A-5 used the Daimler-Benz DB610, which was a coupled pair of DB 605s. This shows the port side of the example in the Munich Technical Museum *(©G. Papadimitriou)*

This is the port side, front of the DB 610 on display at the Munich Technical Museum *(©G. Papadimitriou)*

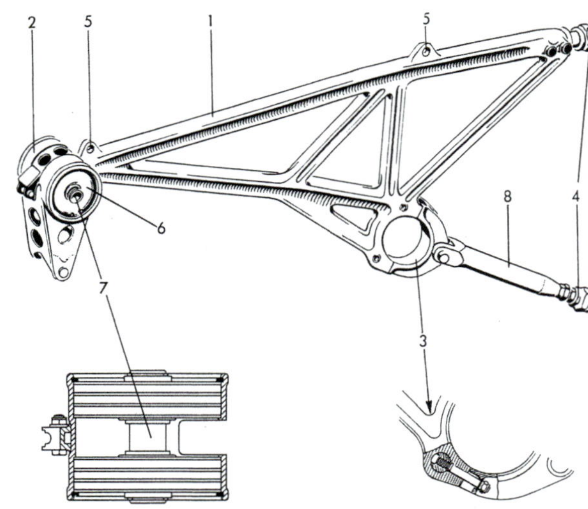

The DB606 and 610 were suspended via an engine bearer that was positioned between the two

1. Profile strut framework
2. Elastic suspension
3. Rear bearing
4. Ball screw connections
5. Eyelets
6. Rubber bearings
7. Support bolts
8. Support strut

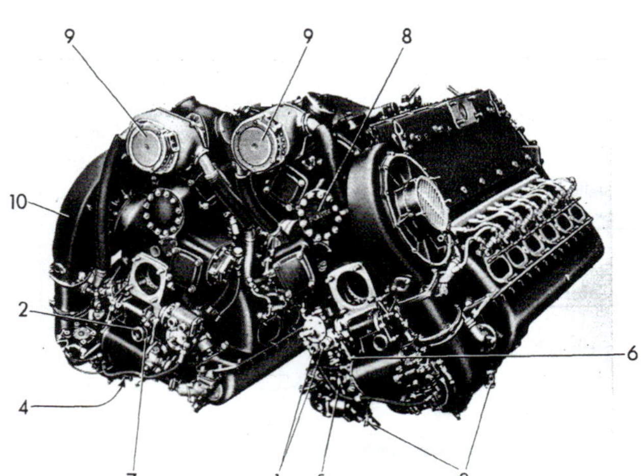

This is the DB606 viewed from the rear, from the He 177A-1 handbook

1. Fuel inlet port
2. Nozzle for lubricant entry
3. Lubricant outlet ports
4. Coolant inlet
5. Ratchet lever on the lubricant filter
6. Throttle lever
7. Drive train for engine shutdown
8. Connection flange for starter motor
9. Bosch twin magneto
10. Supercharger duct

Each engine was coupled to drive a single propeller shaft, as seen here in this image from the He 177A-0 handbook

1. Propeller shaft
2. Support ring
3. Neck bearing
4. Retaining plates

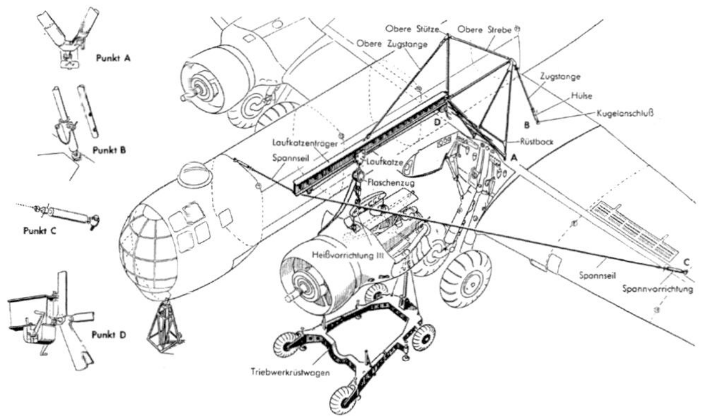

This diagram appears in all the handbooks (seen here from the A-0 handbook, hence the dive brakes in the wing) and is shows, in more detail, the attachment of the gantry crane assembly to the wing and fuselage

Access to the engines was achieved via a series of hinged panels, this image from the He 177A-1 handbook, shows those on top of the wing

1. Top middle flap
2. Upper lateral flaps
3. Shoulder plate
4. Flap support
5. Hand hole cover
6. Cowl flaps

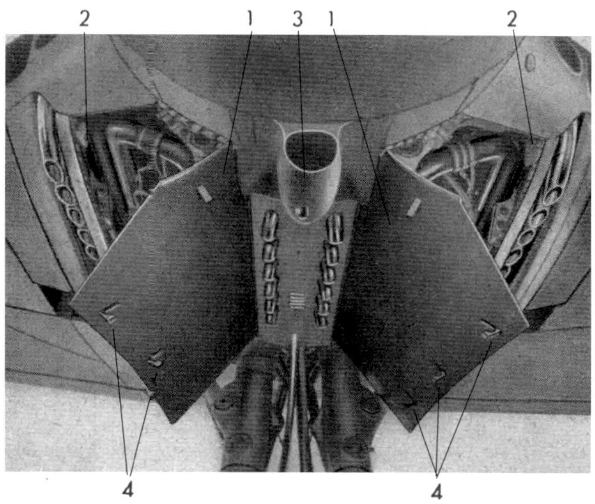

Underneath, access was via two hinged panels as depicted here from the He 177A-0 handbook. Note the exhausts stacks on the side, with the double set down the middle

1. Side flaps
2. Flap carrier
3. Cover panel with ventilation nozzle
4. Closures

This image from the He 177A-1 handbook shows the upper engine area from the rear, with the fixed panel running down the middle and the hinged doors on either side removed

1. Cowling framework
2. Scaffolding arch
3. Hand hole cover
4. Flap in the cowling frame

1. Hood framework
2. Top side flap
3. Scaffolding arch
4. Scaffolding tube
5. Mounts
6. Ventilation and ventilation protection

above left: Here you have the upper/front engine area viewed from the port side, with the access panel aft of the cowl gills removed and the hinged side panels closed

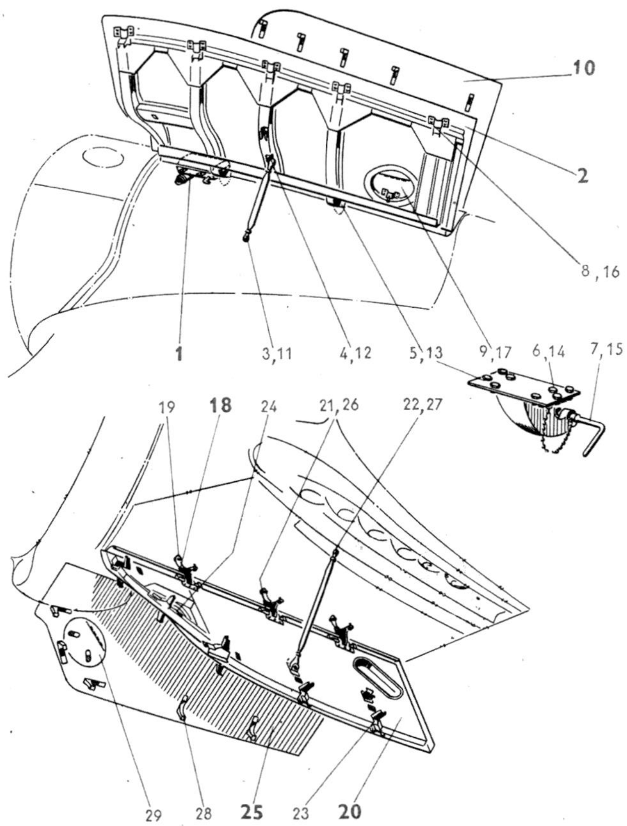

Here are the main upper and lower hinged access panels, as depicted in the He 177A-3 parts manual

This image shows the front engine baffle and the shell around the propeller shaft

1. Carrying tray
2. End frame
3. Support profile
4. Holder for de-icing line
5. Support tubes

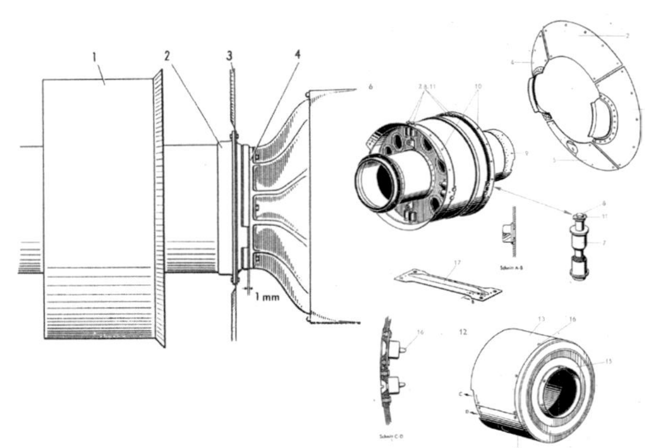

Here are the components of the propeller shaft carrier and engine baffle plate on the right, with how the carrier fits around the propeller shaft on the left

1. Carrying tray
2. Bearing ring
3. End frame
4. Support ring on the gearbox

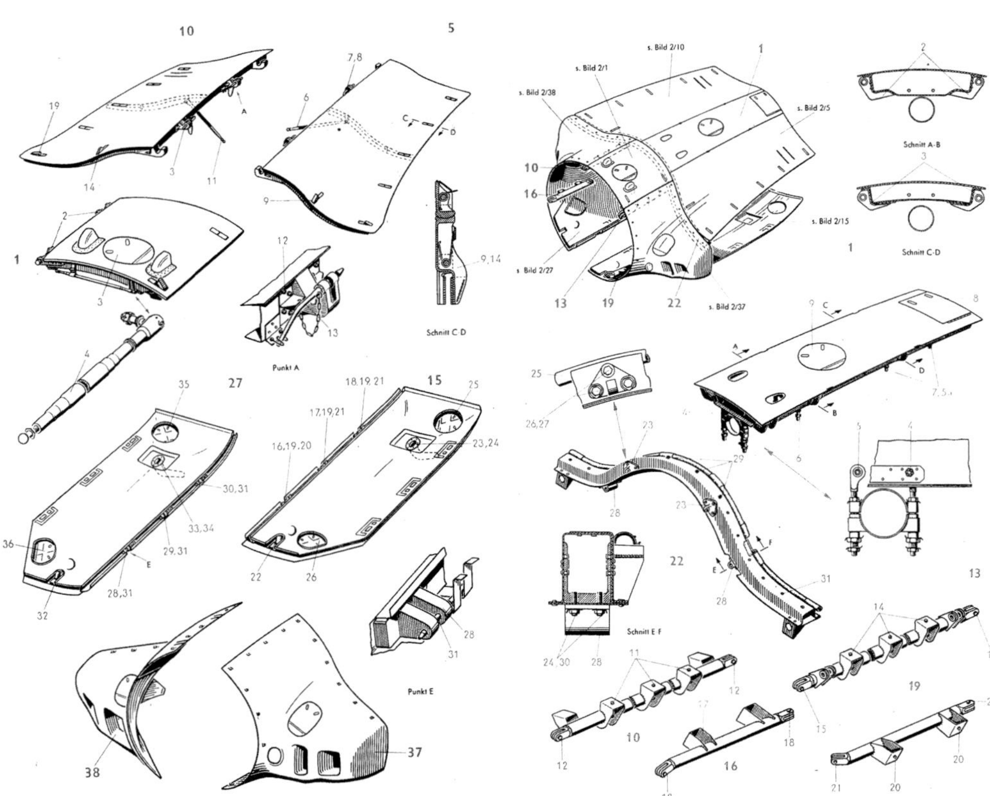

These diagram from the He 177A-3 parts manual depict most of the engine cowlings, as well as their associated mounting frames

This image shows the various section of the radiator

1. Carrying tray
2. Radiator segments
3. Sheet metal strips
4. Cover strips

These diagrams show the elements of the front cowling and apply to all A-series variants

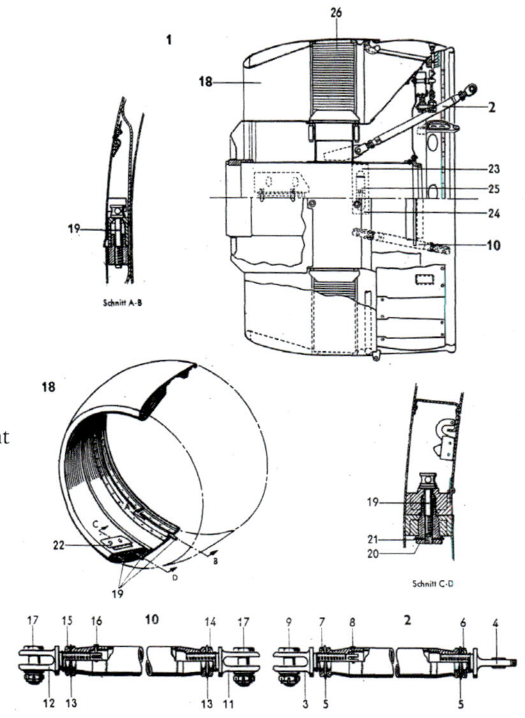

This DB610 displayed at the RAF Museum at Cosford has the front cowling and radiators in situ, but sectioned for display, so this allows you to see how these all fitted within the front section, note the ring behind the radiator that held the cowl flaps in place – the coolant header tank at that top of this area is missing *(©G. Papadimitriou)*

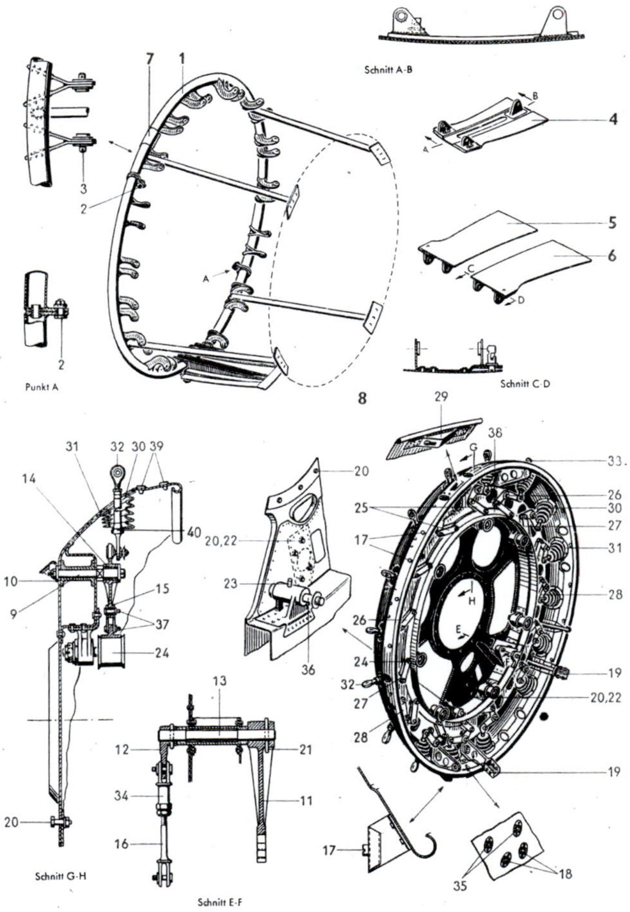

These diagrams show the forward baffle (lower right), as well as the frame that holds the cowl gills (top left) and the gills themselves (top right – '4', '5' & '6')

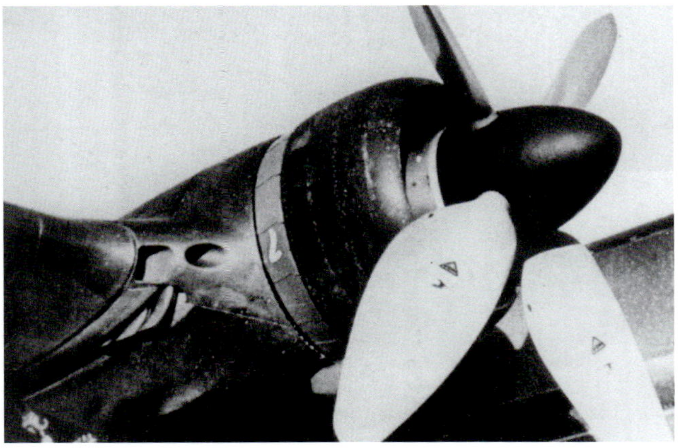

This is the VDM 4.5m diameter, four-blade metal propeller fitted to the He 177 V2 CB+RQ

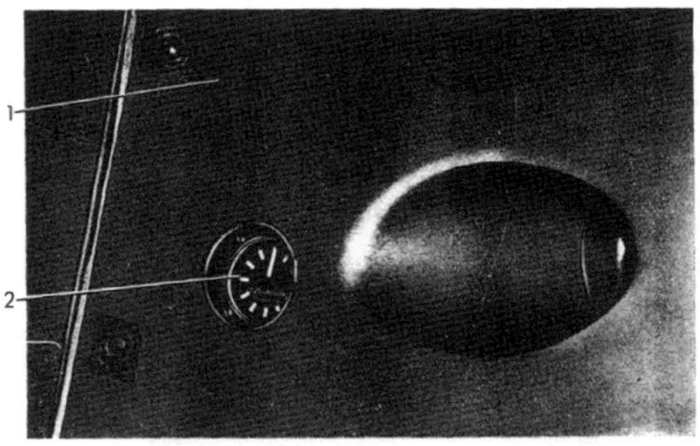

The propeller position indicator was both external (top) and in the cockpit (bottom)

Top
1. Engine cowling
2. Mechanical position indicator

Bottom
1. Equipment tower
2. Electrical position indicators

The He 177A-1 and A-3 still used VDM, four-blade, metal propellers, but they were of narrow chord, as seen here with He 177A-1, VF+RP of KG 1

The He 177A-5 adopted broad-chord, four-blade, metal propellers, with the collar at the base of each blade, as seen here on this close-up of captured example, TS439

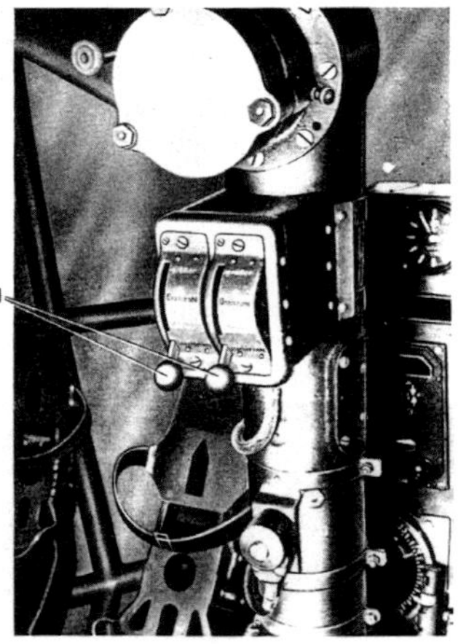

The manual selector switches for the propeller were mounted on the control column
1. Switch

This period images shows the outer port DB 603A-2 being installed in one of the He 274 prototypes in late 1944. Note the fixed portion of the nacelle, something the type copied from the similar installation in the He 219

When it first flew, the He 274 V1 (AAS.01A) was fitted with three-blade, metal propellers with spinners, as seen at the top, while later it (or maybe the V2?) had four-blade propellers without spinners as seen on the bottom (apologies for poor quality, it is a still from a ciné film)

The He 177 had exhausts on both sides of both units within each coupled DB 606 or DB610, that meant there were exhaust stacks on the outer edge, built into a gully in the wing underside and leading edge fillet, as can be seen here in this close-up of the starboard engine of the He 177 V2

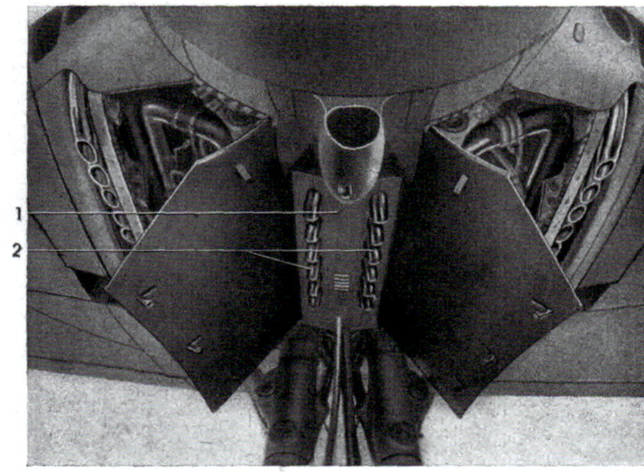

The 'inner' exhausts were set in a gully on the underside of the nacelle, this diagram deals with access to the electric actuators, but it does highlight the inner exhausts ('2')

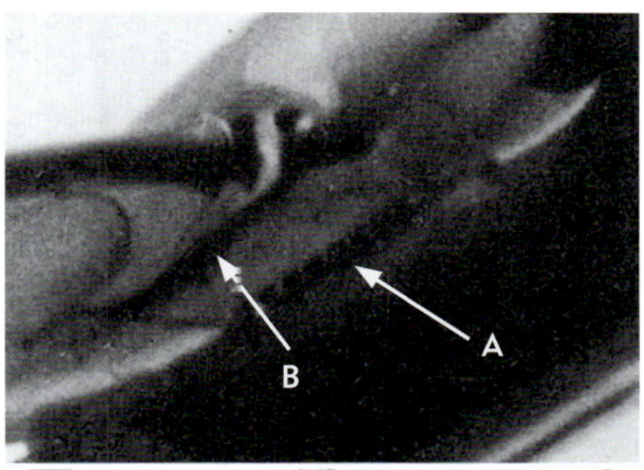

Oddly, in the A-0 and A-1 handbooks there is this image, which deals with the underside of the engine cowlings, but it shows the exhausts without the cover, while the (sorry, rather blurry) image at the top is a close-up of the He 177A-02 and you can see both sets of exhausts down the middle (A), as well as the outer set (B), the former do seem to lack the cover?

1. Lower flaps
2. Flap carrier
3. Cladding panel with ventilation nozzle
4. Closures

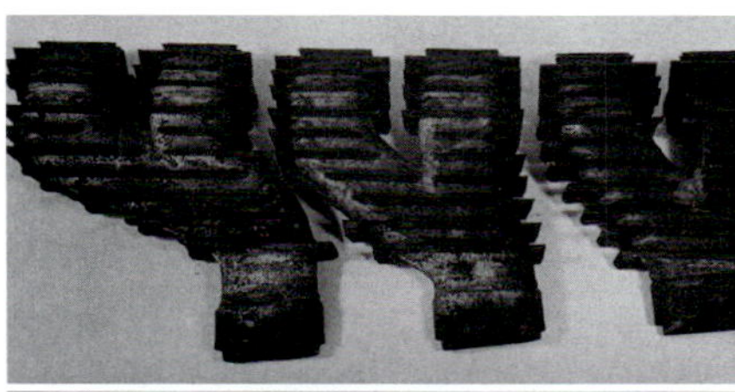

The proximity of the coupled engines meant that from the start the inner exhausts got hot, very hot, so to increase the speed of the airflow over the main bodies of each stack out of the manifold, fins were added, as seen here in these two period images that show the stacks (made from Sicromal 8), tested first by the He 177 V2

This shows the outer exhaust pipes from the He 177A-1 handbook

1. Flange plate
2. Side panel
3. Exhaust nozzle

It would seem that the fins added to the exhausts were simplified later in the war, as seen here in these two images of the DB 610 on display at the Munich Technical Museum *(©G. Papadimitriou)*

The flame visible from the exhausts meant that for night or twilight operations the He 177 had to adopt some form of flame dampers, these Fla.V units were first ground tested as seen in this period image

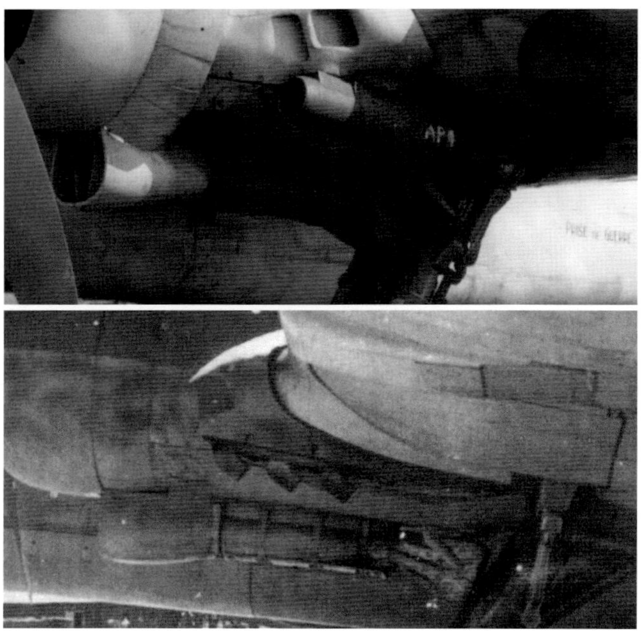

By combining these two close-ups from period images you can see the large intake and box section over the central exhausts plus the tubular ones for the outer stacks on the captured He 177A-5, TS439 at the top, while the bottom image shows an unidentified A-5 with the central intake and damper in place, but with the outer tubular ones not fitted, which allows you to see that with the A-5, these outer exhausts were co-joined at the rear to give just three outlet pipes at the front

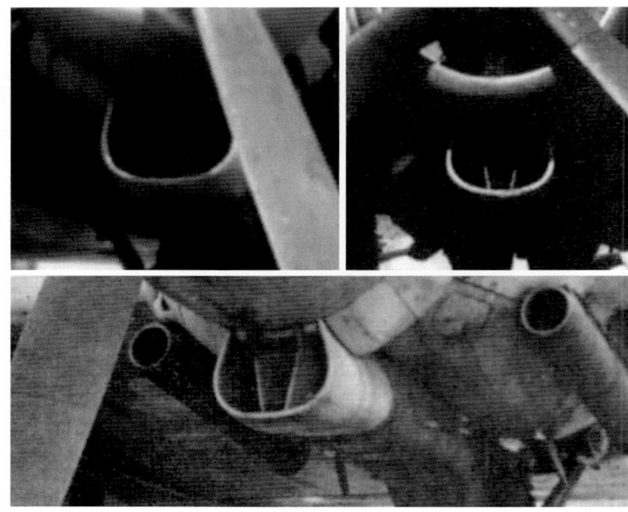

In service flame dampers took the form of a tubular one mounted onto the stacks for the outer position, with a deeper intake with three splitters inside to force air along a big box-section, also split in three, back across and between the middle exhausts. These three close-ups show the intake on a wrecked He 177A-5 found at the end of the war (top right), a He 177A-5 of the II/KG 401 (top left) and the captured He 177A-5, TS439 (bottom), the latter also allows you to see the outer tube dampers. The system, including the large front intake could be fitted to the A-1, A-3 and A-5, so it is not a distinguishing feature for a set variant

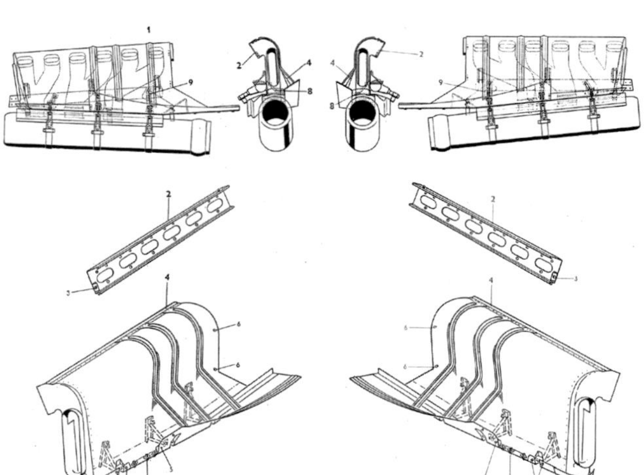

These two diagrams from the He 177A-3 parts manual show the outer flame damper units and their associated panel

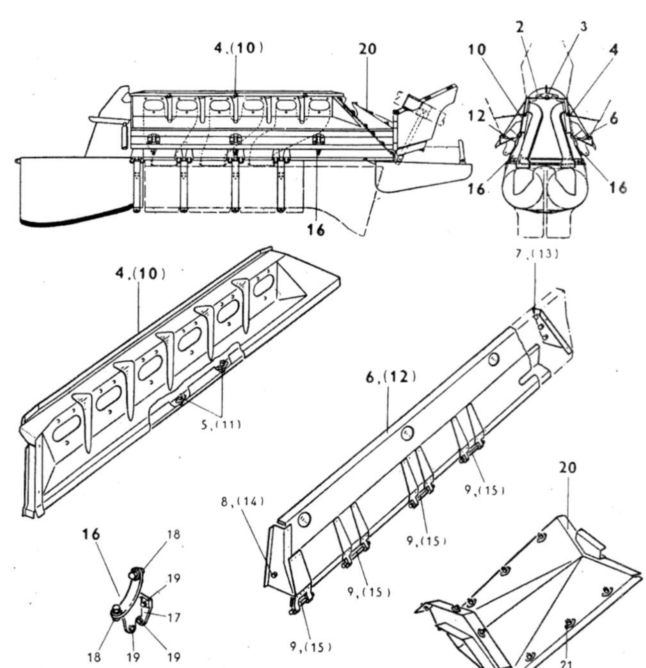

This diagram, also from the He 177A-3 parts manual, show the inner flame damper unit

Note: Whilst the prototypes had a variety of fuel tank sizes/location as the ideal combination was sought, no period images or diagrams exist, so we cannot cover them here

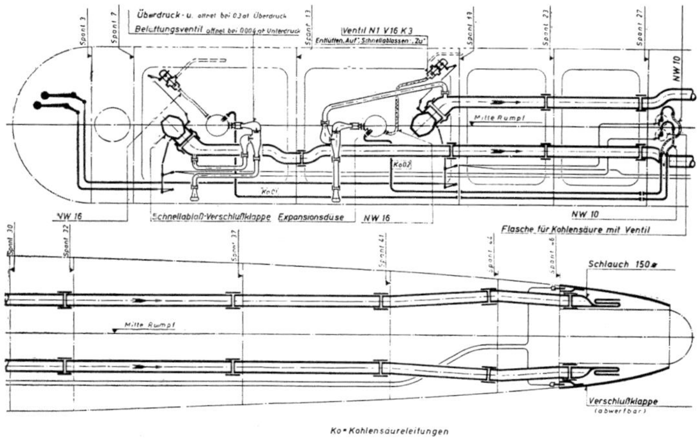

The He 177 had an emergency fuel dump system, as depicted in this diagram and image, both from the He 177A-1 handbook
Stern stand seen from below
(The releasable flaps on the fuel drain have been removed)
1. DBU fabric hoses

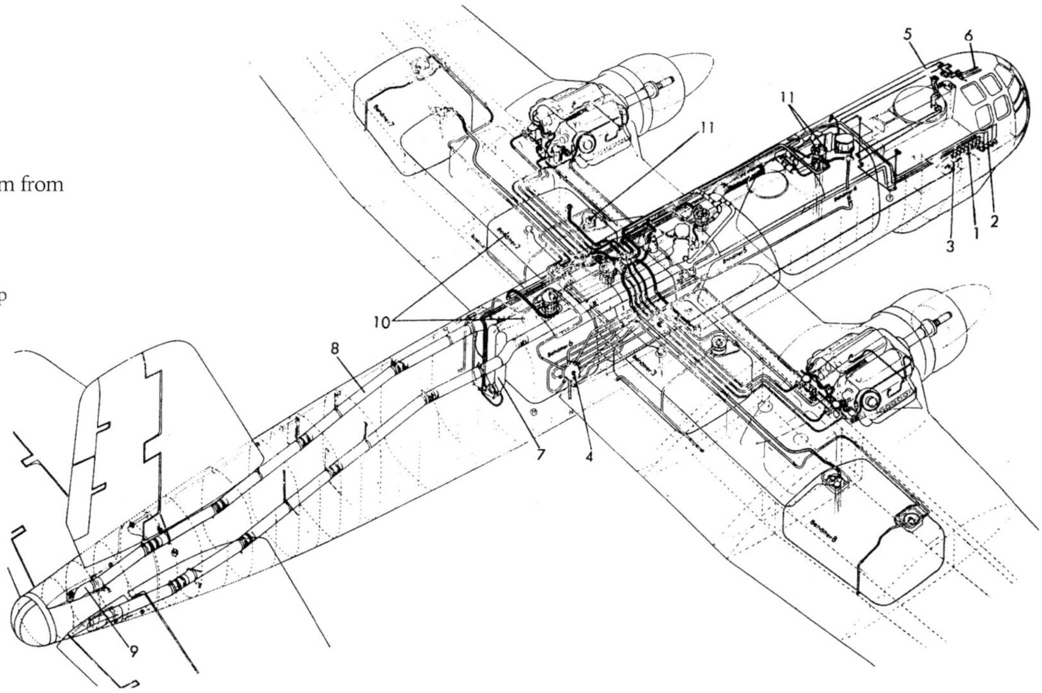

This is the fuel system diagram from the He 177A-1 handbook

1. Fuel level gauge
2. Fuel pressure gauge
3. Crank drive for emergency stop
4. Switching tap for emergency shutdown
5. Filter fire valve actuation
6. Fuel buckle drain hand lever
7. Carbon dioxide bottle with valve
8. Quick drain pipe
9. Hose (rolled up)
10. Fuel tank
11. Fuel filler neck

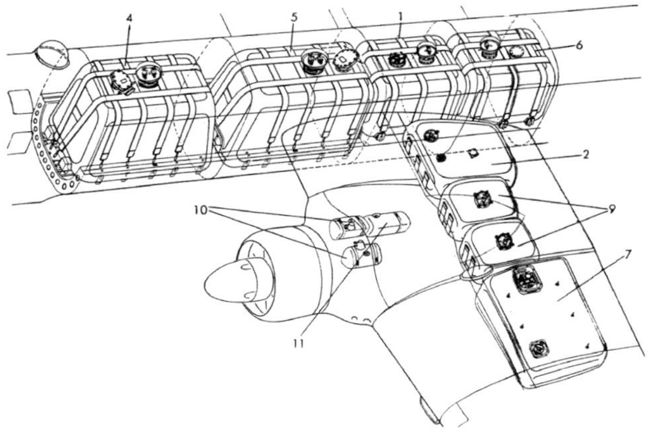

This diagram shows the fuel tanks and their capacities and it comes from the He 177A-1 handbook

1. Removal container 1 with 1140 liters content (between frames 19 and 23)
2. Storage container with 620 liters capacity (wing center section, left)
4. Storage container with 3530 liters capacity (between frames 7 and 13)
5. Storage container with 3530 liters capacity (between frames 13 and 19)
6. Storage container with 1140 liters capacity (between frames 23 and 27)
7. Storage container with 1120 liters capacity (wing center section, left)
8. Lubricant container
10. Transmission lubricant reservoir
11. Coolant container

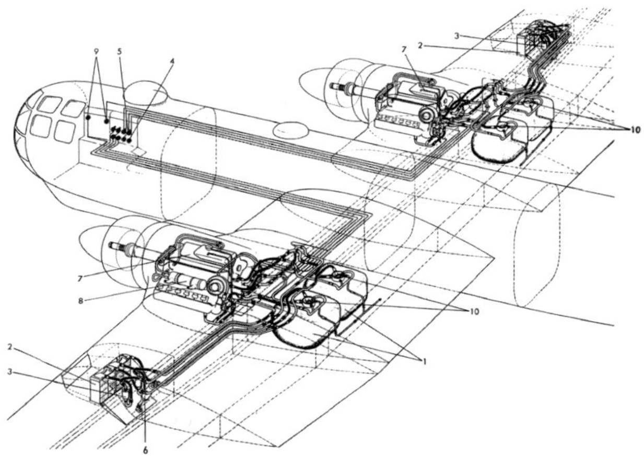

This diagram shows the oil system and comes from the He 177A-1 handbook

1. Lubricant container
2. Lubricant cooler
3. Lubricant filter
4. Lubricant pressure gauge
5. Lubricant temperature meter
6. Hydraulic oil cylinder for radiator flap adjustment
7. Gear lubricant container
8. Heat exchanger
9. Transmission lubricant pressure gauge
11. Lubricant filling head

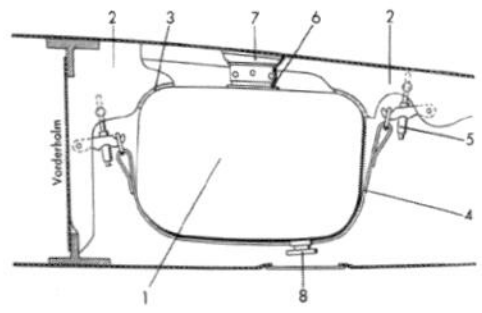

These three images give various details about the oil system tanks

Lubricant container storage (top right)
1. Container
2. Container storage
3. Liners
4. Carrying strap
5. Tension screws
6. Container head
7. Cuff
8. Sum drain valve

Lubricant container (lower right)
1. Container
2. Container head

Lubricant container in the centre wing section (left)
1. Container storage
2. Strap
3. Container

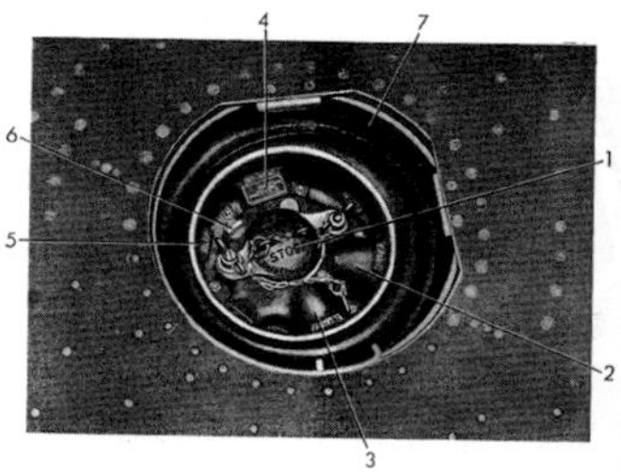

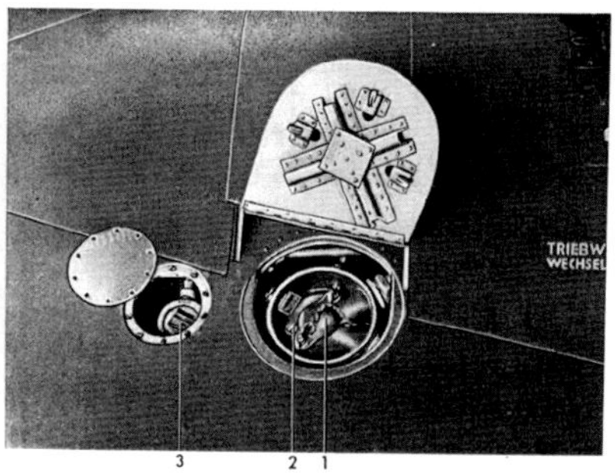

This is the filler point for the oil reservoir on the right, with a more detailed look at it on the left

Fittings of the lubricant container (right)
1. Filling nozzle
2. Dipstick
3. Supply giver

Lubricant container head (left)
1. Filling nozzle
2. Flow connection
3. Return connection
4. Venting
5. Process
6. Dipstick
7. Cuff

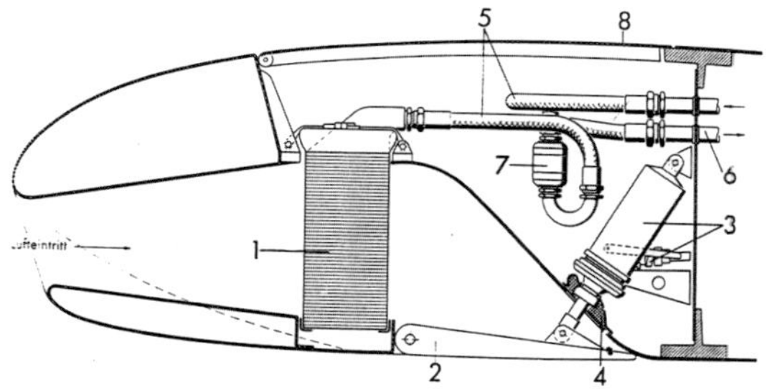

This diagram shows the the cooler in the wing

1. Lubricant cooler
2. Radiator flap
3. Thermost. fittings
4. Sealing sleeve
5. Supply lines
6. Return line
7. Lubricant filter
8. Lid in the wing

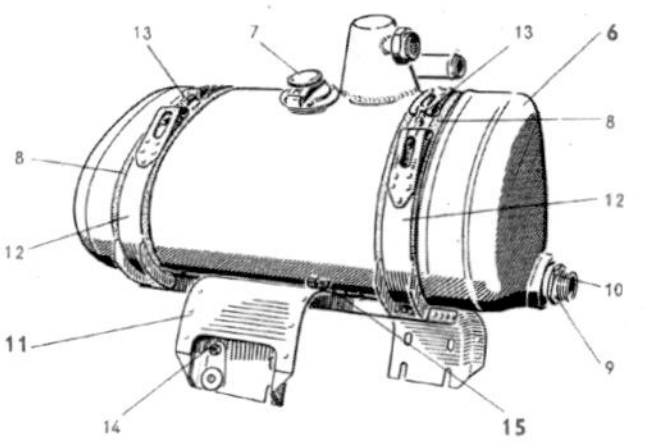

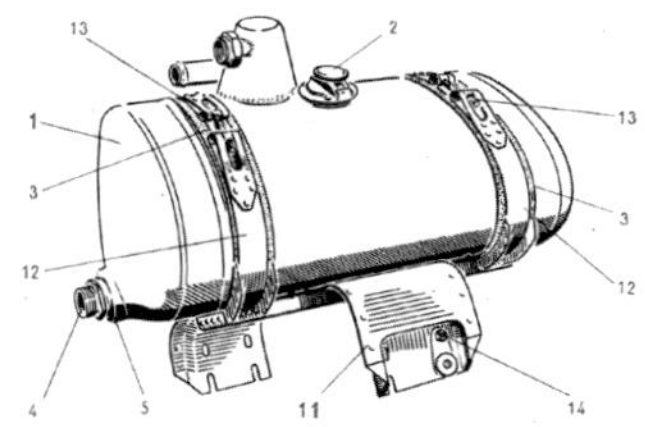

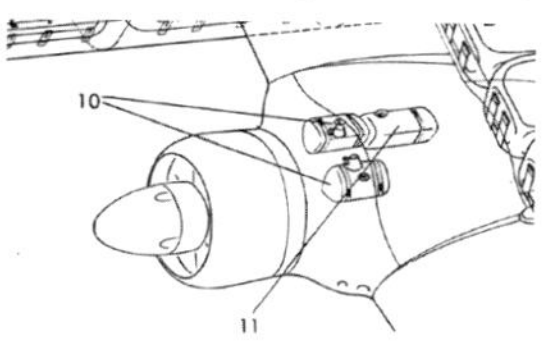

The engine coolant system used two reservoirs (top and middle images) situated above and on either side of the engine (marked as '10' in the lower diagram)

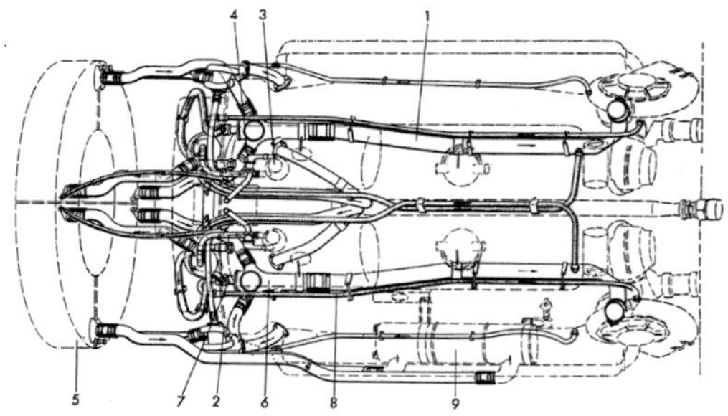

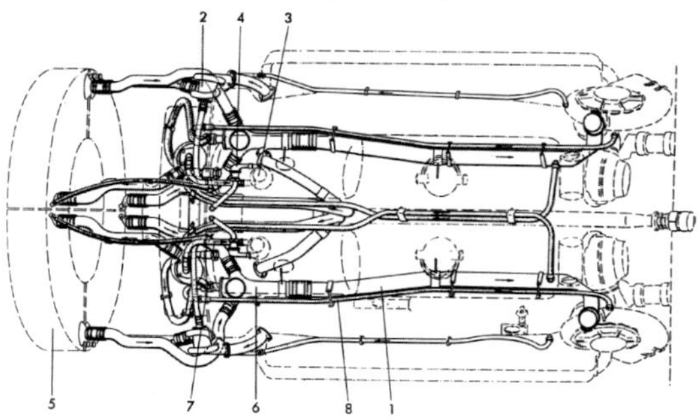

These two diagrams show the coolant system for the left (top) and right (bottom) engines

Overview plan (top) – coolant system (left engine)
1. Collector pipe
2. Steam air separator
3. Steam Dome
4. Pressure maintaining valve
5. Radiator segment
6. Branch piece
7. Injector nozzle
8. Pressure line
9. Heat exchanger

Overview plan (bottom) – coolant system (right engine)
1. Collector pipe
2. Steam air separator
3. Steam Dome
4. Pressure maintaining valve
5. Radiator segment
6. Branch piece
7. Injector nozzle
8. Pressure line

The main undercarriage remained the same throughout production of the A-series, only some of the later projected variants had a revised layout. These two diagrams, all showing the He 177A-01, W/ Nr.0016, DL+AP used to illustrate the undercarriage down (top) and during retraction with the doors open (bottom)

This period image shows the main undercarriage leg, viewed from the front

These two period images show the main undercarriage legs from behind on the port and starboard sides

This diagram from the He 177A-1 handbook gives an overview of the main undercarriage and applies to all production A-series variants

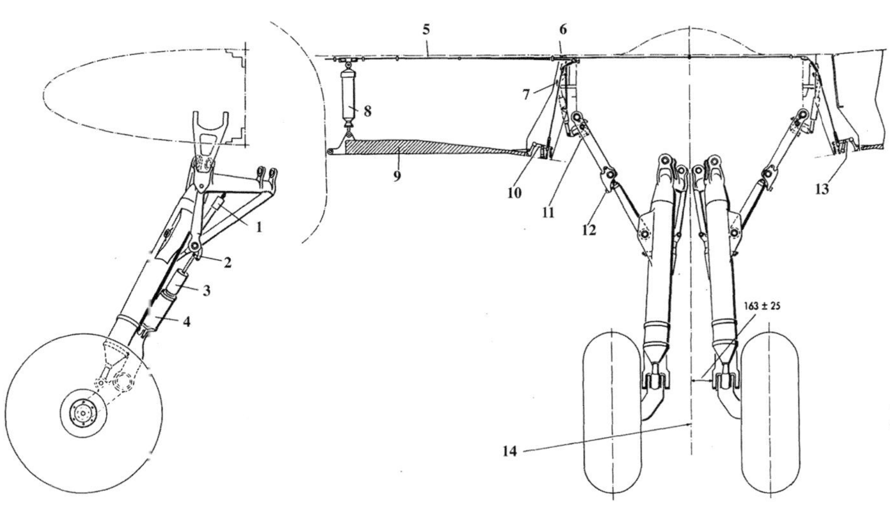

1. Compression spring
2. Crank
3. Sheet metal sleeve
4. Landing gear retraction cylinder
5. Landing gear door retraction control
6. Surface rib
7. Control switch in lower end position
8. Single cylinder for landing gear door
9. Landing gear door
10. Arrangement of the landing gear door catch
11. Adjusting screw
12. Large buckle brace stop screw
13. Arrangement of the landing gear door catch
14. Plumb line position. The machine is jacked up and aligned according to the spirit level

This shows a cutaway of the main undercarriage support leg with shock absorber

1. Shock absorber
2. Connection bolts
3. Packing piece
4. Pivot pin
5. Bumper
6. Lower spherical shell
7. Ring nut
8. Viewing holes
9. Air filling valve
10. Axle control arm
11. Wooden wedge
12. Cuff

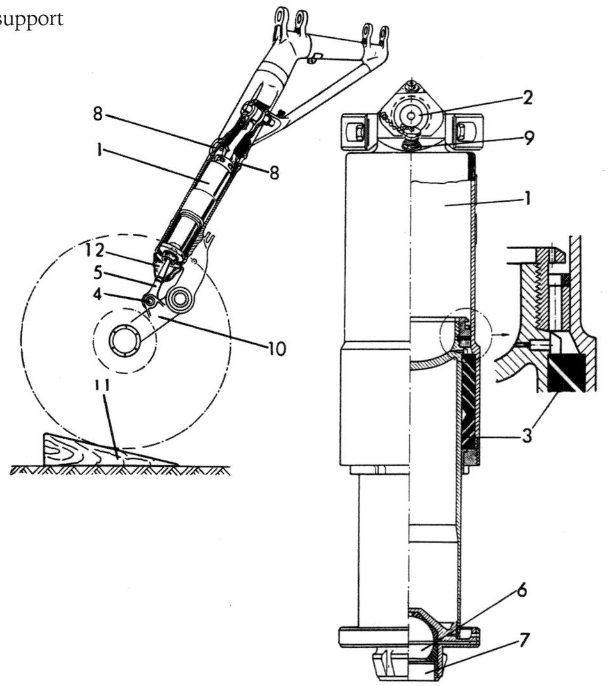

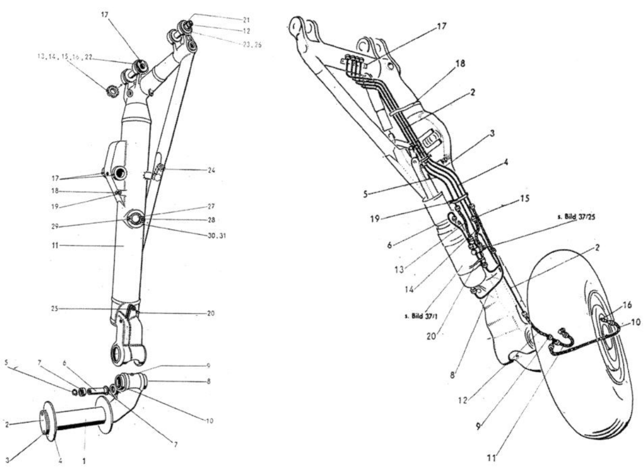

These two diagrams from the He 177A-5 parts manual show the route of the brake lines on the right, and the main components of the main leg on the left

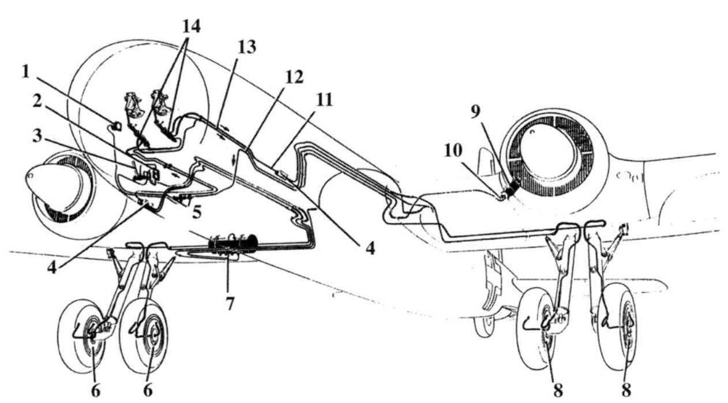

This diagram shows the brake system of the He 177

1. Pressure gauge
2. Emergency operation switch
3. Hand pump
4. Pipe burst protection
5. Check valves
6. Wheel brakes on the right
7. Special return to the main container
8. Wheel brakes on the left
9. Pressure accumulator
10. Circulation line
11. Feed to the brake
12. Feed from the pressure vessel
13. Feed to the container
14. Foot brake valve

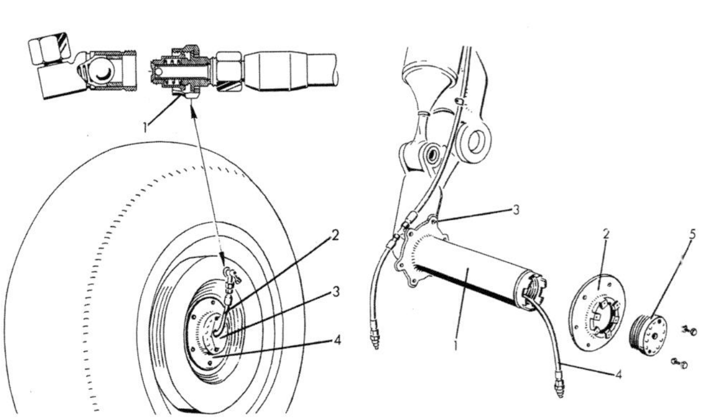

These two diagrams, from the He 177A-5 parts manual, show the axle and brake line on the right, and the connection of the brake line to the outer face of the hub on the left

Axle control arm
Argus pipe coupling upwards
Right
1. Wheel axle
2. Loose brake flange
3. Fixed brake flange
4. Brake hose
5. Axle cap

Wheel
Argus pipe coupling loosened
Flow blocked on both sides
Left
1. Red union nut
2. Hex screws
3. Axle cap
4. Brake hub

The main wheels were large, 1220mm x 445mm and lacked any tread, as seen in these two period images

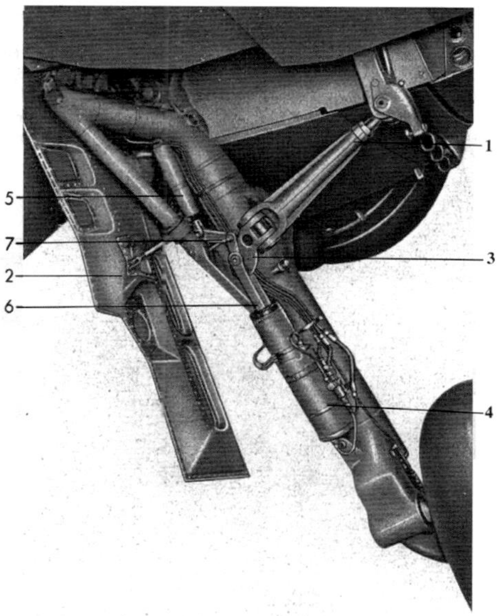

This shows the inner undercarriage door and its linkage and applies to all variants

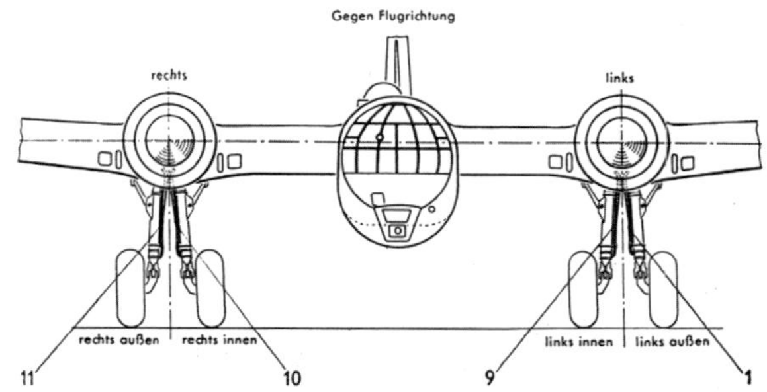

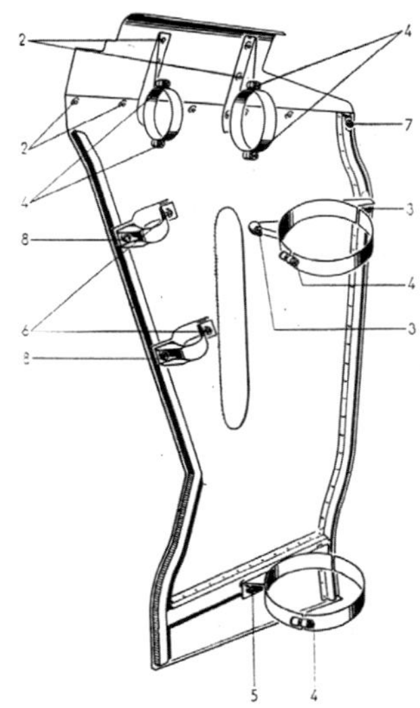

This diagram shows the inner undercarriage door

This diagram shows the outer undercarriage door

Landing gear door
1. Landing gear door cylinder
2. Rest roller
3. Latching hook
4. Landing gear door

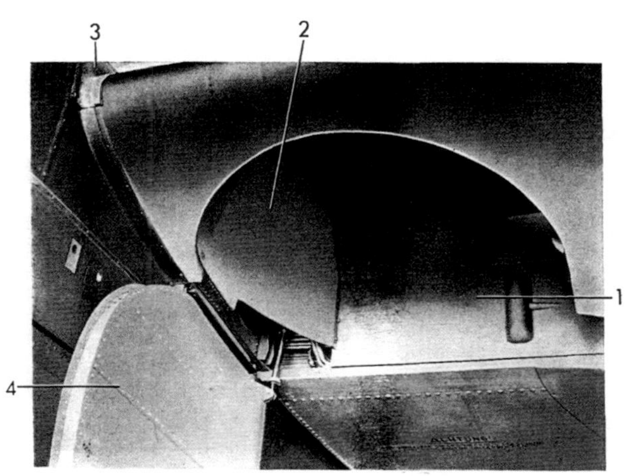

This image from the He 177A-1 manual shows the main undercarriage bay, outboard left looking aft

Landing gear compartment of the nose box on the left (view from below against the direction of flight)
1. Hole trim panel
2. Nose rib trim panel 1
3. Fuselage (wing root) fairing
4. Landing gear door

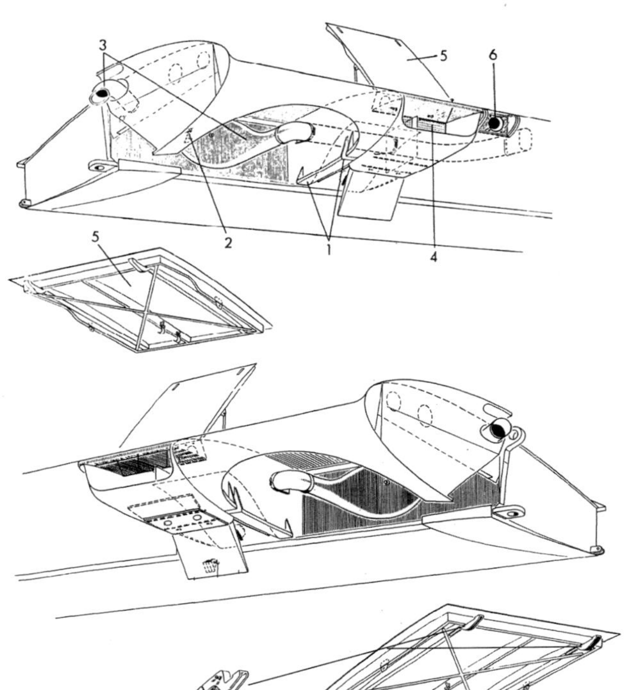

These two diagrams show the undercarriage bay in the port (upper) and starboard (lower) outer wing panels

1. Landing gear door bearing (door removed)
2. Landing gear catch
3. Warm air supply
4. Lubricant cooler
5. Flap with quick-release fasteners
6. Landing light (left only)

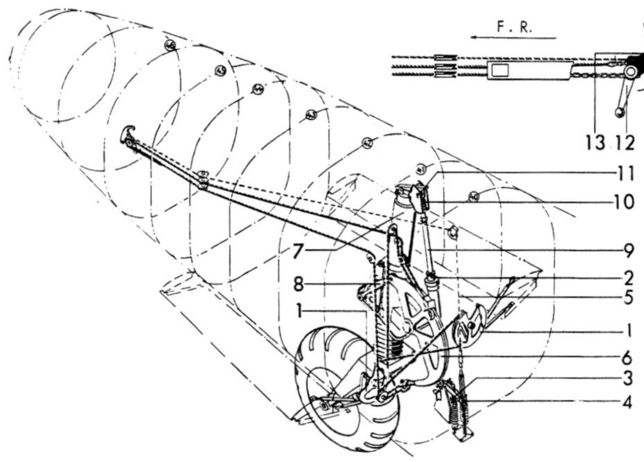

This diagram from the He 177A-1 shows the tailwheel system

1. Valve segments
2. Retraction cylinder
3. Detent cylinder
4. Detent lever
5. Cable for emergency tensioning
6. Spur segment
7. Suspension strut
8. Connecting rod
9. Retraction cylinder piston rod
10. Compression spring
11. Pawl
12. Hand crank for emergency retraction of the tailwheel
13. Hand lever for tailwheel retraction

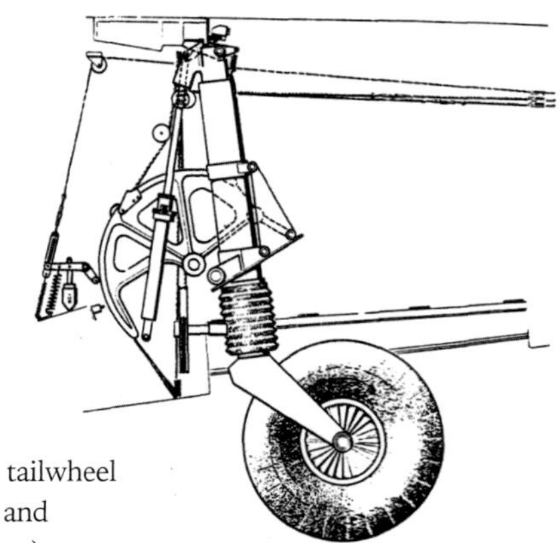

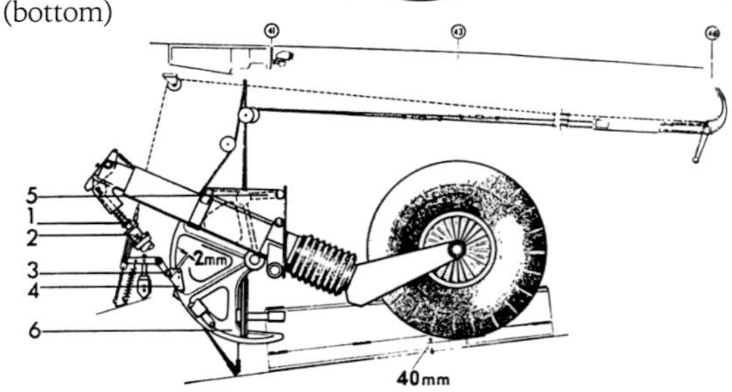

This shows the tailwheel extended (top) and retracted (bottom)

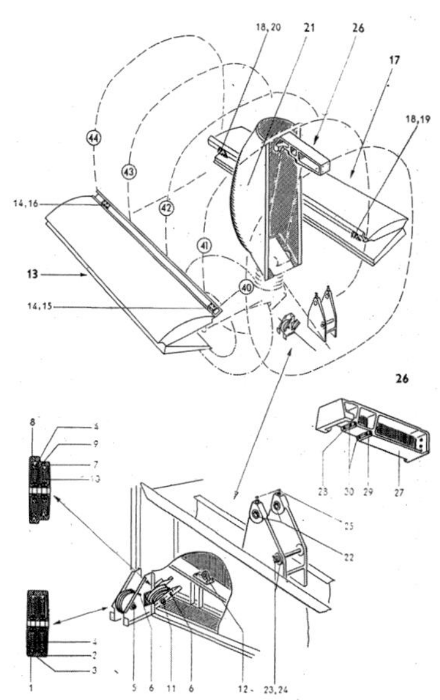

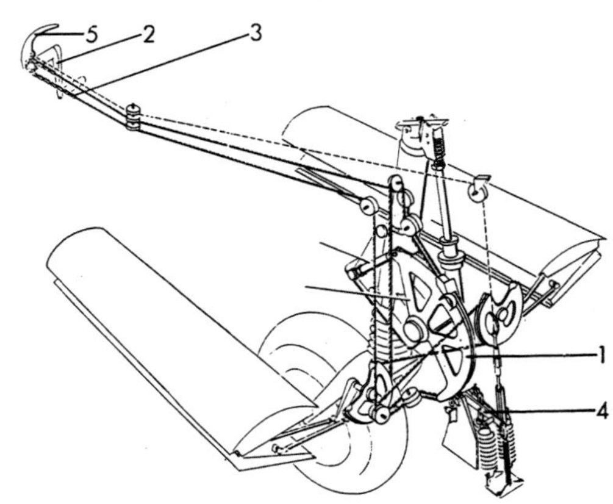

These two diagrams show how the tailwheel was extended in an emergency (right), as well as the various components in the tailwheel bay plus the doors (left)

1. Spur segment
2. Crank
3. Roller chain
4. Detent lever
5. Hand lever for unlocking

This image from the handbook shows the tailwheel extended and the doors open

1. Undercarriage doors
2. Retraction linkage

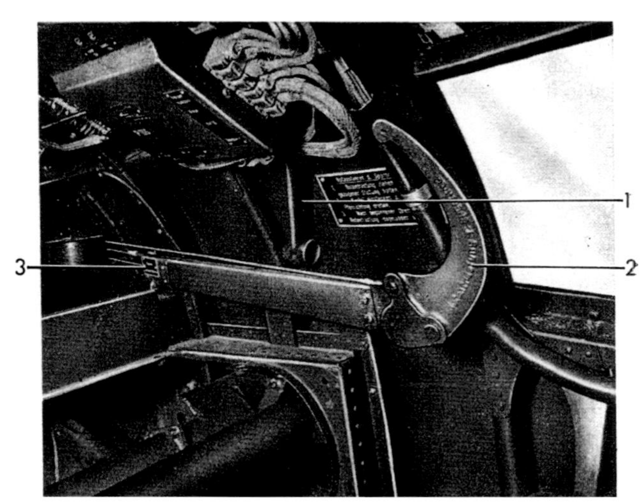

This image from the handbook shows the locking lever for the emergency deployment of the tailwheel in the rear gunner's position

1. Hand crank
2. Detent lever
3. Marking plate

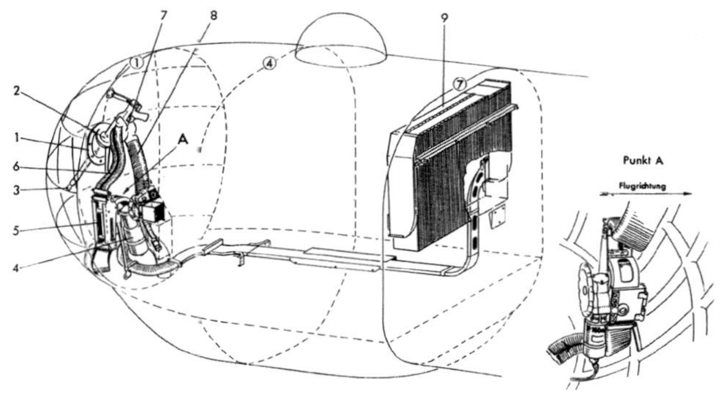

This is an overview of the upper A-*Stand* position and applies to the A-0 and A-1

1. Gun mount
2. MG bearing 81, 110ø
3. MG 81
4. Belt conveyor GF-3A
5. Gear roller box
6. Belt guide hose 81 with connector
7. Sleeve arrester
8. Spent cartridge hose
9. Full belt container

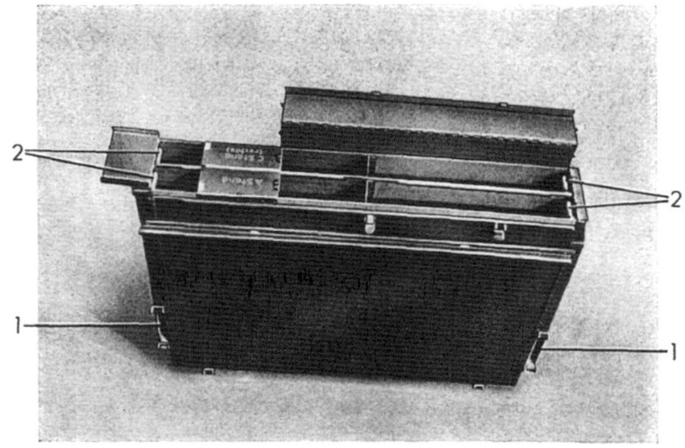

This image shows the ammunition box for the A-*Stand* that was marked as '9' in the previous diagram

1. Belt discharge shaft
2. Sliding rollers

These two images from the He 177A-1 handbook show the A-*Stand* with 140/81 mount viewed from the inside

1. Fabric cuff
2. Lashing
3. Sleeve arrester
4. Belt discharge neck
5. Spent cartridge/belt hose
6, Mouthpiece for spent cartridge/ belt hose
7. Snap clamp

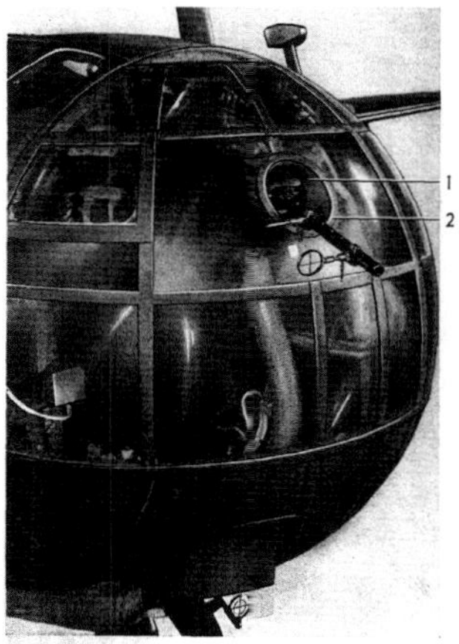

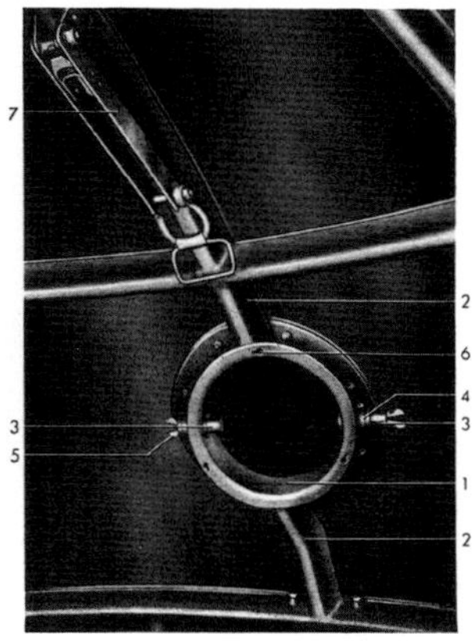

These three images show the 140/81 mount for the A-*Stand* in more detail

Gun mount (right)
1. Funnel plate
2. Mounting flange
3. Corner plate
4. Support strut

Carriage bearing for bearing ball 140/81 (middle)
1. Ring plate
2. Profile pipe
3. Trunnion
4. Bushing for pivot pin
5. Double spring
6. Rest hole
7. Lashing in rest position

A-stand above with bearing ball 140/81, external view (left)
1. Funnel plate
2. Cover ring

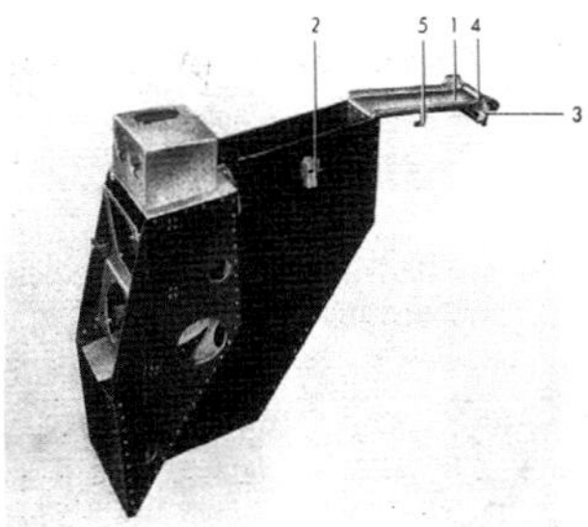

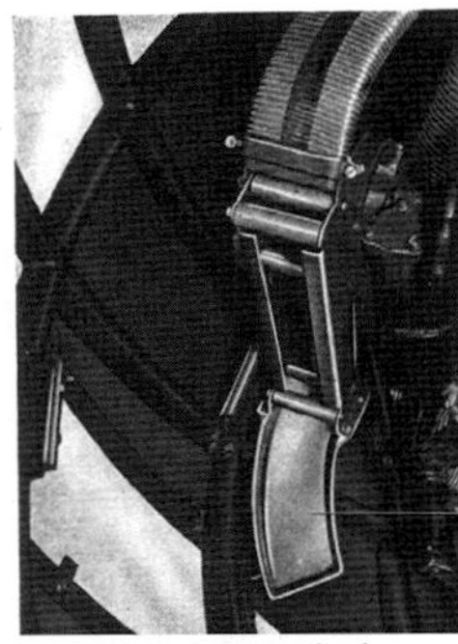

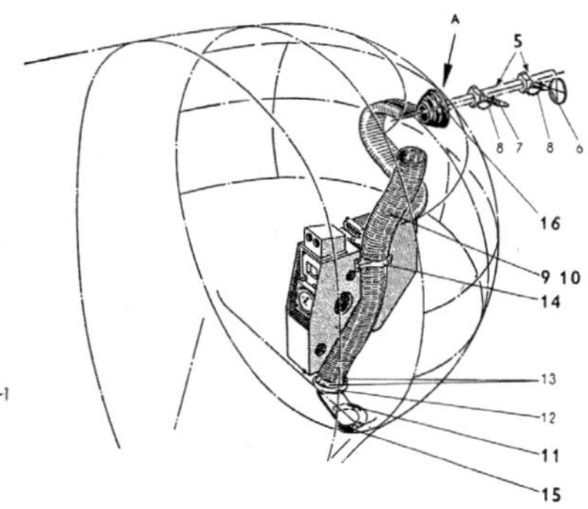

These diagrams and images show the ammunition box (top left), feed (middle top and bottom left) and spent cartridge chute (middle bottom) for the A-*Stand*

Switch roller box installed (top right)
1. Storage box

Sleeve discharge (bottom right)
1. Spent cartridge/belt hose
2. Exhaust shaft
3. Flange

Full belt container (top left)
1. Lid
2. Tension lock
3. Clamp for belt guide hose
4. Sliding roller for full belt
5. Spring clamp for belt guide hose

Belt conveyor motor (bottom left)
1. Belt conveyor
2. Belt conveyor gear

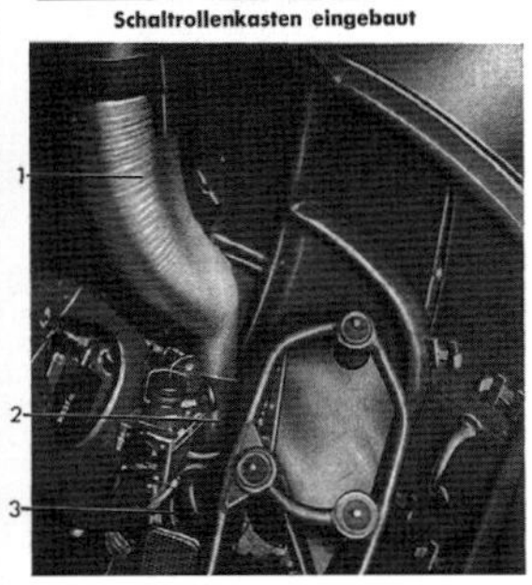

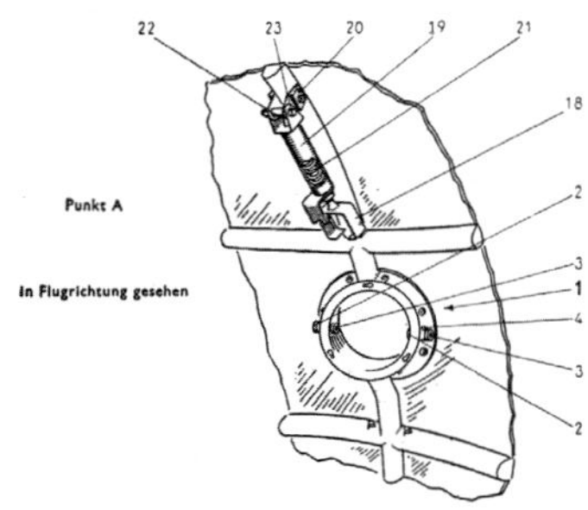

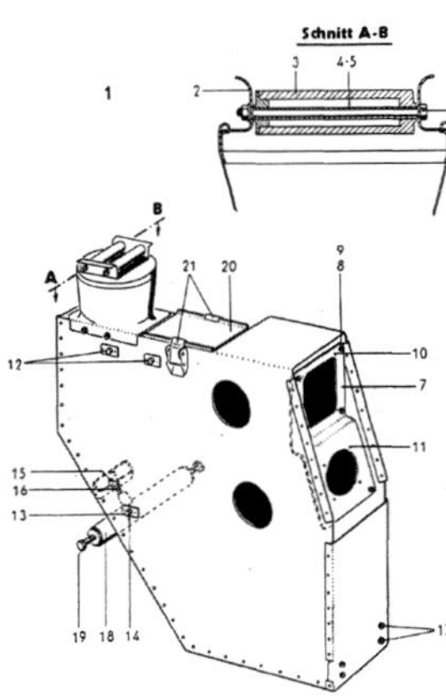

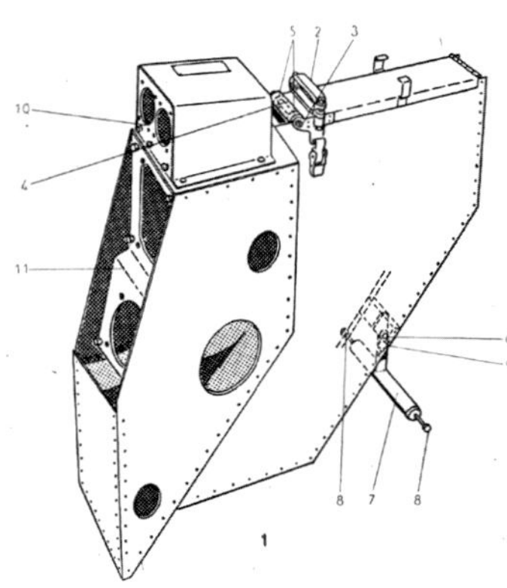

These diagrams show the ammunition box for the upper A-*Stand* as used by the A-0, A-1 and A-3 on the right, with the revised version used by the A-5 on the left

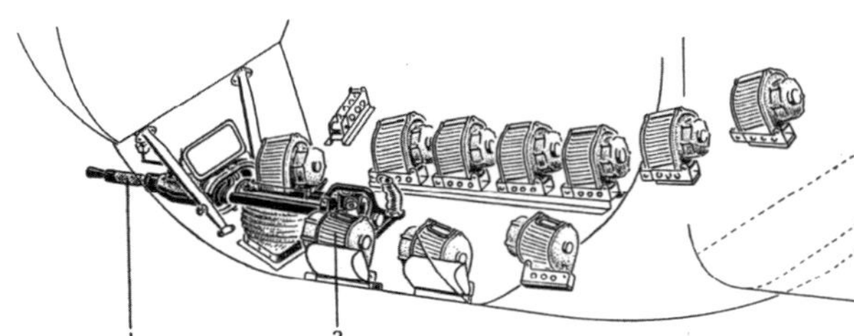

This diagram gives an overview of the lower A-*Stand*
1. MG-FF/M
2. Gun mount T 30-FF

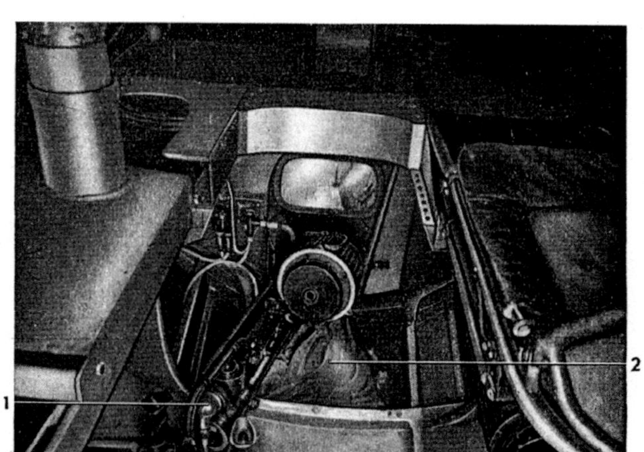

This shows the interior of the lower A-*Stand* with L-FF/6 mount and MG-FF/M cannon
1. Connector plug
2. Spent cartridge/belt discharge sleeve

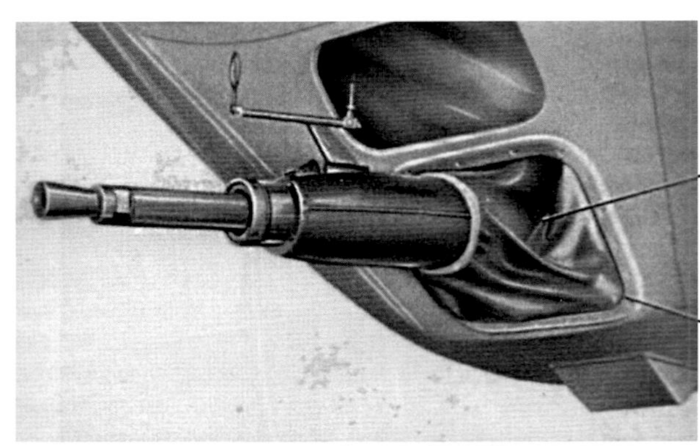

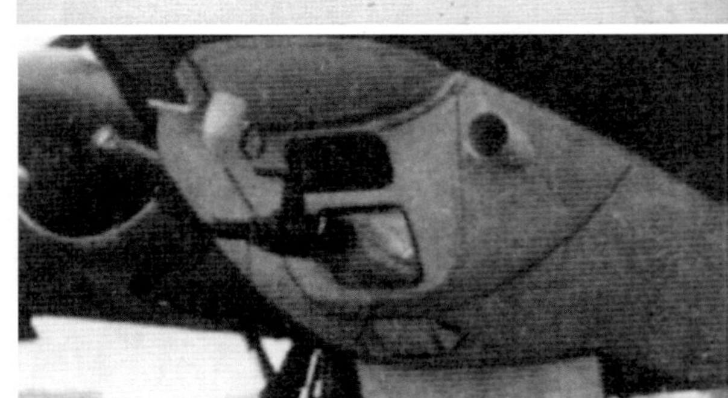

These show the MG-FF/M in the lower A-*Stand* from the outside
1. Leather waterproofing
2. Frame sheet

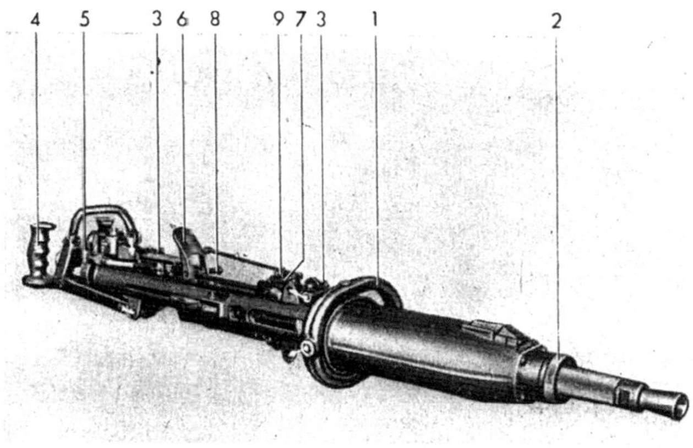

This is the MG-FF/M in detail

1. Weapon storage
2. Bearing screw
3. Screws for clamping cylinder attachment
5. Connector of the connection cable
6. Magazine release
7. Magazine release lever on the weapon
8. Fastening bolts for ZV SK-FF
9. Hex screw

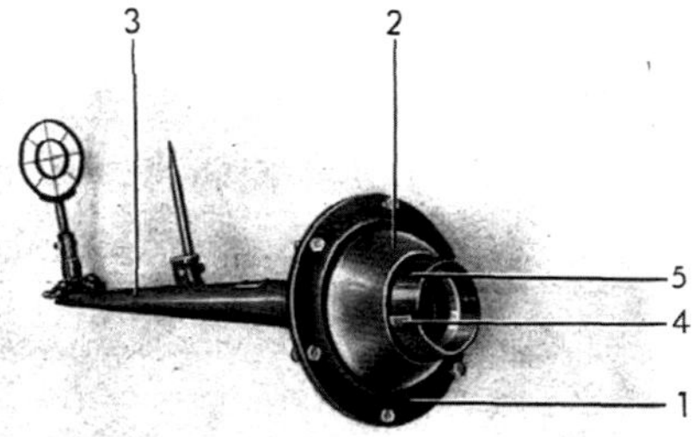

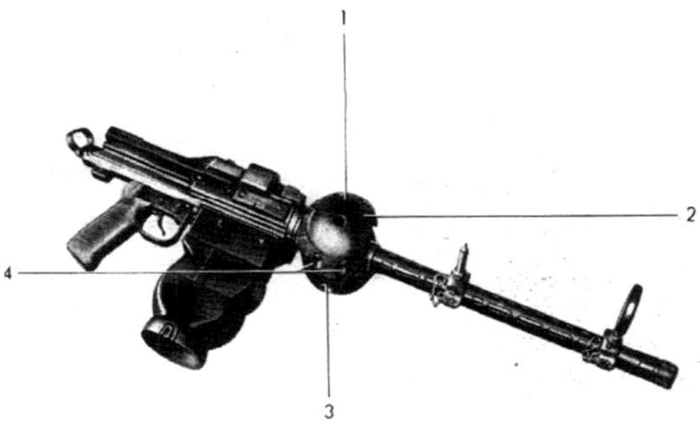

These two images show the MG 81 with the 100mm diameter ball mount (below), and the 110mm mount with the ring and bead sight (top)

MG 81 with attached bearing ball (bottom)
1. Installation arrow
2. Upper half of the ball
3. Lower half of the ball
4. Connecting bolts

MG storage 81, 110ø (top)
1. Bearing ring
2. Bearing ball
3. Sight carrier with sight
4. Rest
5. Knurled ring

The other armament option in the lower A-*Stand* was the MG 151, seen here in the diagram of the installation on the right and the exterior view on the left

Overview of A stand below L 151/3A with MG 151/20A (right)
1. MG 151/20A
2. Mount L 151/3 A with V 43/L 151A
3. Outer frame with bolts
4. Belt 151
5. Full belt container
6. Wind compensation spring
7. Feed channel with deflection roller
8. Spent cartridge chute

A stand below with L 151/3 A, outside view (left)
1. Sight V 43/L 151 A
2. Flap for empties ejection
3. Frame for cuff

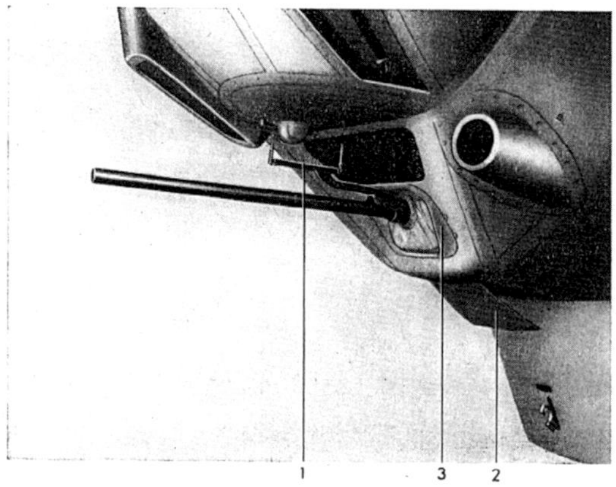

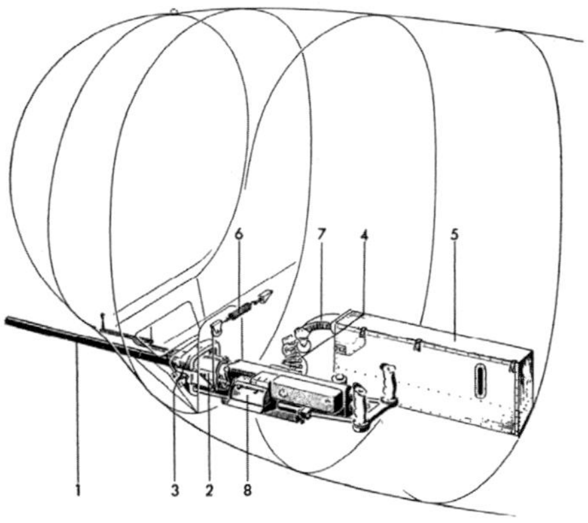

A-*Stand* below with L 151/3A, interior view (right)
1. Electrical connection cable for the weapon
2. Electrical through-charging switch box EDSK 151-B 1
3. Fuse and distribution box SVK 1

View A-stand below with L 151/3A without carriage (left)
1. Bearing blocks with spring bolts
2. Cuff
3. Lashing with snap button
4. Eye screw for wind compensation spring

These two diagrams show the lower A-*Stand* MG 151 installation with the cannon in place (right) or without (left)

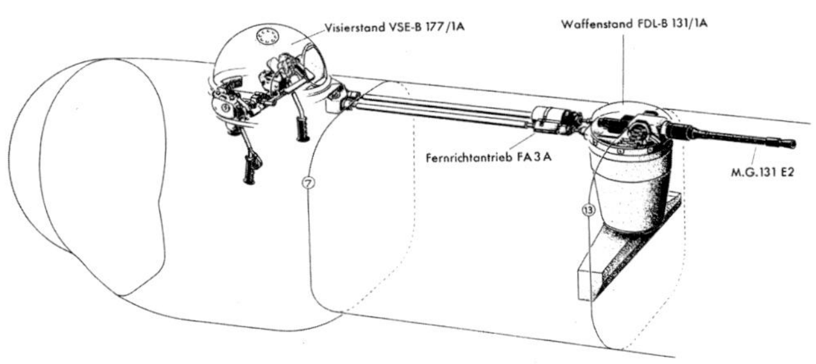

This diagram shows the FDL-B 131/1a B-*Stand* remote-controlled turret and the VSE-B 177/1A sighting position, fitted to the He 177A-0 and He 177A-1

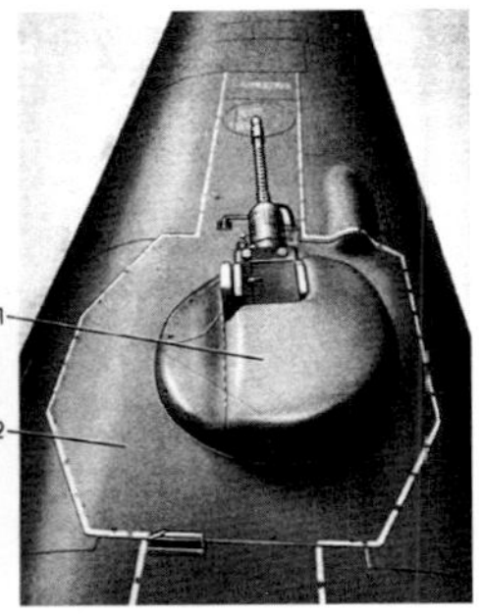

The B1-*Stand* in the A-0 and A-1 had a single MG 131 as depicted in these two images from the handbook

Right
1. Hood
2. Fairing panel

Weapon stand with belt inserted (left)

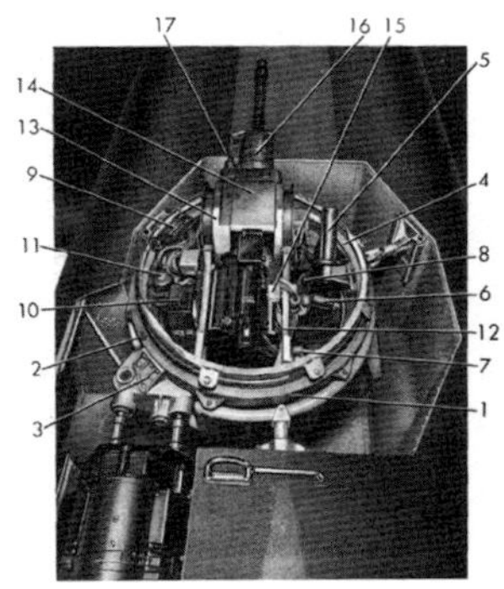

These two images show the B1-*Stand* turret support ring (right) and the gun without the cover (left)

Turret range support ring (right)
1. Bearing block
2. Support ring
3. Baffle for hood derivation
4. Attachment flange for the slip ring clutch

Turret without cover (left)
1. Outer ring
2. Lid ring with eyelets
2. Transmission gel gears
4. Inner ring
5. Introductory role
6. Guiding role
7. Shift roller
8. Drum drive motor switch
9. Shot lock
10. Mount control box LSK 5 B
11. Ignition converter
12. Cradle carrier
13. Cradle
14. Cradle lid with lever
15. Distributor
16. Buffering
17. Buffering lever

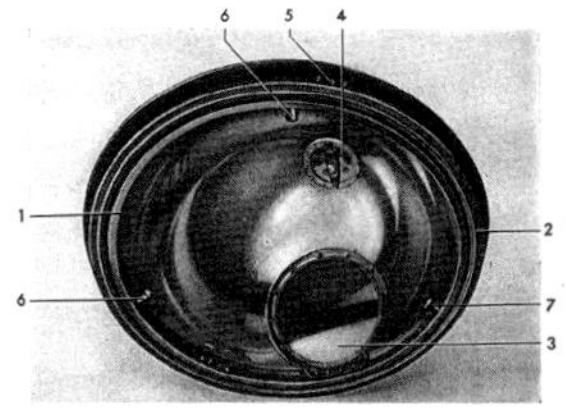

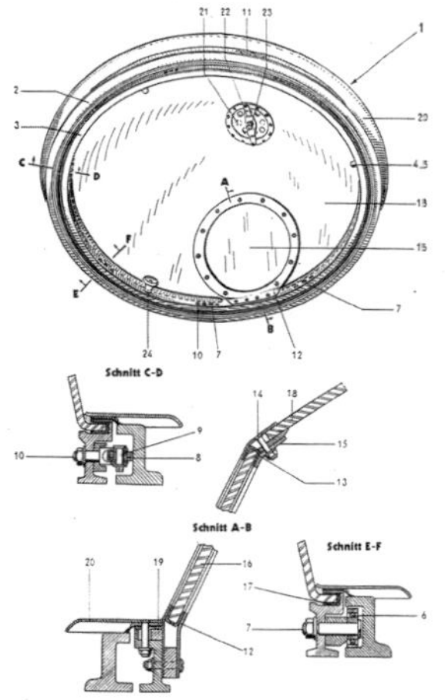

These diagrams and images deal with the VSE-B 177/1A sighting position used for the B1-*Stand*

Plexiglass hood for B-1 sighting stand (top left)
1. Guide ring
2. Support ring
3. Navigation disc
4. Turntable
5. Angle plates for inserting the hood
6. Handle
7. Clamp handwheel

B-1 sighting stand, exterior view (middle left)
1. Visor stand hood
2. Upper cover plate
3. Lower cover plate

B-1 sight stand (hood removed) (lower left)
1. Support
2. Clamping ring
3. 0° adjustment mark on LSK 4B
4. Installation mark on the outer ring
5. Flat surface with contact edge
6. 10° adjustment mark on the outer ring
7. Directional locking curve for B-2 stand
8. Directional locking curve for B-1 sight stand
9. Installation location of the direction lock roller on the visor bracket (roller has been removed)

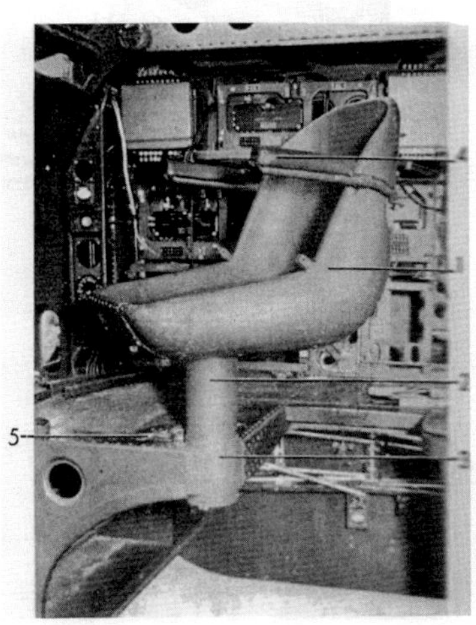

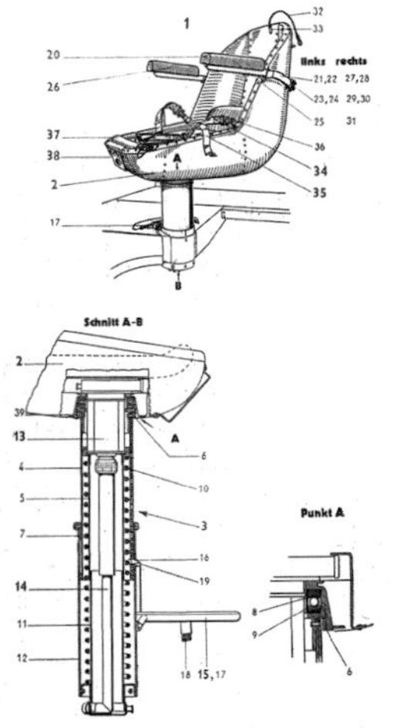

This diagram and image show the swivel seat used by the gunner operating the sight for the B1-*Stand* position

1. Belt feed
2. Belt lock
3. Mouthpiece of the spent cartridge hose
4. Shift handle with push buttons
5. Fork
6. Bolts
7. Auxiliary side drive (hand crank in-use position)

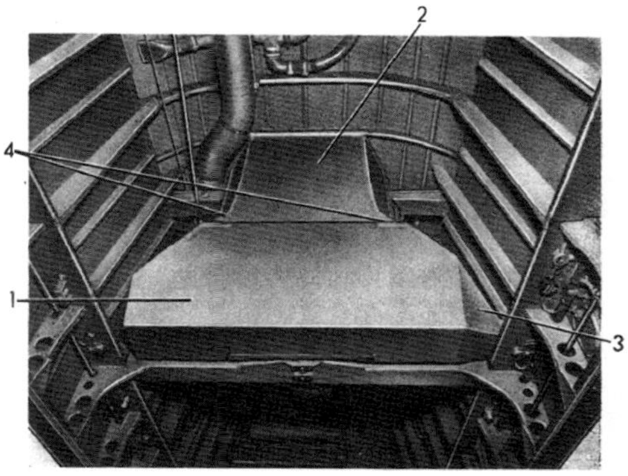
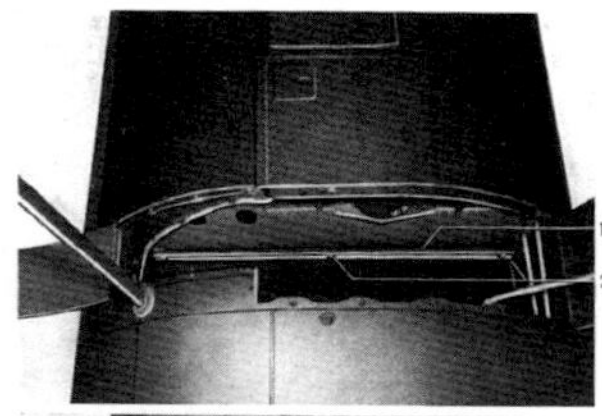

These images from the handbook show the ammunition bins (right) from underneath and the spent cartridge and belt box (left) inside the fuselage for the B1-*Stand*

Full belt container fastening (A-profile) (top right)
1. A-profile
2. Threaded piece

Full belt container installed (bottom right)
1. Transmission shafts for B-1 stand

Sleeve and belt link box (left)
1. Sleeve and belt link box
2. Weapon range fairing
3. Drainage shaft
4. Hex bolt attachment points

From the He 177A-3, the B1-*Stand* was fitted with two MG 131s, which resulted in removal of the step in the turret cover

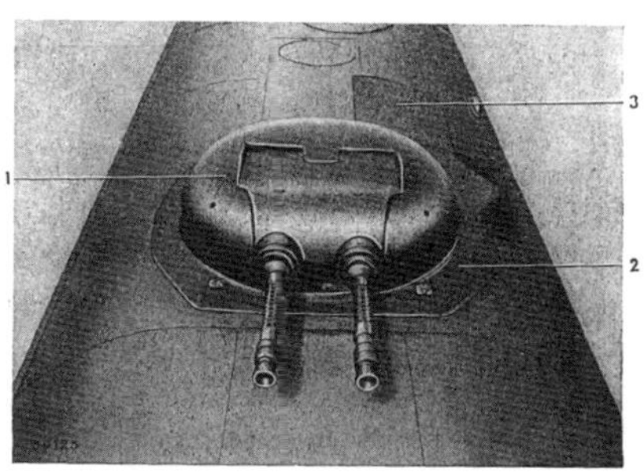
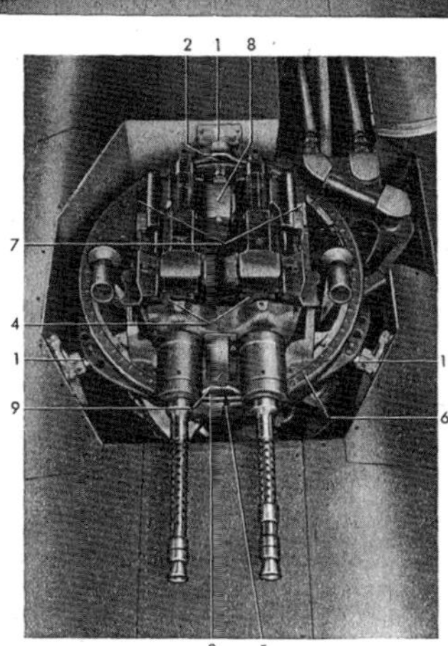

These two illustrations from the He 177A-3 handbook show the B1-*Stand* installation

B-1 turret with cover (top)
1. Hood
2. Cover plate for weapon stand
3. Cover plate for shaft gear

B-1 turret, installed (bottom)
1. Attachment points
2. Weapon deflector to protect B-1 sights
3. Weapon deflector to protect B-2 stand
4. Locking button
5. Line mark on the cradle carrier (covered by weapon deflector)
6. Deck ring with 360° pitch
7. Plane-parallel surfaces on the cradle support
8. EDSK-B
9. Low deflector

From the A-1 a DL 131, manually-controlled, electrically powered turret was installed in the mid-fuselage dorsal spine as the B2-*Stand*. This was deleted initially with the A-1, but reinstated from the 61st airframe

B2 stand, exterior view
1. Weapon deflector
2. Hood
3. Wind vane
4. Vent slider

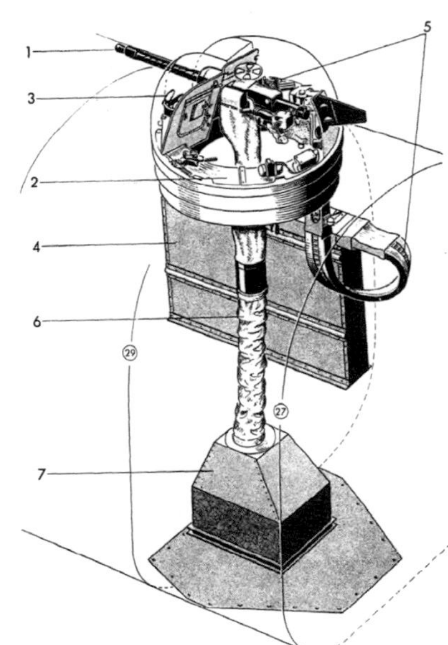

This is an overview of the B2-*Stand* used by the A-1, A-3 and A-5

1. MG 131 A2
2. Rotating ring mount DL 131/1 C
3. Rev 16A
4. Full belt container (reserve)
5. Belt 131 (500 links)
6. Spent cartridge and belt hose
7. Spent cartridge and belt containers

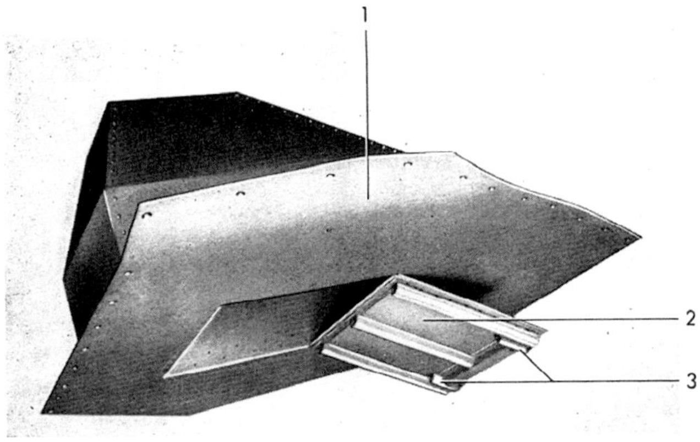

This image shows the spent cartridge container access door for the B2-*Stand*

1. Cover plate
2. Removal flap
3. Latch closure

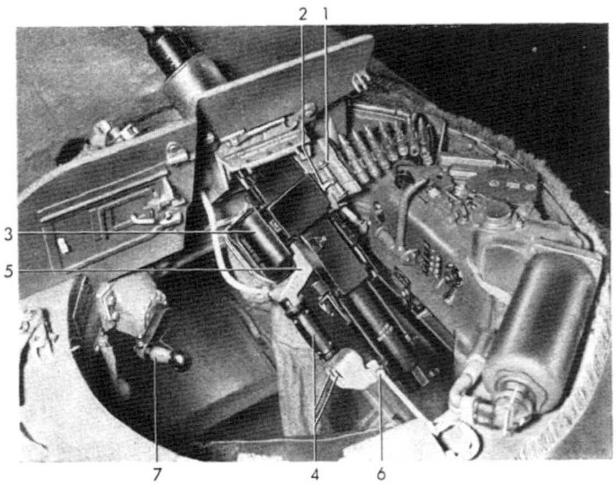

This shows the B2-*Stand* with ammo belt engaged (set at 45°)

These two images from the handbook show the rotating ring and seat etc. from below for the B2-stand

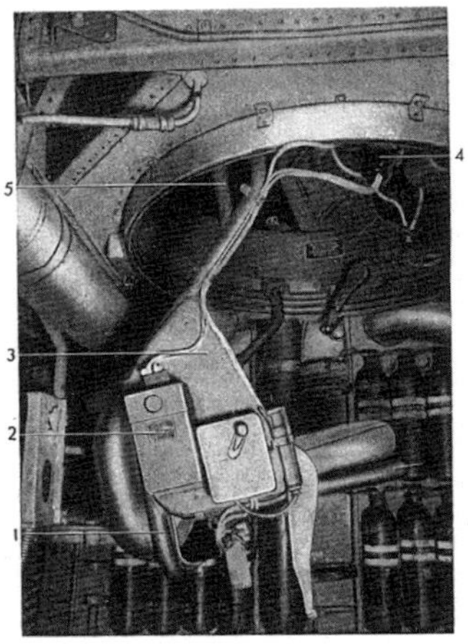

Rotating (gun) ring carriage seen from below (right)

1. Slip ring
2. Mounting ring for rotating ring mount
3. Pantograph
4. Cover for slip ring

Hanging seat with weapon ignition battery box (left)

1. Hanging seat
2. Weapon ignition battery box WZBK 1A
3. Equipment panel
4. Plug connection for WZB 1 A with the emergency switch
5. Limitation strut for hanging seat

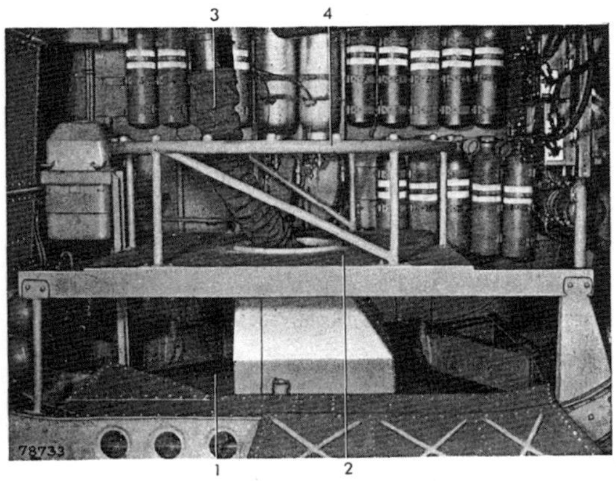

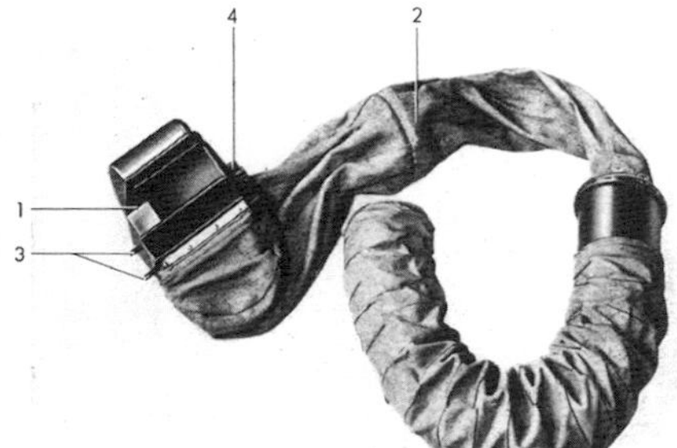

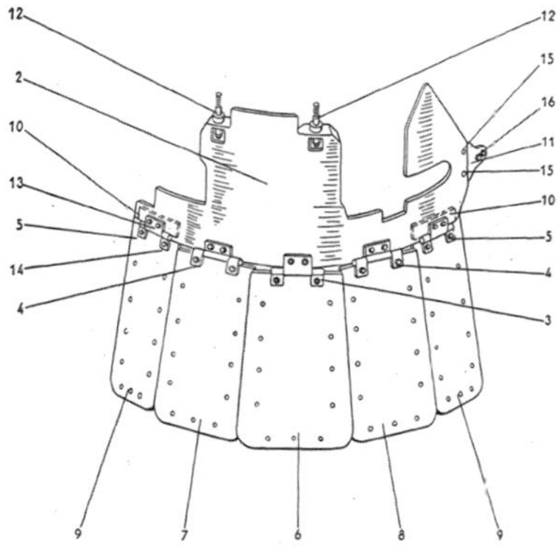

These images and diagrams from the He 177A-3 handbook show the built-in spent cartridge and belt container (top right), the reserve full ammo belt (top left) spent cartridge chute (lower right) and the armour plate skirt that is fitted below the turret ring, inside the fuselage (lower left)

Spent cartridge/belt container, installed (middle)

1. Cover plate
2. B-2 floor
3. Spent cartridge/belt hose
4. Foot ring

Storage of the reserve full belt (top left)

1. Full belt container
2. Full belt duct connector
3. Frame for rowing machine
4. Console
5. Pick-up piece
6. Belt retaining lever

Discharge hose (top rght)

1. Mouthpiece
2. Hose
3. Fork plate
4. Spring locking mechanism

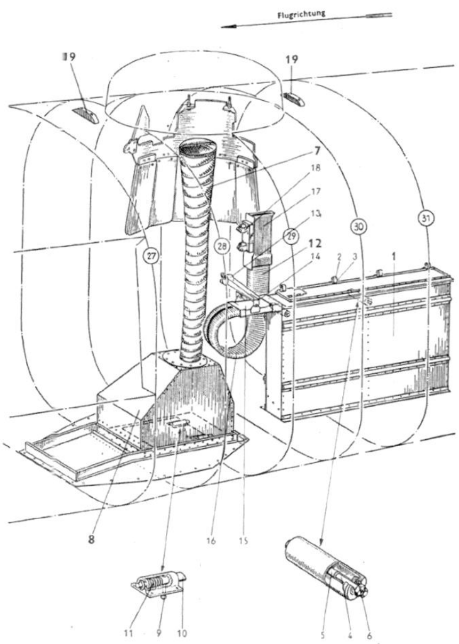

This diagram shows the B2-*Stand* installations ammo box, feed and spent cartridge and belt chute and box

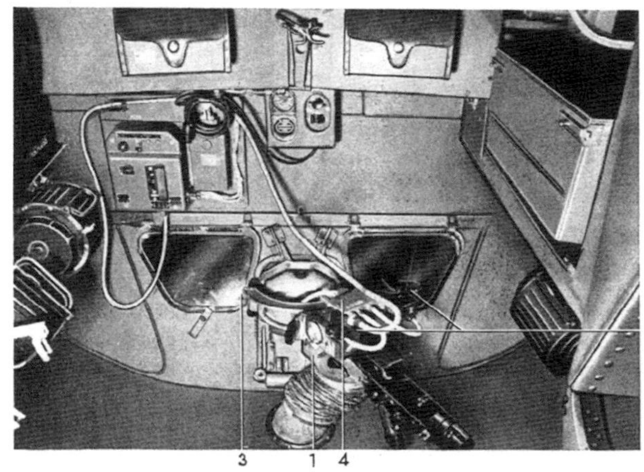

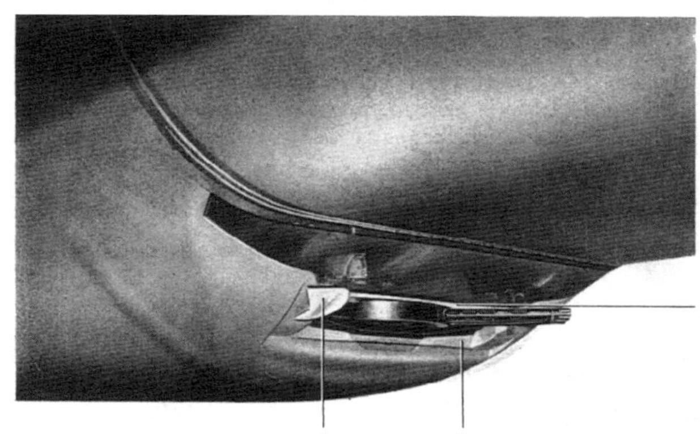

This image from the He 177A-1 handbook shows the C-*Stand* with WL 81/Z1 from the interior (top) and exterior (bottom)

Roller carriage WL 131/1 swivelled to the left (top)
1. Empty belt derivation
2. Rev 16a
3. Left adjustment slide
4. Double visor holder

C-*Stand*, exterior view (bottom)
1. Shot limitation plates
2. Upper sealing plate
3. Lower sealing plate

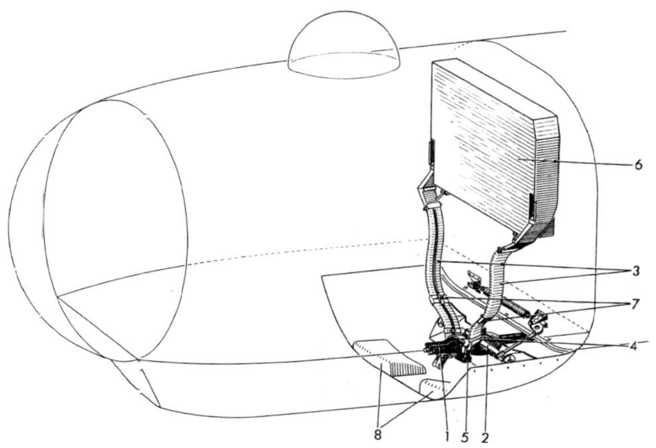

This diagram from the He 177A-1 handbook shows the C-stand with WL 81/Z1

1. MG 81Z
2. Roller carriage WL 81 Z/1
3. Belt guide hose
4. Connector
5. Sleeve box 81Z
6. Full belt container
7. Belt brake
8. Padding

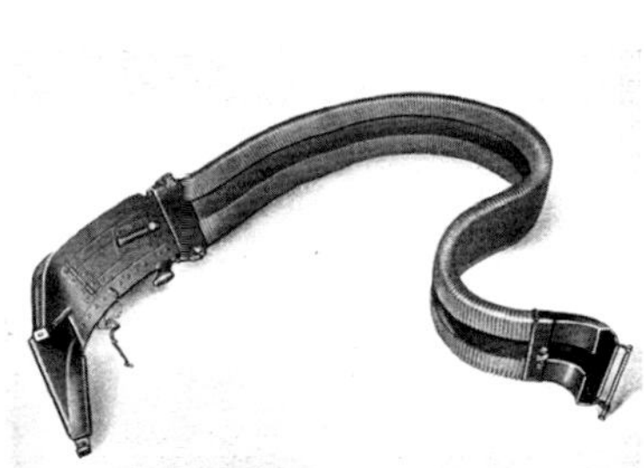

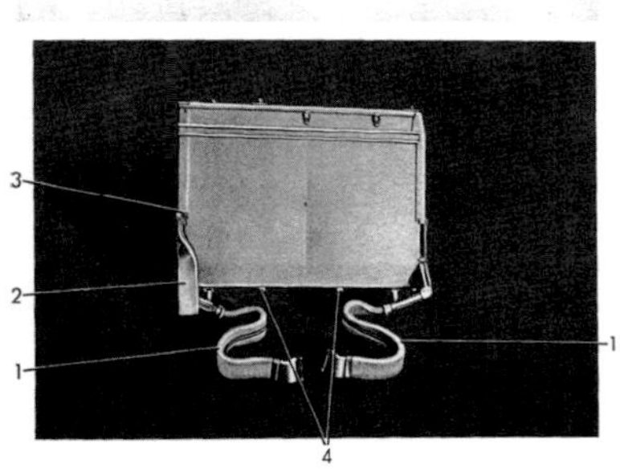

The image on the bottom shows the C-stand ammo box with feed belts, while on the top is detailed image of a feed belt

Belt channel fasteners on the full belt container
1. Belt guide hose for C-*Stand*
1. Belt guide channel for the A-*Stand* above
3. Drop bolt
4. Supports

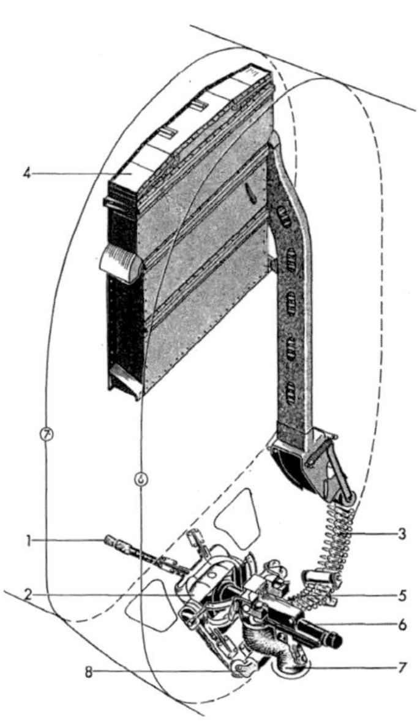

From some stage in A-1 production the C-stand had the option of a MG 131 cannon in place of the MG 81Z, as seen here in this diagram of the WL 131AR set-up

Overview of C-*Stand* WL 131/AR with MG 131 A 2
1. MG 131 A 2
2. Roller carriage WL 131/1 AR
3. Belt 131 (1000 links)
4. Full belt container
5. Feed neck
6. Purging neck
7. Empty belt and sleeve arresters
8. Wind and weight balance

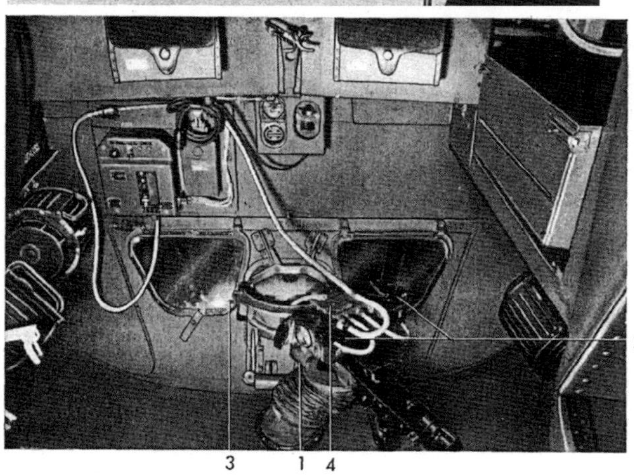

These two images from the handbook show the WL 131/AR installation from the exterior (top) and interior (bottom)

C-*Stand* with WL 131/AR, exterior view (top)
1. Buffering

Roller carriage WL 131/AR, swiveled to the left (bottom)
1. Empty belt derivation
2. Rev 16A
3. Left locking button
4. Double visor holder

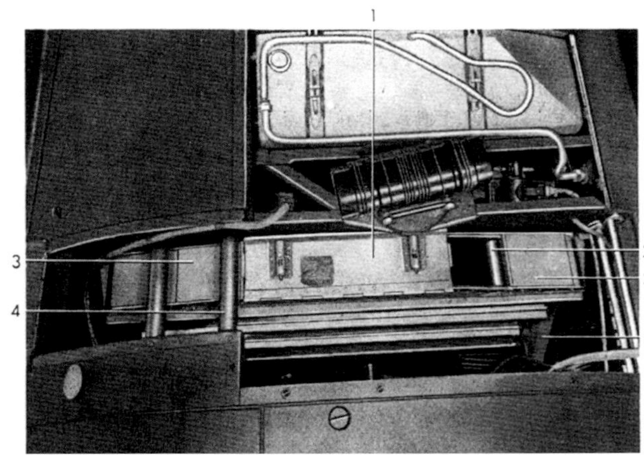

This image from the handbook show the access to the ammunition bins for the C-*Stand* in the dorsal spine – note the DF loop visible at the top

Full belt container installed
1. Full belt container
2. Sliding roller
3. Slider
4. Transmission shafts for B-*Stand*
5. Belt guide channel

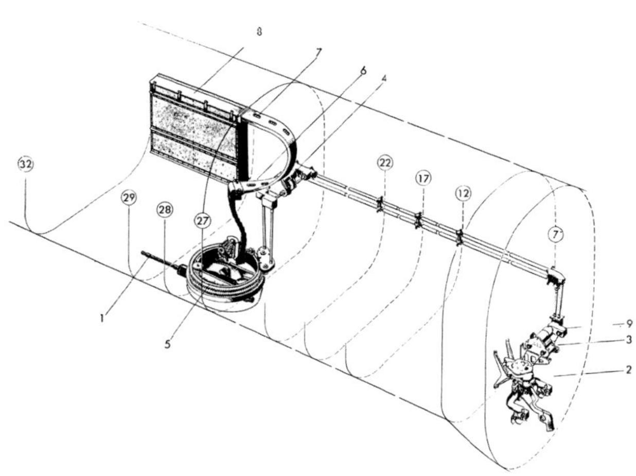

The He 177A-1 manual includes details of a C-stand, installed aft and comprising a remotely-controlled FDL 131/1A turret with MG 131 as depicted in this diagram

C-*Stand* FDL 131/A with MG 131, overview
1. MG 131 E2
2. Sighting stand VSE-C 177 1a
3. Long-range directing drive FA 3 V
4. Long-range directing drive FA 3 A
5. Rotary ring carriage FDL-C 131/1A
6. Belt conveyor
7. Belt 131
8. Full belt container
9. Angle gear on frame 7, below

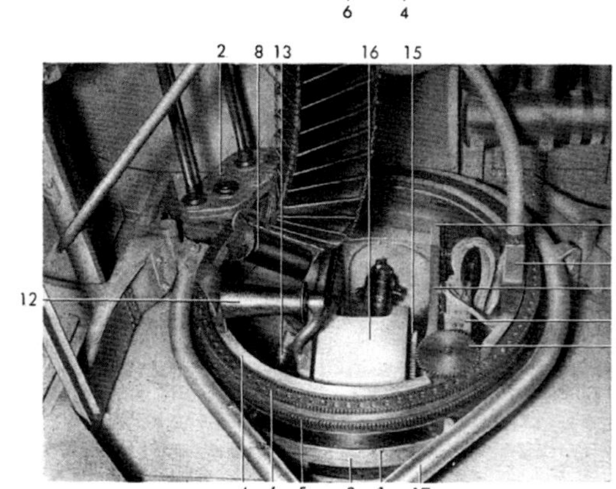

These two images show the aft C-stand installation used by the A-1/R2, A-1/R3 and A-5/R3

Turret exterior view (top)
1. Hood
2. Hood flap
3. Cover plate
4. Empty belt and sleeve drain opening
5. Buffering
6. Locking or unlocking lever
7. Deflector

Turret seen from above (bottom)
1. Outer ring
2. Transmission gear
3. Lid ring
4. inner ring
5. Lateral alignment gear
6. Height alignment gear
7. Height gear spur gear
8. Shift roller
9. Electrical cable holder
10. Cradle carrier
11. Adjustment surface
12. Guiding roller (ammo)
13. Introductory roller (ammo)
14. Mount control box LSK 7A
15. Height adjustment arch of the cradle
16. Cradle
17. Support ring for weapon stand

This shows the rear gunner's position of the V1 which lacked any actual armament

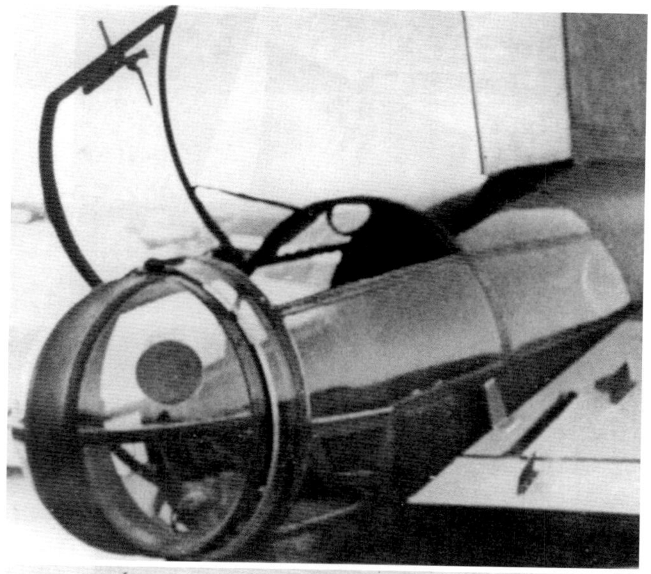

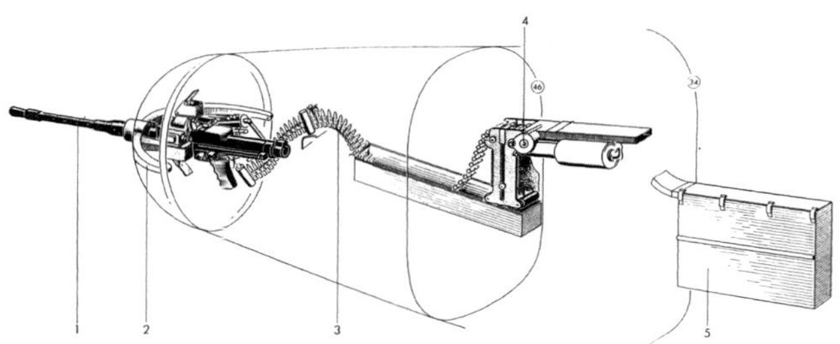

This diagram shows the MG 131A in the rear gunner's position and applies to the He 177A-0 and He 177A-1

1. MG 131 A 1
2. Rear mount HL 131
3. Belt 131
4. Belt conveyor GF 1 A
5. Full belt box

These two period images show the tail gunner's position in the V2 in its initial form without armament at the top and in revised form with MG 131 installed at the bottom

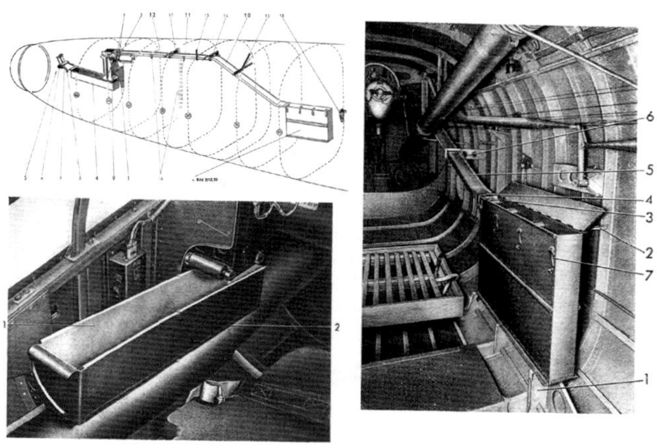

This shows the ammo container and belt feed (right and top left) for the rear MG 131, while the lower left image shows the full ammunition belt container for emergency demand

Full belt box
Key (right)
1. Consoles
2. Angle plates
3. Sliding rollers
4. Connector
5. Belt channel part 1
6. Frame mount
7. Spring clasp

Full belt tray for emergency demand
Key (left)
1. Full belt tub
2. Mounts

This image from the manual shows the rear gunner's position viewed forward from frame 44 and applies to the A-0 and A-1

1. Belt conveyor
2. Gear roller box
3. Belt conveyor flap
4. Connection for ammo counter
5. Connection for hand crank
6. Hand crank in rest position
7. Roller box pulse generator
8. Web plate
9. On-board bag holder
10. Carriage disc system
11. LSK 2 A
12. LSK 3 A

These two period images show the experimental HL 151Z turret intended for He 277 but tested in an unknown He 177

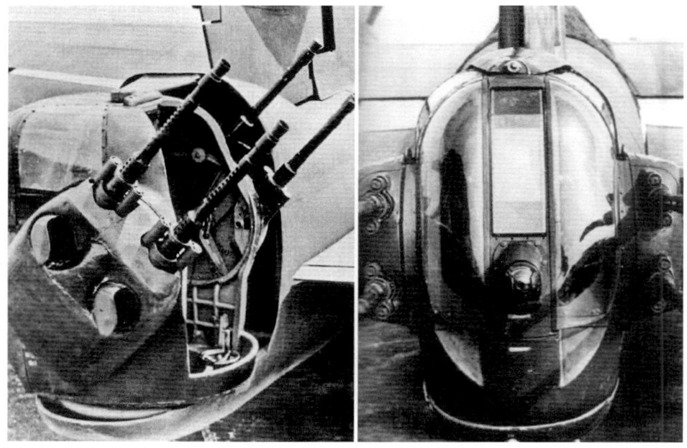

A He 177A-3 was experimentally fitted with this HL 131V armed with four MG 131s

These two images give interior details of the HL 131V turret

The HL 131V turret used a HL 121 sight situated in the middle (arrowed), which is shown in close-up detail in the lower images of an example found by 2nd TAF Intelligence Officers at Tarnewitz

He 177A-3, 6N+AS, W/Nr.332618 of KG 100 with fitted with this experimental installation of a MG 131Z as used by Ju 288, it was never adopted by the He 177

The He 177 V12, GI+BL, was experimentally fitted with two manually-operated MK 101 cannon in the nose. There are accounts of large calibre cannon being carried by the He 177, sadly no images exist of these

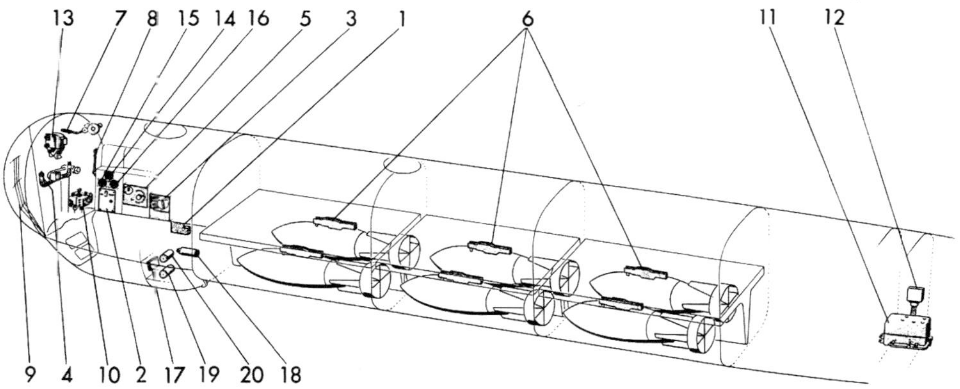

1. Ignition battery box ZBK 241/1
2. Igniter switch box ZSK 244 A
3. Additional timer device ZZG 1/24
4. B Button XI
5. RAB 14 d
6. Castle 500/XII or 1000/XIb
7. Emergency throw lever
8. Blind arming lever
9. Course sighting wires
10. Target device Lofte 7B or 7C, 7D or BZG 2-E
11. Retention calculator IVR 1
12. Relay box IRK 1
13. Stuvi 5B
14. Self-speed sensor VE-Geb. IEG 1
15. Wind speed sensor VW-Geb. IWG 1
16. Height correction sensor Zh and Qff IHKG 1
17. Capacitor box IKK 1
18. Switch box SKVe
19. Converter GDU 87/30 f. BZA
20. Converter GDU 87/30 f. BZG 2E

This is an overview of the bombs carried by the He 177A-0, along with the sighting equipment and systems used

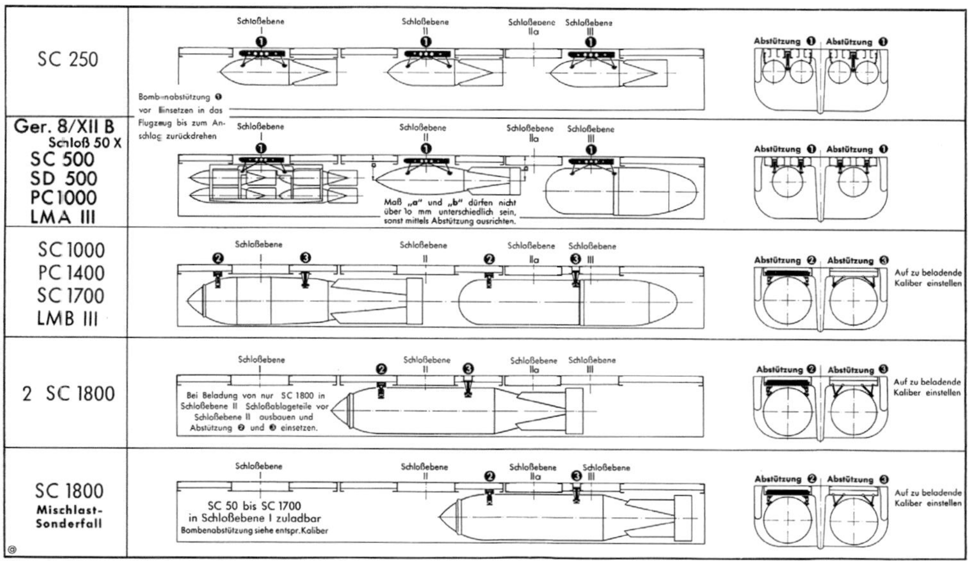

This shows the bomb loads for the He 177A-0

These images (below) show the Schloß 100/XI0 and 500/XII in the bomb bay of the He 177A-0, along with detailed images of the Schloß 1000/IX and Schloß 500/XII itself

Bomb carrier 1000/500/XI installed (left)
1. Contact plate
2. Mounting plates
Bomb carrier 1000/XI
Bomb carrier 500/XII (right)
1. Locking fitting
2. Auxiliary support
3. Loader device

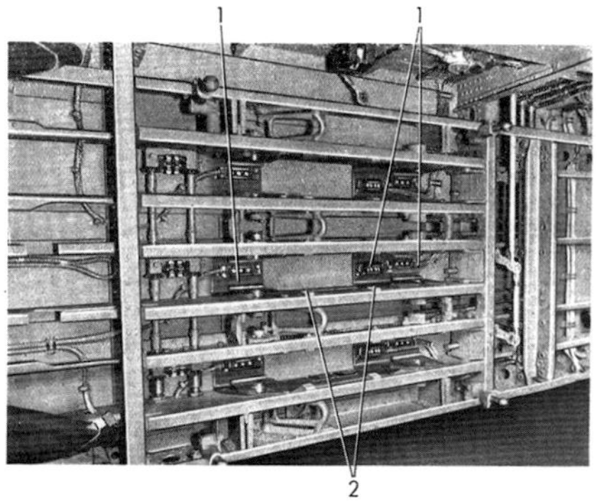

Schloßlafette 1000/500/XI eingebaut

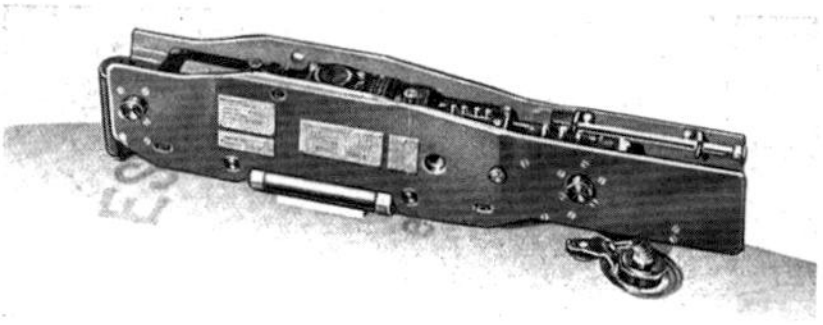

Schloß 1000/XI

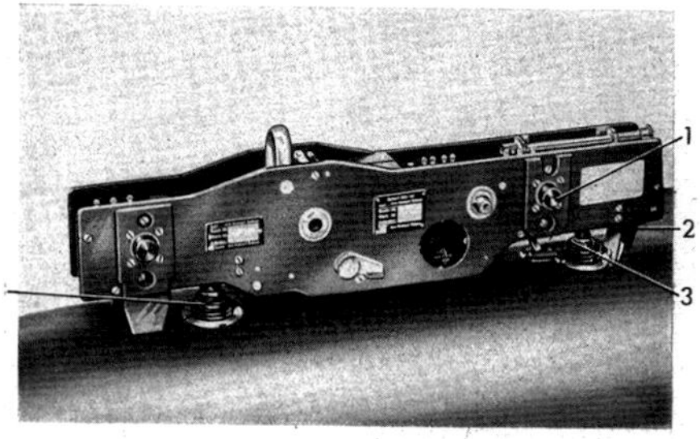

Schloß 500/XII

Vorderer Bombenträger

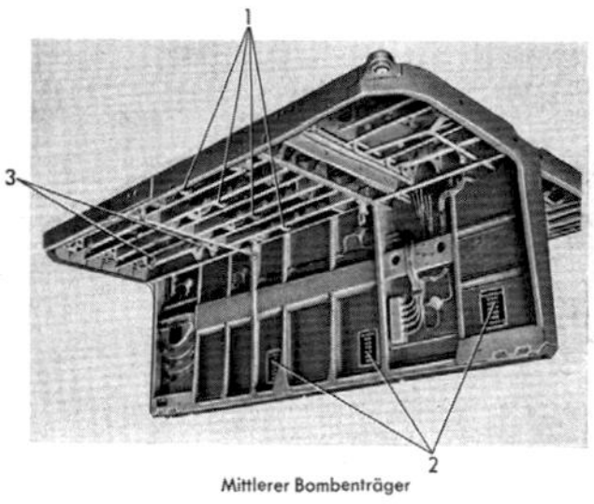

Mittlerer Bombenträger

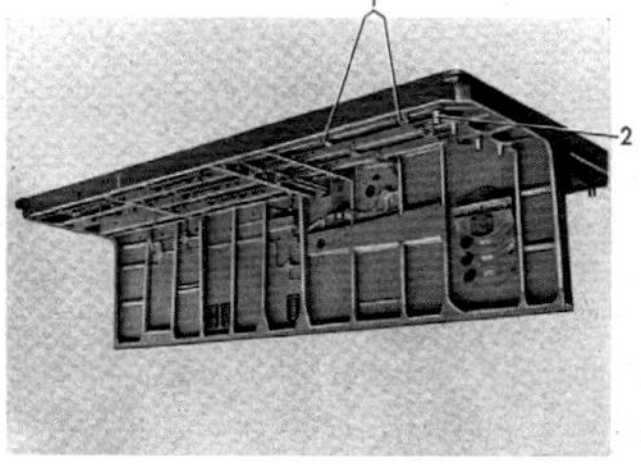

Hinterer Bombenträger

These three images show the front (left), middle (middle) and aft (right) bomb bays of the He 177A-0

Front bomb carrier (left)
1. Carrier fitting
2. Fittings for supports
3. Parachute hanging loop
4. Labels
Medium bomb carrier (middle)
1. Carrier fitting
2. Labels for supports
3. Trays
Rear bomb carrier (right)
1. Storage
2. Pin for deflection pulleys

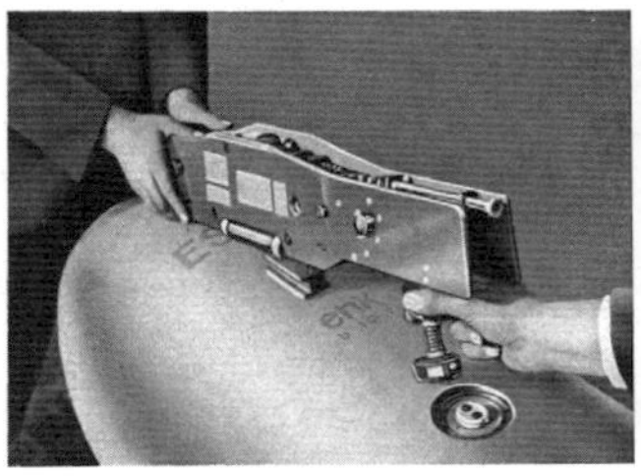

Herausziehen der Ladevorrichtung

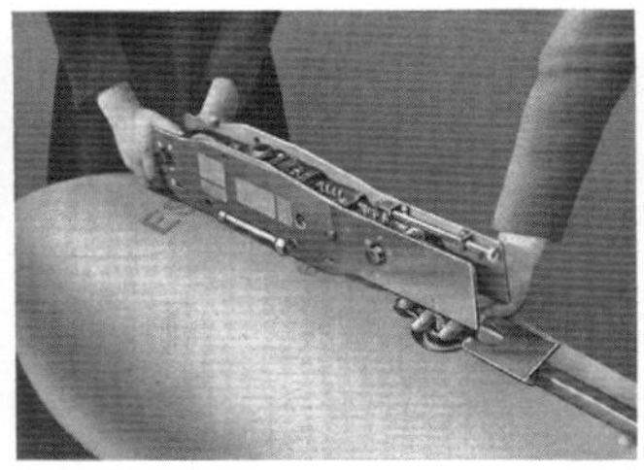

Aufsetzen der Ladevorrichtung

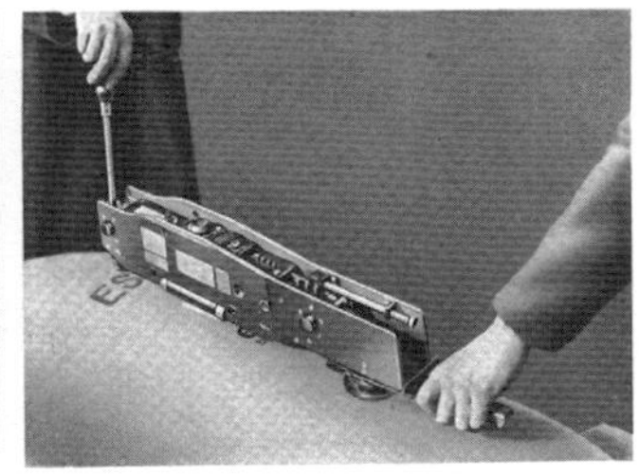

Einstellen der Hilfsbratze

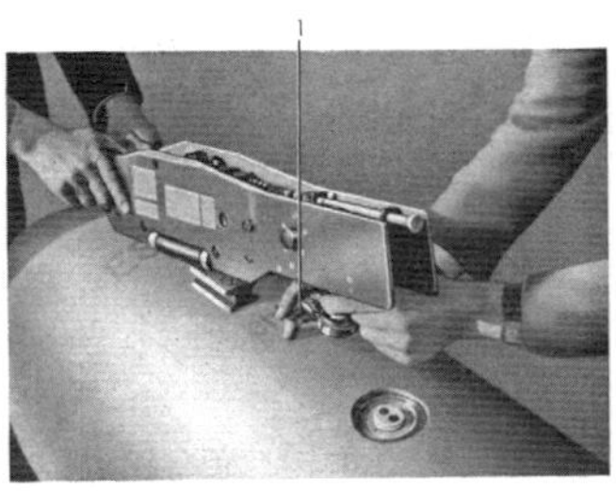

Öffnen des Schutzdeckels der Ladevorrichtung

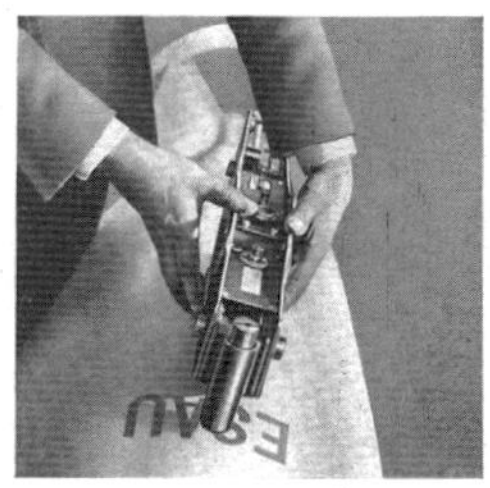

Schließen der Traghaken

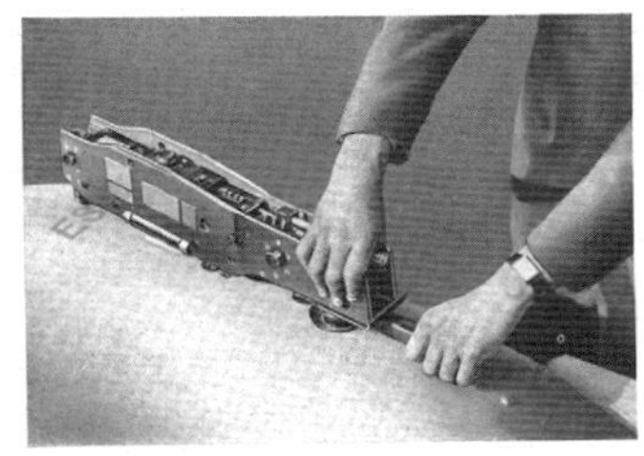

Herausziehen der Beladelehre

These images from the He 177A-0 handbook show the steps taken in attaching the electrical release unit (ETC) to the bomb, which was done prior to each bomb being hoisted up into the bomb bay

Bomb carrier 1000/500/XI installed
Pulling out the loader device (top left)
Open the protective cover of the charging device (bottom left)
1. Protective cover
Attach the loading device (middle top)
Closing the carrying hooks (middle bottom)
Adjusting the auxiliary bracing (top right)
Pull out the loading gauge (bottom right)

This image from the He 177A-1 handbook shows one of the bomb bay doors

1. Upper spar
2. Nose spar
3. Recess of the emergency release arm
4. Bearing rib

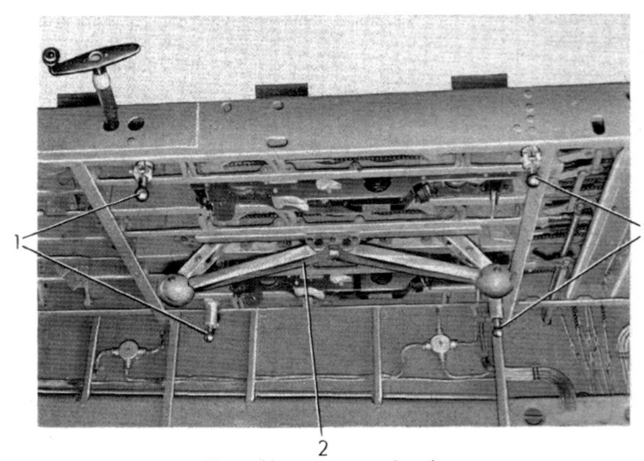

Feste Abstützungen, eingebaut

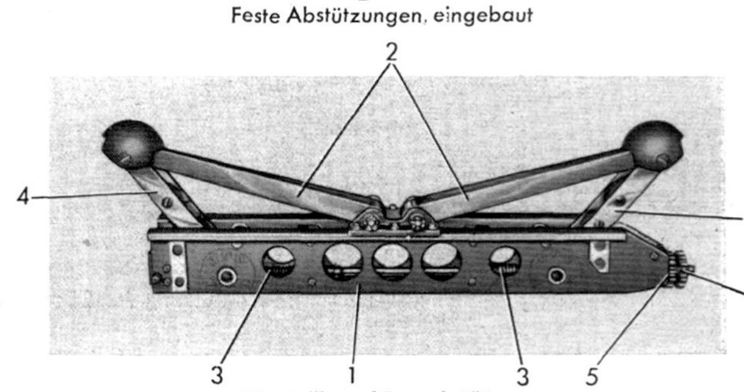

Verstellbare Längsabstützung

These two images from the He 177A-0 handbook show the additional timing device ZZG 1/24 (right) and B-Button XI (left) to release the ordnance

Timer additional device ZZG 1/24, installed (right)
1. Closing plate
2. Main switch
3. Time selector switch

B-button XI installed (left)
1 – B-button XI

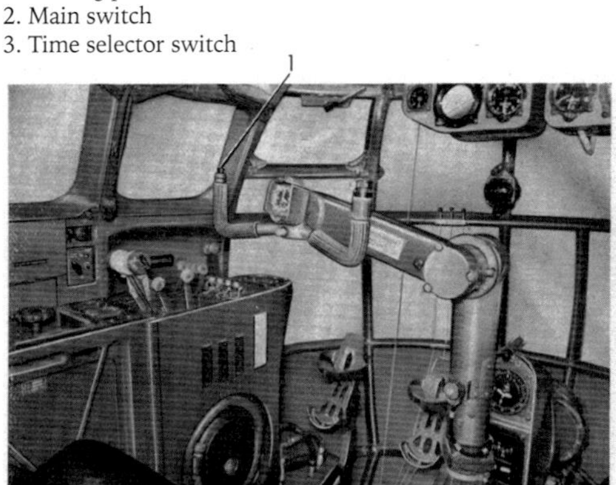

B-Knopf XI eingebaut

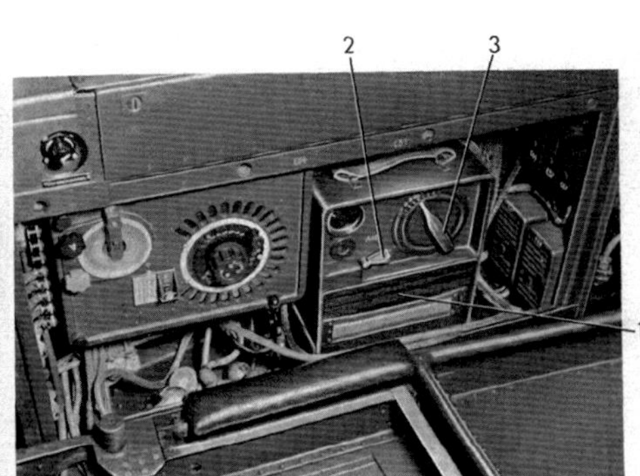

Zeitzünderzusatzgerät ZZG 1/24, eingebaut

Each bomb bay had built-in solid supports for the bombs as well as adjustable longitudinal supports

Fixed supports installed (top)
1. Fixed supports
2. Adjustable longitudinal support

Adjustable longitudinal support (bottom)
1. Housing
2. Lever
3. Spindle
4. Guide arm
5. Front gear
6. Rear gear

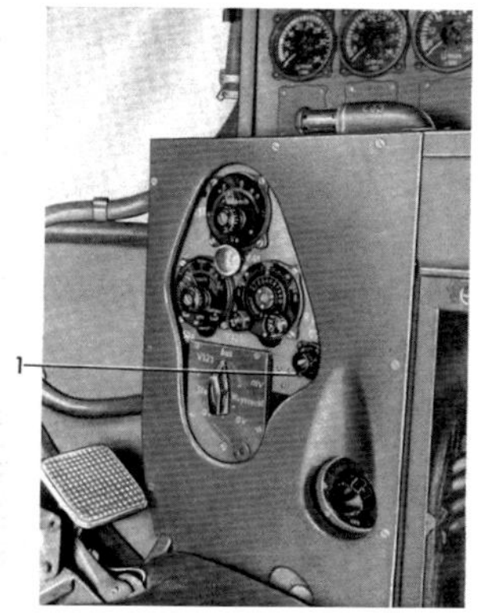

The image on the right shows the bomb ignition switch box ZSK 233A fitted in the cockpit, while the one on the left shows the bomb emergency release lever in the overhead panel

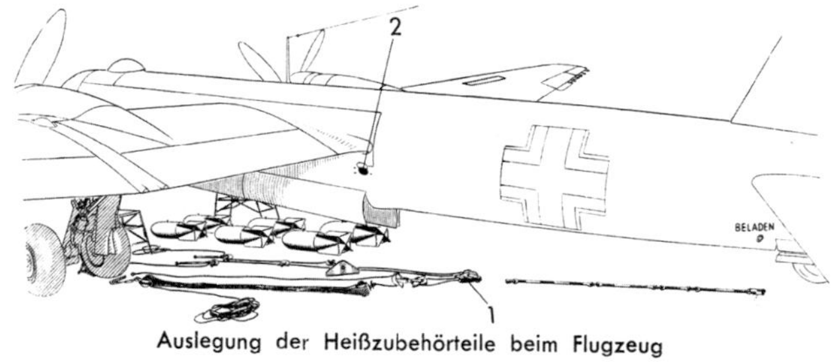

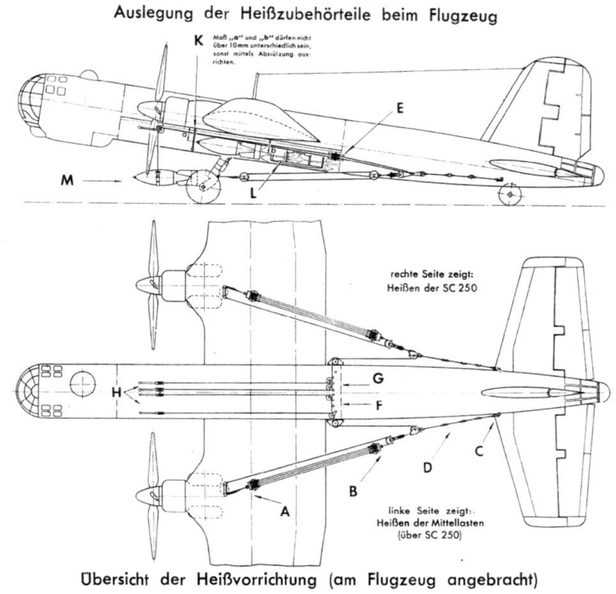

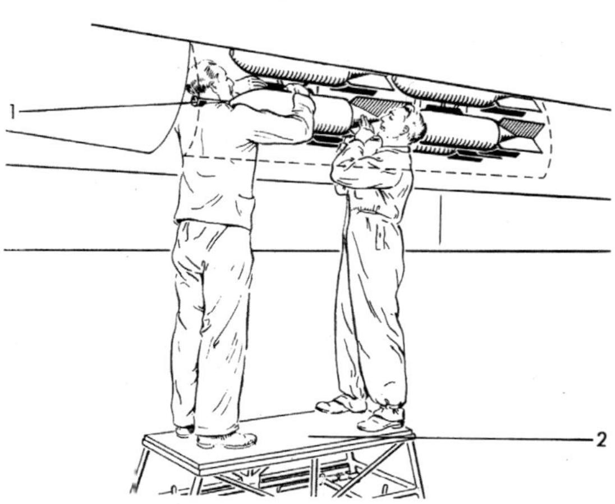

Smaller capacity bombs like the 50kg, could be loaded by hand, as depicted here

1. Loading handle
2. Loading ladder

In common with all Luftwaffe bombers, the He 177 used a series of hoisting devices and accessories to load the bombs inside the bomb bay, as depicted in these two diagrams

Auslegung der Heißzubehörteile beim Flugzeug – Design of hoisting accessories on aircraft
1. *Doppelrolle* – Dual role
2. *Rüstklappe* – Preparation flap
recht Seite zeigt: Heißen der SC250 – right side shows: SC250 load
linke Seite zeigt: Heinßen der Mittellasten (über SC250) – left side shows: Middle loads (above SC250)
Übersicht der Heißvorrichtung (am Flugzeug angebracht) – Overview of the hoisting device (mounted on the aircraft)

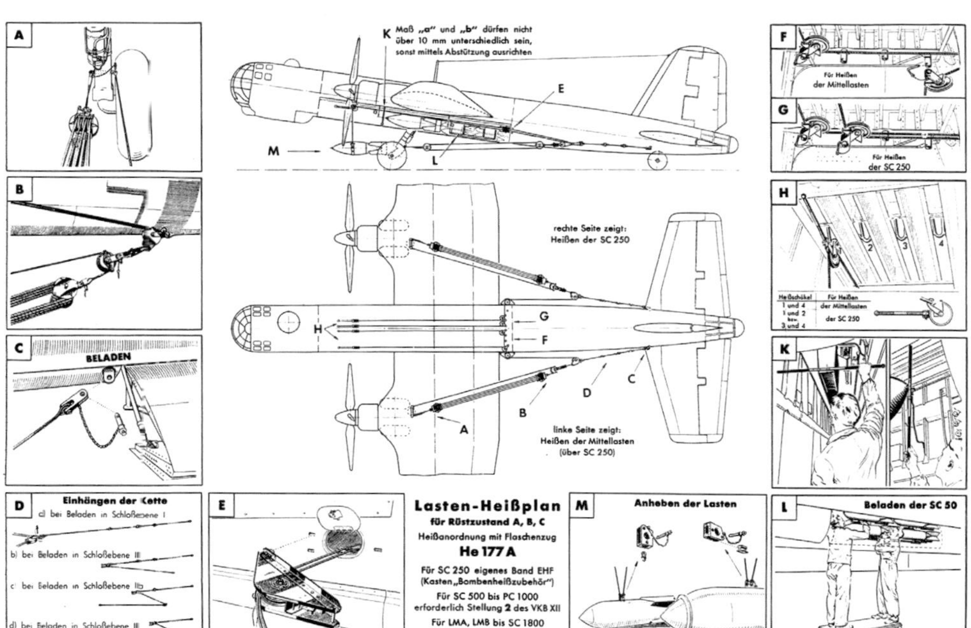

These diagrams show the various attachment points and pulleys used to hoist the ordnance into the bomb bay

Lasten-Heißplan für Rüstzustand A, B, C – Load plan for setup status A, B, C
Heißanordnung mit Flaschenzug – Hoisting arrangement with pulley system

He 177A
Für SC 250 eingened Band EHF (Kasten, 'Bombenheißzubehör) – For SC 250 integrated band EHF (box, hosting bomb accessories)
Für SC 500 bis PC 1000 erforderlich Stellung 2 des VKB XII – For SC 500 to PC 1000, position 2 of VKB XII is required
Für LMA, LMB bis SC 1800 erforderlich Stellung 5 des VKB XII – For LMA, LMB up to SC 1800, position 5 of VKB XII is required

Ripple release of the bombs was achieved via the RAB 14b control in the cockpit

1. Neck screws
2. Trigger lever

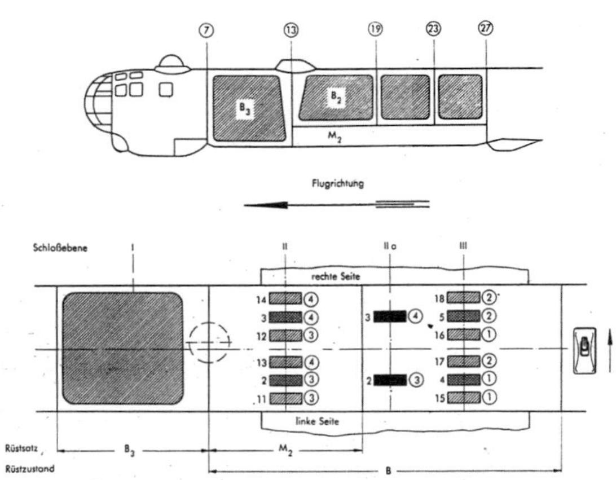

Rüstzustand B

Munition Anz.	Art	Behälter-Rüstsätze ×	Waffen-Rüstsätze	Einbausätze	Schloß	Schloß-ebene	Schauzeichen RAB	Notwurf-hebel Nr.	Schalter-stellung
32	SC 50	B_2 B_3	M_2	2 × E_1	L-Gerüst 8 Schloß 50/B	II III	2 bis 5	① bis ④	
8	SC 250	B_2 B_3	M_2	2 × E_2	500/XII A	II III	11 bis 18	① bis ④	
4	SC 500 SD 500 PC 1000 LMA III	B_2 B_3	M_2	2 × E_3 2 × E_3 2 × E_4 2 × E_4	500/XII A 500/XII A 2000/XIII A 2000/XIII A	II III	2 bis 5	① bis ④	
2	SC 1000 PC 1400 PC 1700 LMB III	B_2 B_3	M_2	E_5 E_5 E_5 E_5	2000/XIII A	II a	2 und 3	③ und ④	
2	SC 1800	B_2 B_3	M_2	E_5	2000/XIII A	II a	2 und 3	③ und ④	

× Füllen der Behälter nach Ladeplan

This diagram shows the bomb and fuel tank layout with *Rustzustand* B

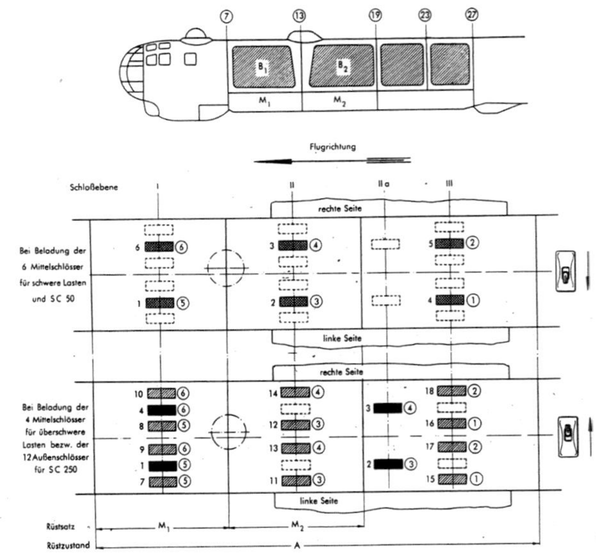

Rüstzustand A

Munition Anz.	Art	Behälter-Rüstsätze ×	Waffen-Rüstsätze	Einbausätze	Schloß	Schloß-ebene	Schauzeichen RAB	Notwurf-hebel Nr.	Schalter-stellung
48	SC 50	B_1 B_2	M_1 M_2	3 × E_1	L-Gerüst 8 Schloß 50/B	I II III	1 bis 6	① bis ⑥	
12	SC 250	B_1 B_2	M_1 M_2	3 × E_2	500/XII A	I II III	7 bis 18	① bis ⑥	
6	SC 500 SD 500 PC 1000 LMA III	B_1 B_2 B_1 B_2 B_1 B_2 B_1 B_2	M_1 M_2 M_1 M_2 M_1 M_2 M_1 M_2	3 × E_3 3 × E_3 3 × E_4 3 × E_4	500/XII A 500/XII A 2000/XIII A 2000/XIII A	I II III	1 bis 6	① bis ⑥	
4	SC 1000 PC 1400 PC 1700 LMB III	B_1 B_2 B_1 B_2 B_1 B_2 B_1 B_2	M_1 M_2	2 × E_5	2000/XIII A	I II a	1 bis 4	③ bis ⑥	
2	SC 1800	B_1 B_2	M_1 M_2	E_5	2000/XIII A	II	2 und 3	③ und ④	

Mischlast-Sonderfall

Anz.	Art	Behälter-Rüstsätze	Waffen-Rüstsätze	Einbausätze	Schloß	Schloß-ebene	Schauzeichen RAB	Notwurf-hebel Nr.	Schalter-stellung
2	SC 1800 und	B_1 B_2	M_1 M_2	E_5	2000/XIII A	II a	2 und 3	③ und ④	
16	SC 50 oder			E_1	L-Gerüst 8 Schloß 50/B	I	1 und 4	⑤ und ⑥	
4	SC 250 oder ab			E_2	500/XII A	I	7 bis 10	⑤ und ⑥	
2	SC 500 bis PC 1700			E_3 bezw. E_4 E_5	500/XII A bezw. 2000/XIII A	I	1 und 4	⑤ und ⑥	

× Füllen der Behälter nach Ladeplan

This diagram shows the bomb and fuel tank layout with *Rustzustand* A

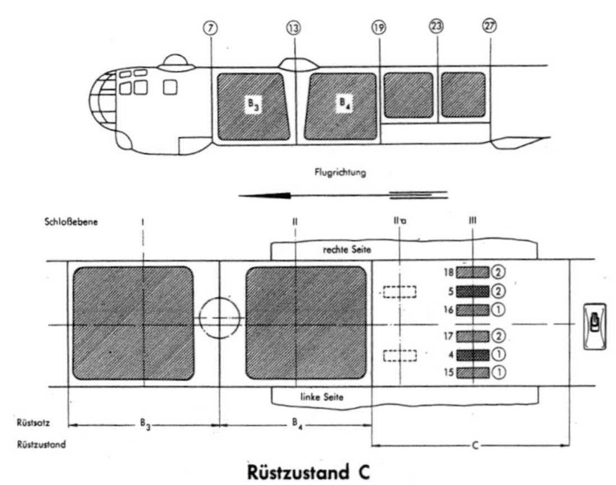

Rüstzustand C

Munition Anz.	Art	Behälter-Rüstsätze ×	Waffen-Rüstsätze	Einbausätze	Schloß	Schloß-ebene	Schauzeichen RAB	Notwurf-hebel Nr.	Schalter-stellung
16	SC 50	B_3 B_4	-	E_1	L-Gerüst 8 Schloß 50/B	III	4 und 5	① und ②	
4	SC 250	B_3 B_4	-	E_2	500/XII A	III	15 bis 18	① und ②	
2	SC 500 SD 500 PC 1000 LMA III	B_3 B_4	- - - -	E_3 E_3 E_4 E_4	500/XII A 500/XII A 2000/XIII A 2000/XIII A	III	4 und 5	① und ②	

× Füllen der Behälter nach Ladeplan

This diagram shows the bomb and fuel tank layout with *Rustzustand* C

This is an overview of the bombs carried by the He 177A-1, along with the sighting equipment and systems used – this is slightly different from the He 177A-0

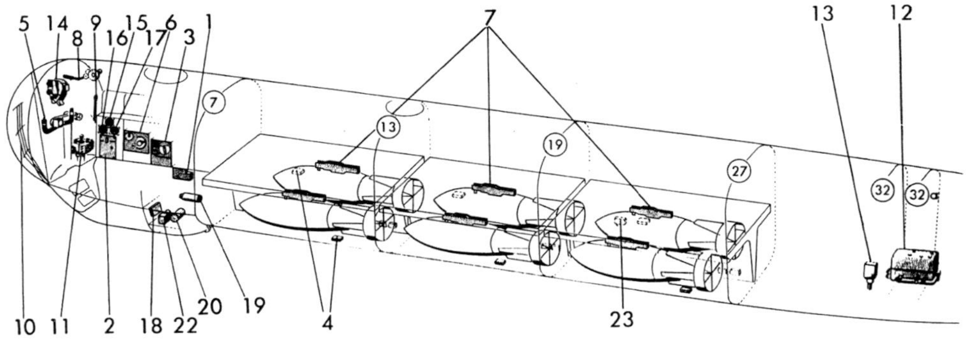

1. Zünderbattieriekasten ZBK 241/1 – Ignition battery box ZBK 241/1
2. Zünderschaltkasten ZSK 244 A – Igniter switch box ZSK 244 A
3. Zeitzünderzusatzgerät ZZG l/24 – Additional timer device ZZG l/24
4. Zeitzündeklappenschalter – Timer ignition flap switch
5. B-Knopf XI – B-Button XI
6. RAB 14 d – RAB 14 d
7. Schloß 500/XII bzw. 1000/XIb – Bomb rack 500/XII or 1000/XIb
8. Notwurfhebel – Emergency release lever
9. Blind-Scharfhebel – Blind arming lever
10. Kursvisierdrähte – Course sighting wires
11. Zielgerät Lofte 7B bzw. 7C, 7D – Bombsight Lofte 7B or &C, 7D
12. Vorhalterechner IVR 1 – Retention calculator IVR 1
13. Relaiskasten IRK 1 – Relat box IRK 1
14. Stuvi 5B – Stuvi (sight) 5B
15. Eigengeschw.-Geber VE-Geb. IEG 1 – Aircraft-speed sensor VE-Geb. IEG 1
16. Windgeschw.-Geber VW-Geb. IWG 1 – Wind speed sensor VW-Geb. IWG 1
17. Höhenkorrektur-Geber Zh u. Qff IHKG 1 – Height correction sensor Zh and Qff IHKG 1
18. Kondensatorkasten IKK 1 – Capacitor box IKK 1
19. Schaltkasten SKVe – Switch box SKVe
20. Umformer GDU 87/30 für BZA – Converter GDU 87/30 for BZA (bombsight)
22. Kommandofahrtgeber – Command speed transmitter
23. Endschalter R36 – Limit switch R36

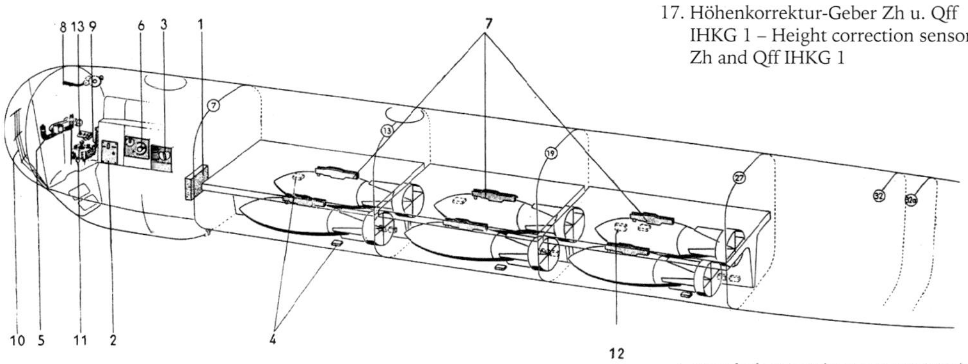

This is an overview of the bombs carried by the He 177A-3, along with the sighting equipment and systems used

1. Zünderbattierieksten ZBK 241/1 – Ignition battery box ZBK 241/1
2. Zünderschaltkasten ZSK 244 A – Igniter switch box ZSK 244 A
3. Zeitzünderzusatzgerät ZZG L/24 – Additional timer device ZZG L/24
4. Zeitzündeklappenschalter – Timer ignition flap switch
5. B-Knopf XI – B-Button XI
6. RAB 14 d – RAB 14 d
7. Schloß 500/XII bzw. 1000/XIb – Bomb rack 500/XII or 1000/XIb
8. Notwurfhebel – Emergency relese lever
9. Blind-Scharfhebel – Blind arming lever
10. Kursvisierdrähte – Course sighting wires
11. Zielgerät Lofte 7D – Bombsight L:ofte 7D
12. Endschalter R36 – Limit switch R36
13. Gerätetafel mit R 172, R 171, R 174 – Device panel with R 172, R 171, R 174

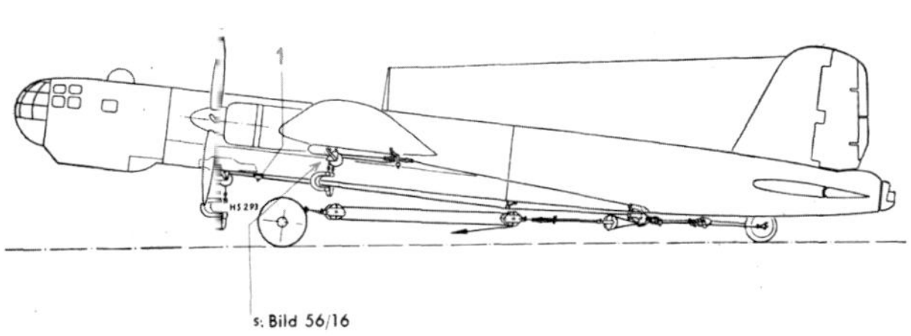

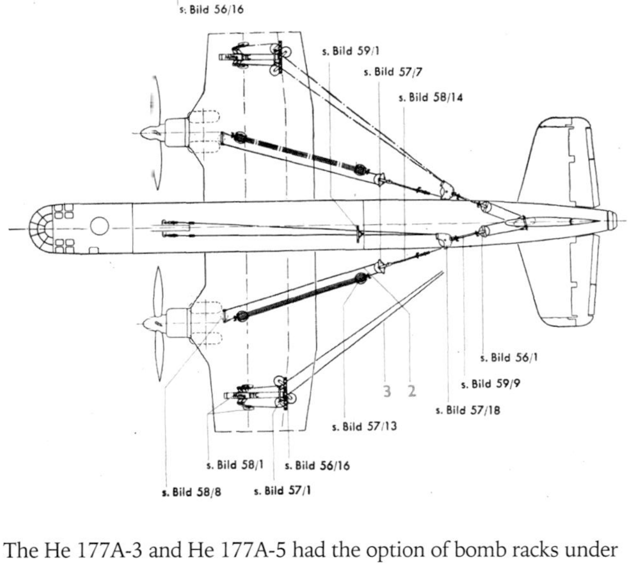

The He 177A-3 and He 177A-5 had the option of bomb racks under the wings and forward fuselage bomb bay, this diagram shows the hoisting devices and accessories used to load the bombs, glide bombs etc.

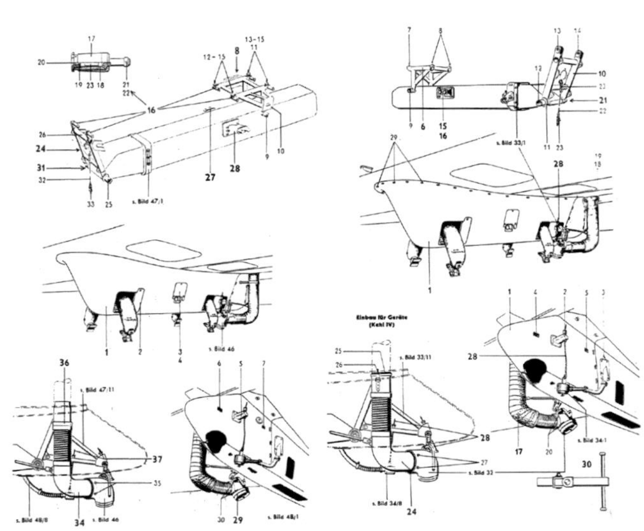

These diagrams show the racks used for the Hs 293 or Fritz X

Two view of a Kramer SD 1400X Fritz-X glide-bomb, in its crate as found by an RAF armament disposal team at the end of war

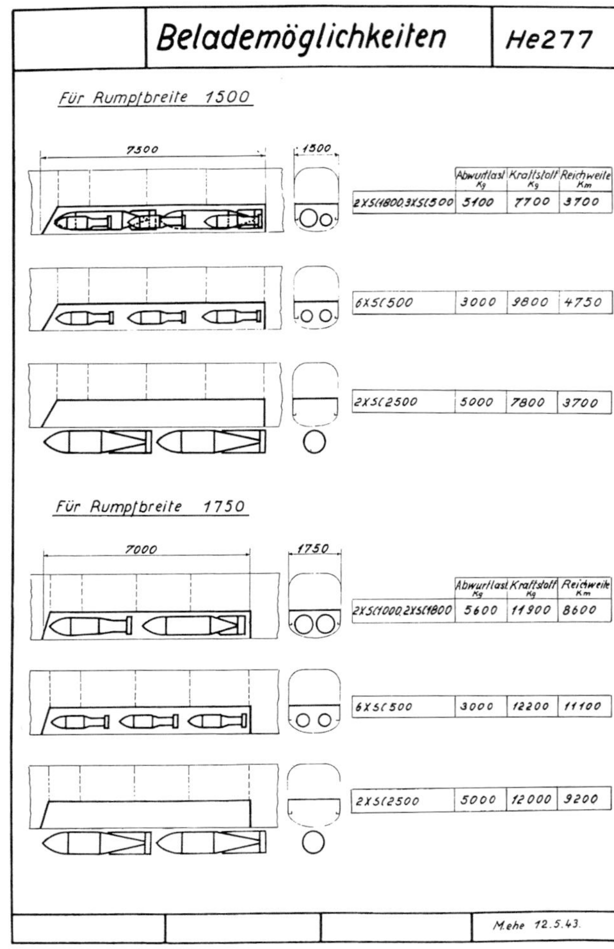

Little exists relating to the bomb bays of the He 277, although they would have been much like the He 177. This diagram shows the proposed bomb loads for the series

These four period images show an SC1800 (some state SC200, others SC2500) bomb being loaded under the port wing of a He 177A-3

The Hs 293 had a 500kg warhead and a top speed of 500km/h, but it was an advanced system and its operational use was problematic

The Blohm & Voss L-10 glider (2.80m span) attached to a LT F5b torpedo was known as the LT 950C Friedensengel [Peace Angel] and the carriage of this was tested by the V31. The weapon was intended to be used by the A-3/R6, but it never went into series production, so was never adopted

This shows a Friedensengel under the port wing of the He 177 V31, a production He 177A-5 used to test the use of the glide-bomb by the He 177

The Hs 295 was a developed version of Hs 293 powered by two HWK 507 rocket motors and was intended for use with He 177A-5, but never went into series production

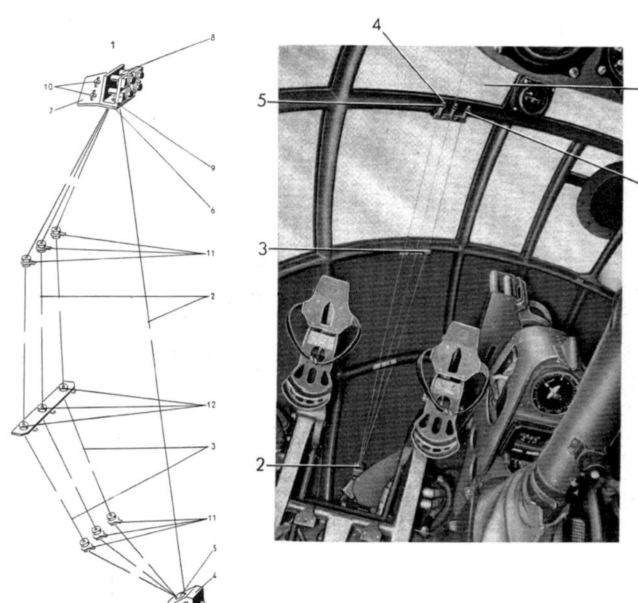

This image and diagram show the armament course setting wires fitted in the port side of the nose/cockpit in all He 177 variants

Course sighting wires
1. Rear sight wire
2. Bracket with ball piece
3. Bracket with clamp and threaded piece
4. Thumbscrew
5. Knurled nut
6. Sleeve

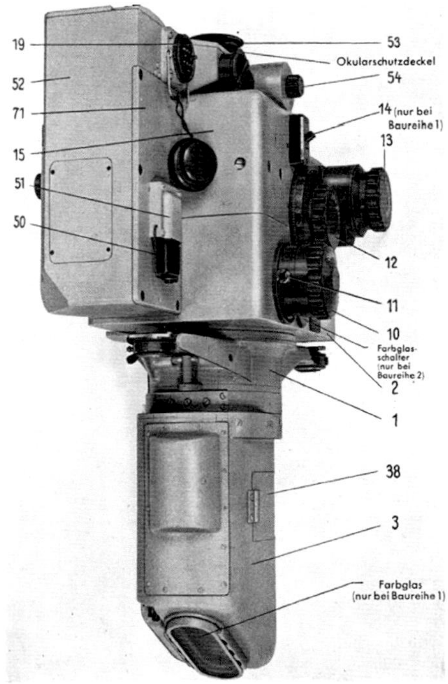

Abb. 1
Lotfe 7C. Ansicht der linken Bedienungsseite von vorn

The main bombsight used by the He 177 was the Lofte 7B, C or D. This period illustration shows the 7C

The other bombsight used early He 177 (A-0 and some A-1s) was the BZG 2, as seen here in this period image of the type installed in a Ju 88

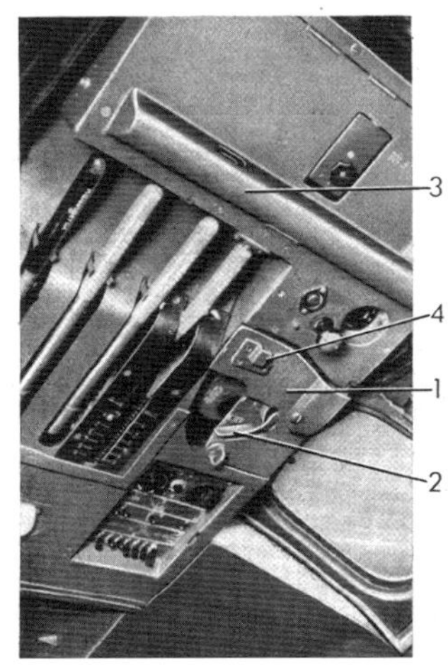

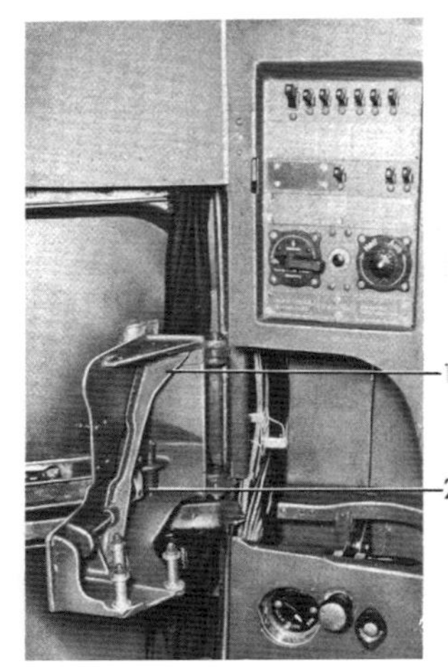

This shows the Stuvi 5B mount swivelled in and swung up

Stuvi holder swivelled in
1. Stuvi mount
2. Trigger lever
3. Cover plate
4. Fittings for support struts

Stui holder swung out
1. Stuvi mount
2. Rest support

The He 177 also used the Stuvi 5B sight, these two images from the handbook show how it was adjusted (top) and mounted (bottom)

Adjusting the Stuvi 5B (top)
1. Setup angle
2. Bracket 1 B
2. Bracket adjusting button
4. Adjusting screws

Stuvi support (bottom)
1. Stuvi mount
2. Support strut

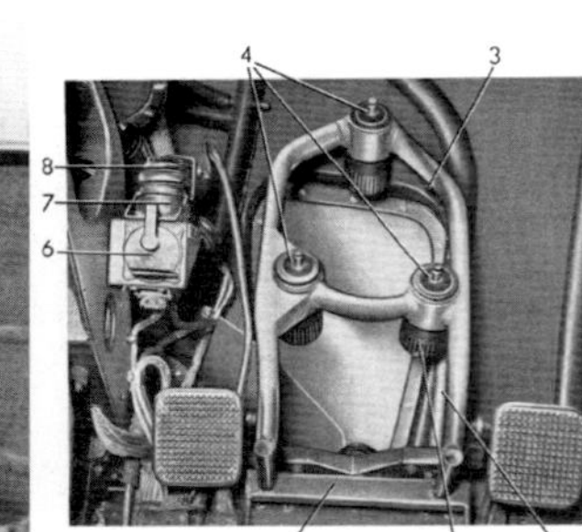

The image on the right shows the mounts for the Lofte or BZG2-E bombsight in the He 177, while the image on the left shows the raised surround and flat clear panel (arrowed) in the starboard side of the nose glazing, through which is bombsight operates

1. Foot pedal holder
2. Support strut
3. Tab for ground cable connection
4. Spring buffer
5. Knurled tension nut
6. Direction indicator LRg 5
7. Blind socket R 56b
8. Target device plug R 56

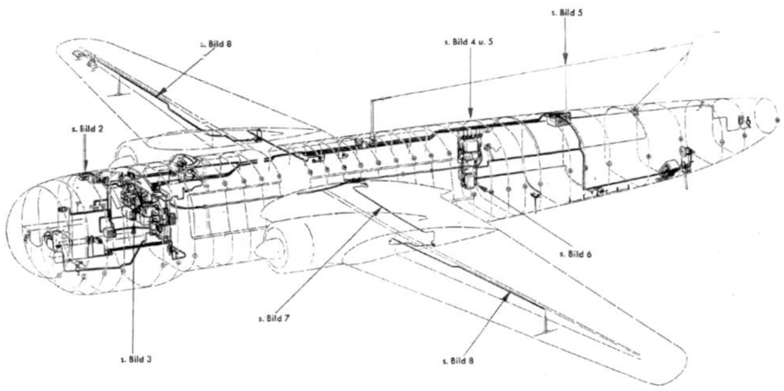

This is an overview of radio equipment and comes from the He 177A-3 handbook, but applies to all variants

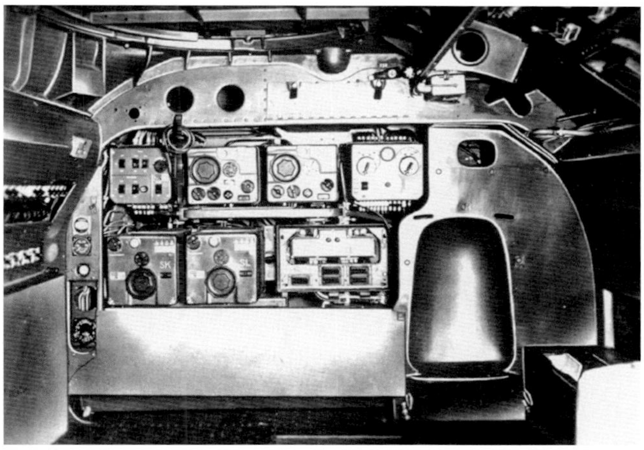

The rear bulkhead in the cockpit contained the FuG X radio equipment

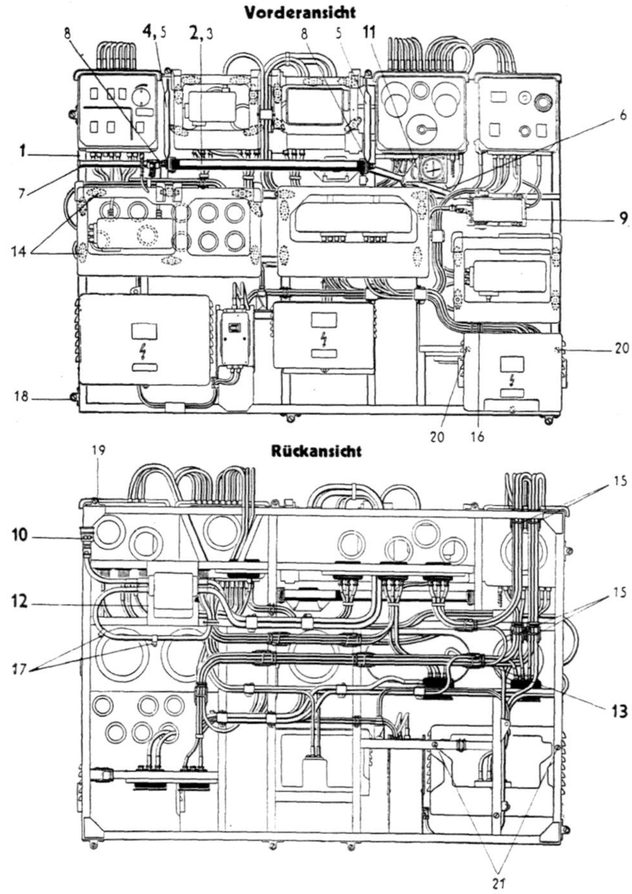

This is the radio equipment that was installed in the rear fuselage, between Frames 29 and 30

This close-up of the radio equipment in the rear fuselage includes the trailing aerial (15), the main radio antenna lead (1) and secondary one into the dorsal spine (18), which relates to the radio equipment in the rear fuselage (visible between frame 29 & 30)

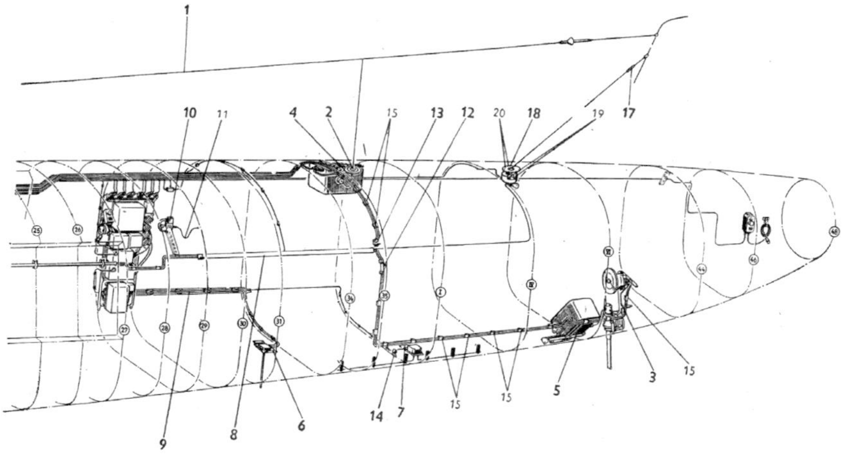

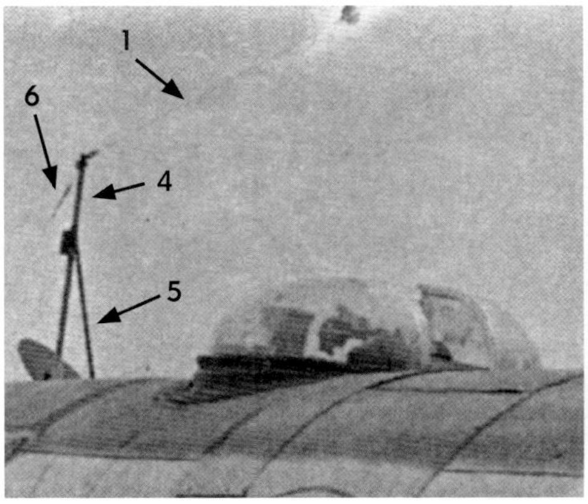

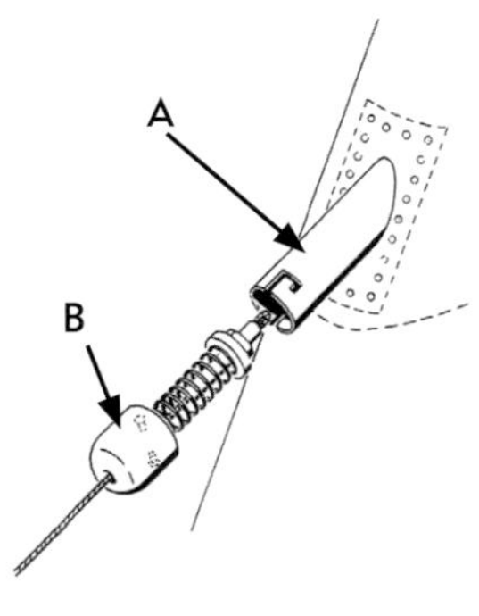

The diagram on the right shows the connection of the radio antenna to the vertical fin, while the image in the middle and left are views showing the antenna lead (1), the secondary lead into the dorsal spine (2), the insulator (3) and the radio mast (4) with support strut (5) and lead running forward down to the dorsal spine (6)

A. Tube
B. Insulator (capsule)

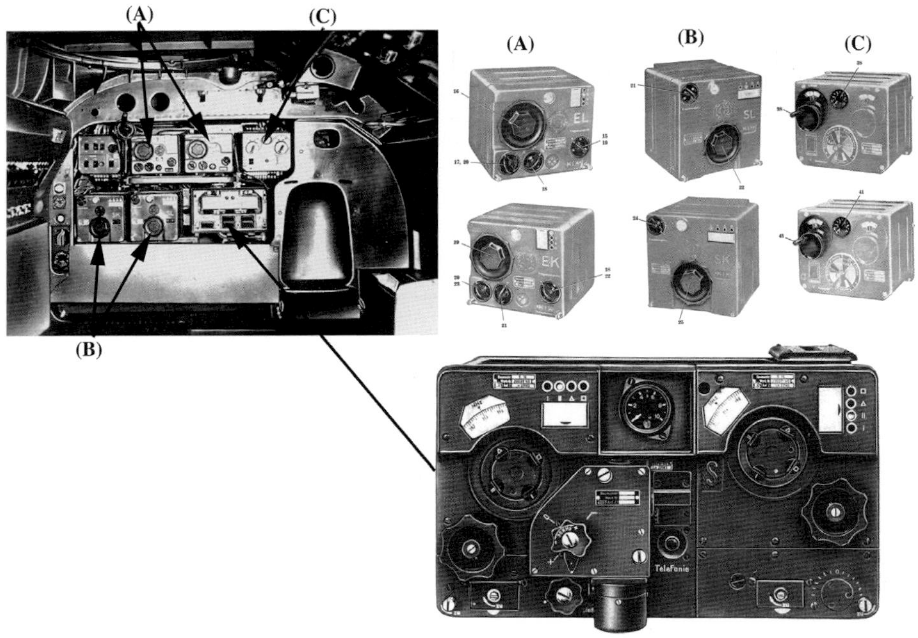

Gerätblock FuG 16 mit aufgesetztem Fernantrieb

Sadly, none of the handbooks include images of the radio equipment, however it was all pretty standard for Luftwaffe bombers on the type, so this image shows the type of radio transmitter and receiver fitted on the rear bulkhead (A & B), as well as the tuner (C). The FuG 16 would have been mounted on the rack as indicated (arrowed) in the bottom right corner, while the image of the FuG 16 unit in the bottom right is one fitted with a remote tuner, used by single-engine types, so that unit would not have been fitted to the FuG 16 in the He 177

Some He 177s used in the anti-shipping role used FuG 200 Hohentwiel radar, the antennae for which can be seen on either side and underneath the nose of this KG 40 example

As far as we can tell, no period images (or diagrams in the handbook) exist showing the FuG 200 radar scope inside the cockpit, so this is a period image of this unit in the nose of a Ju 188 – the He 177 set-up would have most likely have been similar

There are no any clear images of the FuG 200 Hohentwiel radar antenna on the He 177, so this close-up of the installation in the nose of a Ju 188A-3 clearly shows the complex shape of each of the three antenna arrays used by the FuG 200

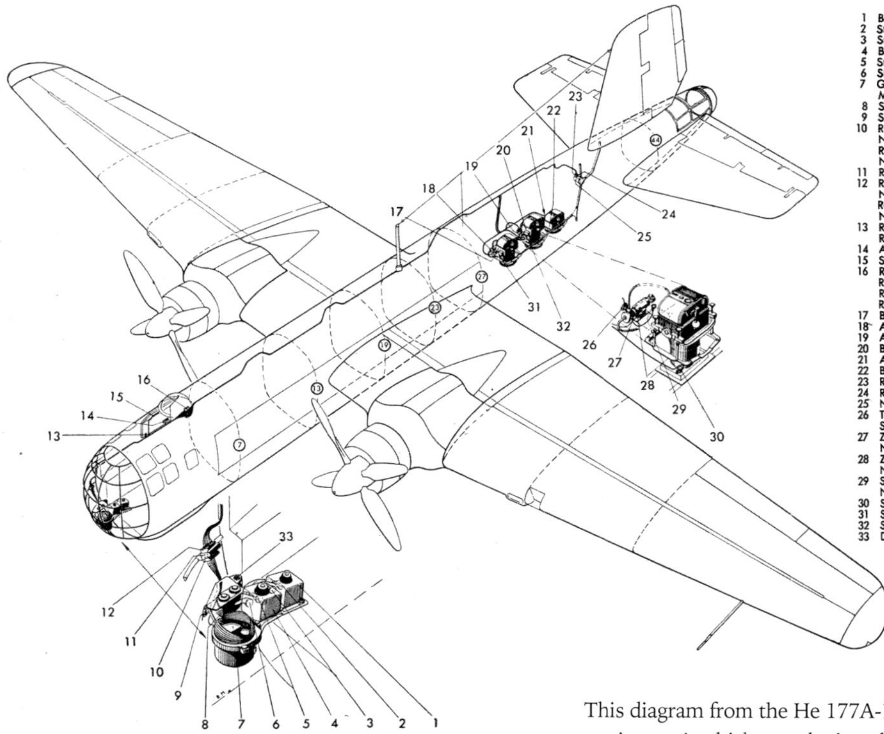

1 Bildfolgeregler, N 23
2 Steckdose, N 27a (N 27 an N 23)
3 Stecker, N 26 (N 26a an N 23)
4 Bildfolgeregler, N 22
5 Steckdose, N 25a (N 25 an N 22)
6 Stecker, N 24 (N 24a an N 22)
7 Grundgeschwindigkeit- und Abtriftmesser, M 17, L 53
8 Schaltkasten, L 51
9 Stecker, Steckdose, L 52, L 52a
10 Reihensteckdosen, N 28a bis N 31a, N 33a, N 34a, L 54a
Reihensteckverteiler, N 28 bis N 31, N 33, N 34, L 54
11 Reihensteckvorrichtung, V 174
12 Reihensteckdosen, V 175a, E 226a, N 36a, N 37a, N 40a, N 41a
Reihensteckverteiler, V 175, E 226, N 36, N 37, N 40, N 41
13 Reihensteckdose, V 76a
Reihensteckverteiler, V 76
14 Aufbauverteiler, V 74
15 Selbstschalter, L 4, N 2, N 3, E 126
16 Reihensteckvorrichtung, V 181
Reihensteckdos., N 6a, N 8a bis N 10a, E 172a
Reihenstecker, N 6, N 8 bis N 10, E 172
Reihensteckdos., N 6b, N 8b bis N 10b, E 172b
17 Bildgerät, N 58
18 Antriebsmotor, N 57
19 Antriebsmotor, N 61
20 Bildgerät, N 62
21 Antriebsmotor, N 65
22 Bildgerät, N 66
23 Reihensteckdose, E 269a
24 Reihensteckdose, E 270a
25 Nachlaufschalter, E 268
26 Temperaturgeber, E 271
Steckdose, E 271a
27 Zentralstecker, N 43, N 48, N 53, N 43a, N 48a, N 53a
28 Zentralstecker, N 42a, N 47a, N 52a, N 42, N 47, N 52
29 Stecker, Steckdose, N 44, N 49, N 54, N 44a, N 49a, N 54a
30 Signalschalter, N 7
31 Stecker, N 45
32 Stecker, N 50
33 Drehschauzeichen, N 20

This diagram from the He 177A-1 handbook shows the 'N equipment', which was the installation of cameras in the rear fuselage and the controls in the starboard side of the cockpit (including the ground speed and drift meter (7))

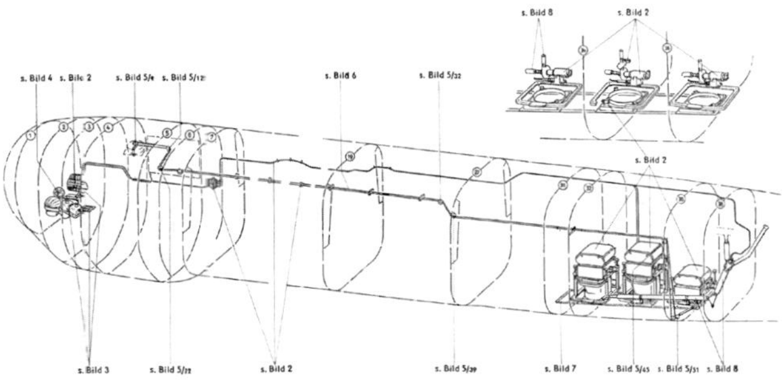

This shows the three-camera installation and comes from the He 177A-3 handbook

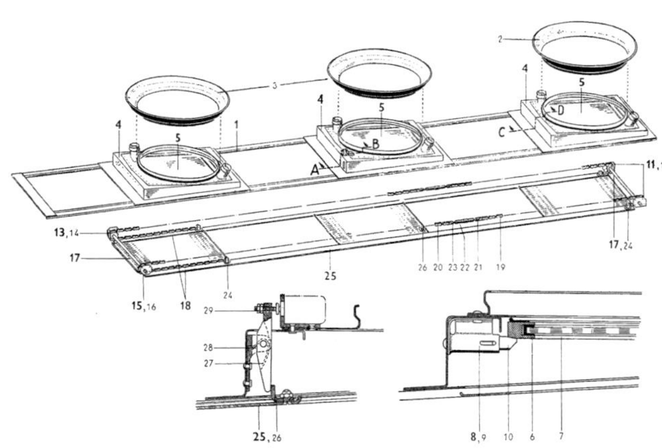

This shows the three camera ports in more detail

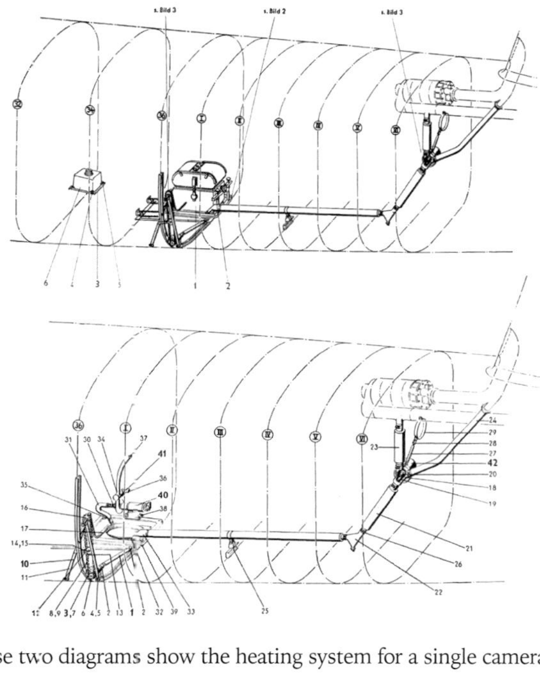

These two diagrams show the heating system for a single camera installation

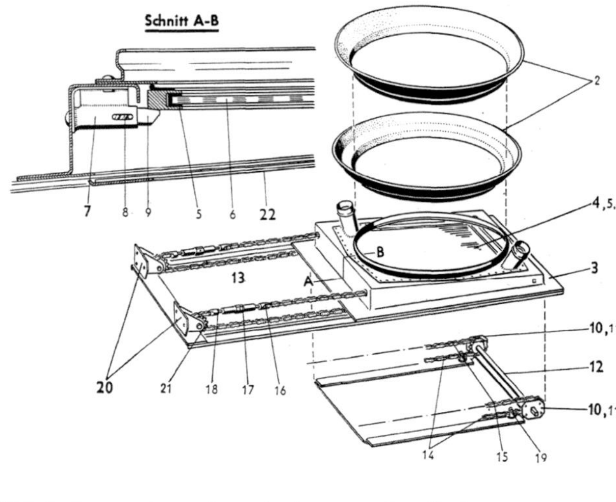

This is the port/cover for a single camera installation

This shows the cabin heating system for those without the B2-*Stand*

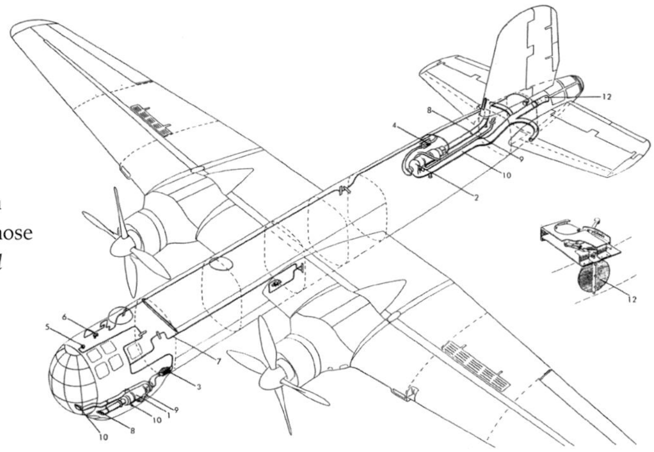

1. Kärcher heater (cockpit)
2. Kärcher heater (rear part of fuselage)
3. Ignition box (cockpit)
4. Ignition box (rear part of fuselage)
5. Toggle switch (Kärcher heaters)
6. Toggle switch (throttle valve)
7. Electrical system
8. Fresh air intake pipe
9. Exhaust gas outlet pipe
10. Heating air outlet pipe
11. Butterfly valve
12. Throttle valve with linkage

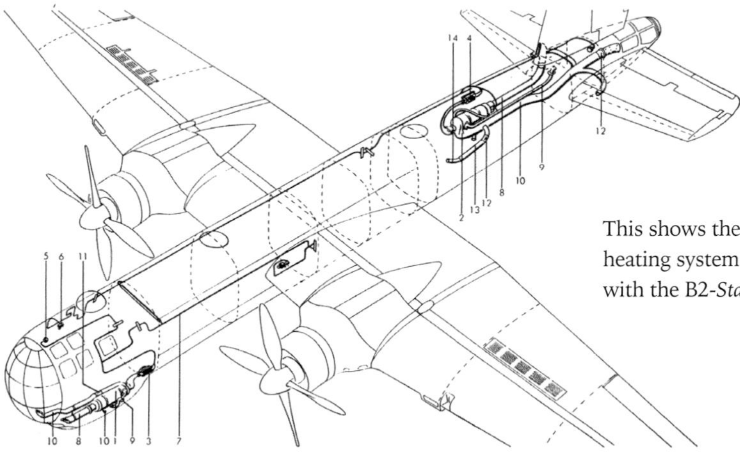

This shows the cabin heating system for those with the B2-*Stand*

1. Kärcher heater (cockpit)
2. Kärcher heater (rear part of fuselage)
3. Ignition box (cockpit)
4. Ignition box (rear part of fuselage)
5. Toggle switch (Kärcher heater)
6. Toggle switch (throttle valve)
7. Electrical system
8. Fresh air intake pipe
9. Exhaust gas outlet pipe
10. Heating air outlet pipe
11. Butterfly valve
12. Throttle valve with linkage
13. Heating air outlet pipe e.g. B2-*Stand*
14. Flexible pipe

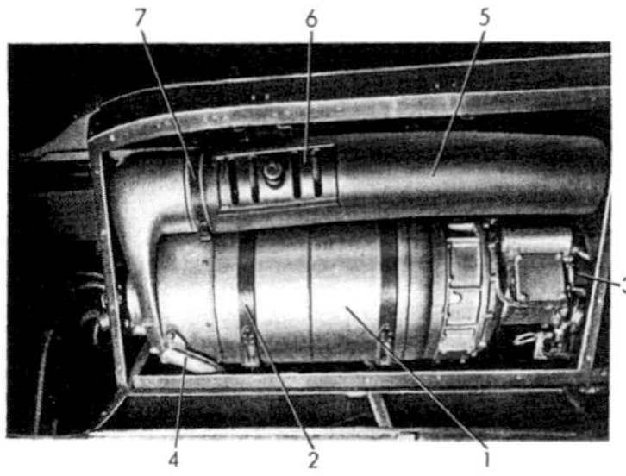

These period images from the handbook show the (Kärcher) cabin heater in the cockpit without (top) and with panelling (middle), plus the cabin heating control panel in the overhead panel in the cockpit (bottom)

Cabin heater (top)
1. Kärcher heater
2. Tension band (Kärcher heater)
3. Fresh air inlet pipe
4. Exhaust gas outlet pipe
5. Heating air outlet pipe
6. Slider
7. Tension band

Air outlet pipe (middle)
1. Fairing panel
2. Mounting screws

Control panel (bottom)
1. Rotary switch
2. Toggle switch

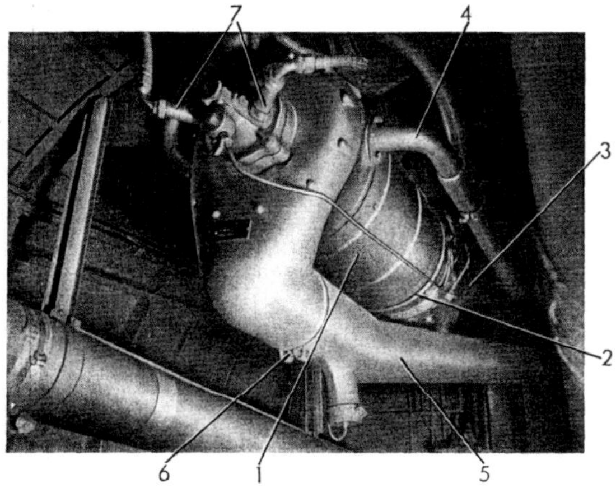

This shows the (Kärcher) cabin heater in the rear of the fuselage
1. Kärcher heaer
2. Tension band (Kärcher heater)
3. Fresh air inlet pipe
4. Exhaust gas outlet pipe
5. Heating air outlet pipe
6. Tension pane (heating air outlet pipe)
7. Ignition cable

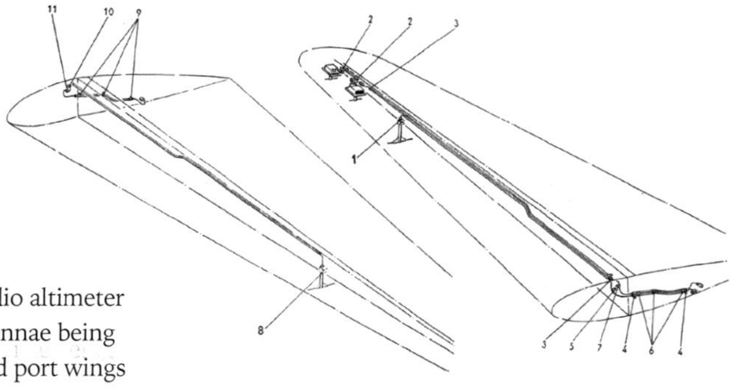

When installed, the FuG 101 radio altimeter resulted in these 'T' shaped antennae being installed under the starboard and port wings

Please note that we have not included any narrative element with these access panel diagrams, mainly because the system used by the Luftwaffe during WWII rarely listed the actual use of the access panel, it was more likely that it stated a general phrase and the type of panel and the method by which it was fixed (e.g. screws, bolts etc.). As many of the phrases make little sense once translated into English, plus many of the terms used in WWII are no longer in use, we felt that they would be more confusing than helpful, so have not included them.

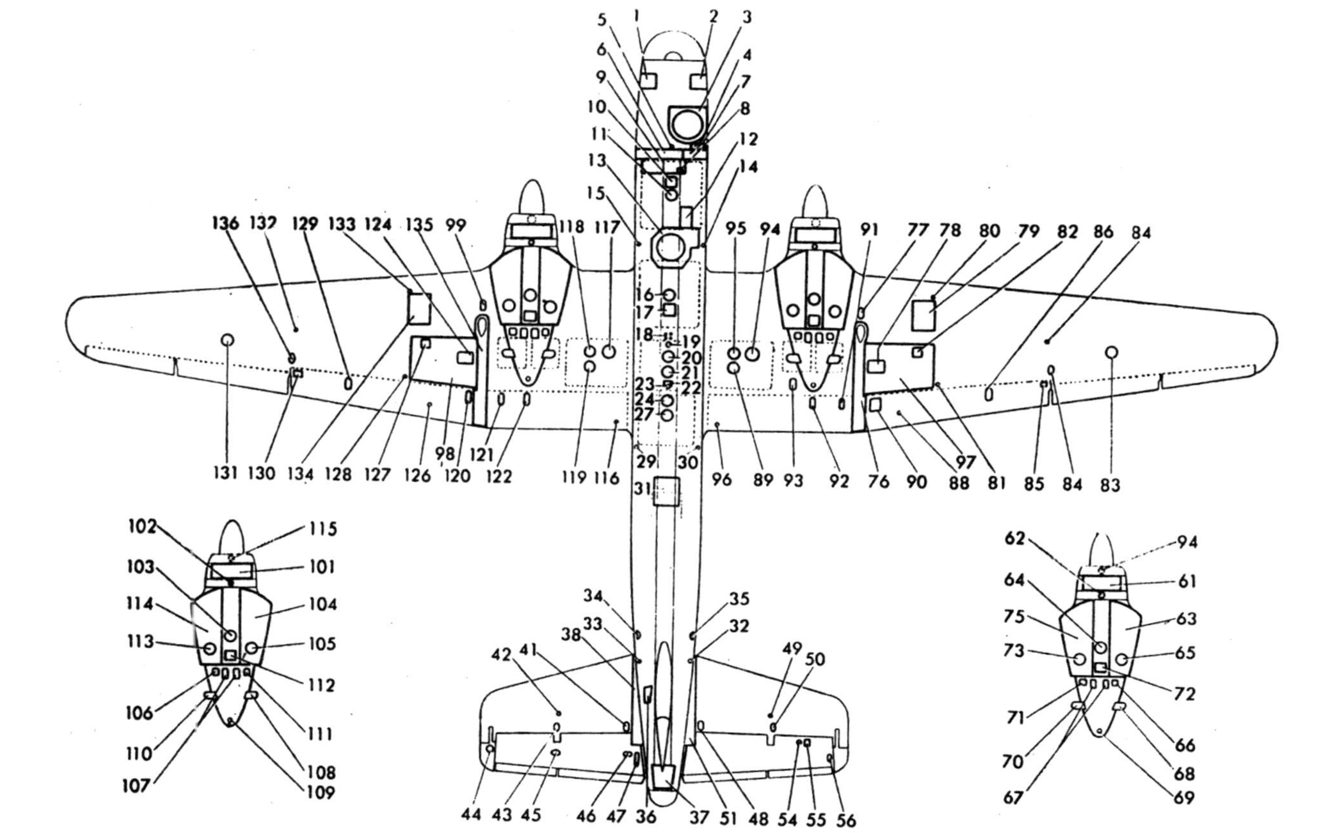

Access panels for the He 177A-1, top views

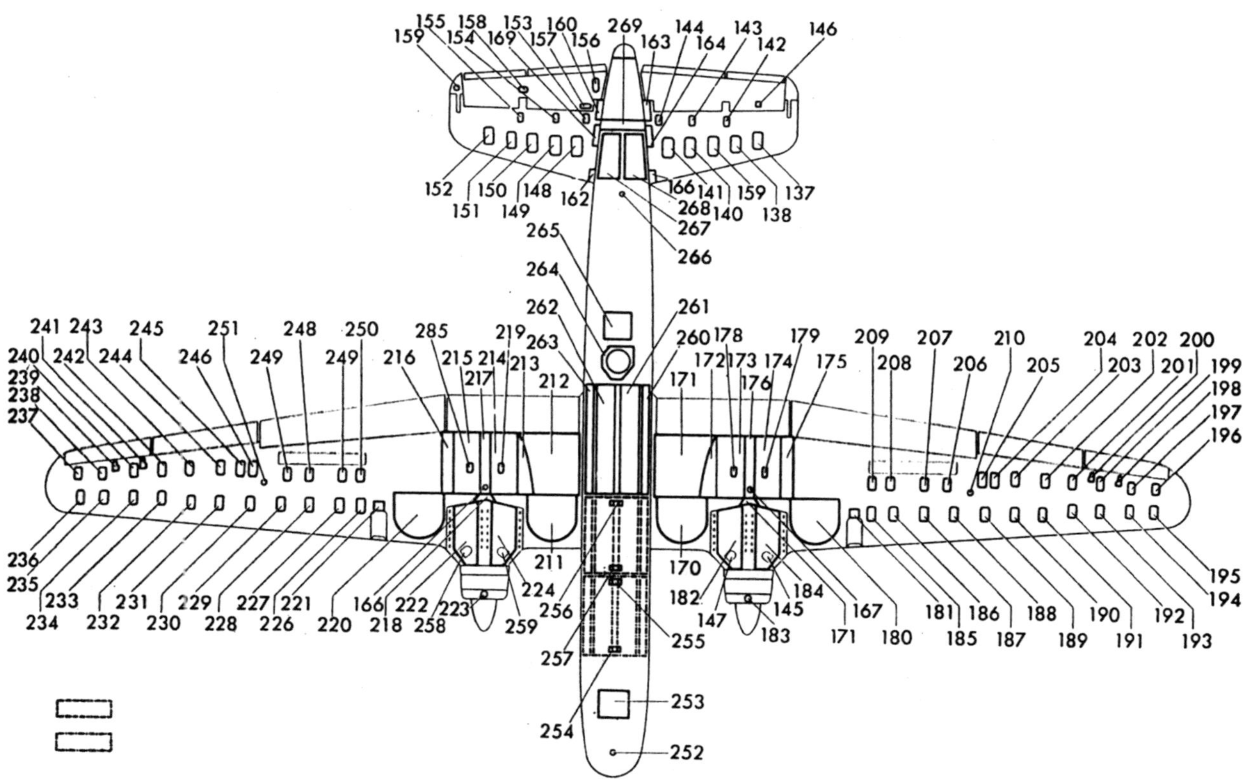

Access panels for the He 177A-1, underside views

Group 8 – Side 4
Miscellaneous 1

106 Ground Equipment

These two diagrams show how to towing the aircraft from the front or back

Normal: Rückwärts – Normal: Reverse
Ausnahmefall: Vorwärts – Exception: Forward
Fahrwerkbein außen – Gear leg outside

This shows the covers for all variants of the He 177A

Bei Tag – By Day
Bei Nacht und ungünstiger Witterung – At night and in unfavorable weather

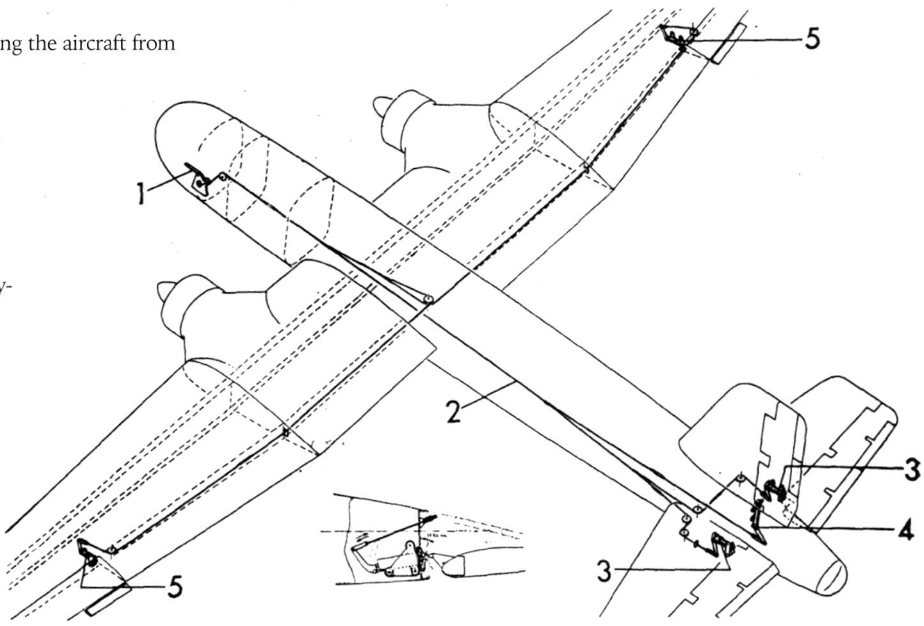

The size of the He 177 meant that it did not rely on manually-fitted control locks, this was all via a mechanical system as depicted here

1. Operating lever
2. Cable pull
3. Locking latch, elevator
4. Locking latch, rudder
5. Locking latch, aileron

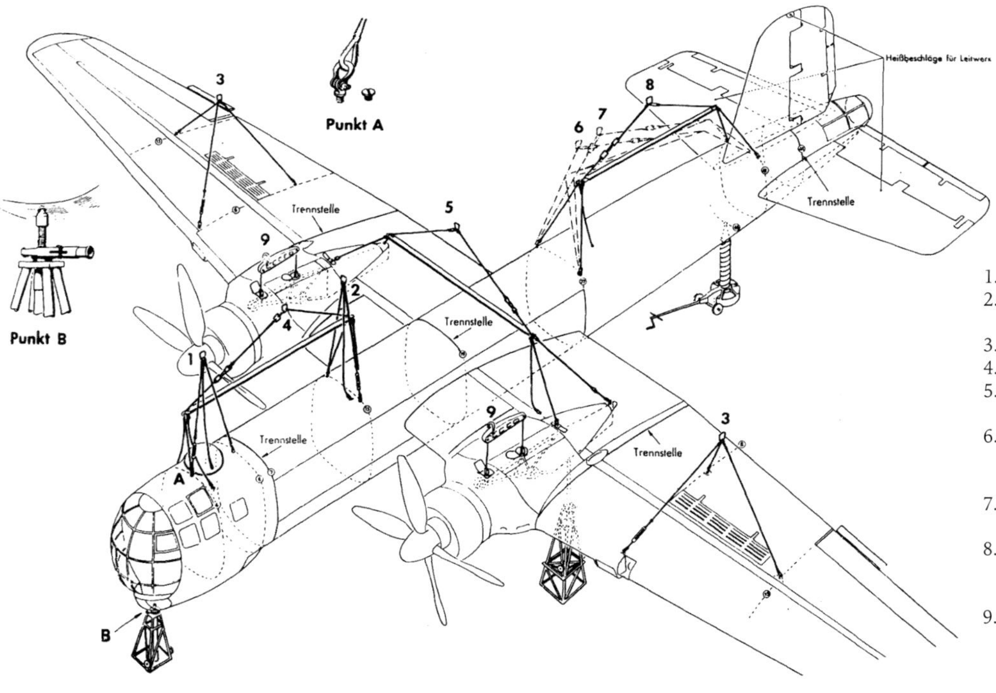

1. Cockpit
2. Front part of the fuselage without cockpit
3. Wing outer parts
4. Front part of fuselage with cockpit
5. Wing centre section without engines
6. End of fuselage with bomb rack and container, without tail stand and tail unit
7. End of fuselage without tail stan, tailplane, bomb rack and container
8. End of fuselage with tail stand and tailplane, without bomb rack and container
9. Engines (auxiliary crane for engine changes see special plan)

This diagram shows the transport and salvage, hoisting and jacking details for the He 177

Please note that we have not included any narrative element with these access panel diagrams, mainly because the system used by the Luftwaffe during WWII rarely listed the actual use of the access panel, it was more likely that it stated a general phrase and the type of panel and the method by which it was fixed (e.g. screws, bolts etc.). As many of the phrases make little sense once translated into English, plus many of the terms used in WWII are no longer in use, we felt that they would be more confusing than helpful, so have not included them.

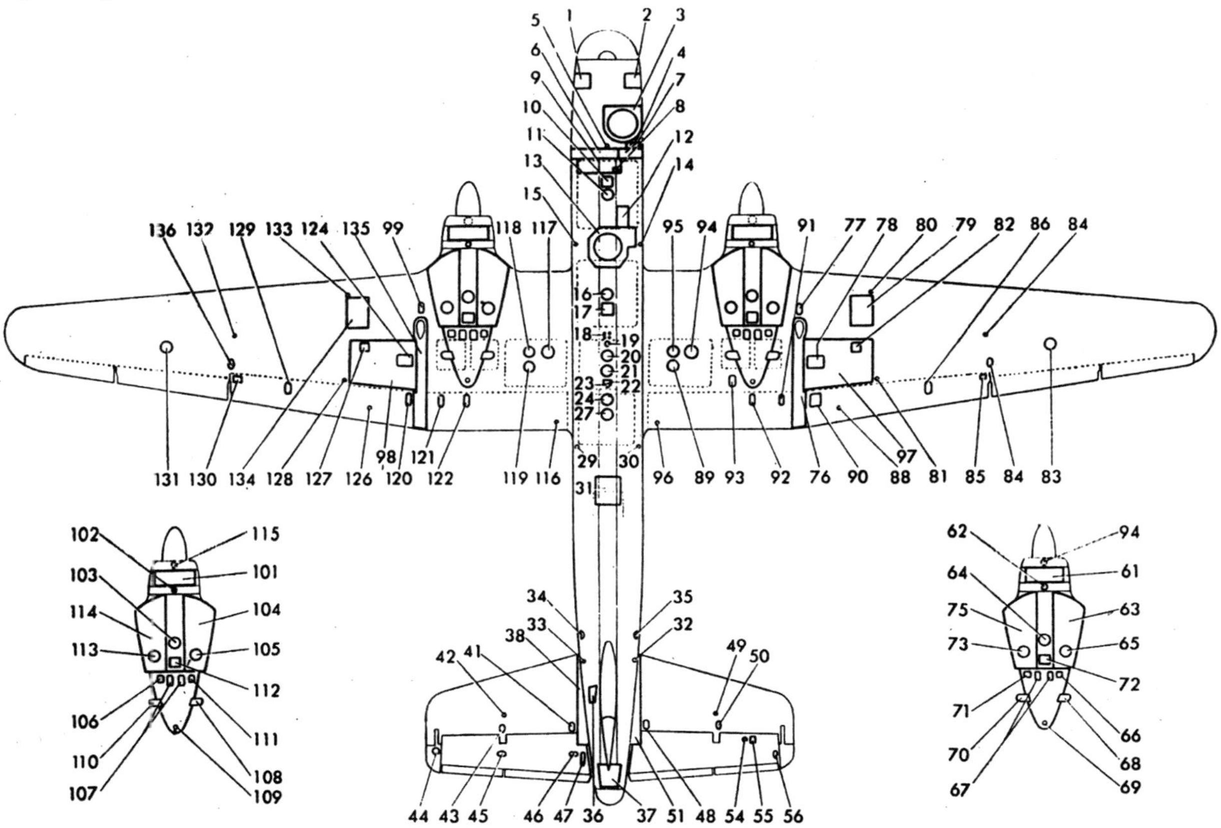

Access panels for the He 177A-1, top views

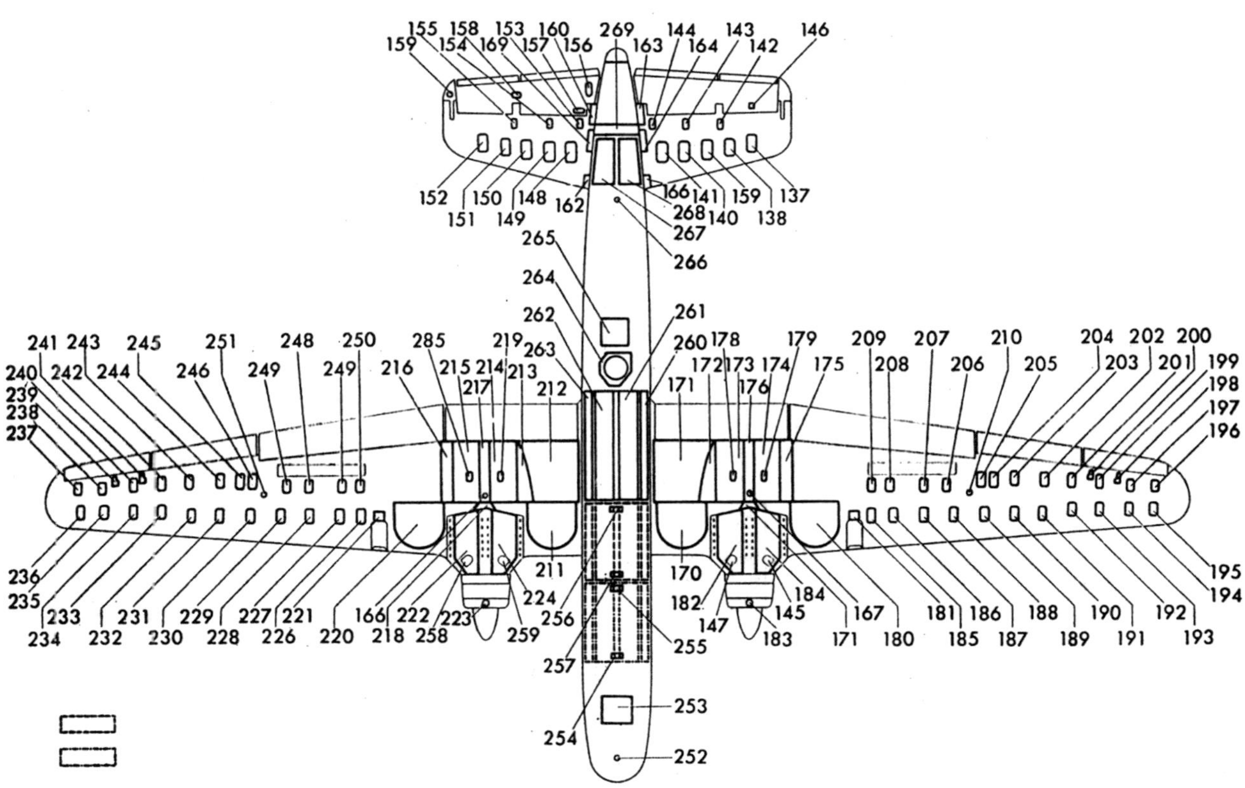

Access panels for the He 177A-1, underside views

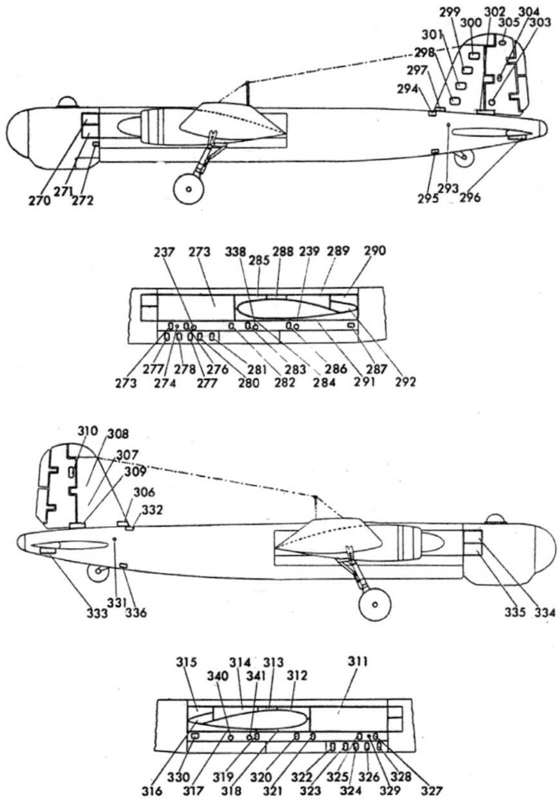

Access panels for the He 177A-1, port and starboard sides

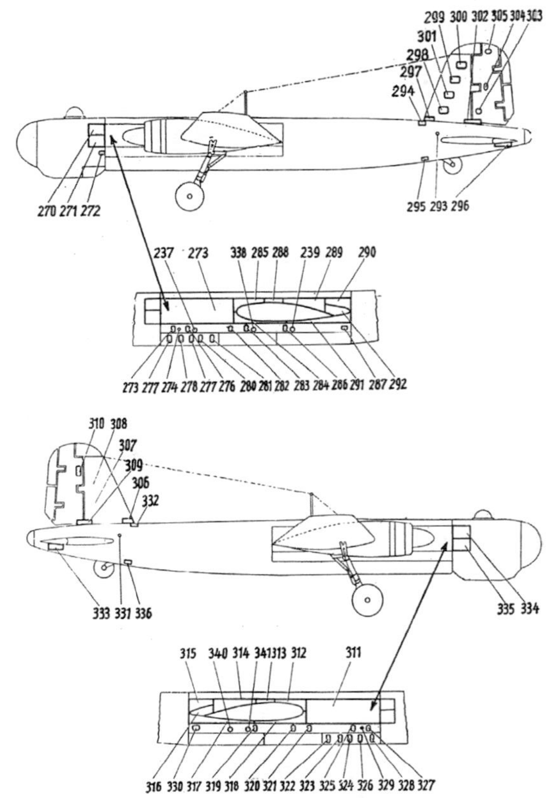

Access panels for the He 177A-3*, port and starboard sides

**The diagram is the same as that used for the A-1, so lacks the B2-Stand*

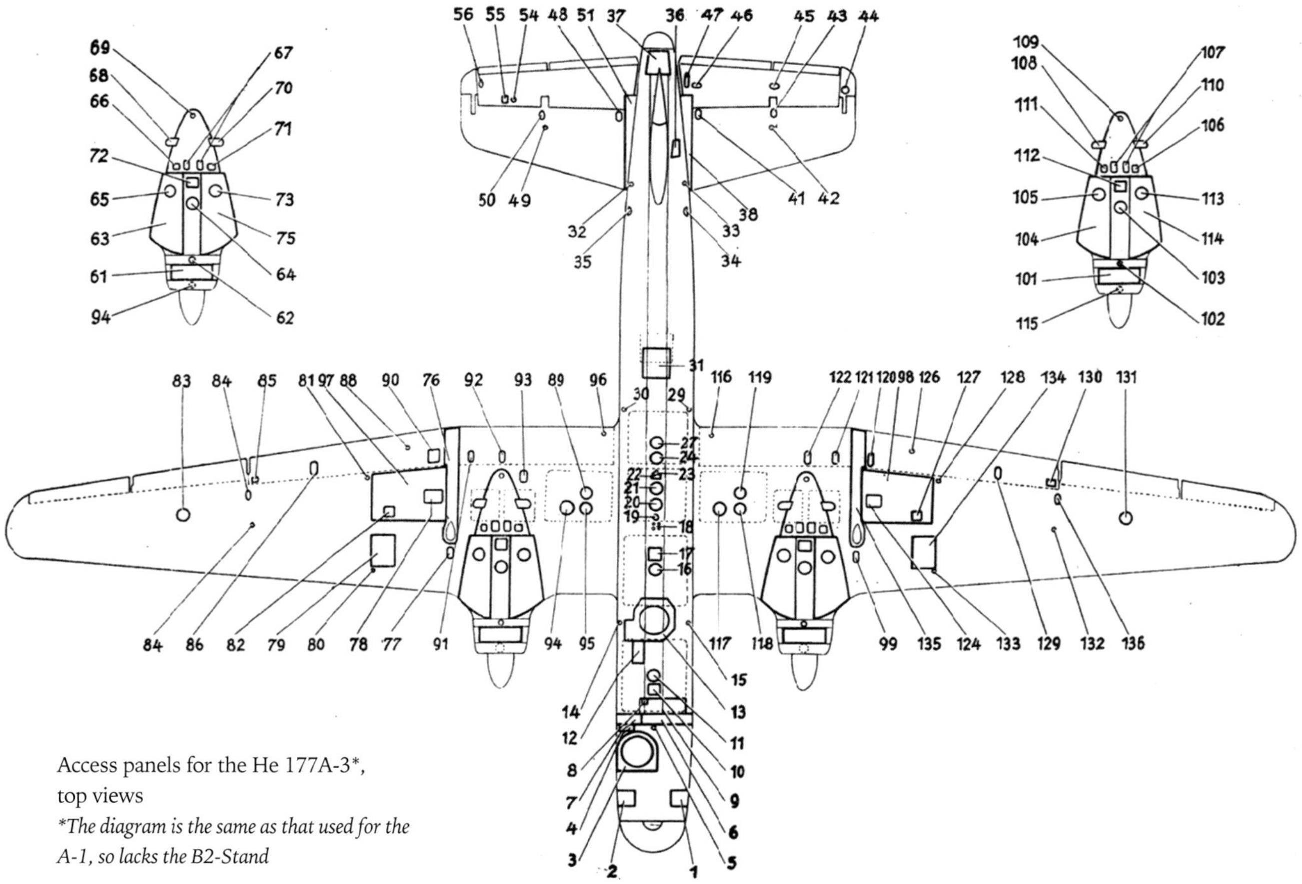

Access panels for the He 177A-3*, top views

**The diagram is the same as that used for the A-1, so lacks the B2-Stand*

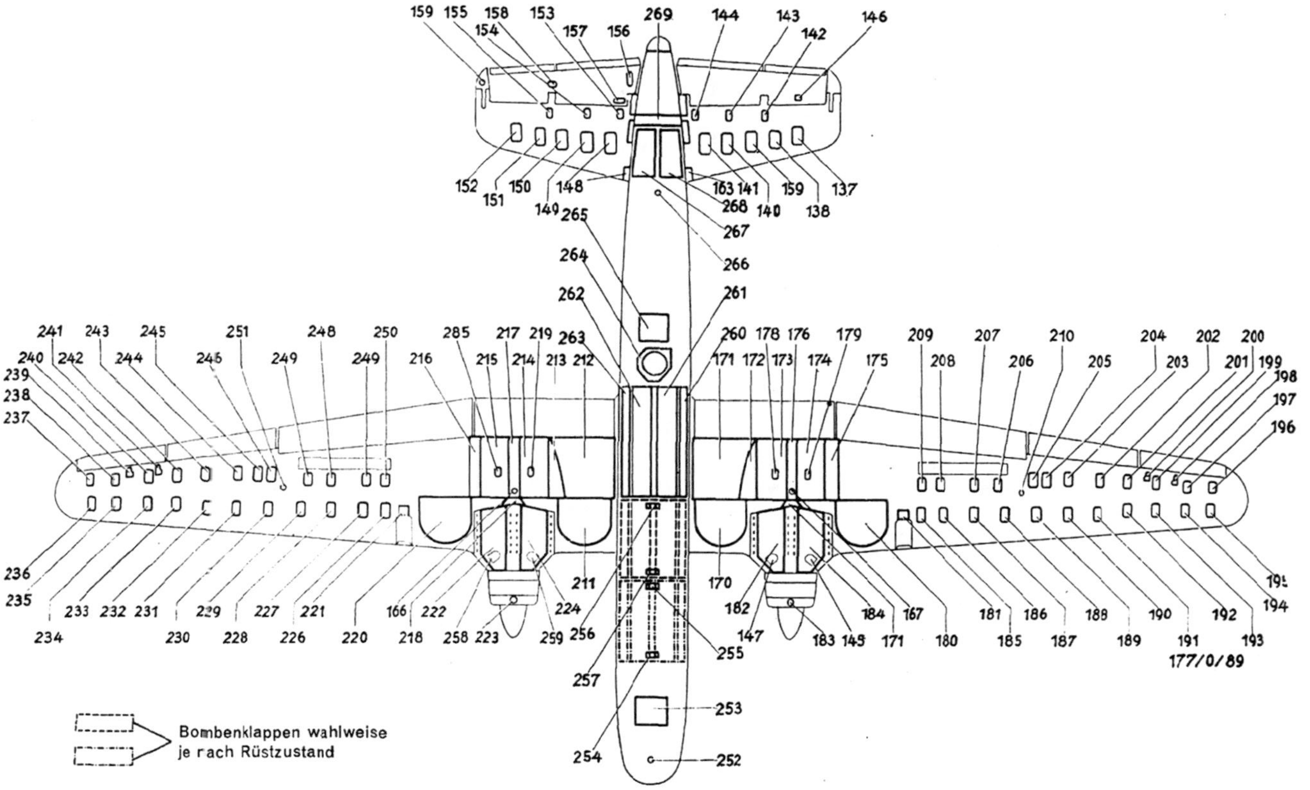

Access panels for the He 177A-3, underside views

This diagram shows the walkable areas and applies to all variants

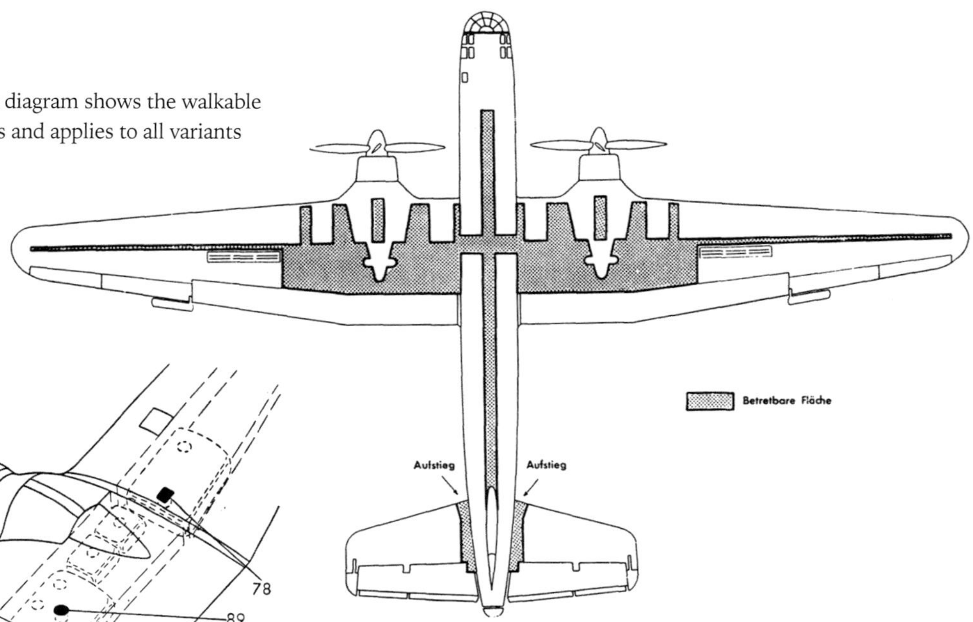

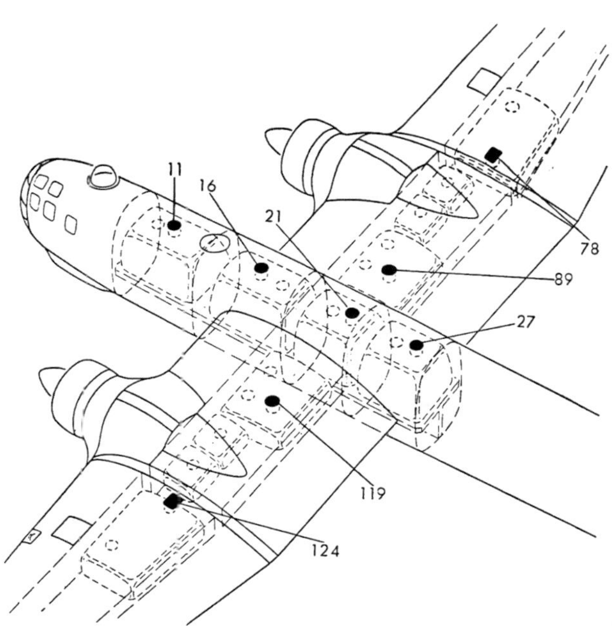

This diagram shows the access panels for the fuel gauges on the dorsal spine and wings and apply to all A-series

11, 16, 21 and 27, cover with quick-release fastener
78, 89, 119 and 124, cover with countersunk screws

This shows the covers for all variants of the He 177A

Bei Tag – By Day
Bei Nacht und ungünstiger Witterung – At night and in unfavorable weather

These two diagrams show how to towing the aircraft from the front or back

Normal: Rückwärts – Normal: Reverse
Ausnahmefall: Vorwärts – Exception: Forward
Fahrwerkbein außen – Gear leg outside

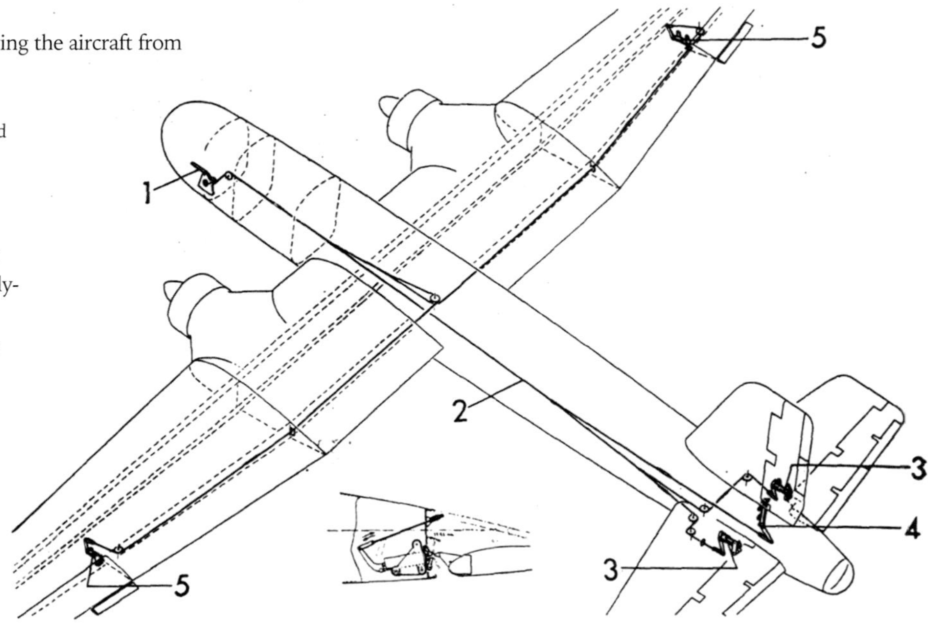

The size of the He 177 meant that it did not rely on manually-fitted control locks, this was all via a mechanical system as depicted here

1. Operating lever
2. Cable pull
3. Locking latch, elevator
4. Locking latch, rudder
5. Locking latch, aileron

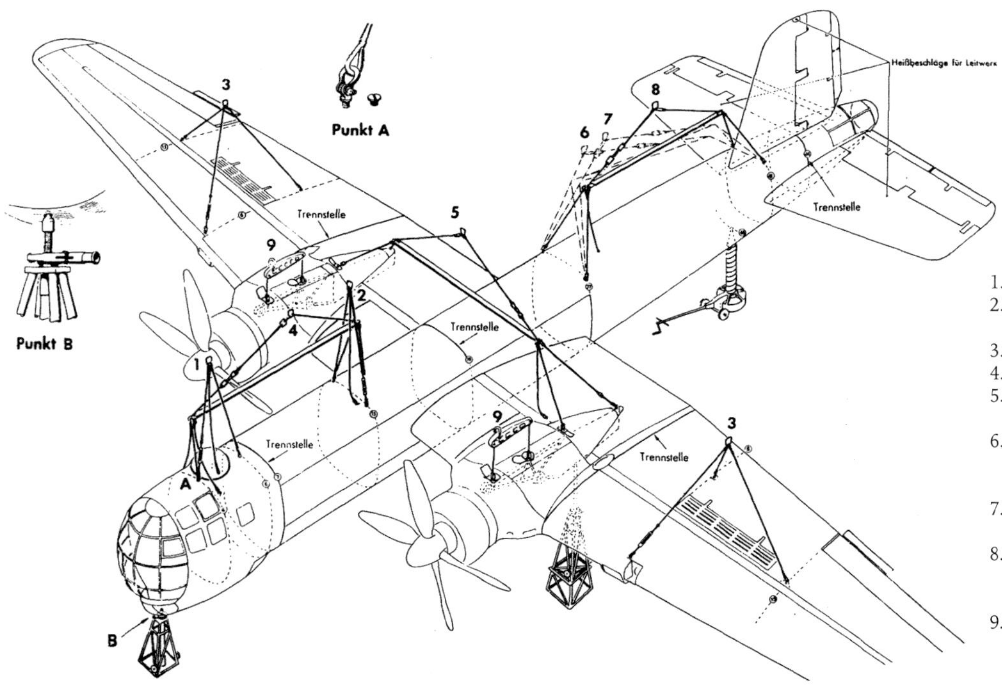

1. Cockpit
2. Front part of the fuselage without cockpit
3. Wing outer parts
4. Front part of fuselage with cockpit
5. Wing centre section without engines
6. End of fuselage with bomb rack and container, without tail stand and tail unit
7. End of fuselage without tail stan, tailplane, bomb rack and container
8. End of fuselage with tail stand and tailplane, without bomb rack and container
9. Engines (auxiliary crane for engine changes see special plan)

This diagram shows the transport and salvage, hoisting and jacking details for the He 177

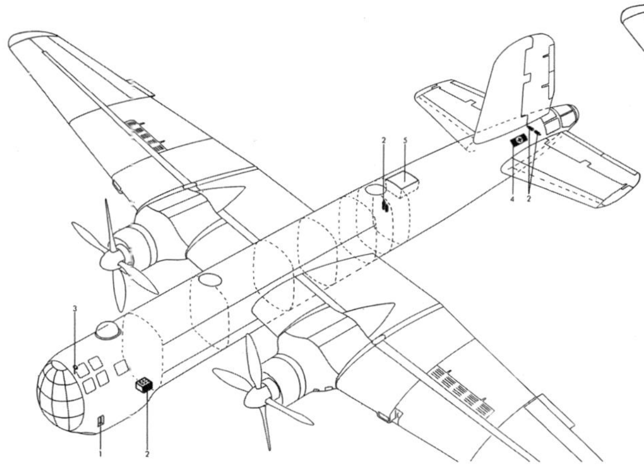

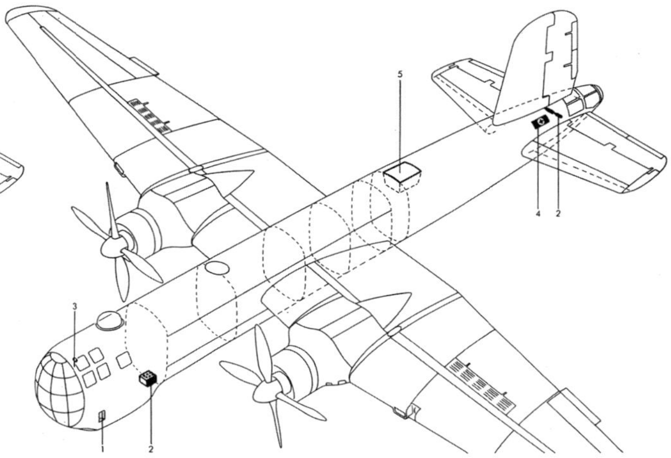

These two diagrams show the rescue and safety devices for those aircraft without a B2-*Stand* (right) and with a B2-*Stand* (left)

1. Medical bag
2. Thermos bottles
3. Rear view mirror
4. Medical pack
5. Rescue inflatable boat with emergency transmitter and emergency provisions

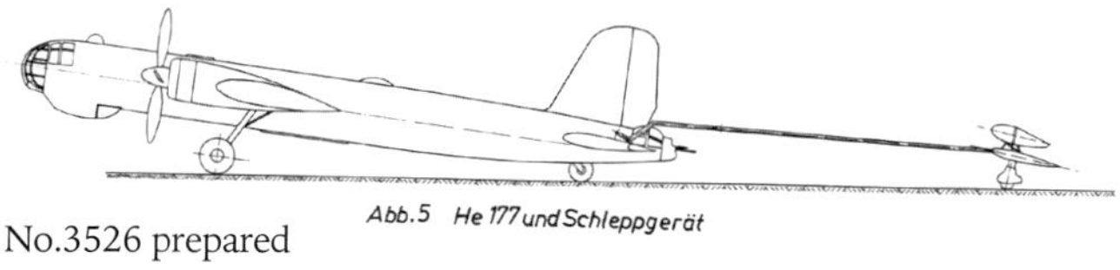

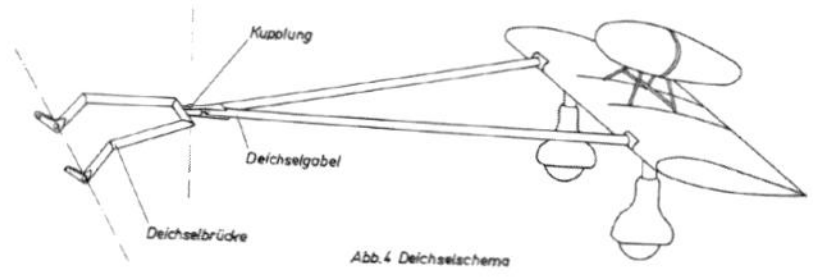

These two diagrams from a report No.3526 prepared by the DFS (Deutsche Forschungssanstalt für Segelflug E.V. 'Ernst Udet' z.Zt at Ainring) published on the 22nd June 1944 and covering the fittings for stability trials for towing an external winged fuel tank by He 177A-3, W/Nr.332236, TM+IU

Two views of the 300lt drop tank fitted above the DFS-designed 'air trailer' towed behind He 177A-3, W/Nr.332236, TM+IU

These two images show the attachment for the 12m-long towing arms above the *Heckstand* of TM+IU

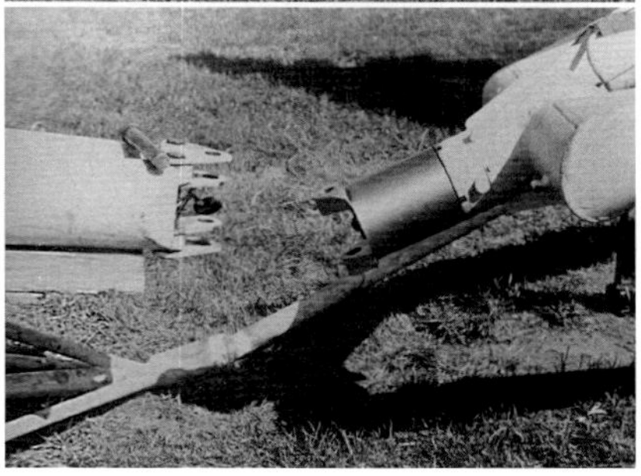

These two period images show the swivel-joint between the towing pole and the 'air trailer', the top one shows how the pole is detached in flight, while the lower image shows how they are disconnected on the ground

Two views of He 177A-3, W/Nr.332236, TM+IU prior to and in flight with the 'Schleppgerät' ('air trailer') behind it

Evolution

Prototype, Production and Projected Variants

The evolution of the Heinkel He 177 series involved a number of prototype and various batches of pre and production series airframes along with a number of conversions and projected variants. What follows therefore is a list of all those airframes that were built, plus details of the known projected development variants.

Please note that there are many errors and omissions in period Nazi German and Allied records of the He 177, He 274 & He 277, many of which have been compounded by post-war accounts that have muddied the waters even more so. As far as we can find, no complete set of Heinkel/Arado production data survives, and that which does, is split over numerous official and private collections all over the world. We have therefore tried to create a complete list of all airframes built, along with projected sub-variants using period and modern accounts as well as a study of period images. As always, all conflicting data is quoted, so you can make your own minds up on the most likely scenario.

Prototypes

Note: The W/Nr. series for the prototypes is often shown as just '0001' etc., but we have shown them in their entirety (e.g. type code [177], production batch [000] and individual airframe number [0001] etc.)

He 177 V1 – Initial Form

W/Nr. 177 000 0001
Stammkenzeichen: CB+RP
First Flight: 20th (others state 19th) November 1939 (Dipl-Ing Franke at controls)
(see photograph of tail on page 52 top left)

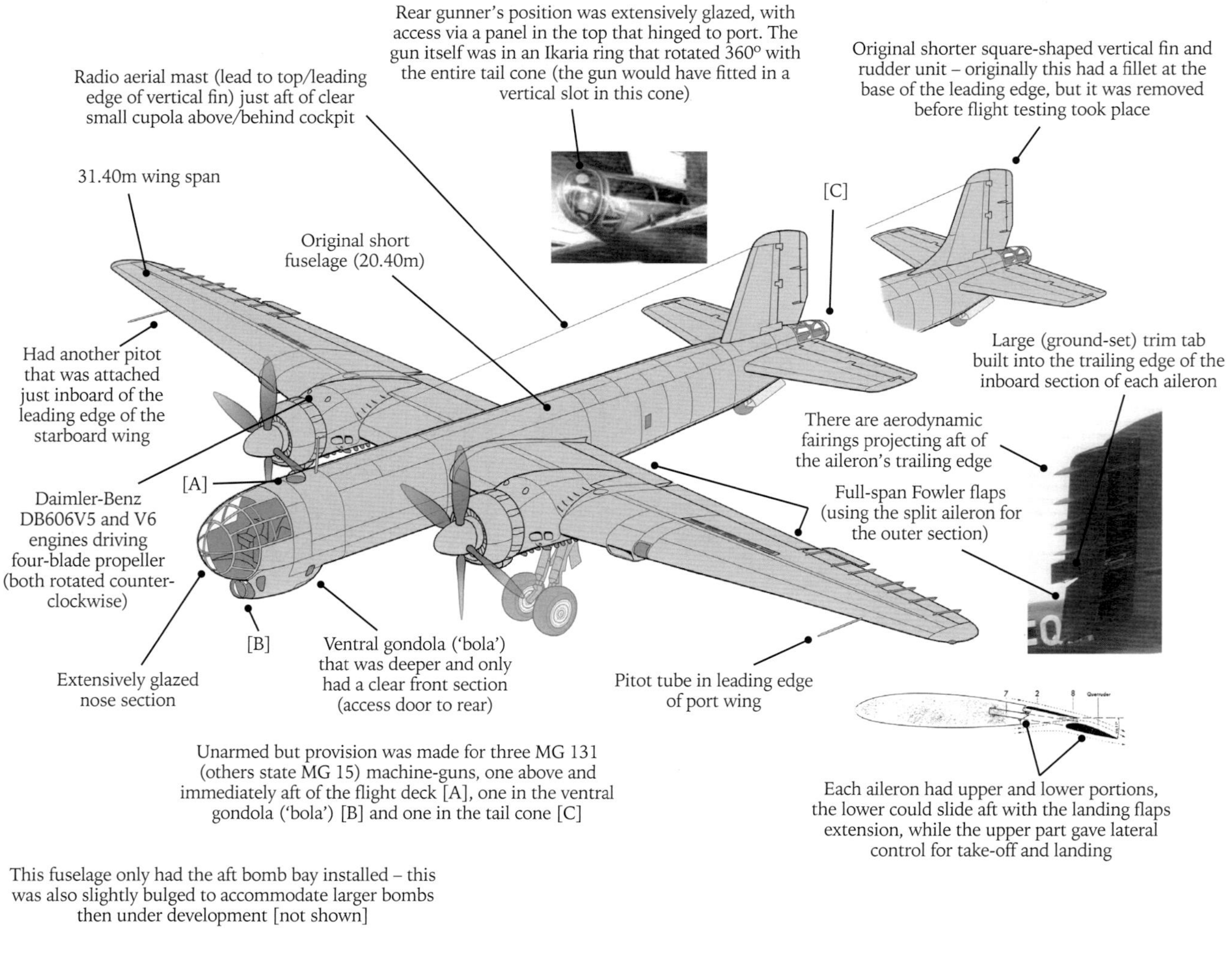

He 177 V1 – Revised Form

Same as He 177 V1 – Initial Form except:

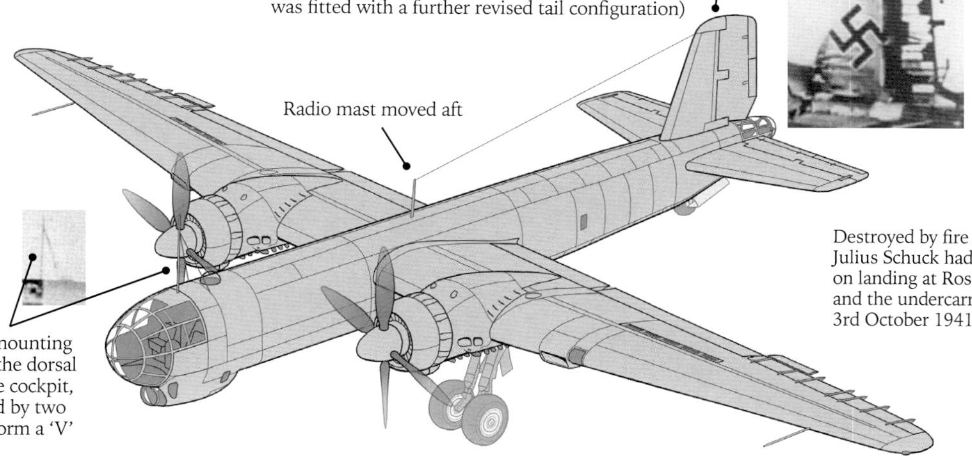

Here the V1 in revised form comes in to land

Often mis-identified as being the V1, this actually shows the V2 prior to receiving an overall coat of paint and *Stammkenzeichen*

He 177 V2

W/Nr. 177 000 0002
Stammkenzeichen: CB+RQ
First Flight – Probably late March/early April 1940, the exact date is unknown (first recorded flight was the 21st April 1940)

Same as He 177 V1 – Initial Form except:

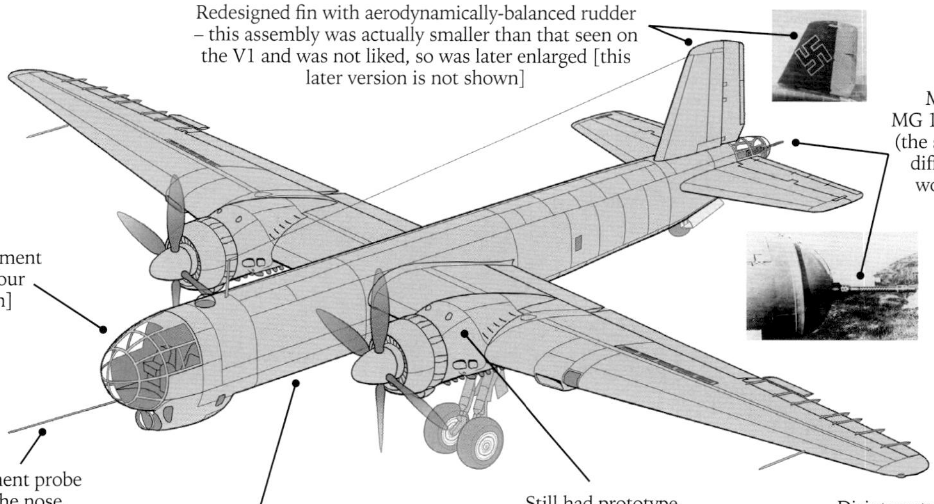

He 177 V3

W/Nr. 177 000 0003
Civil Registration: D-AGIG
Same as He 177 V2 except:

Crashed near Gehlsdorf whilst being flown by Dipl-Ing Rickert due to inadequate balancing of the rudder (some sources state faulty trimming) caused failure of the tail surfaces during diving trials on the 24th April 1940. All crew killed

Note: There is much contradiction in written accounts as to which V-series airframe was the first to be armed, some claim the V4, others the V6, while there are those that state different machines in the same title!

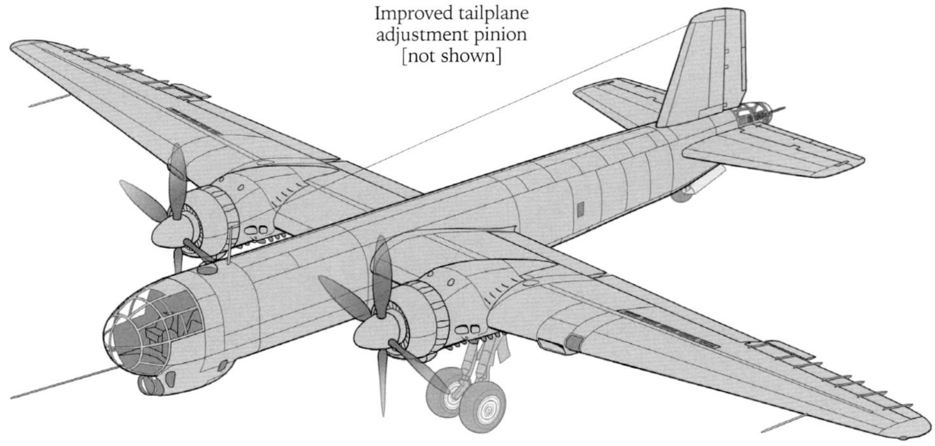

He 177 V4 – Initial Form

W/Nr. 177 000 0004
First Flight – 4th September 1940
Same as He 177 V3 except:

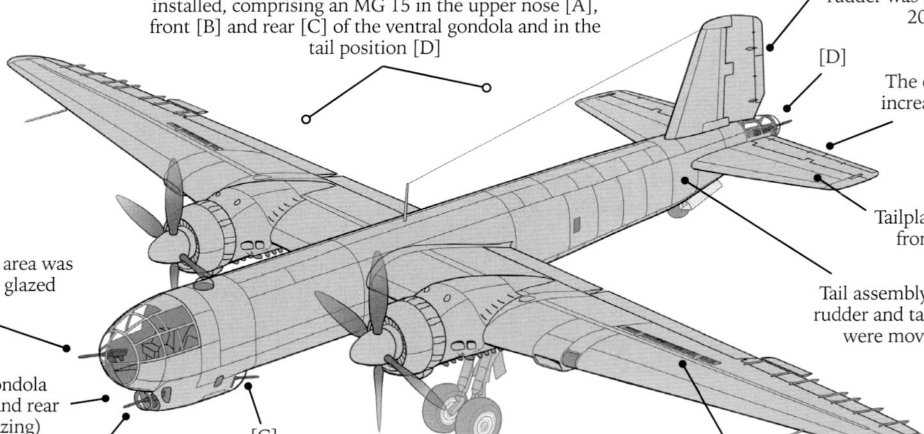

Third bomb bay added [not shown]

This airframe also tested a simplified drop-load release mechanism along with the V5 [not shown]

The bulge around the bomb bay was eliminated [not shown]

Had increased fuel tankage (raising weight to 24,820kg) [not shown]

He 177 V4 – Revised

The same as He 177V4 – Initial Form, except period documents list the following 'revisions':

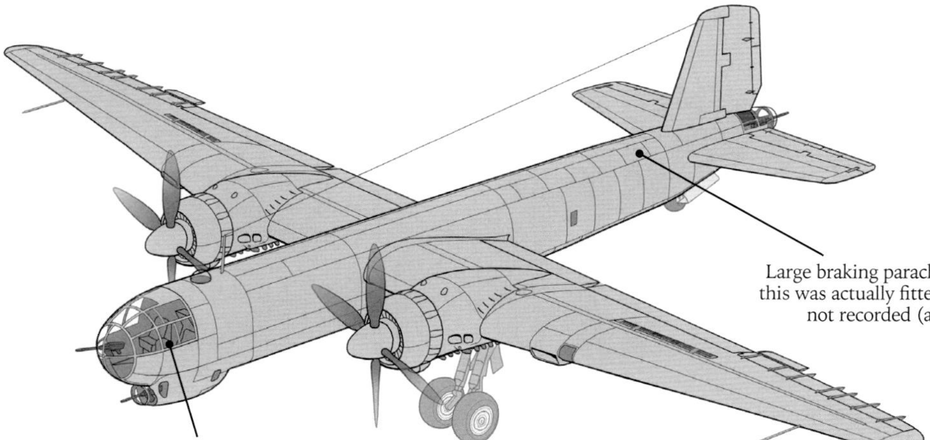

Used for inclined flight tests but lost in crash-landing at Marienehe due to engine failure 8th June 1941

He 177 V5

W/Nr. 177 000 0005
Stammkenzeichen: PM+OD
First Flight – 30th September 1940
Generally similar to He 177 V4 except:

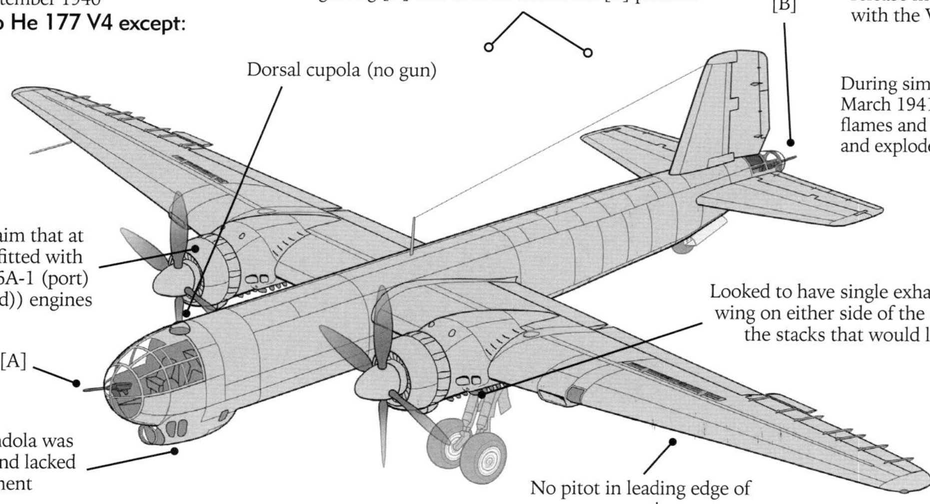

He 177 V6 – Initial Form

W/Nr. 177 000 0006
Stammkenzeichen: BC+BP
First Flight – 18th December 1940
Similar to the He 177 V5 except:

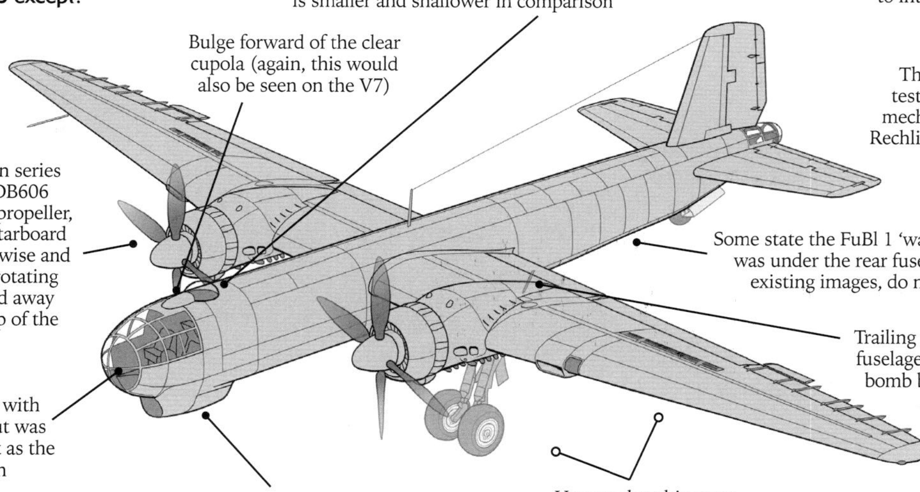

This shows the V6 in initial form taking off, the revised shape of the ventral gondola being obvious from this angle

He 177 V6 – Revised Form

Same as He 177 V6 – Initial Form except:

Fitted with flexible armament prior to operational evaluation comprising:
[A] MG FF cannon in modified gondola under the nose (known as Kanzelform 2 – [cabin type 2] A2-*Stand*) – this lacked any side glazing
[B] MG 15 in Ikaria ball-mount in the nose (A1-*Stand*) – period images do not confirm this
[C] MG 131 in manually-operated dorsal turret above cockpit (B1-*Stand*)
[D] MG 151 in Ikaria ball-mount in rear of ventral gondola (C1-*Stand*)
[E] MG 131 in tail (*Heckstand*)

Prototype DB606 engines replaced with pre-production DB606A-1 (port) and B-1 (starboard) versions

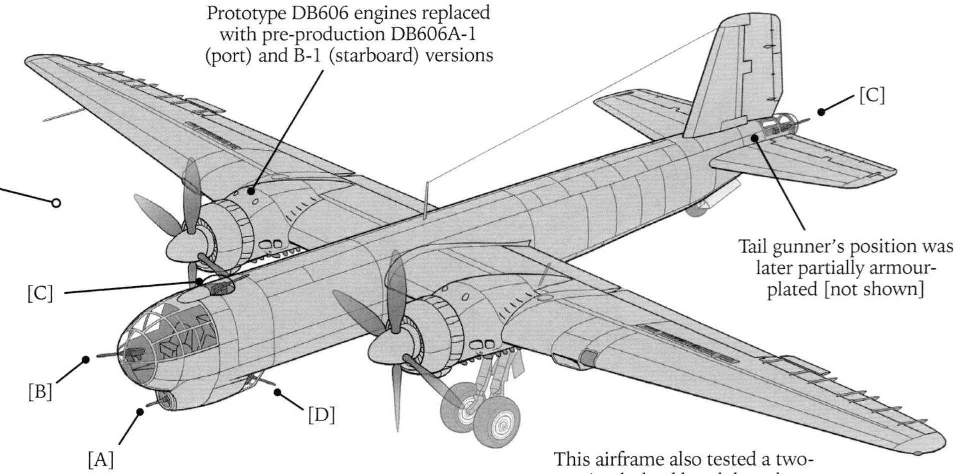

Tail gunner's position was later partially armour-plated [not shown]

Laster transferred to *Erprobungsstaffel 177* and also tested by IV.(Erg)/KG 40 at Lechfeld (some sources state Orléans), but crash-landed on the 28th June 1943 and was never flown again

This airframe also tested a two-section bulged bomb bay along with the V8 [not shown]

A very poor, blurry image, but the only one that exists that seems to show the V6 in revised form with armament installed

The V7 was very well photographed, this shot shows it at Rechlin during a visit from Reichmarschall Göring (who, in his white uniform, is just visible in the front of the middle of the group of officials)

He 177 V7

W/Nr. 177 0000 0007
Stammkenzeichen: SF+TB
First Flight – 14th March 1941

Similar to He 177 V6 – Revised Form except:

Fuselage was 18cm shorter

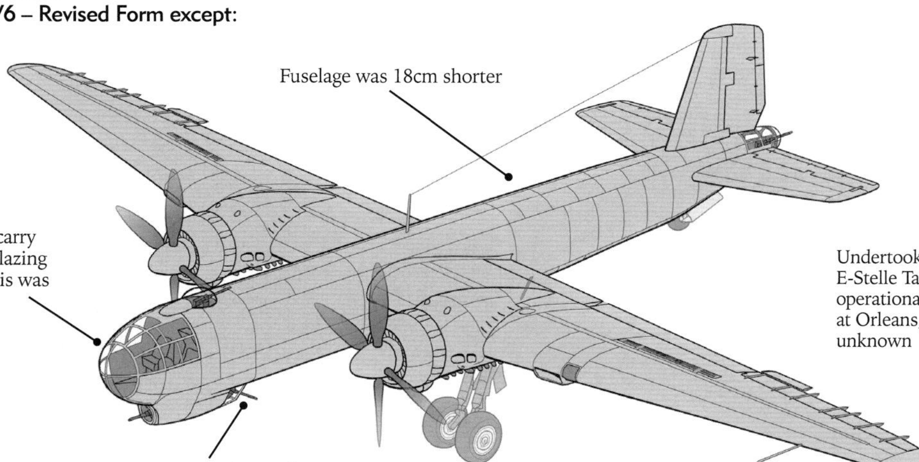

Had capacity to carry MG 131 in nose glazing (A1-*Stand*), but this was not fitted

Undertook armament trials at E-Stelle Tarnewitz then was operationally evaluated by IV/KG40 at Orleans, France, ultimate fate unknown

MG 131 in rear of ventral gondola (C1-*Stand*)

He 177 V8

W/Nr. 177 000 0008
Stammkenzeichen: SF+TC
First Flight – 24th April 1941
Similar to He 177 V7 except:

Last airframe to be built from the outset as a pure prototype

Although surviving period images do not show any actual armament fitted*, it had the capacity to carry the following armament [not shown]:
1x MG 131 in manually-operated dorsal turret aft of the cockpit (B1-*Stand*)
1x MG 15 in Ikaria ball-mount in the aft ventral position (C2-*Stand*)
1x MG 131 in tail (*Heckstand*)

**Some sources claim it had an MG 131 in the A1-Stand and MG 15s in the B1-Stand, C2-Stand and Heckstand, but all surviving images show it without armament fitted*

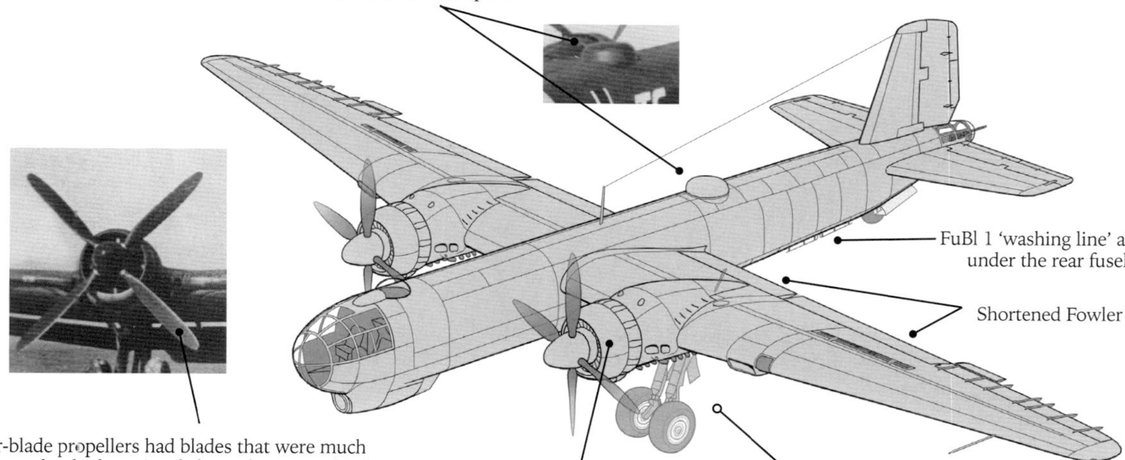

Used to test cooling equipment and flaps and was later fitted with de-icers on the wing leading edges [not shown]

This airframe also had the bulged bomb bay seen on the V6 and V7 [not shown]

The early style of cockpit/nose glazing used by the prototype is well illustrated in this head-on view of the V8

The following Versuch numbers relate to other airframes used for research purposes:

He 177 V9 – See He 177A-08/V9
He 177 V10 – See He 177A-09/V10
He 177 V11 – See He 177A-10/V11
He 177 V12 – See He 177A-1/V12
He 177 V13 – Probably never built
He 177 V14 – See He 177A-1/V14
He 177 V15 – See He 177A-0/V15
He 177 V16 – See He 177A-0/V16
He 177 V17 – See He 177A-0/V17
He 177 V18 – See He 177A-015/V18
He 177 V19 – See He 177A-1/V19
He 177 V20 – See He 177A-1/V20
He 177 V21 – See He 177A-1/V21
He 177 V22 – See He 177A-1/V22
He 177 V23 – See He 177A-1/V23
He 177 V24 – See He 177A-1/V24
He 177 V25 – See He 177A-1/V25
He 177 V26 – See He 177A-04/V26
He 177 V27 – See He 177A-1/V27
He 177 V28 – See He 177A-1/V28
He 177 V29 – See He 177A-1/V29
He 177 V30 – See He 177A-1/V30
He 177 V31 – See He 177A-3/V31
He 177 V32 – See He 177A-1/V32
He 177 V33 – See He 177A-1/V33
He 177 V34 – See He 177A-1/V34
He 177 V35 – See He 177A-1/V35
He 177 V36 – See He 177A-1/V36
He 177 V37 – See He 177A-5/V37
He 177 V38 – See He 177A-5/V38
He 177 V39 – See He 177A-5/V39
He 177 V40 – See He 177A-1/V40

Whilst in a sense the following were all pre-production A-0s, they were specifically ordered for test purposes and thus were allocated identity numbers '1' to '20', which we have shown here as 'A-01' to 'A-020' to differentiate them from the true pre-production A-0 series.

He 177A-01

W/Nr. 177 000 0016
Stammkenzeichen: DL+AP
First Flight – 7th February 1941
Similar to He 177 V8:
(see photograph on page 11)

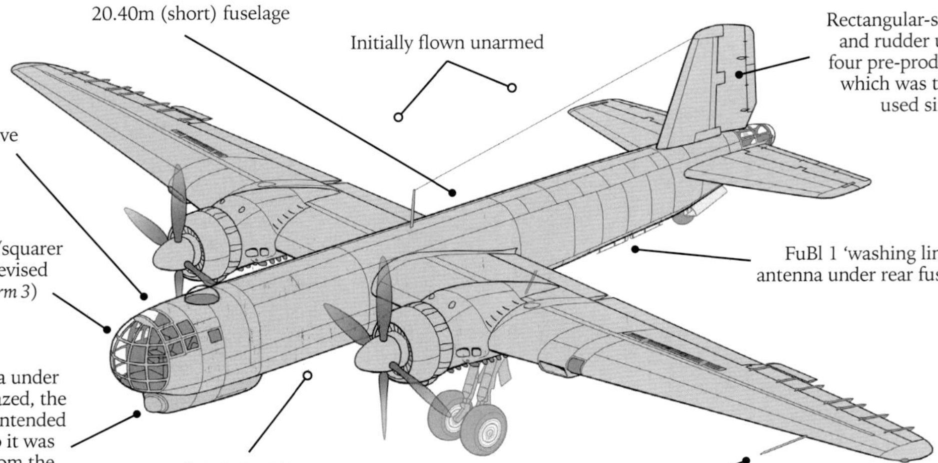

He 177A-02

W/Nr. 177 000 0017
Stammkenzeichen: DL+AQ
First Flight – 5th May 1941
Same as He 177A-01 except:

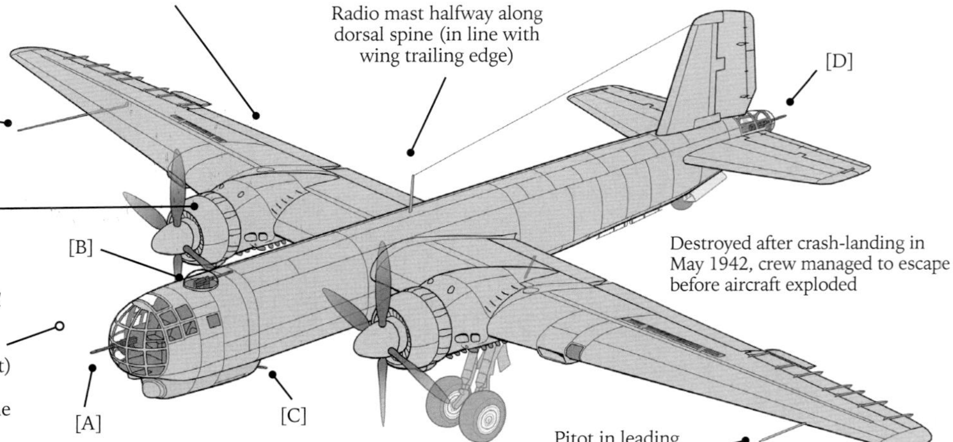

The A-02 was well photographed, this shot is one of a series taken during an air-to-air sortie. By this stage the type had adopted a more familiar overall shape

He 177A-03

W/Nr. 177 0000 0018
Stammkennzeichen: DL+AR
Same as He 177A-02 except:

Used for electrical, radio and hydraulic tests at Rechlin

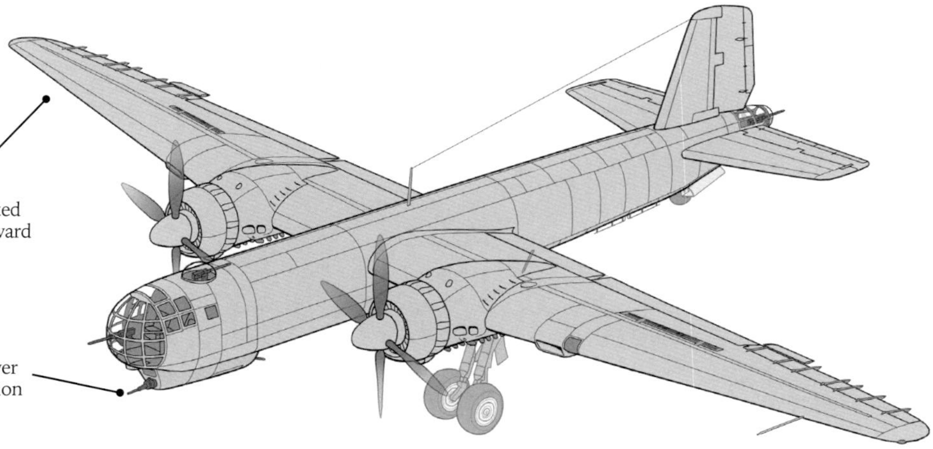

No instrument probe fitted below, and projecting forward of the starboard wing

MG FF cannon in lower nose (A2-*Stand*) position

He 177A-04 (V26)

W/Nr. 177 000 0019
Stammkennzeichen: GA+QM*
Same as He 177A-03 except:

**The Stammkennzeichen was out of sequence here, as the next number (DL+AS had been allocated to the He 280 V1)*

Selected for testing remotely-controlled defensive armament (as V26) and sent to E-Stelle Tarnewitz (other state Lärz) on the 28th October 1941.
The only surviving images show this aircraft without any armament fitted, probably before it went to Tarnewitz (when it was like the A-03), as no photographs, diagrams of written description survives of what exactly the ‘ remotely-controlled defensive armament’ was, we have done our isometric with it fitted with the aft dorsal turret as per the A-3 production series and the sighting done via the cupola aft of the cockpit

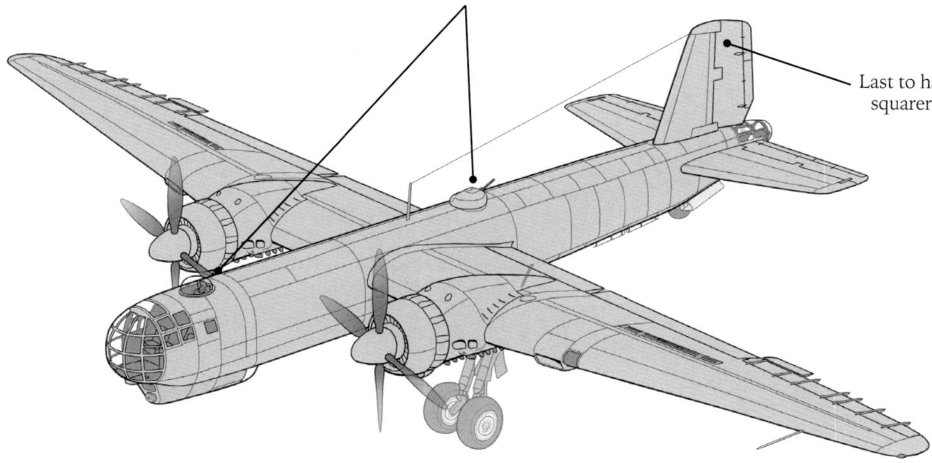

Last to have the early squarer fin/rudder

He 177A-04 – Revised

Same as He 177A-04 (V26) except:

The remote-controlled armament fitted at Tarnewitz would most likely have been removed

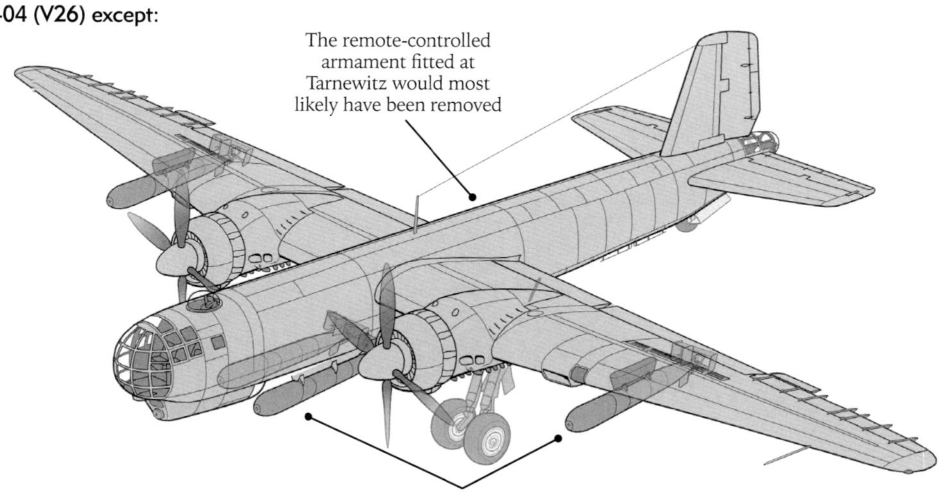

Used for testing the carriage of aerial torpedoes, modified by Lufthansa at Berlin-Staaken to carry two LT 5 torpedoes under the forward fuselage and one under each wing

No images survive of this configuration, so our isometric is purely based on written accounts

He 177A-05

W/Nr. 177 000 0020
Stammkenzeichen: GA+QN
Same as He 177A-03 except:

Some sources list this as the V9, but that was converted from the A-08

Crashed and destroyed at Priepert 13th June 1942 after a con-rod failed in one engine

No images survive of this airframe (other than a close-up of the tail), so our isometric is purely based on written accounts

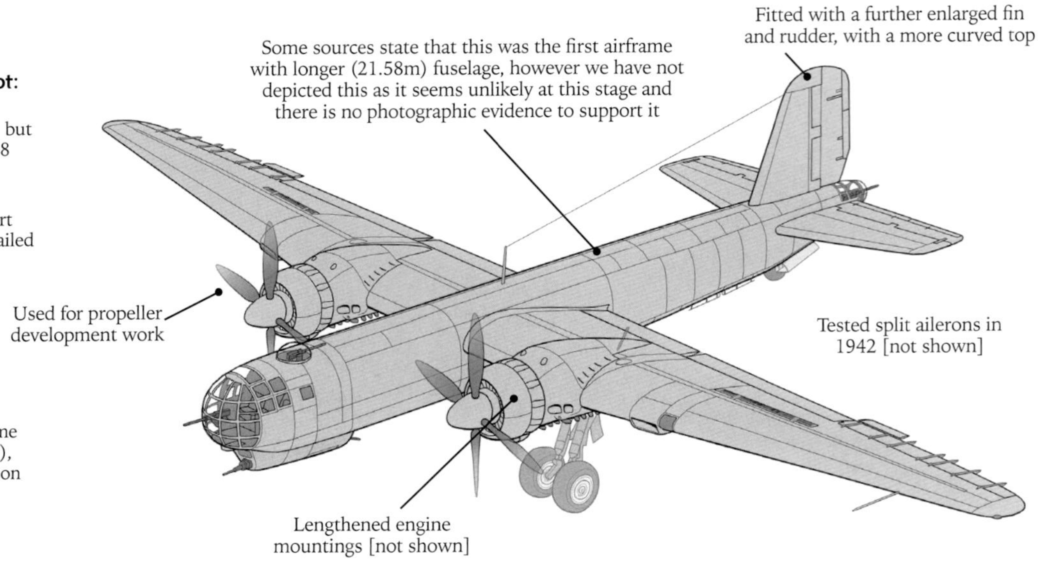

He 177A-06

W/Nr. 177 000 0021
Stammkenzeichen: GA+QO
First Flight – 21st October 1941
No data or images are available for this airframe, so we assume it is similar/the same as the A-05 (*see above*)
• Some sources list this as the V10, but that was converted from the A-09

He 177A-07

W/Nr. 177 000 0022
Stammkenzeichen: GA+QP
Same as He 177A-03 except:

Delivered to *Erprobungsstaffel 177* at Rechlin for evaluation

90% damaged at Rechlin on the 10th February 1942 (some sources state 70% damage on the 11th February) after it caught fire during static testing of the heating system when the fuel was jettisoned

Some sources list this as the V11, but that was converted from the A-10

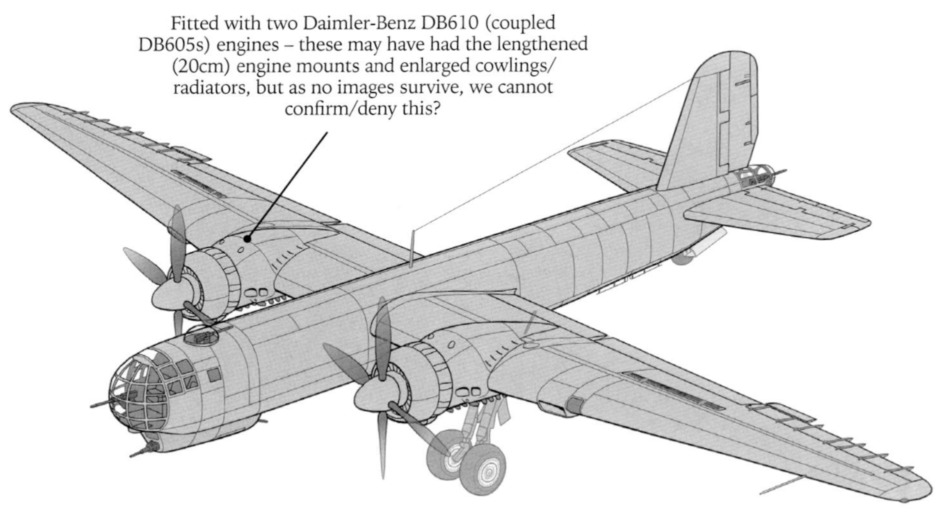

He 177A-08 – Initial

W/Nr. 177 000 0023
Stammkenzeichen: GA+QQ
First Flight – 6th February 1942
Same as He 177A-03 except:

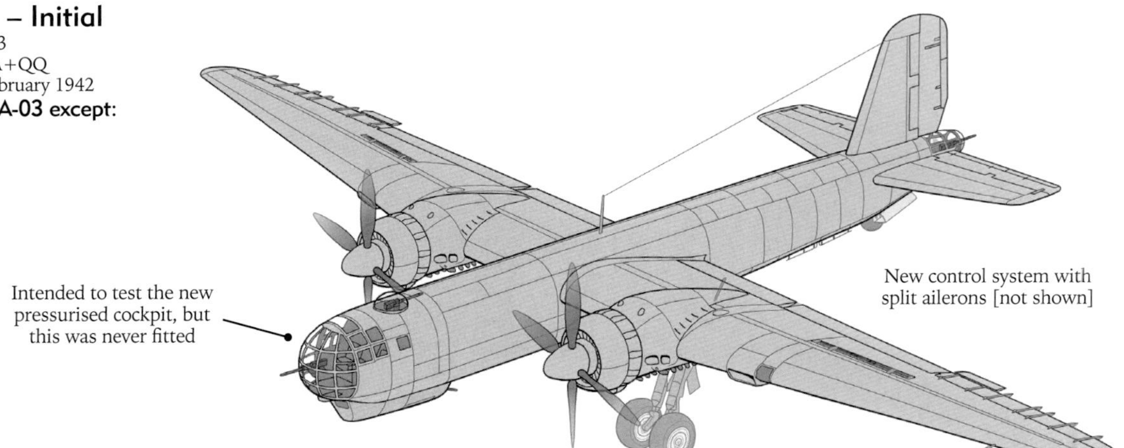

He 177A-08 as the V9

Same as He 177A-08 – Initial except:

This was later rebuilt to become the He 177 V102 (see elsewhere)

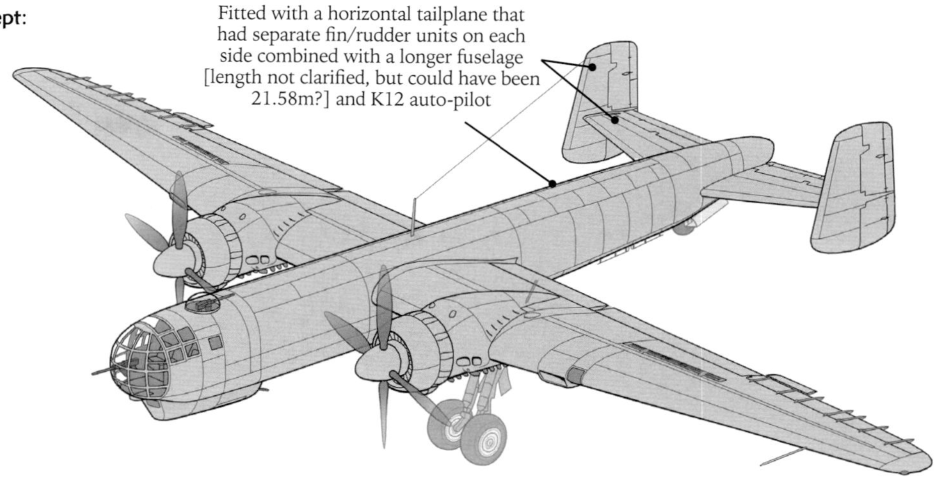

He 177A-09 (V10)

W/Nr. 177 000 0024
Stammkenzeichen: GA+QR
First Flight – 5th February 1942

Same as He 177A-03 except:

Crash-landed on the 20th February 1943

All testing abandoned from 3rd November 1943

By 2nd May 1944 it was listed to be cannibalised for spares, but by 28th June 1944 it was with Heinkel for training purposes, ultimate fate unknown

No images survive of this airframe, so our isometric is purely based on written accounts

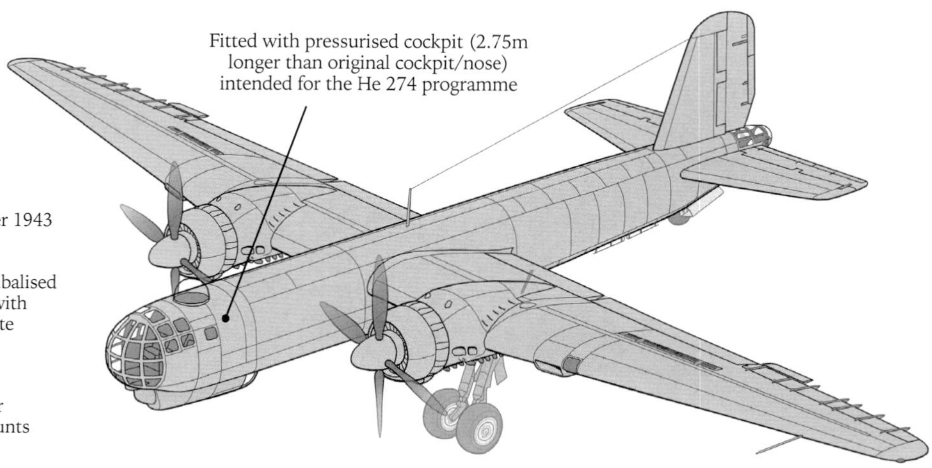

He 177A-010 (V11)

W/Nr. 177 000 0025
Stammkenzeichen: GA+QS

Same as He 177A-03 except:

All testing abandoned from 3rd November 1943

On the 2nd May 1944 it was grounded due to staff shortages, but its ultimate fate is unknown

No images survive of this airframe, so our isometric is purely based on written accounts

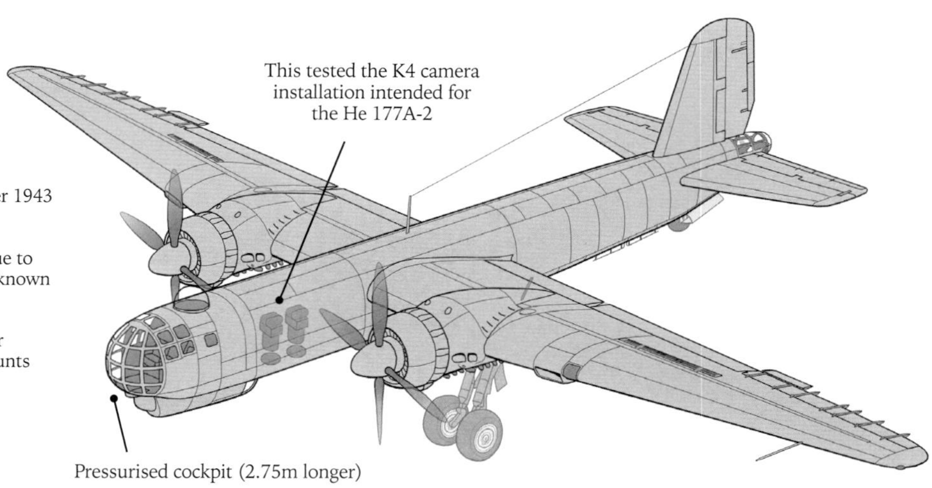

He 177A-011

W/Nr. 177 0000 0026
Stammkenzeichen: GA+QT
Same as He 177A-03, but as no images exist, we cannot offer an isometric

- Crashed and caught fire (probably due to fuel leak) in the Müritzsee region on the 18th February 1942 (all crew killed)

He 177A-012

W/Nr. 177 0000 0027
Stammkenzeichen: GA+QU
First Flight – 7th November 1941
Same as He 177A-03, but as no images exist, we cannot offer an isometric

- To *Erprobungsstaffel 177*
- Two reports of loss exist, one states it was 60% damaged on the 12th June 1942 at Rechlin due to elevator failure in shallow dive, the other states it was badly damaged at Fassberg on the 14th October 1942

He 177A-013

W/Nr. 177 0000 0028
Stammkenzeichen: GA+QV
Same as He 177A-03, but as no images exist, we cannot offer an isometric

- To *Erprobungsstaffel 177*
- Lost when the wing broke off after too fast a pull-out from a dive was initiated over the Plauer lake near Rechlin on the 16th July 1942

He 177A-014

W/Nr. 177 000 0029
Stammkenzeichen: GA+QW
Just a single front-view image of this airframe exists, which is not enough really to produce an isometric, we have however included one

Based on the He 177A-03 except:

(see the only known photograph on page 13)

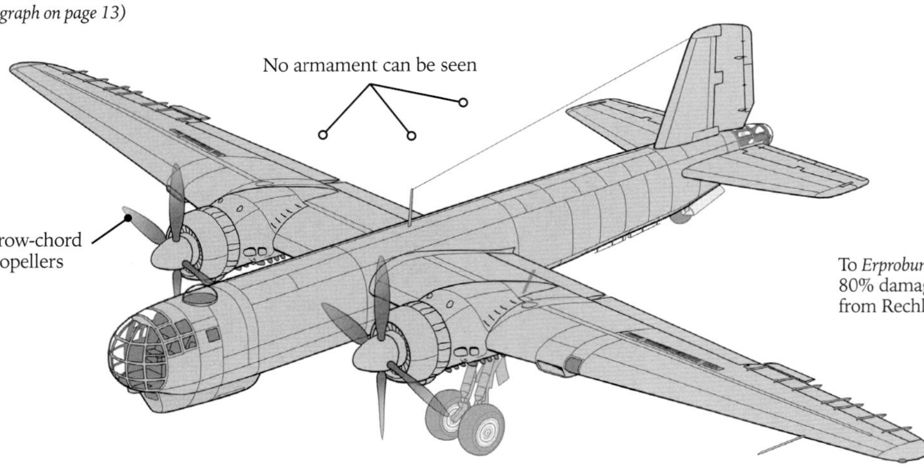

He 177A-015 (V18)

W/Nr. 177 0000 0030
Stammkenzeichen: GA+QX
Just a single close-up image of the armament exists, which is not enough really to produce an isometric, we have however included one

Based on the He 177A-03 except:

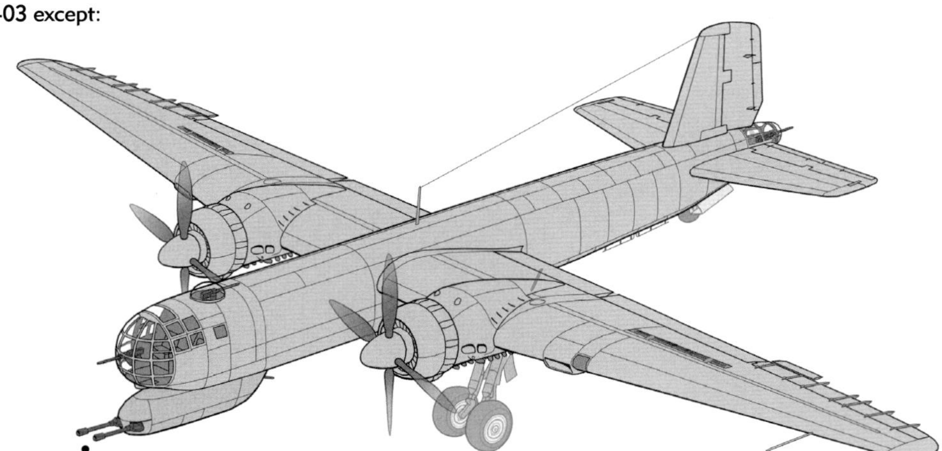

As the V18 this was the second pattern aircraft (after A-1/U1 GI+BR) fitted with heavy armament of two Mk 101 30mm cannon in revised/deep chin position with rear access hatch

These had canvas convers at the base of each cannon, which may indicate these had limited movement

He 177A-016

W/Nr. 177 0000 0031
Stammkenzeichen: GA+QY
Nothing known, but some accounts state the A-016 to A-020 were the last airframes to have dive brakes?

He 177A-017

W/Nr. 177 0000 0032
Stammkenzeichen: GA+QZ
Same as He 177A-03, but as no images exist, we cannot offer an isometric

- To *Erprobungsstaffel 177*

He 177A-018

W/Nr. 177 0000 0033
Nothing known

He 177A-019

W/Nr. 177 0000 0034
Same as He 177A-03, but as no images exist, we cannot offer an isometric

- Destroyed at Tarnewitz due to oil loss

He 177A-020

W/Nr. 177 0000 0035
Same as He 177A-03, but as no images exist, we cannot offer an isometric

- To *Erprobungsstaffel 177*
- Crashed on the 16th April 1942

Note: The A-01 to A-20 (W/Nrs.177 0000 0001 to 0035) were all built by Heinkel at Rostock-Marienehe, although some accounts state that the 'A-016 to A-021'(?) were built by the Marnemunde plant, while others state the A-01 to A-015 were built at Rostock-Marienehe and A-016 to A-020 were built at the Oranienburg factory and given W/Nrs.32001 to 32015, however those were the fifteen true pre-production A-0s built by Heinkel at Oranienburg (*see next entry*)

Pre-Production

He 177A-0 – Early Production

W/Nrs. 2001 to 2015
Stammkenzeichen: DR+II to DR+IW
All built by Heinkel at Oranienburg
W/Nrs. 5001 to 5005
All built by Arado at Brandenburg
Short, medium or long-range bombers

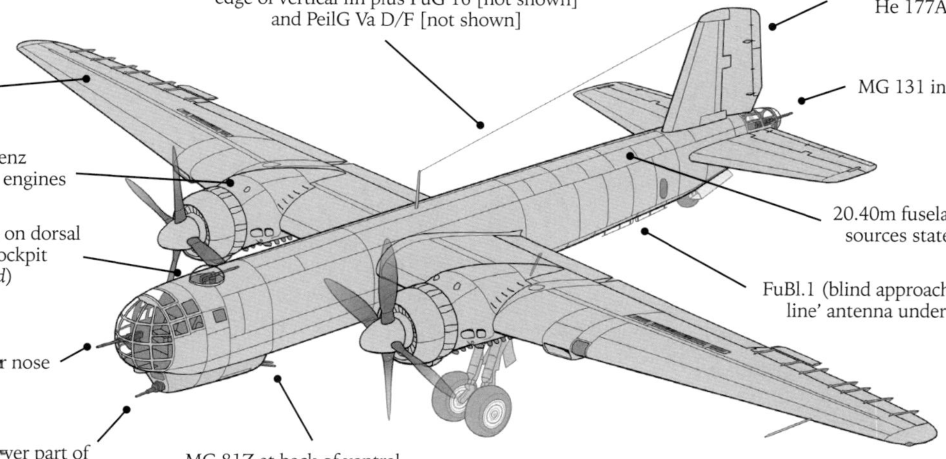

Note: 5001 was the V15, 5004 was the V16 and 5005 was the V17 (all see elsewhere)

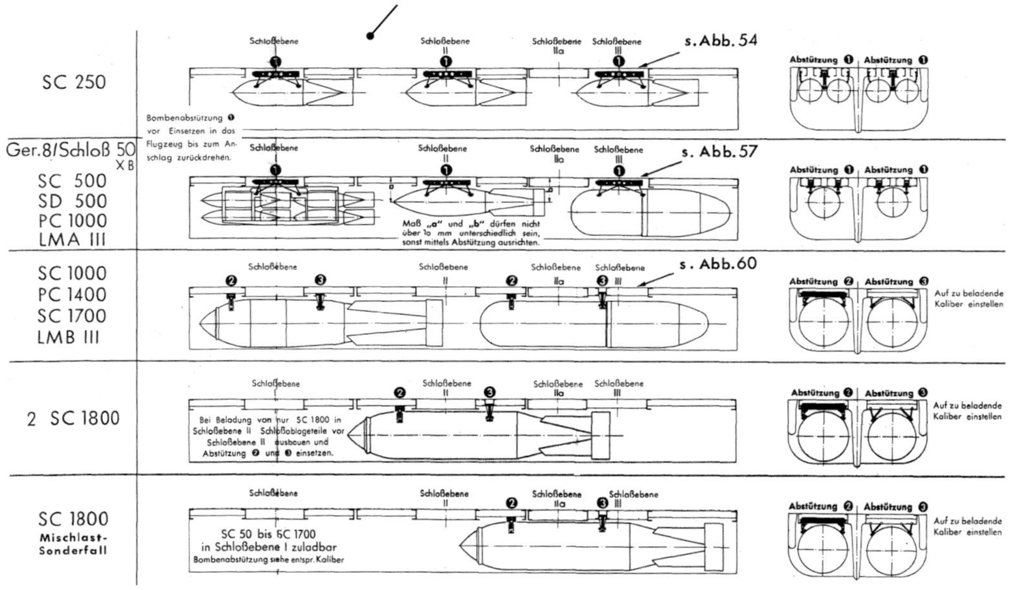

An He 177A-0 (unlikely to be the A-03 as some sources state) used by E-Stelle Rechlin in relation to the planned 20mm MG FF installation in the A2-*Stand* - the shape of gondola and the A2-stand are very different from that which would be used by production aircraft

He 177A-0 – Late Production

Same as He 177A-0 – Early Production except:

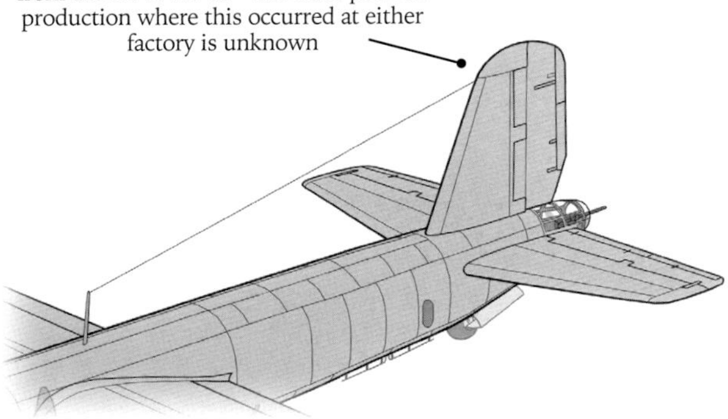

He 177A-0 (V15)

Stammkenzeichen: W/Nr.5001

Same as He 177A-0 – Early Production, but as no images exist, we cannot offer an isometric

- Used for test flight vibrations up to 700km/h
- Split ailerons
- From 2nd May 1944 carried out vibration test with slotted ailerons up to 710km/h
- Undertook Katapultkanzel (cockpit ejection seat) and braking parachute trials
- Destroyed in accident 24th June 1944

He 177A-0 (V16)

W/Nr.5004

Same as He 177A-0 – Early Production, but as no images exist, we cannot offer an isometric

- Used for He 177A-3 development work
- Tested radio equipment

He 177A-0 W/Nr.32913

Same as He 177A-0 – Late Production except:

(see photopraph on page 13)

Note: This looks to have been an A-0-series airframe that has been mated with an A-3 fuselage, or the existing fuselage was upgraded to A-3/R2 standard?

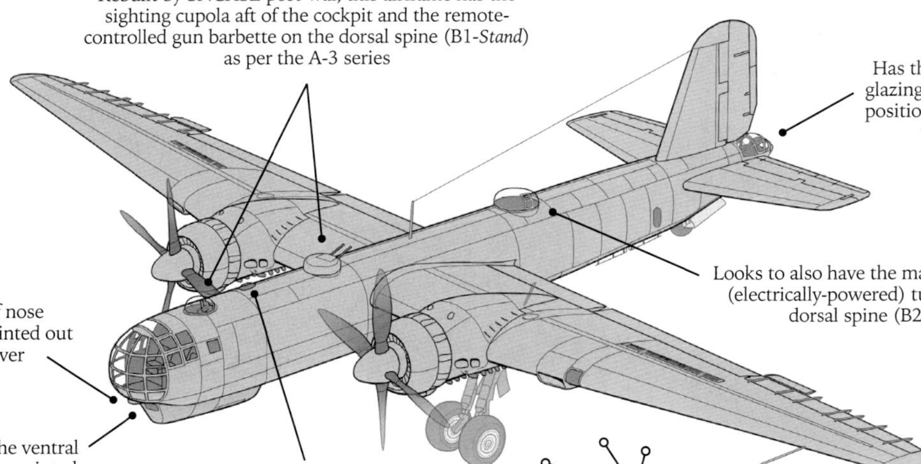

He 177A-0 (V17)

W/Nr.5005

Same as He 177A-0 – Early Production except:

Used for He 177A-3 development work

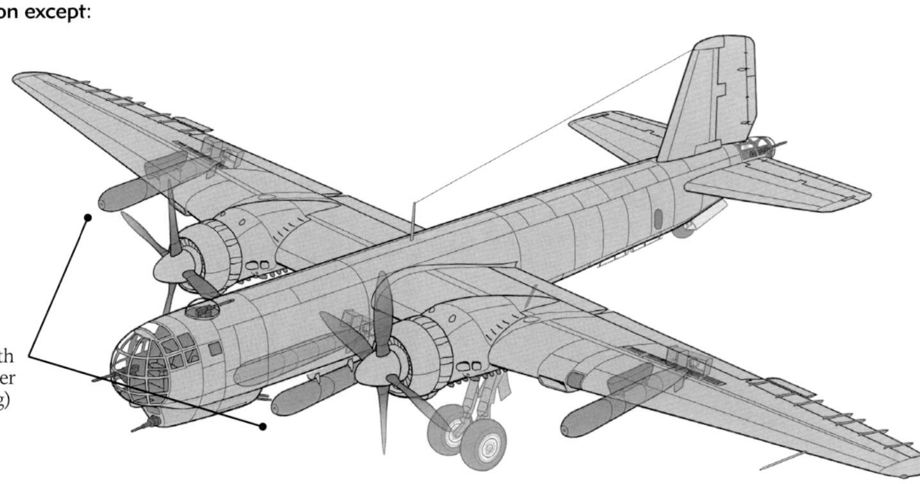

Production

He 177A-1 (W/Nrs. 332101 to 332142)

Stammkenzeichen: VF+QA to VF+XR
Not all W/Nrs had the '33' prefix
Short, medium or long-range bombers

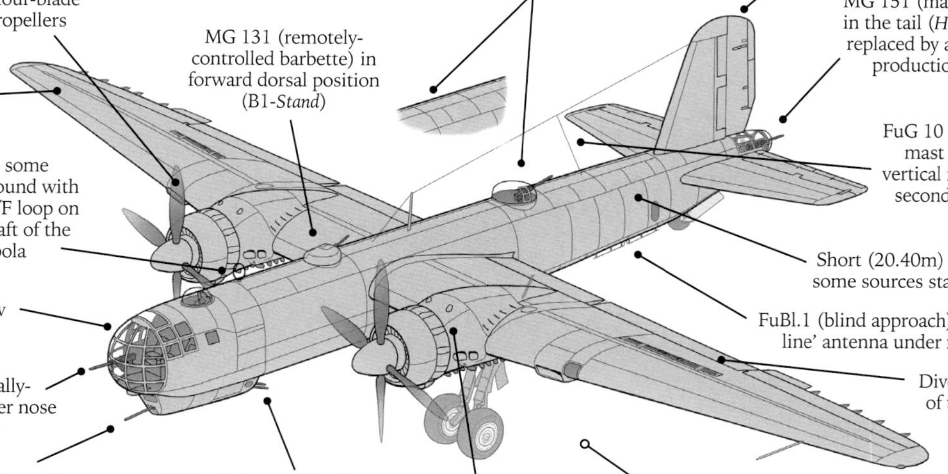

After operational evaluation by I./KG40 at Bordeaux-Mérignac in July to Sept 1942, the type was pronounced unfit for operational use and all were returned to Germany for use in second-line role. All production ceased in October 1942 in favour of the A-3 series

Note: W/Nr.2101 was fitted with DB610s as the V19 and became the prototype for the A-3 series, W/Nr.2103 became the V21 as the He 177A-5 prototype, W/Nr.2104 became the V22 as the second He 177A-5 prototype, W/Nr.2112 became the V23 as the He 177A-5 and engine development prototype – *see separate listings elsewhere*

Whilst it is almost impossible to determine the W/Nr. batches for known images of the A-1 series, this does show what is obviously an early machine attracting quite a lot of attention at Lechfield in June 1943

He 177A-1 (W/Nrs. 135006 to 135025)

Stammkenzeichen: ND+SA to ND+SS
Not all W/Nrs had the '13' prefix (official documents express the W/Nr. as '177.0135xxx')

Same as He 177A-1 (W/Nrs. 332101 to 332142) except:

Built by Arado at Brandenburg-Neuendorf

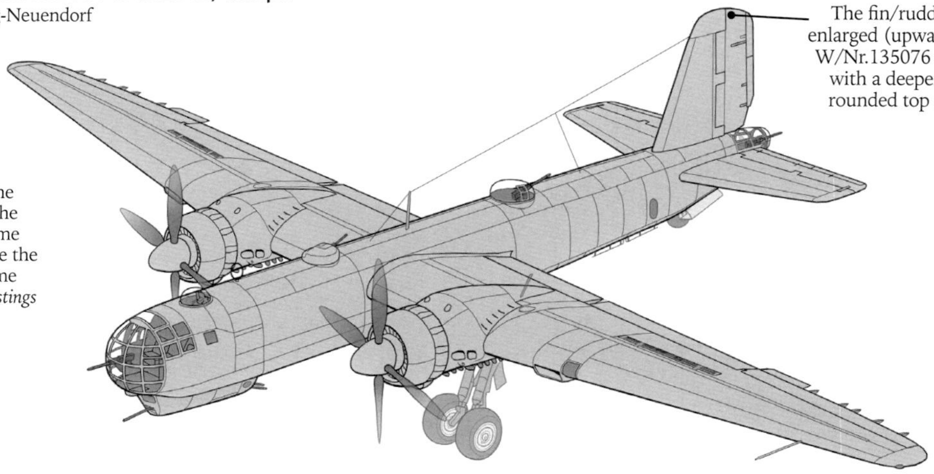

Note: W/Nr.135018 became the He 177 V30, 135024 became the He 177 V24, W/Nr.2121 became the V36, W/Nr.135018 became the He 177 V30 and 135024 became the He 177 V24 – *see separate listings elsewhere*

He 177A-1 (W/Nrs. 15151 to 15280)

Not all W/Nrs had the '1' prefix
Same as He 177A-1 (W/Nrs. 332101 to 332142) – *see isometric previous page*
Built by Arado at Brandenburg-Neuendorf

Note: W/Nr.15151 (GI+BL) became the He 177 V12, W/Nr.15152 (GI+BM) became the He 177 V14, W/Nr.15153 (GI+BN) became the He 177 V25, W/Nr.15155 (GI+BP) became the He 177 V29, W/Nr.15203 (VE+UC) became the He 177 V27, W/Nr.15254 (VF+RD) became the He 177 V20 – *see separate listings elsewhere*
W/Nr.15154, 15158, 15161, 15164, 15180, 15191, 15214, 15215, 15217, 15231, 15232, 15233, 15241, 15242, 15250, 15256, 15259, 15263 and 15269 all crashed without seeing any operational use

He 177A-1, W/Nr.15266, VF+RP at Bourges in 1944

He 177A-1 (V12)

W/Nr. 15151
Stammkenzeichen: GI+BL
Same as He 177A-1 (W/Nrs 15151 to 15280) except:

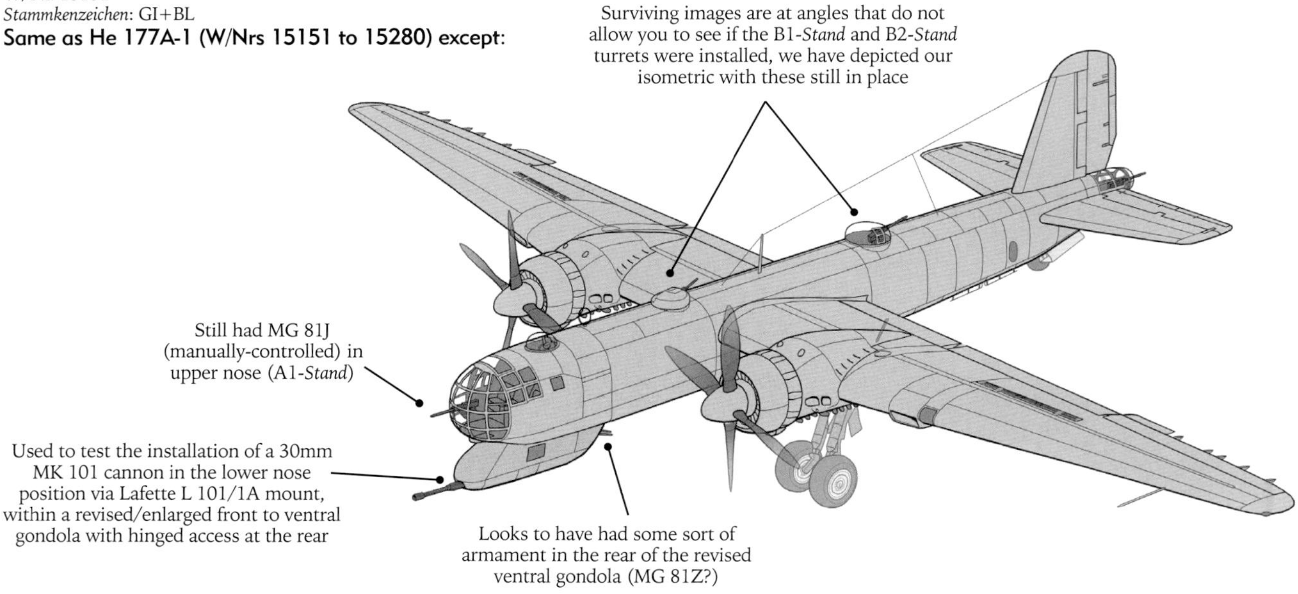

The He 177A-1, W/Nr.15141 as the V12 (GI+BL) on jacks prior to undercarriage retraction tests

He 177A-1 (V14)

W/Nr. 15152
Stammkenzeichen: GI+BM
Same as He 177A-1 (W/Nrs 15151 to 15280) except:

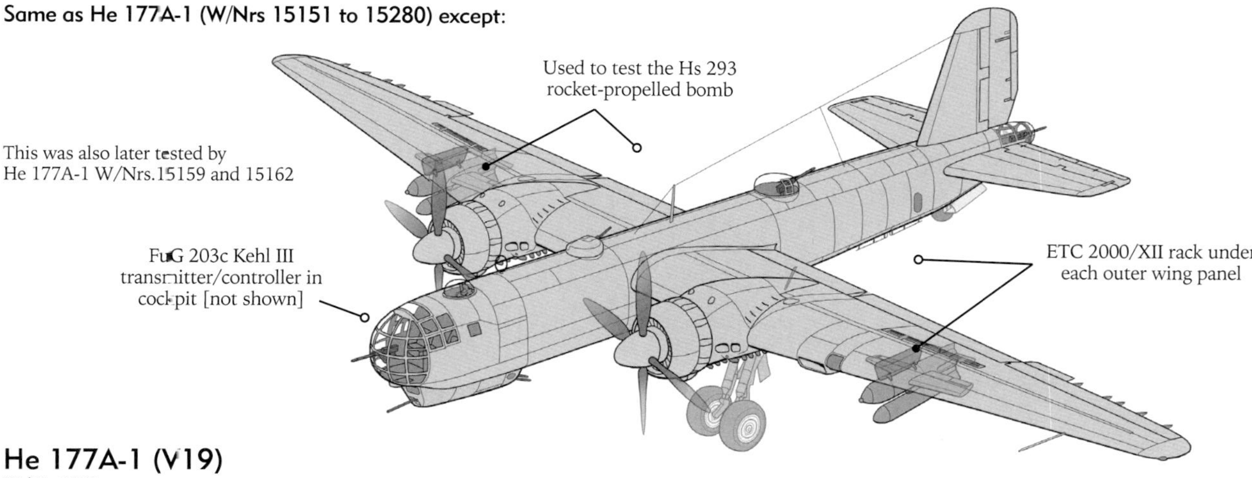

He 177A-1 (V19)

W/Nr. 2101
Stammkenzeichen: VF+QA
First Flight – 22nd March 1943
Same as He 177A-1 (W/Nrs 2101 to 2142)

- First to be fitted with Daimler-Benz DB610 (coupled DB605) engines
- These were mounted 20cm further forward and had enlarged cowlings and radiators
- Also tested split ailerons
- Lost in an engine fire at Rechlin 13th November 1943

He 177A-1 (V20)

W/Nr. 15254
Stammkenzeichen: VF+RD
Same as He 177A-1 (W/Nrs 15151 to 15280) except:

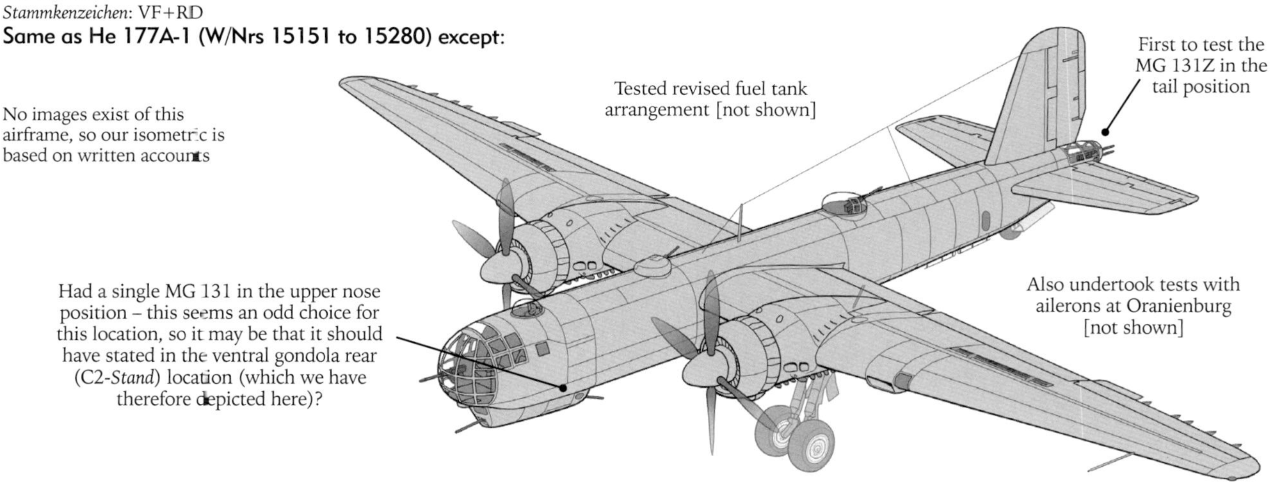

He 177A-1 (V21)

W/Nr. 2103
Stammkenzeichen: VF+QC (other sources state VF+QB, but that was W/Nr.2102)
Same as He 177A-1 (W/Nr.2101 to 2142) except:

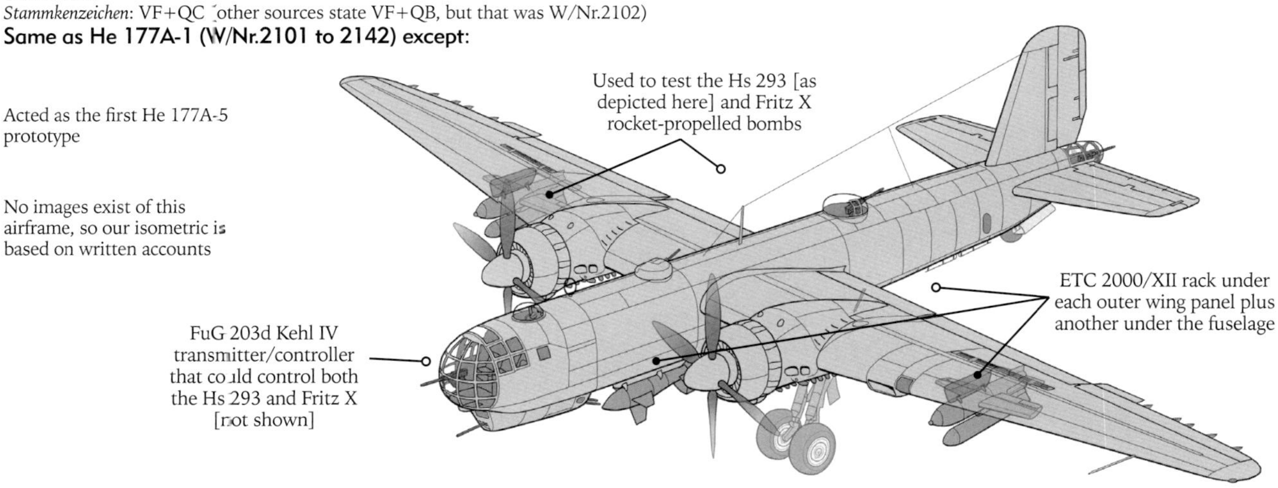

He 177A-1 (V22)

W/Nr. 2104
Stammkenzeichen: VF+QD
Same as He 177A-1 (W/Nr.2101 to 2142) except:

- Acted as the second He 177A-5 prototype
- Fitted with split ailerons
- Tested superchargers and exhaust systems at Rechlin
- Same as He 177A-1 (W/Nrs 2101 to 2142), but as no images exist, we cannot offer an isometric
- 75% damaged after crash-landing at Chateaudun airfield on the 19th April 1943 due to an engine fire
- Many sources list this was the prototype for the A-6 series, but this is incorrect
- No images exist of this airframe, so we are unable to offer an isometric

He 177A-1 (V23)

W/Nr. 2112
Stammkenzeichen: VL+QL
Same as He 177A-1 (W/Nr.2101 to 2142) except:

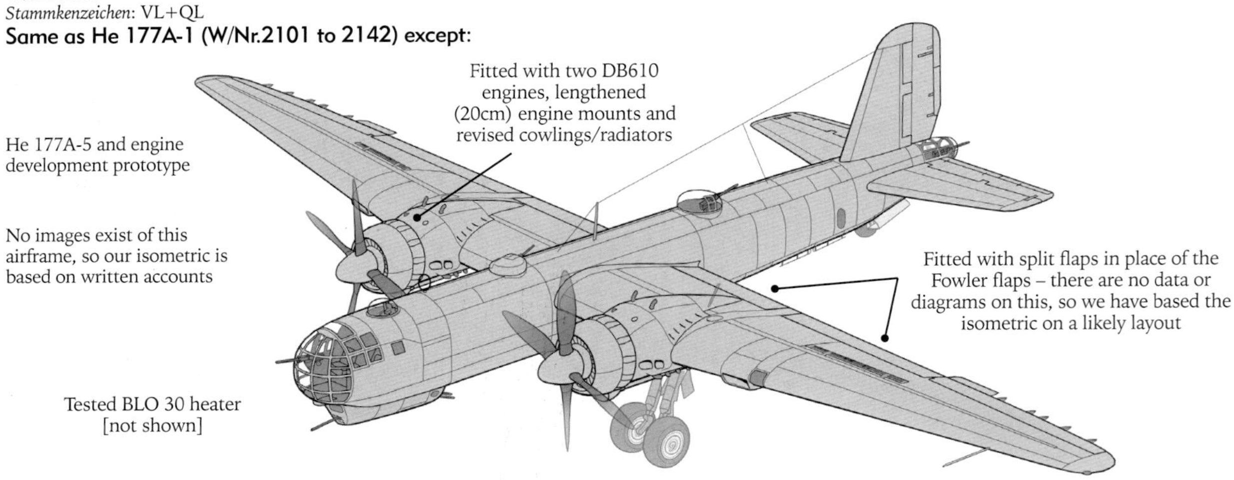

He 177A-1 (V24)

W/Nr. 5024
Stammkenzeichen: ND+SS
Same as He 177A-1 (W/Nrs 135006 to 135024) except:

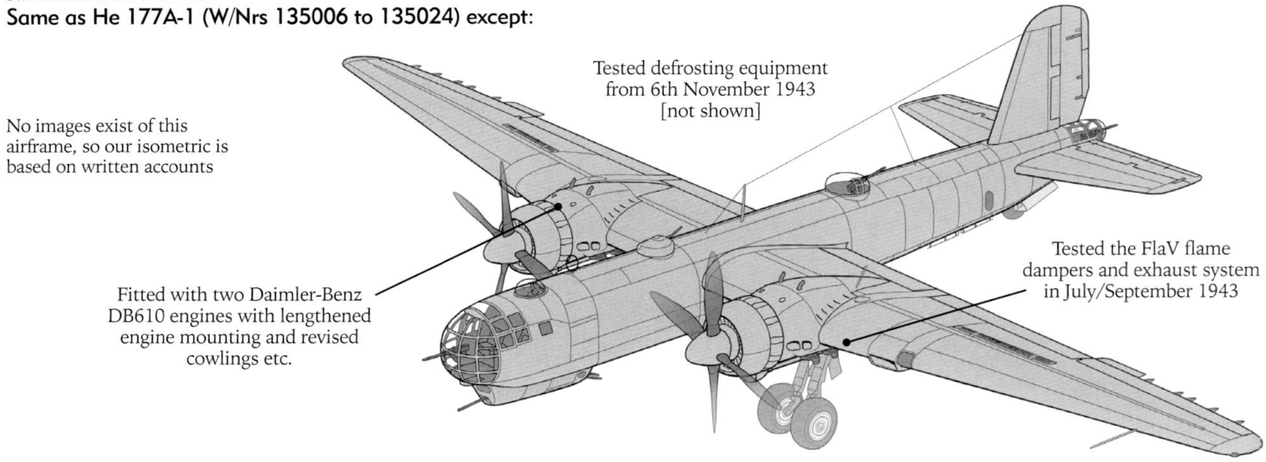

He 177A-1 (V25)

W/Nr. 15153
Stammkenzeichen: GI+BN
Same as He 177A-1 (W/Nrs 15151 to 15280) except:

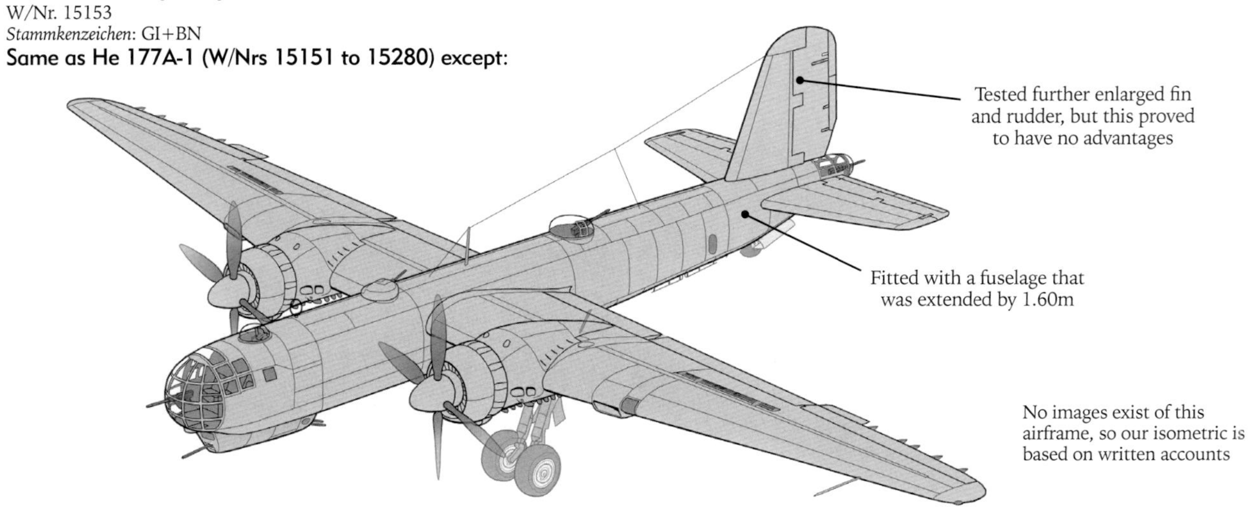

He 177A-1 (V27)

W/Nr. 15203
Stammkenzeichen: VE–UC

Same as He 177A-1 (W/Nrs 15151 to 15280) except:

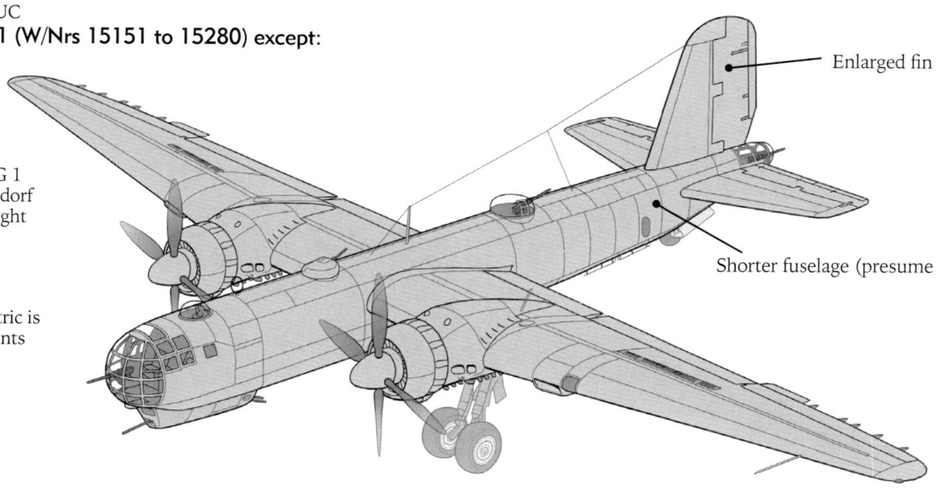

Enlarged fin and rudder

Shorter fuselage (presume 20.40m)

Later delivered to I./KG 1 but crashed at Wichersdorf 5th April 1944 and caught fire (98% damage)

No images exist of this airframe, so our isometric is based on written accounts

He 177A-1 (V28)

W/Nr. 535356
Same as He 177A-1 (W/Nrs 15151 to 15280) except:

- Tested Patin auto-pilot system, 22nd July 1943
- As no images exist of this airframe and the Patin system makes no external changes, we have not offered an isometric of this airframe

He 177A-1 (V29)

W/Nr. 15155
Stammkenzeichen: GI+BF

Same as He 177A-1 (W/Nrs 15151 to 15280) except:

Used at Lärz to test the installation of a twin-barrel, remote-controlled turret in place of the MG 151/20 in the lower nose position – although all surviving images show it without any guns in this position?

A poor image, but one of the few that shows the V29, seen here after running off the edge of the taxiway at E-Stelle Rechlin

He 177A-1 (V30)

W/Nr.135018
Stammkenzeichen: ND+SM

Same as He 177A-1 (W/Nrs 135005 to 135024) except:

No images exist of this airframe, so our isometric is based on written accounts

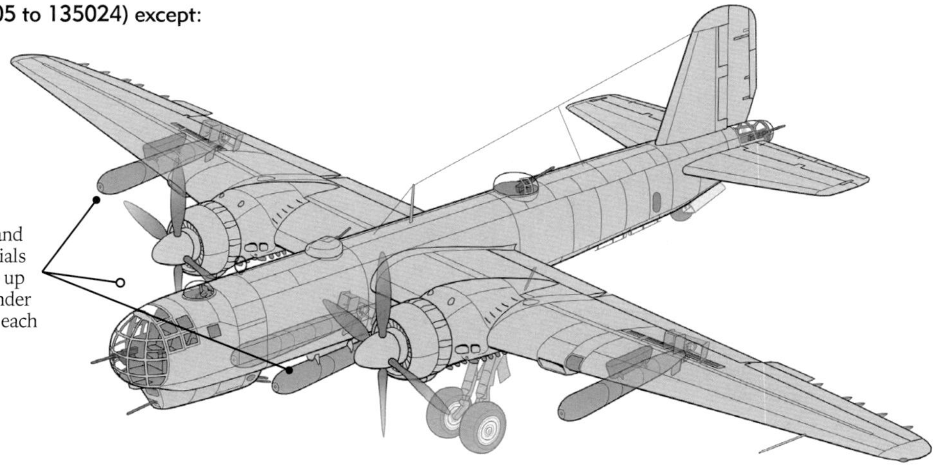

Used at E-Stelle Travemünde and Gotenhafen-Hexengrund for trials with LT F5b aerial torpedoes – up to four could be carried (two under forward fuselage and one under each outer wing panel)

He 177A-1 (V36)

W/Nr. 332121
Stammkenzeichen: VF+QU

Same as He 177A-1 (W/Nrs/332101 to 332142) except:

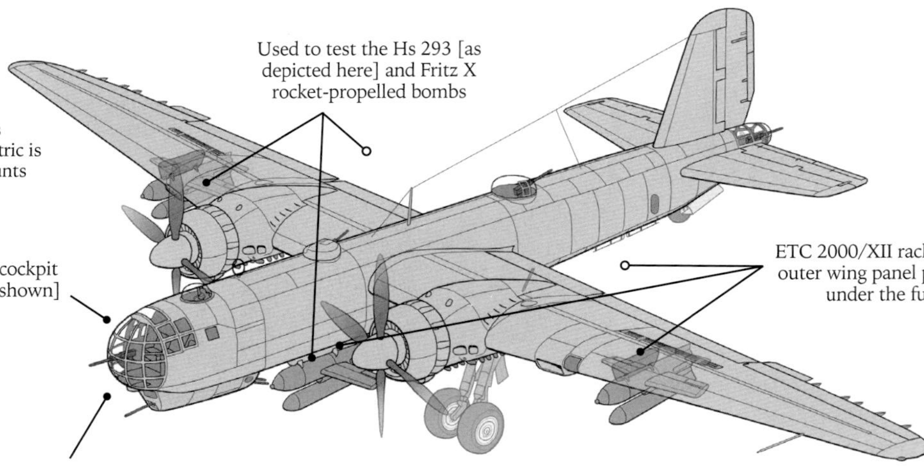

He 177A-1/R1

Same as He 177A-1 except:

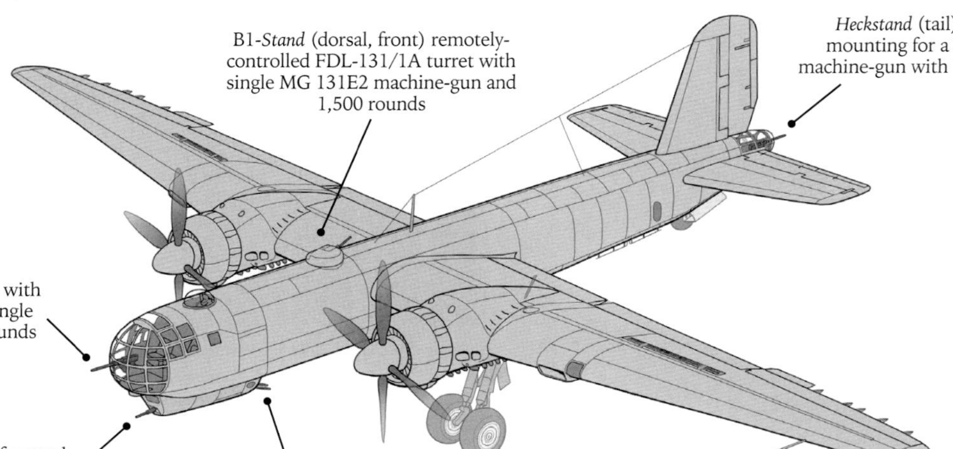

This diagram from the manual shows the revised armament layout of the R1 set

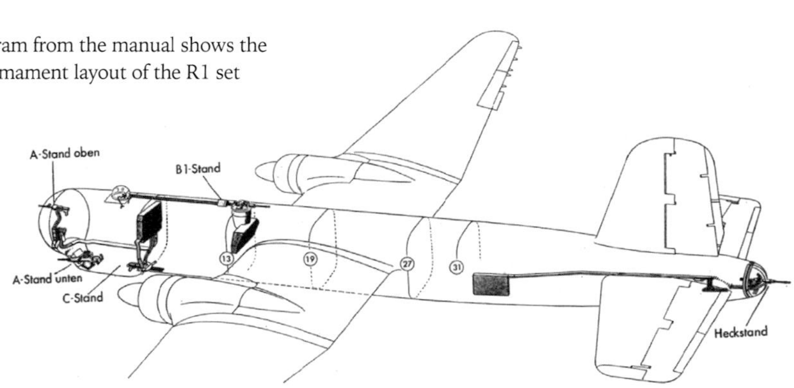

He 177A-1/R2

Same as He 177A-1/R1 except:

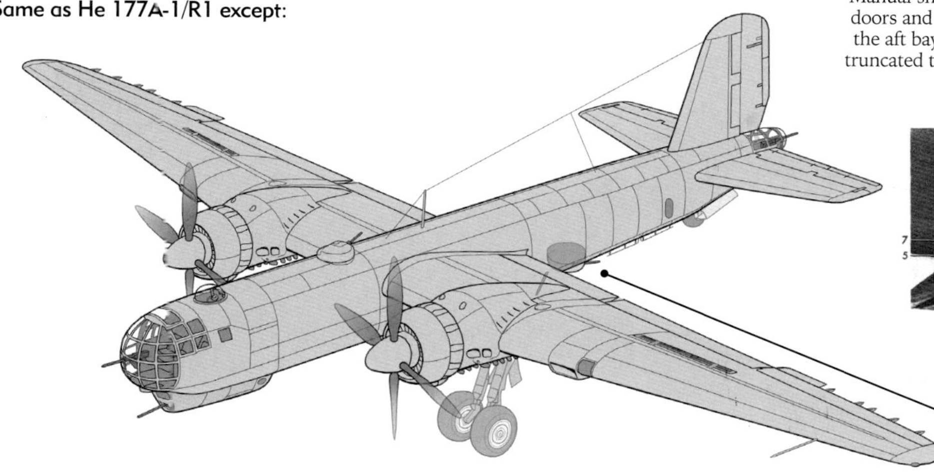

Manual shows the bomb bays had flat (not bulged) doors and although the C2-*Stand* was in the rear of the aft bay, the doors were still there, just revised/truncated to accommodate the turret (which sat in a new plated section)?

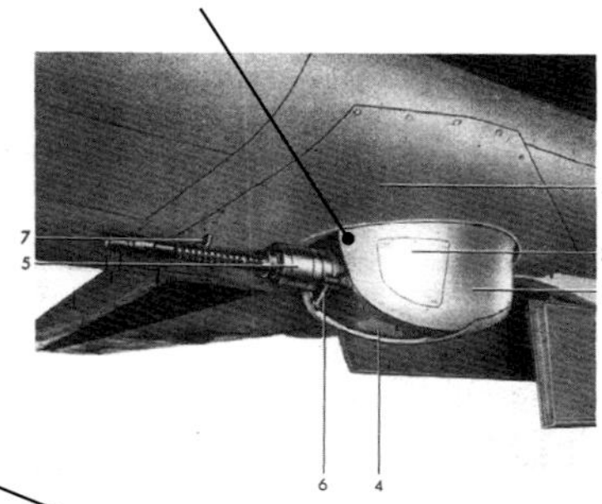

New C2-*Stand* with one FDL 131/1A remote-controlled turret for MG 131 and 1,500 rounds replacing the weapon in the C1-*Stand* (sighting unit was mounted in the rear of the ventral gondola)

This diagram, also from the handbook, shows the revised armament layout of the R2 set

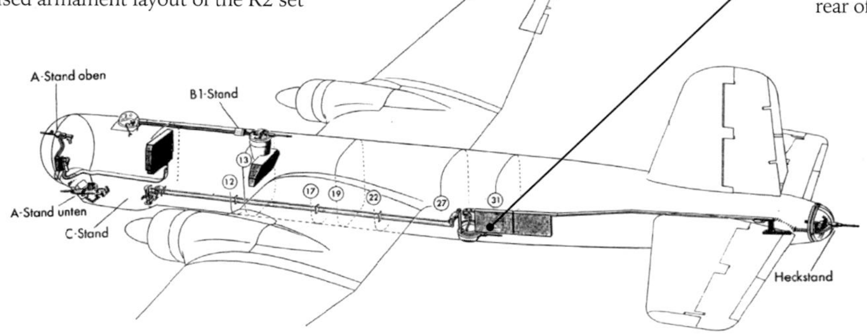

He 177A-1/R3

Same as He 177A-1/R2 except:

A1-*Stand* (nose) revised to 140/81 mount for MG 81J with only 1,000 rounds, but this mount allowed the gun to be elevated further

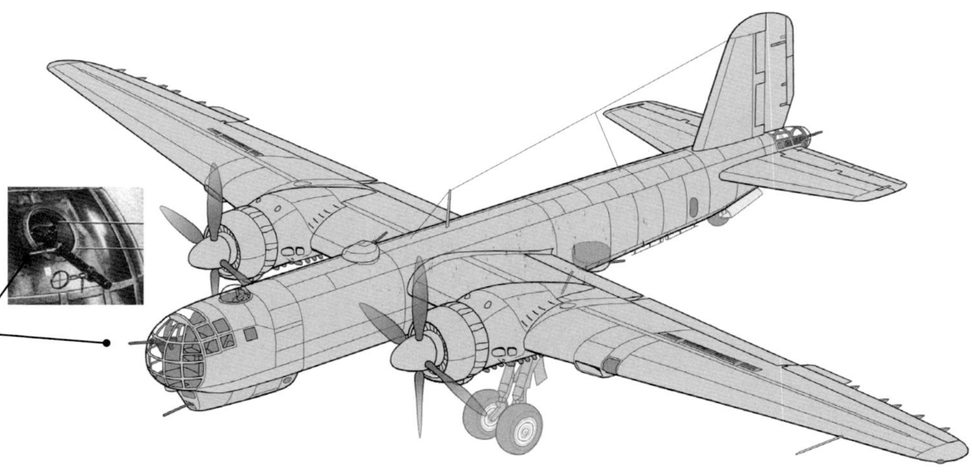

This is the revised armament layout of the R3 set

He 177A-1/R4

Same as He 177A-1/R3 except:

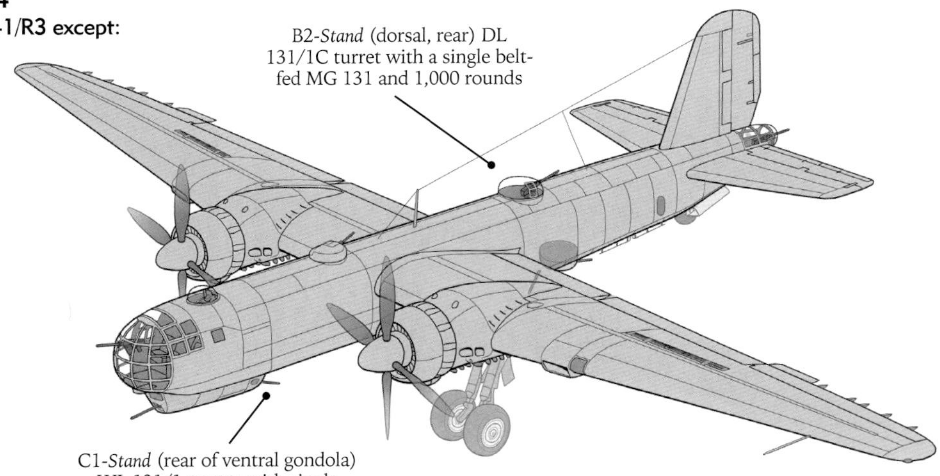

B2-*Stand* (dorsal, rear) DL 131/1C turret with a single belt-fed MG 131 and 1,000 rounds

C1-*Stand* (rear of ventral gondola) WL 131/1 mount with single MG 131 and 1,000 rounds

The revised armament layout of the R4 set

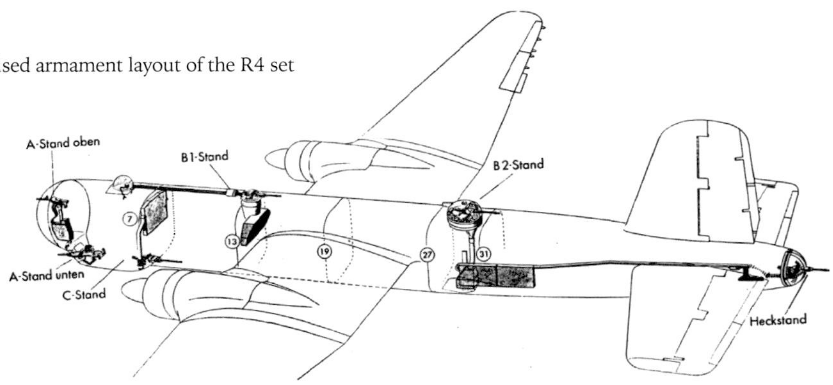

He 177A-1/U1*

Same as He 177A-1 except:

**Some sources list this as the A-1/U2, but that upgrade relates to the carriage of HS 293 and Fritz X*

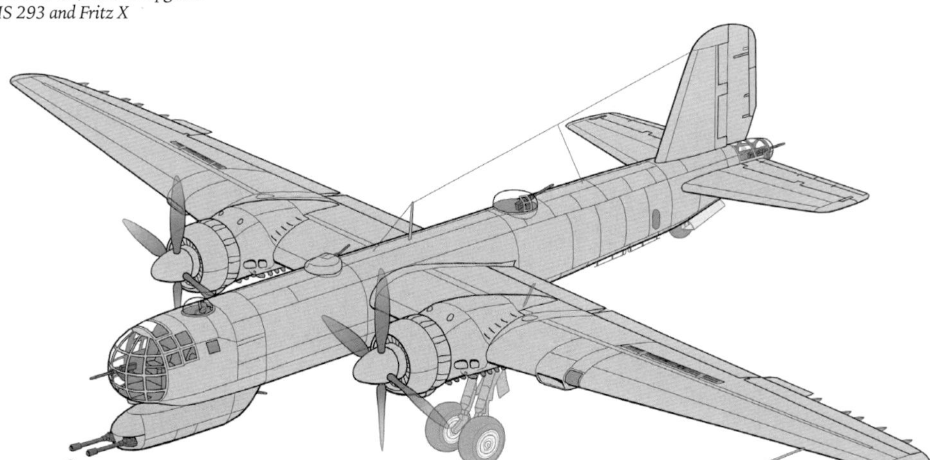

Twin (fixed) 30mm MK 101 cannon in the lower nose position, within a revised/enlarged ventral gondola with hinged access at the rear (as tested in the V18)

Alternative layout was for two semi-fixed MK 101 in the nose position with canvas covers around the base of each barrel [as depicted here]

The first pattern aircraft was GI+BR, while the first delivered to the Luftwaffe was GI+BZ; also known are GI+BX, W/Nr.15170, GI+BQ, GI+BU, W/Nr.15169 and BL+FI

It is believed that two or three of these were issued to 10./KG 40 (which became 15./KG 40 20th May 1942) for long-range, anti-shipping work, but none saw action

He 177A-1/U2

Same as He 177A-1 except:

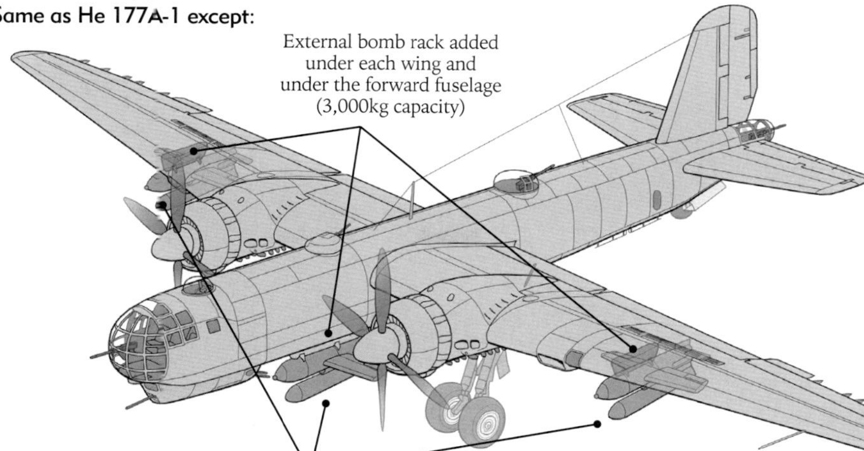

He 177A-2

Special Long-Range Reconnaissance version

- Two Daimler-Benz DB610 engines
- Pressurised cockpit
- MG FF in nose removed
- Fitted with GM-1 nitrous oxide power-boost system for engines
- Fitted with camera equipment (precise types not known, some sources state 'K4', but no period reference or diagrams can be found of this equipment/installation) in bomb bay
- Range of 5,800km was to be increased to 9,500km with the use of in-flight refuelling
- It was intended to make a limited production run of 40 such aircraft, but in the end, none were built

Note: He 177A-1s W/Nr 5215 (VE+UQ), W/Nr 5161 (GI+BV), W/Nr 5210 (VE+UJ), W/Nr 5211 (VE+UK) and W/Nr 5212 (VE+UL) were all used by Versuchsstelle für Höhenflüge (Experiment Establishment for High-Altitude Flights) in temporary support of this proposed reconnaissance version of the He 177

He 177A-3 (W/Nrs. 332143 to 332252)

Stammkenzeichen: VD+XS to VD+XZ (W/Nr.332143 to 332150)
Stammkenzeichen: TP+FA to TP+FZ (W/Nr.332190 to 332215)
Stammkenzeichen: SL+WV (W/Nr.332241)
Note that the prefix '33' was not added to all W/Nrs, but we have listed them all here with it (and official documents, the W/Nr. is expressed as '177.0133xxxx')
All built by Heinkel at Oranienburg

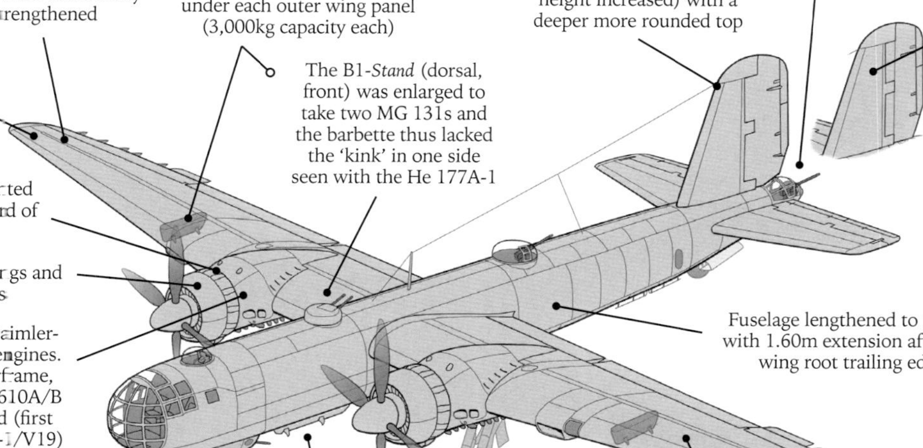

Radio equipment expanded to FuG 10P, FuG 16Z, FuBl 2F, FuG 25A IFF, Fuf 101 (radio altimeter), FuG 102, FuG 200, FuG 216 and FuG 203a (control unit for Hs 293)

As well as armour plate for the pilot's seat, B1-*Stand*, tail turret, ventral gondola and dinghy bay, this series also had additional armour for the B2-*Stand* and the equipment used to guide the Hs 293 or Fritz X (Kehl-unit) [not shown]

Intended to use guided-bombs like the Henschel Hs 293A-1

He 177A-3, WNr.332143, VD+XS of FFS(B) 16 at Burg

He 177A-3 (W/Nrs. 332351 to 332410)

Stammkenzeichen: KP+PA to KP+PZ (W/Nr.332351 to 332376)
Same as He 177A-3 (W/Nrs. 332143 to 332252*) – *see isometric previous page*
All built by Heinkel at Oranienburg

He 177A-3 (W/Nrs. 332471 to 332519)

Stammkenzeichen: DW+CK to DW+CW (W/Nr.332507 to 332519)
Same as He 177A-3 (W/Nrs. 332143 to 332252*) – *see isometric previous page*
All built by Heinkel at Oranienburg

He 177A-3 (W/Nrs. 332536 to 332555)

Same as He 177A-3 (W/Nrs. 332143 to 332252*) – *see isometric previous page*
All built by Heinkel at Oranienburg

He 177A-3 (W/Nrs. 332610 to 332629)

Same as He 177A-3 (W/Nrs. 332143 to 332252*) – *see isometric previous page*
All built by Heinkel at Oranienburg

The experimental fitment of two MG 131s in the tail position of He 177A-3, 6N+AS

He 177A-3 – Twin MG 131 (6N+AS)

W/Nr. 332618
Same as He 177A-3 (W/Nrs. 332610 to 332629) except:

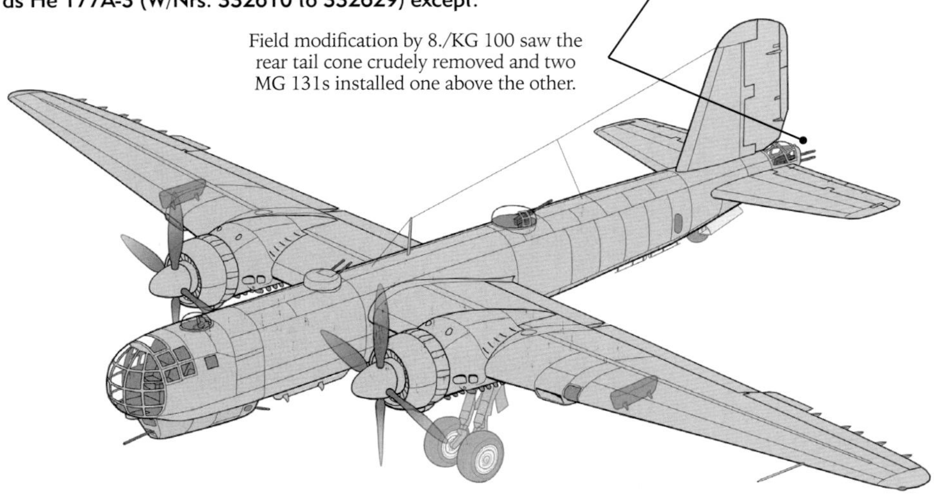

He 177A-3 (W/Nrs. 535351 to 535375)

Stammkenzeichen: GP+WA to GP+WV
Not all W/Nrs had the '53' prefix
Same as He 177A-3 (W/Nrs. 332143 to 332252*) except:
Built by Arado at Brandenburg-Neuendorf

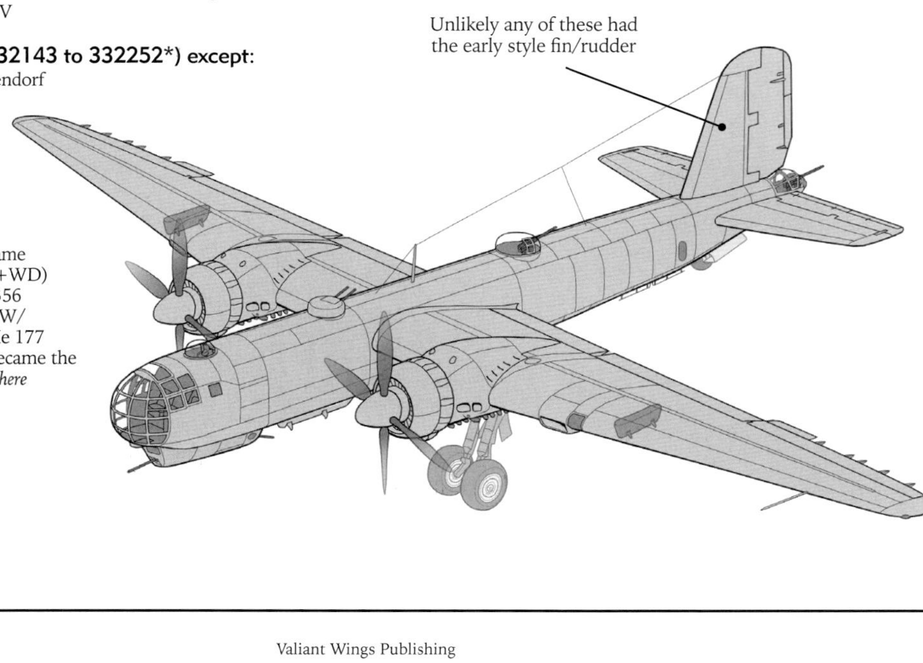

Note: W/Nr.535353 (GP+WC) became the He 177 V32, W/Nr.535354 (GP+WD) became the He 177 V33, W/Nr.535356 (GP+WF) became the He 177 V28, W/Nr.535364 (GP+WN) became the He 177 V34 and W/Nr.535366 (GP+WP) became the He 177 V35 – *see separate listings elsewhere*

He 177A-3 (W/Nrs. 535436 to 535460)
Stammkenzeichen: GP+WW to GP+WY & GJ+RA to GJ+RV
Not all had the '53' prefix to the W/Nr.
Same as He 177A-3 (W/Nrs. 535351 to 535375) – *see isometric opposite*
• Unlikely any of these had the early style fin/rudder
All built by Arado at Brandenburg/Neuendorf

He 177A-3 (W/Nrs. 535531 to 535575*)
Stammkenzeichen: NE–OC, NE+OD (W/Nrs 535549 and 535550) and NN+QR to NN+QZ (W/Nrs.535551 to 535559)
Not all had the '53' prefix to the W/Nr.
Same as He 177A-3 (W/Nrs. 535351 to 535375) – *see isometric opposite*
• Unlikely any of these had the early style fin/rudder
All built by Arado at Brandenburg/Neuendorf
Note: W/Nr.535550 (NE+OD) converted to the He 177 V101
**Other sources quote 535533 to 535570*

He 177A-3 (W/Nrs. 535670 to 535699)
Not all W/Nrs had the '53' prefix
Same as He 177A-3 (W/Nrs. 535351 to 535375) – *see isometric opposite*
• Unlikely any of these had the early style fin/rudder
Built by Arado at Brandenburg-Neuendorf

He 177A-3 (W/Nrs. 535726 to 535760)
Stammkenzeichen: CJ+FA to CJ+FY (W/Nrs535727 to 535751)
Not all had the '53' prefix to the W/Nr.
Same as He 177A-3 (W/Nrs. 535351 to 535375) – *see isometric opposite*
• Unlikely any of these had the early style fin/rudder
All built by Arado at Brandenburg/Neuendorf
Note: W/Nr.535550 (NE+OD) converted to the He 177 V101

He 177A-3 (W/Nrs. 535846 to 535870)
Stammkenzeichen: GR+MD to GR+MZ (W/Nrs. 535846 to 535868)
Not all W/Nrs had the '53' prefix
Same as He 177A-3 (W/Nrs. 535351 to 535375) –*see isometric opposite*
• Unlikely any of these had the early style fin/rudder
Built by Arado at Brandenburg-Neuendorf
Note: W/Nr.535850 (GR+MH) became the He 177 V40

He 177A-3 (V32)
W/Nr. 535353
Stammkenzeichen: GP+WC
Same as He 177A-3 (W/Nrs. 332143 to 332252) except:

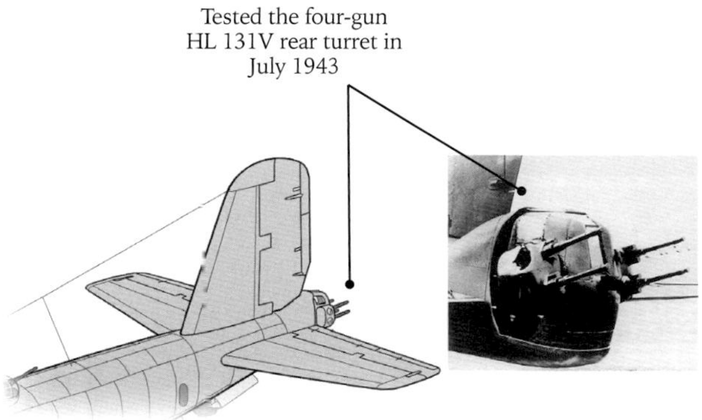

A close-up of the HL 131V turret, as tested by the V32, V33 & V34

He 177A-3 (V33)
W/Nr. 535354
Stammkenzeichen: GP+WD
Same as He 177A-3 (W/Nrs. 332143 to 332252*) except – *see isometric above*:
• Tested the four-gun HL 131V rear turret in July 1943

He 177A-3 (V34)
W/Nr. 535364
Stammkenzeichen: GP+WN
Same as He 177A-3 (W/Nrs. 332143 to 332252*) except – *see isometric above*:
• Tested the four-gun HL 131V rear turret in July 1943

He 177A-3 (V35)
W/Nr. 535366
Stammkenzeichen: GP+WP
First Flown – 19th September 1943
Same as He 177A-3 (W/Nrs. 332143 to 332252) except:
• Carried out single-engine flight trails for A-3 series
• Used for stalling tests and flutter trials with Flettner elevators
• Fitted with anti-spin parachute
• No images survive of this airframe in this configuration, so we cannot offer an isometric

He 177A-3 (V35) – FuG 217

Same as He 177A-3 (V35) except:

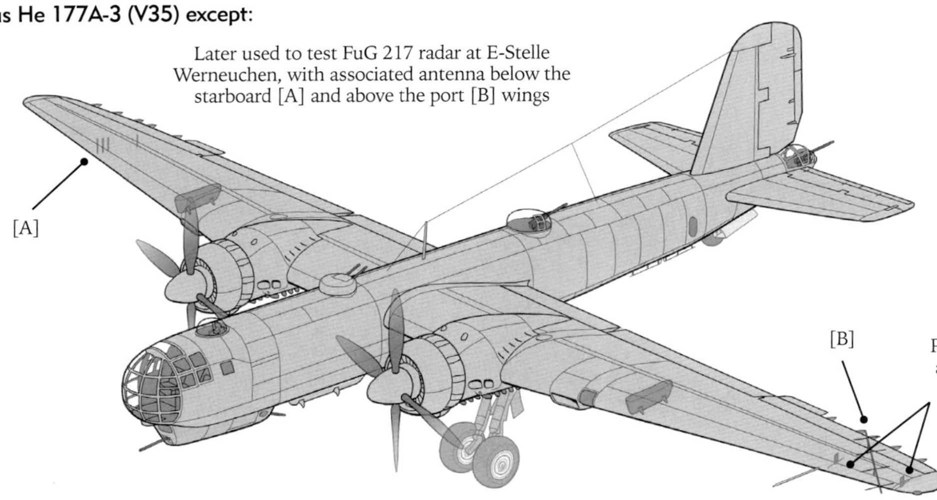

He 177A-3 (V40)

W/Nr.535850
Stammkenzeichen: GR+MH

Same as He 177A-3 (W/Nrs. 535846 to 535870) except:

Built by Arado at Brandenburg-Neuendorf

Some sources state MG 131Z in A-*Stand* [not shown, as it seems unlikely in that location]

Later used to test FuG 240 Berlin airborne-interception radar, the fitment of this radar system would have needed some form of radome for the parabola antenna, but the nose glazing of the He 177 would not allow this to be installed in the usual fashion. As no period images survive of this airframe, we have opted to depict the radar as having been installed in the ventral gondola front, which is revised accordingly – this is purely for illustrative purposes and until such times as evidence comes to light about the actual installation, should be considered as pure conjecture

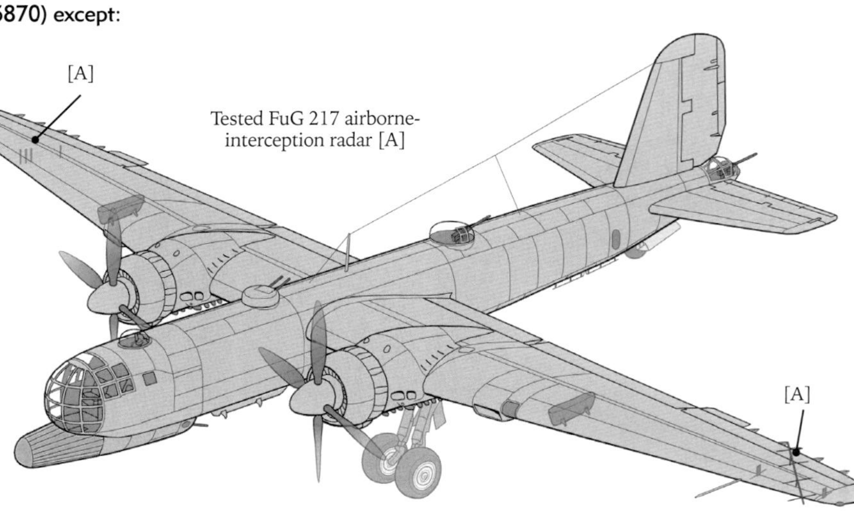

He 177A-3 – MG 151Z

W/Nr. unknown

Same as He 177A-3 except:

Rear fuselage modified to take a turret (the same central element as the HL 131V unit) that contained two MG 151/20 cannon

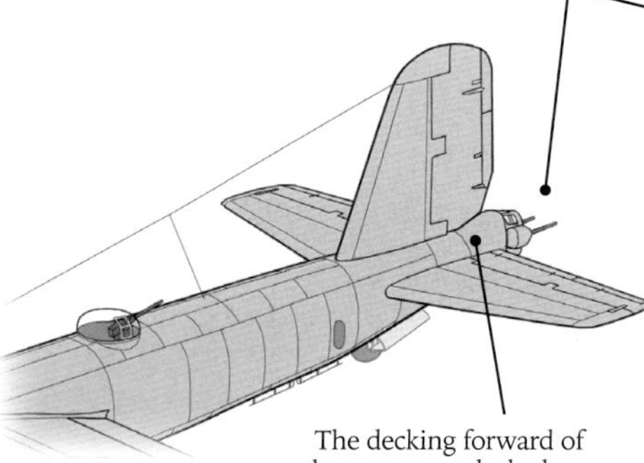

The decking forward of the new turret lacked any glazing, it was all plated over

Port side view of the twin MG 151 installation, as tested in both the A-3 and A-5 airframes

He 177A-3 – Trials (GP+WP*)

**W/Nr. is unknown*

Same as He 177A-3 except:

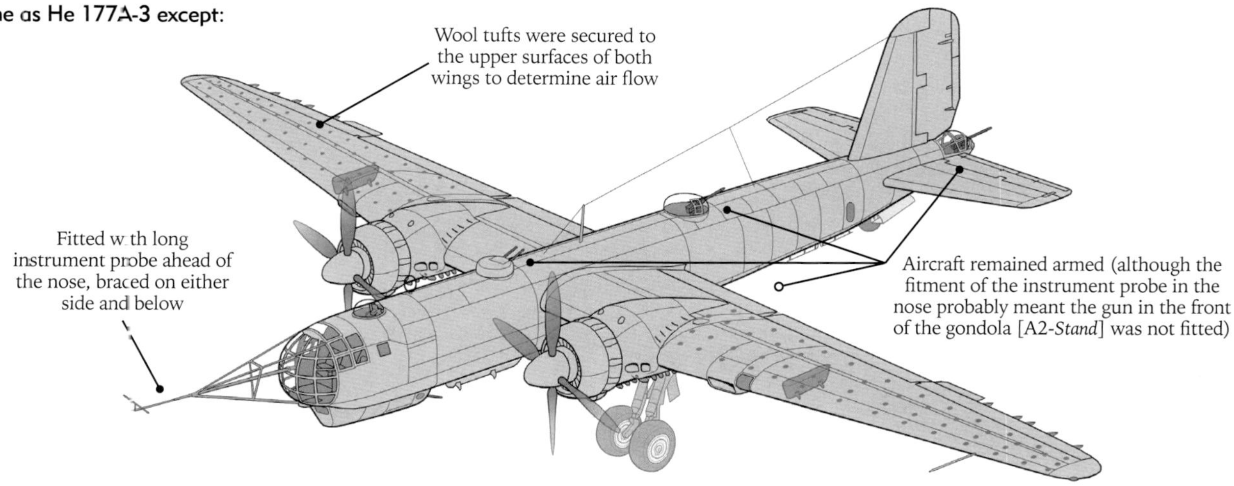

The only known image of GP+WP, highlighting the instrument probe in the nose and the wool tufts on the wings

He 177A-3, W/Nr.332236, TM+IU with the Schleppgerät in tow just after take-off

He 177A-3 with Schleppgerät (1)

Same as He 177A-3 except:

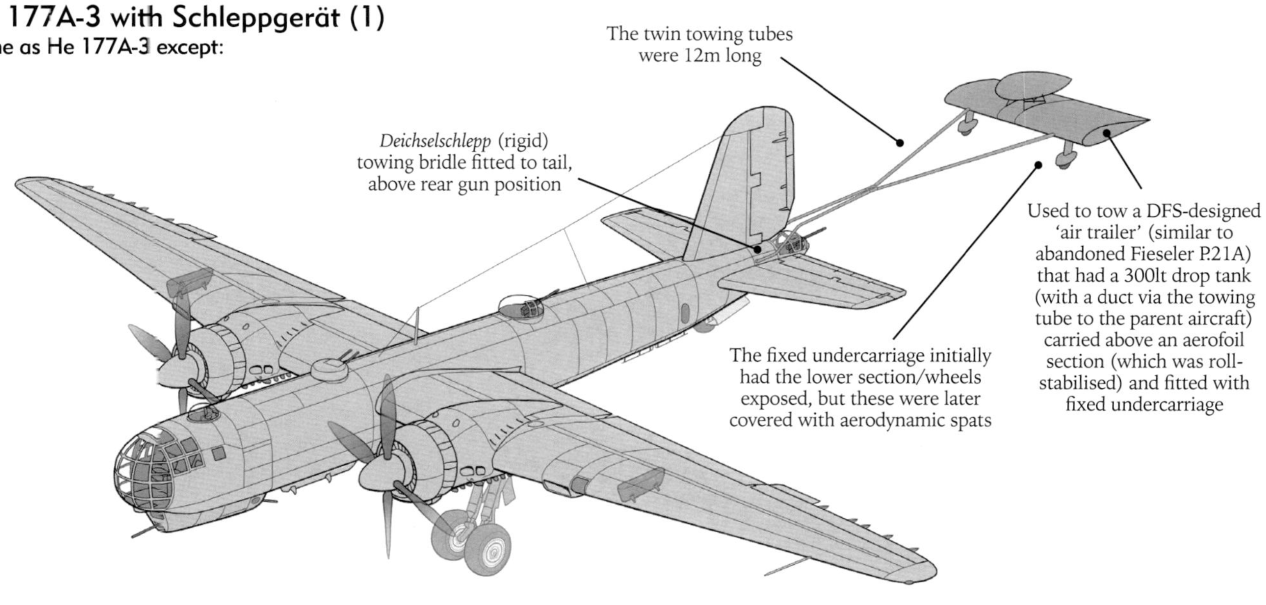

Two He 177As were allocated to the DFS (Deutsche Forschungssanstalt für Segelflug) for trials: W/Nr.332236*, TM+IU was one of them (*some sources state He 177A-5 W/Nr.550229 may also have been used in addition to W/Nr.332236)

He 177A-3 with Schleppgerät (2)

Same as He 177A-3 except:

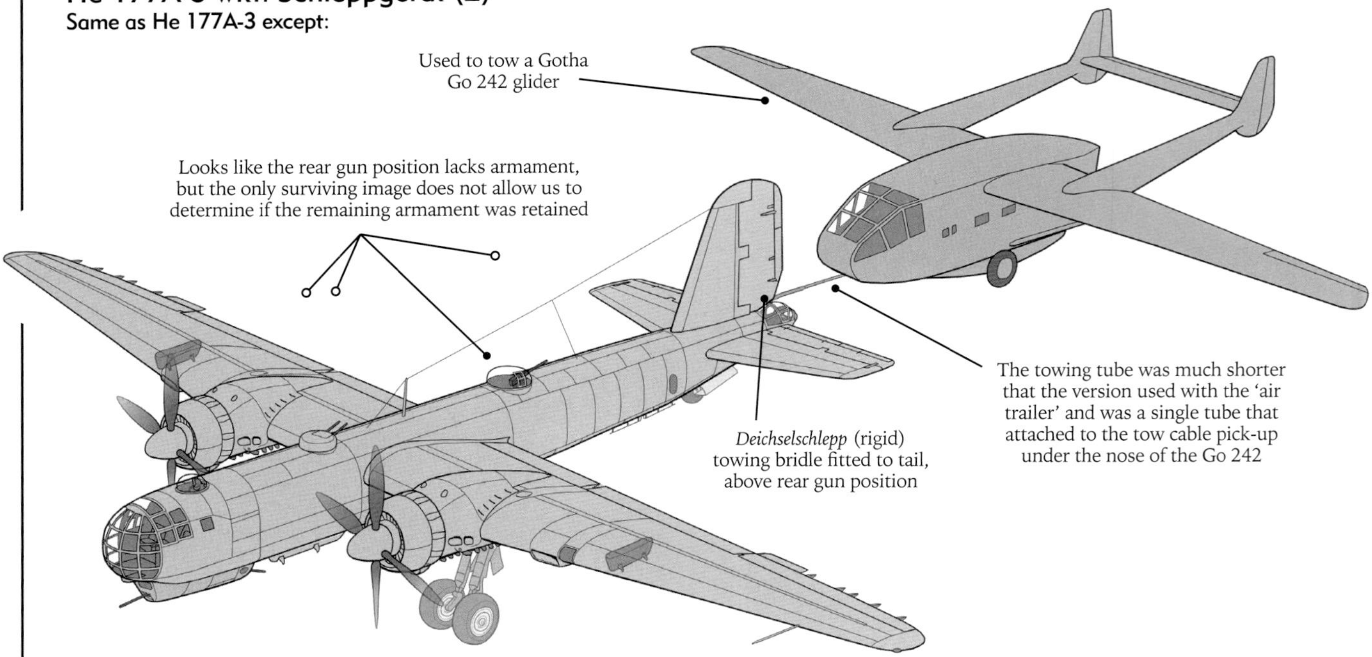

A poor in-flight shot, but nonetheless the only known image of the He 177 towing a Go 242

He 177A-3/R1

Same as He 177A-3 except:

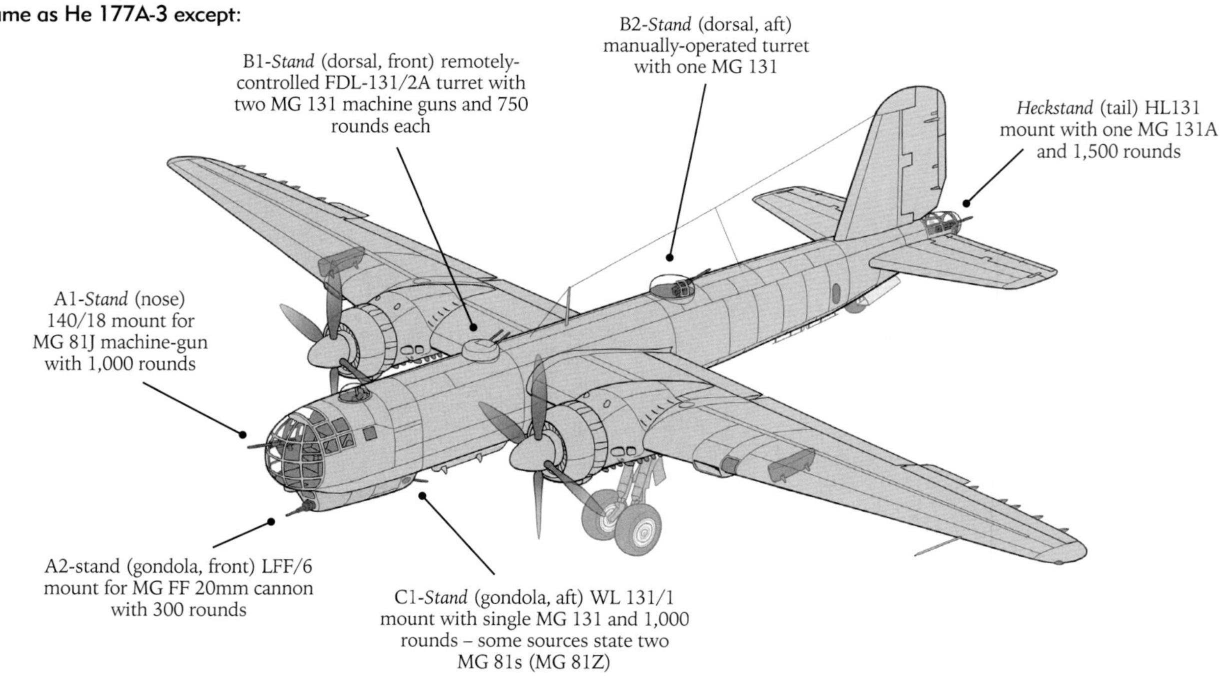

He 177A-3/R2
Same as He 177A-3 except:

The *Heckstand* was fitted with a domed clear cover that allowed the gunner to sit upright, instead of lying prone as had previously been the case. The gun was also changed from a MG 131 to a 20mm MG 151 cannon

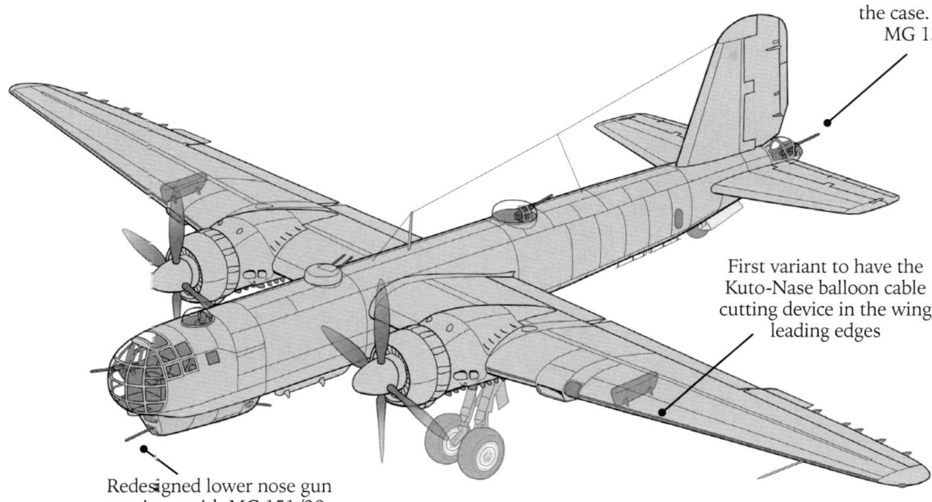

First variant to have the Kuto-Nase balloon cable cutting device in the wing leading edges

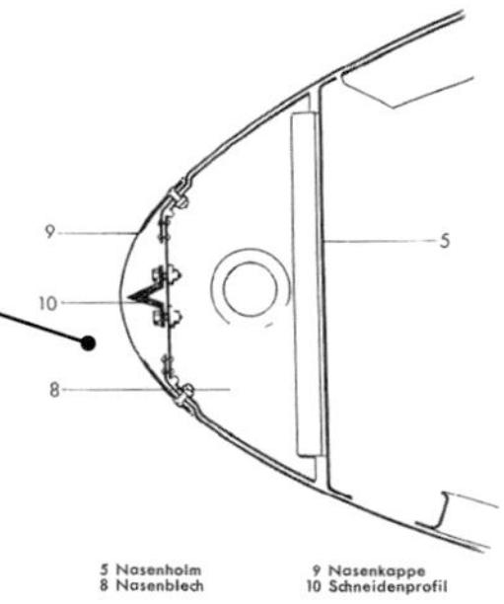

Redesigned lower nose gun position with MG 151/20 replacing the previous MG FF

He 177A-3/R3
Same as He 177A-3 except:

[B]

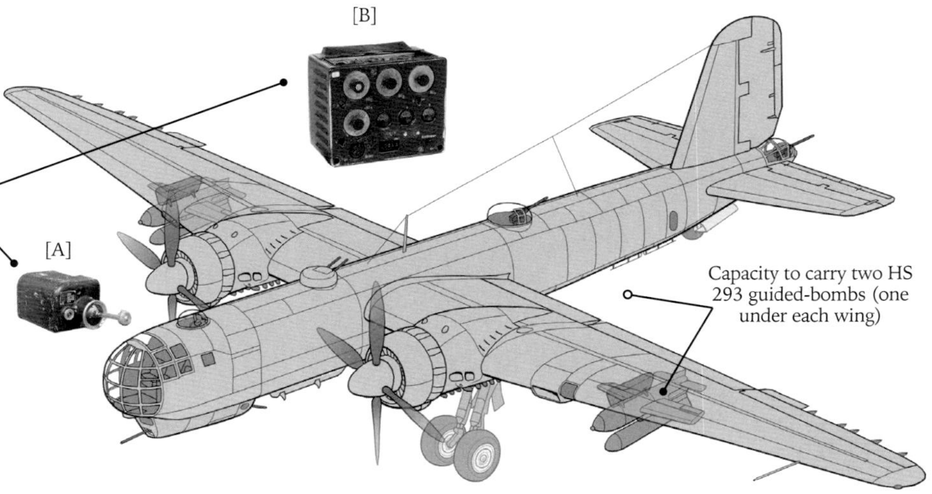

Many sources state that the type had an 'enlarged nose section' for Kehl I or II control equipment, however period documents and images do not support this, the use of these control systems just resulted in the control joystick unit[A] on the starboard side of the cockpit interior, along with the FuG 203 transmitter [B] [not shown]

[A]

Capacity to carry two HS 293 guided-bombs (one under each wing)

He 177A-3/R4
Same as He 177A-3/R3 except:

Used the FuG 203c Kehl III control equipment [not shown]

He 177A-3/R5
Same as He 177A-3 except:

Intended to convert five airframes to carry this weapon, but vibrations when firing proved excessive, so it was abandoned

No images exist of this airframe, so our isometric is based on written accounts combined with known data for the PAK 40

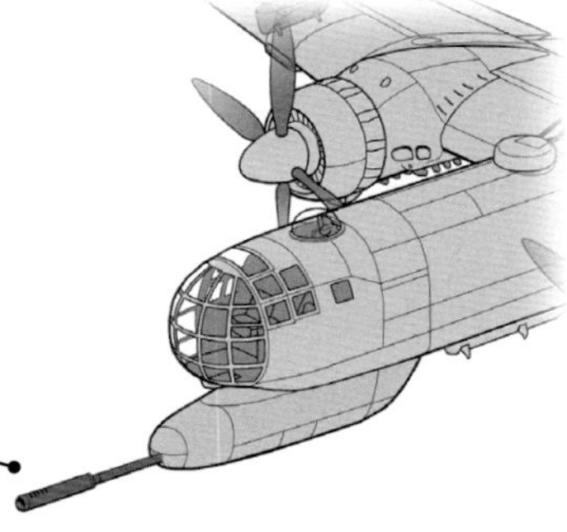

Fitted with heavy armament of one 75mm BK7.5 (PAK 40) cannon in revised/deep chin position with rear access hatch

He 177A-3/R6
Same as He 177A-3 except:

Only six L10s were ever built, so it is unlikely this upgrade option was ever actually available for the A-3 series (It was tested by the V31 [He 177A-5], TM+IF)

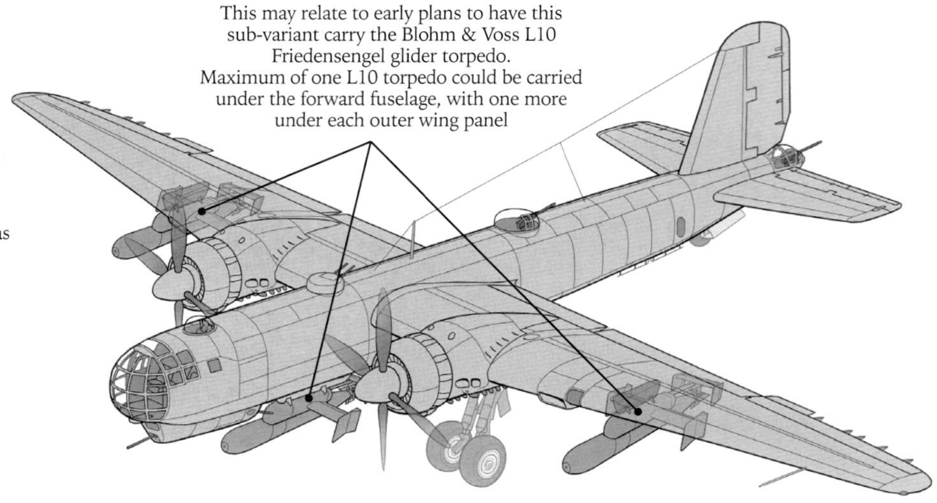

He 177A-3/R7
Same as He 177A-3 except:

Instructions were issued that production of this sub-variant was to start in June 1943, and it is believed that three may have been converted and tested by KG 26, but the Hs 293 was a much better anti-shipping weapon

First tested by He 177A-0 (V17), W/Nr.5005

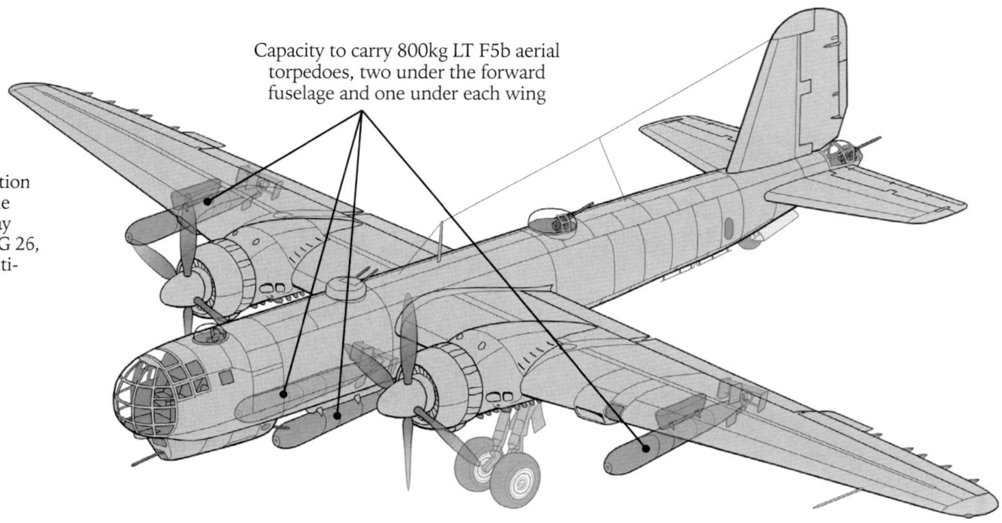

He 177A-3/M5
Same as He 177A-3 except:

FuG 203d Kehl IV transmitter/controller [not shown]

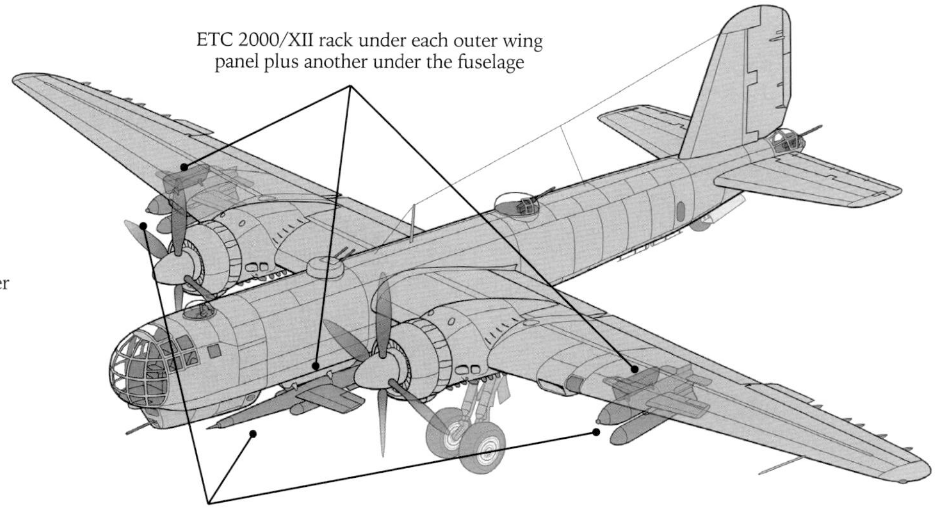

He 177A-3/M6
Same as He 177A-3 except:

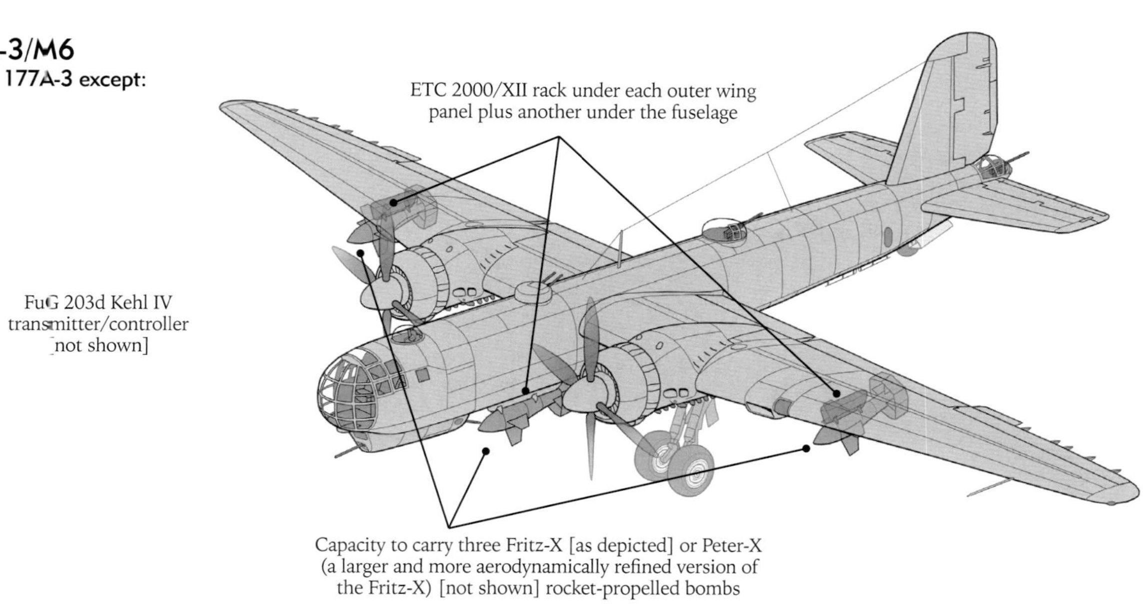

He 177A-3/M7
Same as He 177A-3 except:

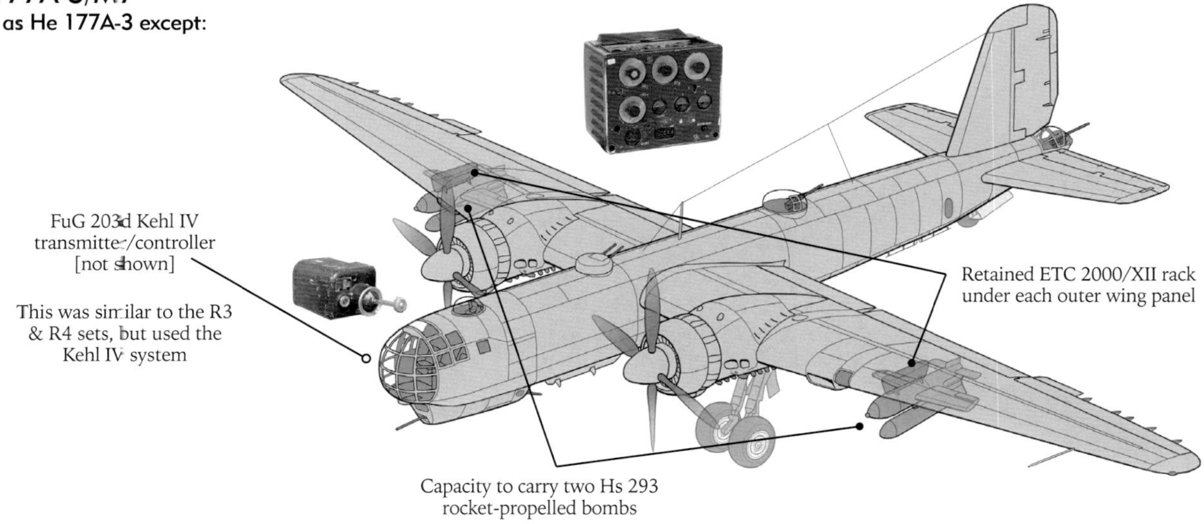

He 177A-3/E7
Same as He 177A-3 except:

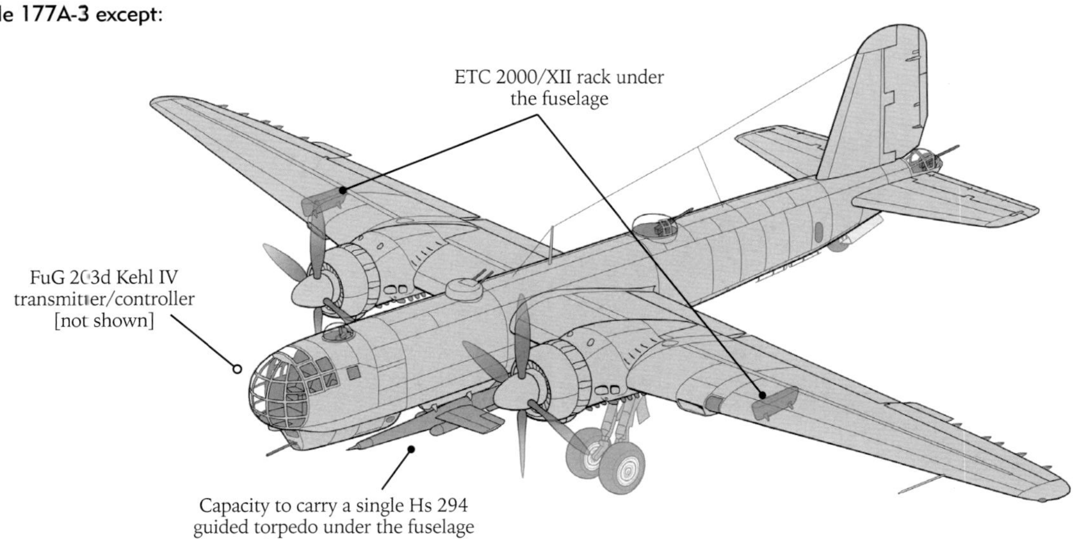

He 177A-3/E8

Same as He 177A-3 except:

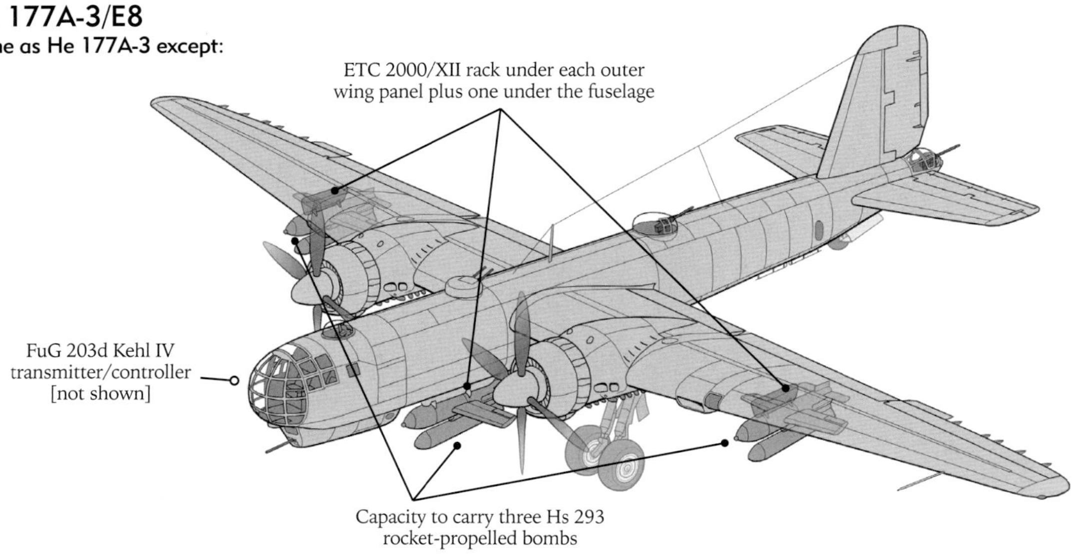

He 177A-3/E9

Same as He 177A-3 except:

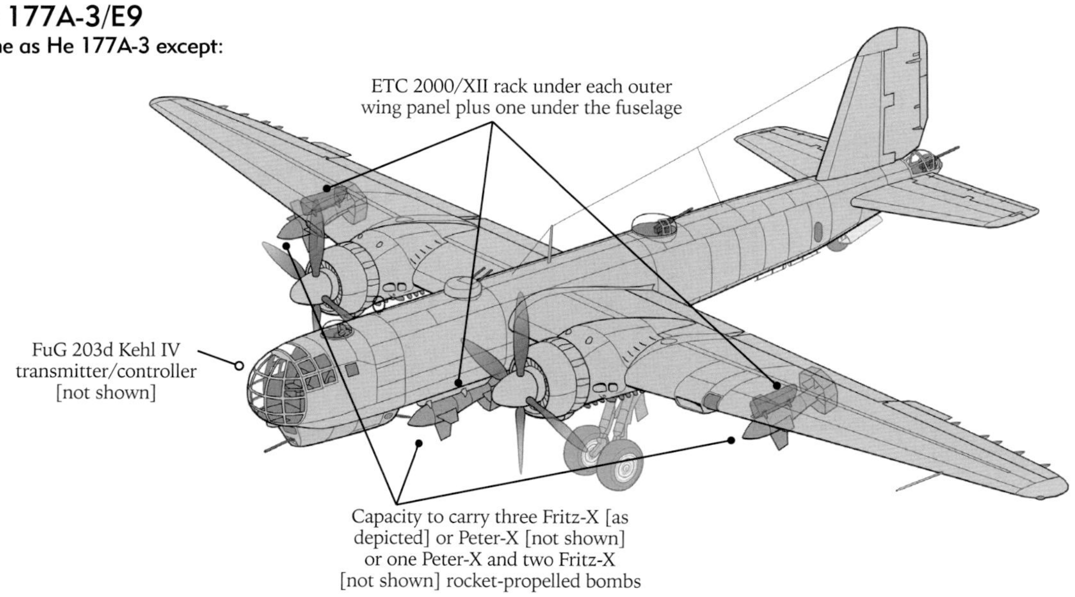

He 177A-3/E10

Same as He 177A-3 except:

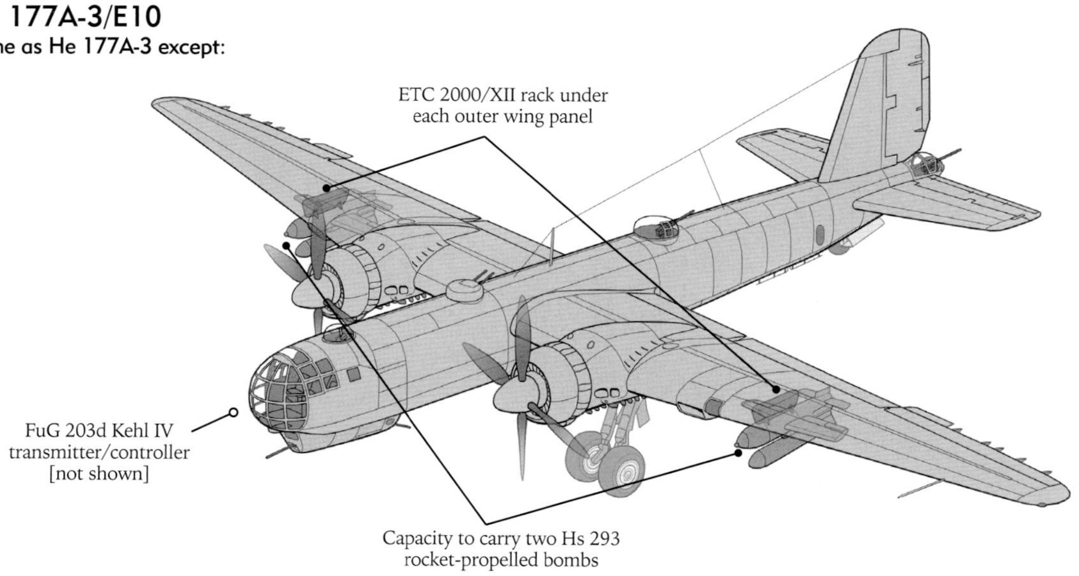

He 177A-3 – Vertical Rockets (Grosszerstörer)
Same as He 177A-3 except:

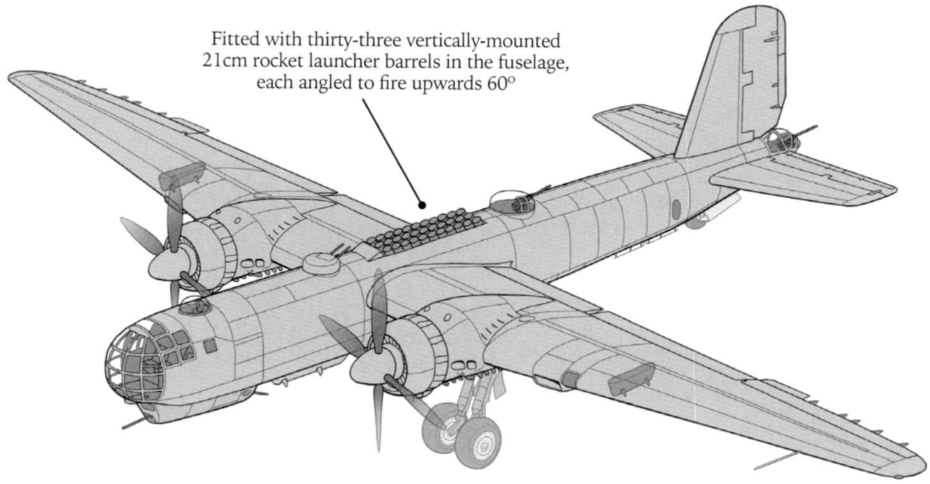

Fitted with thirty-three vertically-mounted 21cm rocket launcher barrels in the fuselage, each angled to fire upwards 60°

Later three were moved to E-Stelle Werneuchen and fitted with FuG 216/217 Neptun radar [not shown]

Four were fitted with FuG 16ZY VHF transmitter/ receiver [not shown]

There is no record of any operational use of this variant, nor any R or U-series set number for this installation

No period images exist, so our isometric is based on written accounts

He 177A-4
High-altitude bomber, derived from He 177A-3 with pressurised cockpit, crew of three and armament comprising, MG 131 (A1-*Stand*), twin MG 131 (B1-*Stand*), MG 131 (C2-*Stand*), MG 131 or MG 151 (*Heckstand*)

• Not built, although the pressurisation system led via the He 177H project to the He 274

He 177A-5 (W/Nrs. 550001 to 550006)
Stammkenzeichen: KM+TA to KM+TF

First Flight – 12th December 1943 (W/Nr.550001)

Similar to He 177A-3 with regard equipment, armament and fuel systems except:

All built by Heinkel at Oranienburg

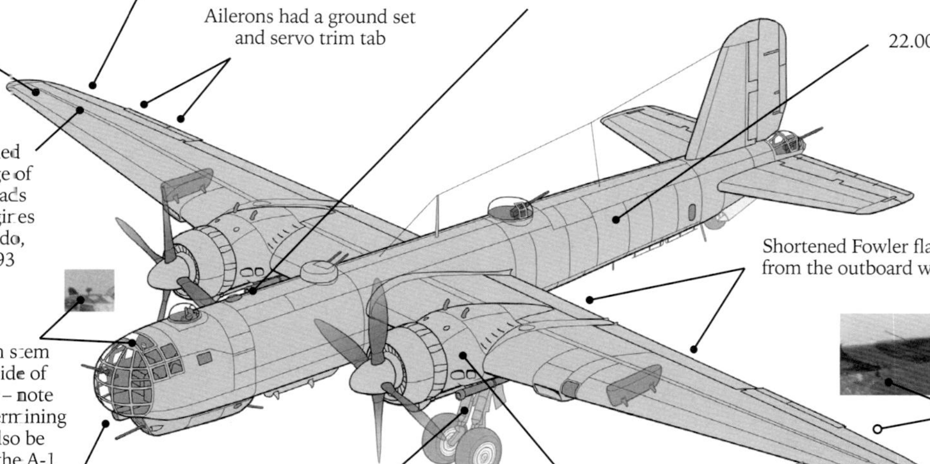

Ailerons no longer dropped with the flaps

Small teardrop-shaped clear cupola added to dorsal spine, just aft of existing larger (sighting) cupola – This can also be found on the last production batches of He 177A-3s

31.44m span (same as A-3)

Ailerons had a ground set and servo trim tab

22.00m fuselage

Wings strengthened to allow the carriage of heavier external loads outboard of the engines such as LT 5 torpedo, Fritz-X and Hs 293

Shortened Fowler flaps (removed from the outboard wing sections)

Rearview mirror on stem mounted on port side of upper nose/canopy – note that this is not a determining feature, as it can also be found in images of the A-1 and A-3 series

Two mass balance weights were added under each aileron

Armour plating on the underside of the nose removed and replaced with Plexiglas to improve forward visibility

Redesigned undercarriage with shortened oleo legs

Had the repositioned engines (moved forward by 20cm) and larger cowling/ radiators for the DB610

Armament varied from aircraft to aircraft, with varying numbers of MG 81Z, although MG 131 and MG 151/20s were also used

Cable-operated, instead of servo-operated controls [not shown]

Bomb bay still divided into three compartments but with revised bomb release system [not shown]

Capacity to carry aerial torpedoes [not shown]

Note: W/Nr.550002 (KM+TB) became the He 177 V38 – *see listing elsewhere*

He 177A-5 (W/Nrs. 550031 to 550090)

Stammkenzeichen: KM+TG to KM+UZ (W/Nrs.550031 to 550076)

Same as He 177A-5 (W/Nrs. 550001 to 550006)

All built by Heinkel at Oranienburg

Note: W/Nr.550036 (KM+TL) became the He 177 V103, W/Nr.550038 (KM+TM) became the He 177 V37, W/Nr.550049 (KM+TX) became the He 177 V39 and W/Nr.550055 (KM+UE) became the He 177 V104 – *see listings elsewhere*

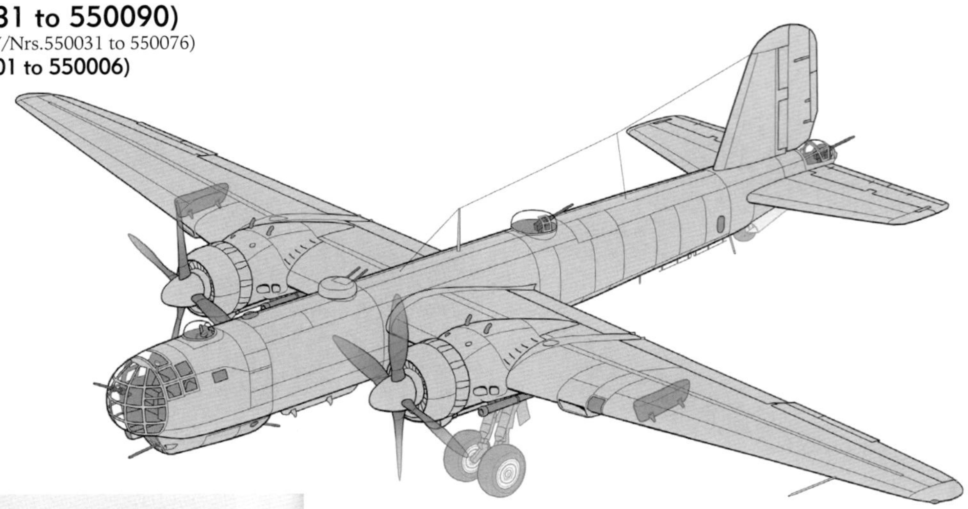

He 177A-5, WNr.550050, captured nearly intact by Allies on an airfield in France in 1944

He 177A-5 (W/Nrs. 550117 to 550175)

Same as He 177A-5 (W/Nrs. 550031 to 550090) – *see isometric above*
All built by Heinkel at Oranienburg

He 177A-5 (W/Nrs. 550191 to 550200)

Same as He 177A-5 (W/Nrs. 550031 to 550090) – *see isometric above*
All built by Heinkel at Oranienburg

He 177A-5, WNr.550131, 6N+DN of 5./KG100 at Alborg in late 1944, early 1945

He 177A-5 (W/Nrs. 550202 to 550266)

Stammkenzeichen: TM+IF to TM+II (W/Nrs.550202 to 550205), BR+CQ ro BR+CV (W/Nrs.550225 to 550230) & GP+RA to GM+DJ (W/Nrs.550231 to 550226)

Same as He 177A-5 (W/Nrs. 550001 to 550006) except:

All built by Arado at Brandenburg/Neueundorf

It is in this batch that some revisions can be noted that many sources claim resulted in these airframes becoming He 177A-7s, however they all lacked things like the extended span, revised cockpit/forward fuselage and tail turret intended for the He 177A-7. It therefore seems that certain revisions were made to some, but maybe not all, from this production batch onwards as follows:

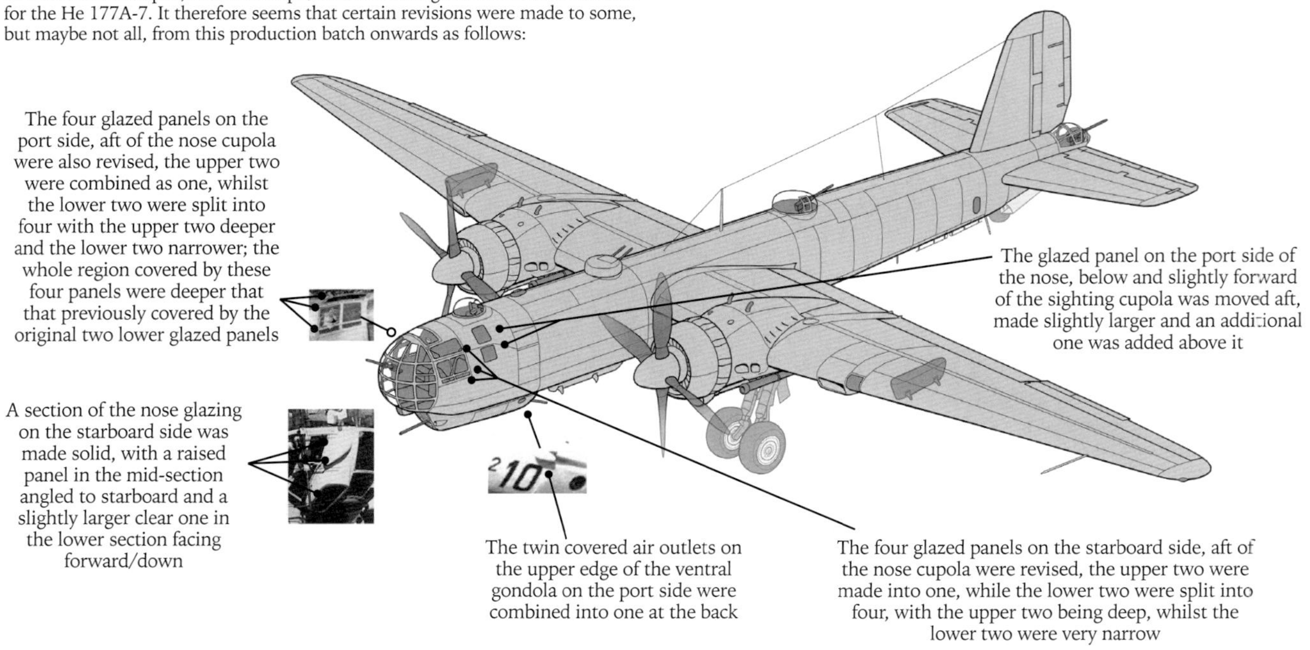

Note: W/Nr.550202 (TM+IF) became the He 177 V31 – *see separate listing elsewhere*

He 177A-5, WNr.550210 of I./KG 40 at Orleans-Bricy in June 1944 prior to move to Toulouse-Blagnac

He 177A-5 (W/Nrs. 550316 to 550333)

Stammkenzeichen: DV+QI to DV+OZ
Same as He 177A-5 (W/Nrs. 550202 to 550266) – *see isometric opposite below*
All built by Arado at Brandenburg/Neueundorf

He 177A-5 – Night Bombers

Same as He 177A-5 except:

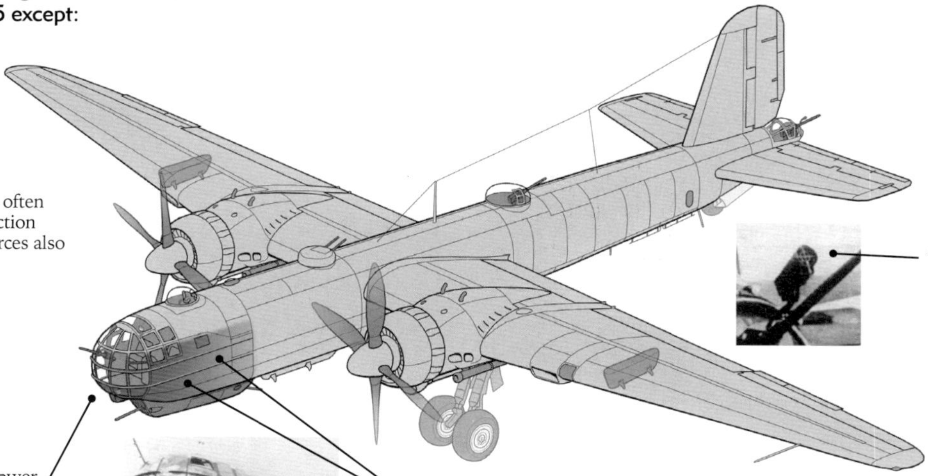

These features can also often be found on late production He 177A-3s (some sources also state the A-1?)

The gunsights were often covered with anti-dazzle cones

Nearly all of the lower section of nose glazing Plexiglas was often painted over

Barrage balloon cable deflectors were fitted around the nose cupola and along each forward fuselage side combined with localised strengthening

He 177A-5 (V31)

W/Nr.550202
Stammkenzeichen: TM+IF
Same as He 177A-5 (W/Nrs. 550202 to 550266) except:
(see photograph page 15)

Used by E-Stelle, Gotenhafen-Hexengrund for trials with Blohm & Voss LT950 (L10 Friedensengel) winged torpedo. Maximum of one L10 torpedo could be carried under the forward fuselage, with one more under each outer wing panel

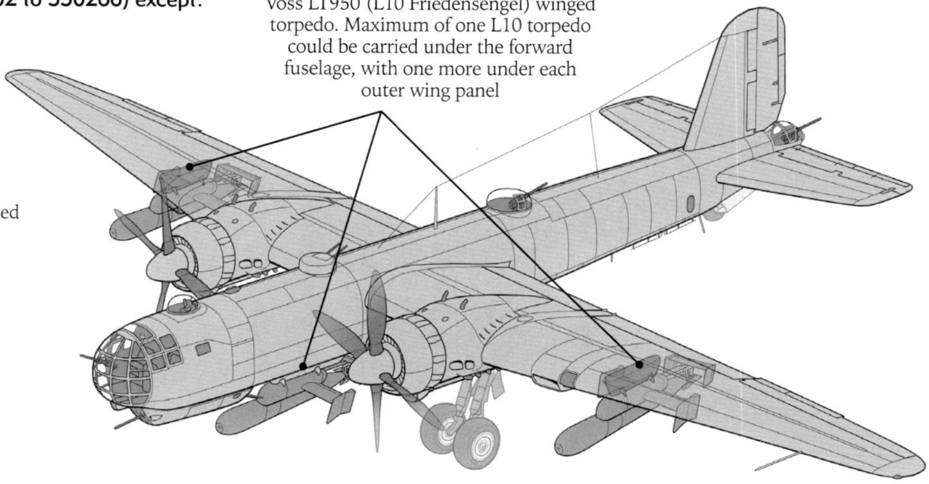

Plans were made in June 1944 to convert twenty-five He 177A-5s to this configuration, but none were ever converted

Transferred to I./KG 40, but blown up at Bordeaux-Mérignac in July 1944

He 177A-5 (V37)

W/Nr. 500038
Stammkenzeichen: KM+TM
Same as He 177A-5 (W/Nrs. 550031 to 550090) except:

Tested FuG 203 radio guidance equipment [not shown]

Later tested FuG 207/208 radio guidance equipment [not shown]

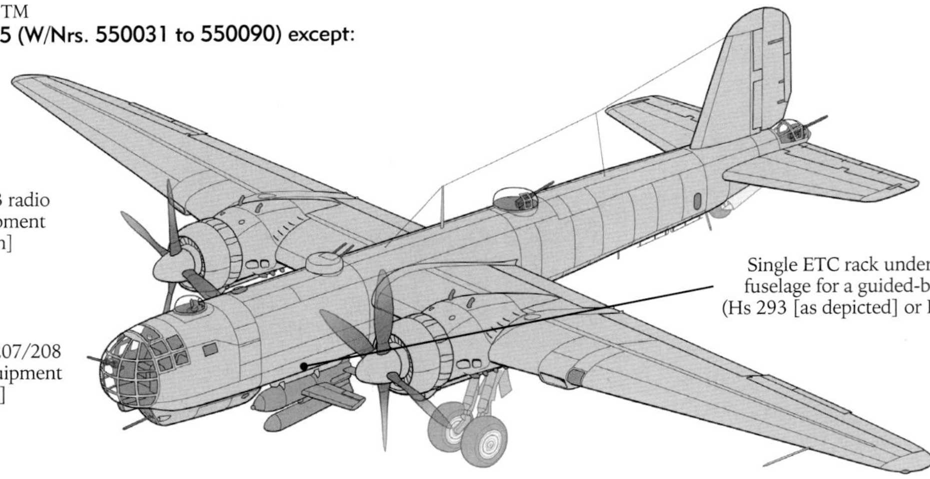

Single ETC rack under the fuselage for a guided-bomb (Hs 293 [as depicted] or Fritz-X)

He 177A-5 (V38) – Initial

W/Nr. 550002
Stammkenzeichen: KM+TB
First Flight – 15th December 1943
Same as He 177A-5 (W/Nrs. 550001 to 550006) except:

Assigned to *Erprobungsstelle Wemeuchen*

Used as the pattern aircraft to test the MG 131J in the dorsal turret [A] and ventral position [B] (some sources state only in the A2-*Stand*)

Tested FuG 216 radar with antennae under each wing [C]

Tested FuG 200 Hohentwiel ASV radar with associated antennae on the nose

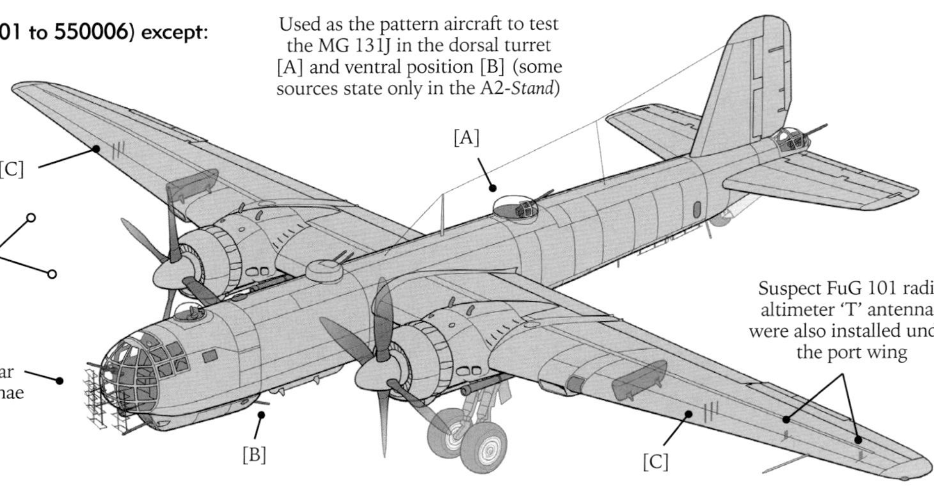

Suspect FuG 101 radio altimeter 'T' antennae were also installed under the port wing

He 177A-5 (V38) – Final

Same as He 177A-5 (V38) – Initial except:

All FuG 101, FuG 200 and FuG 216 radar equipment and antennae most likely removed

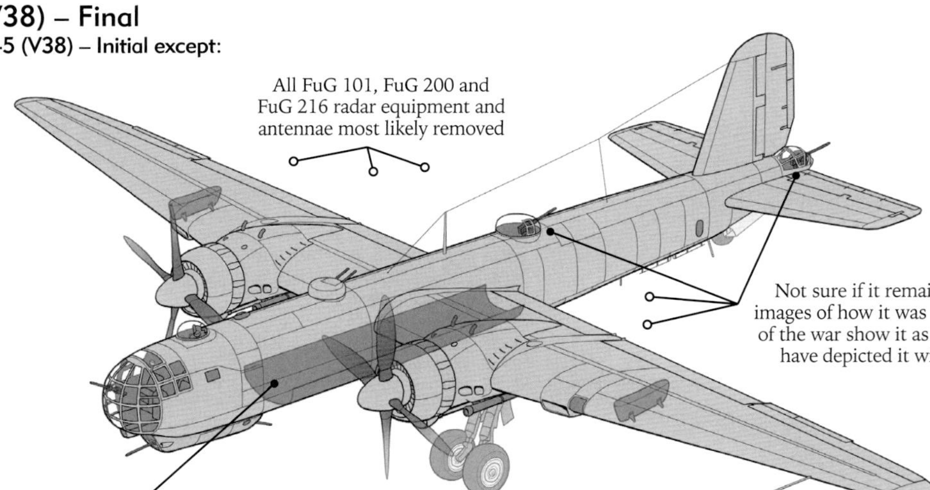

Not sure if it remained armed, as images of how it was found at the end of the war show it as a wreck, but we have depicted it with armament

Used to test the single-bay layout to the bomb bay intended for the production Junkers Ju 287 (the prototype Ju 287 used a He 177 fuselage, so it was an obvious choice to try out the proposed production-standard bomb bay)

Found at the end of the war at Cheb, Czechoslovakia, many say this had the enlarged bomb bay to house a nuclear bomb, but this is untrue, it was only enlarged in the sense that it had a single, not three separate compartments

Often wrongly stated as being intended to carry an atomic bomb, the V38 was used to test the bomb bay layout of the Ju 287 and is seen here in wrecked condition as found at Cheb, Czechoslovakia at the end of the war

He 177A-5 (V39)

W/Nr. 550049
Stammkenzeichen: KM+TX
Same as He 177A-5 (W/Nrs. 550031 to 550090) except:

- Fitted with improved ailerons
- Used to test stalling speeds by KDE and E-Stelle Rechlin
- Fitted with wooden bomb bay doors (tested with these open and closed in flight)
- Later tested leading-edge wing de-icers
- Used to test wing torsion effect at varying aileron deflections
- No images survive of this airframe, so we are unable to offer an isometric

He 177A-5/R1

Same as He 177A-5 except:

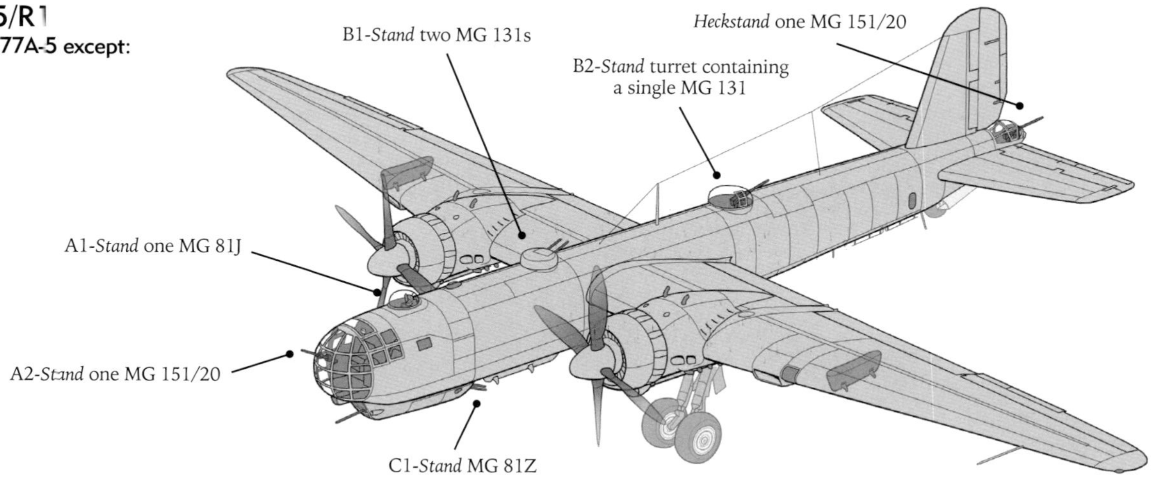

He 177A-5/R2

Same as He 177A-5/R1 except:

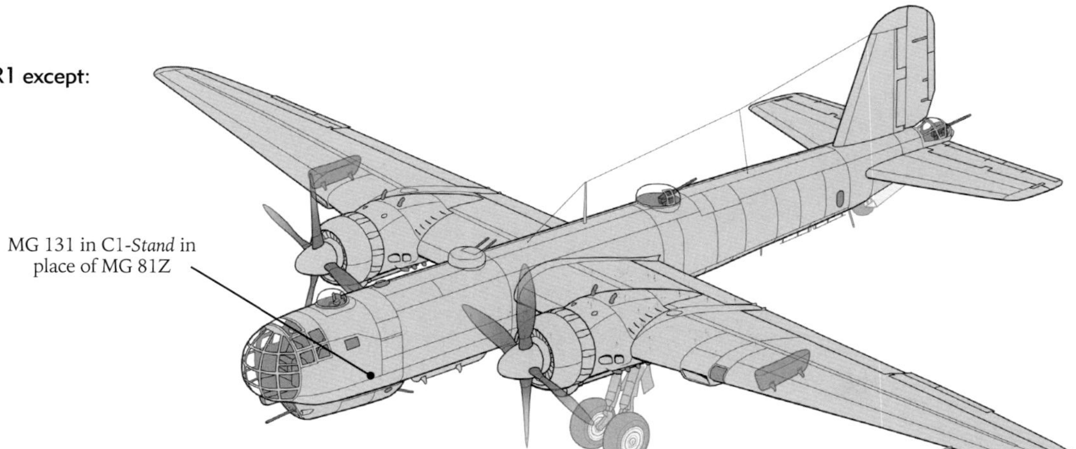

He 177A-5/R3

Same as He 177A-5/R2 except:

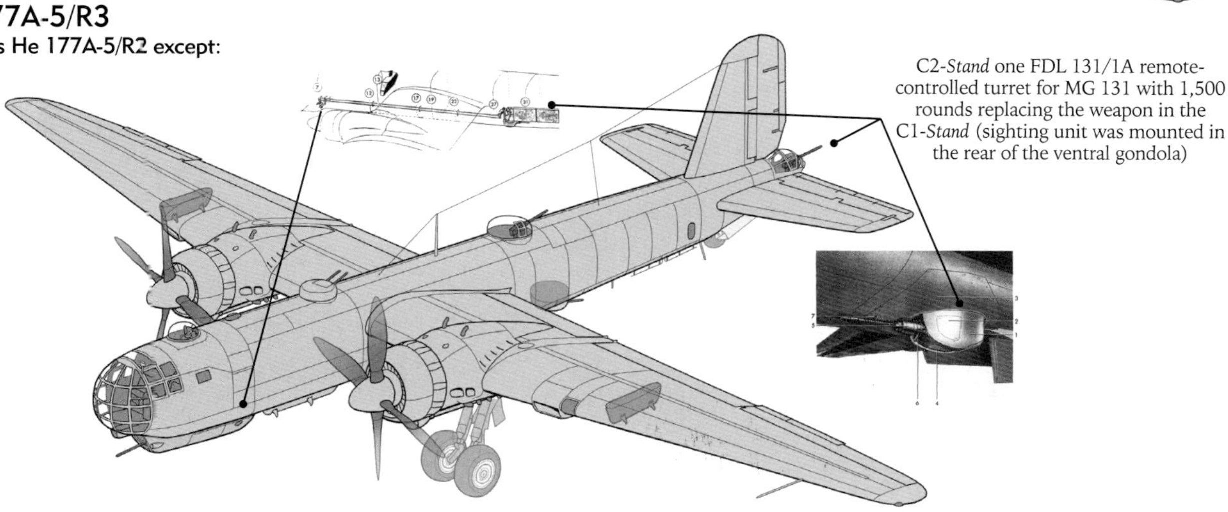

He 177A-5/R4

Same as He 177A-5/R1 except:

- Long-distance bomber
- Simplified release system for special weapons
- Never built

He 177A-5/R5

Same as He 177A-5/R1 except:

- FDL 131/2A* mount in C2-*Stand* (*some sources state FDL C 131/1A)
- No details or period images exist of this gun mount, so we are unable to offer an isometric – the basic layout of the turret's location etc. would have been as per the A-5/R3, it's just the size/ shape of the /2A turret that is unknown

A pilot stands alongside his aircraft fitted with FuG 200 ASV radar, note the square side windows and revisions to the nose glazings, elements often attributed to the A-7 series, but more likely upgrades to late production A-5s

He 177A-5/R6

Same as He 177A-3/R6 except:

Other sources state this had capacity to carry two L10 Friendensengel glider torpedoes* [not depicted], one under each outer wing panel, while captured example TS439, had the capacity to carry a Hs 293/Hs 294 or Fritz-X/Peter-X under each outer wing panel and under the fuselage [as depicted here]

Smaller bomb bay (only aft section) to carry more fuel for long-range missions

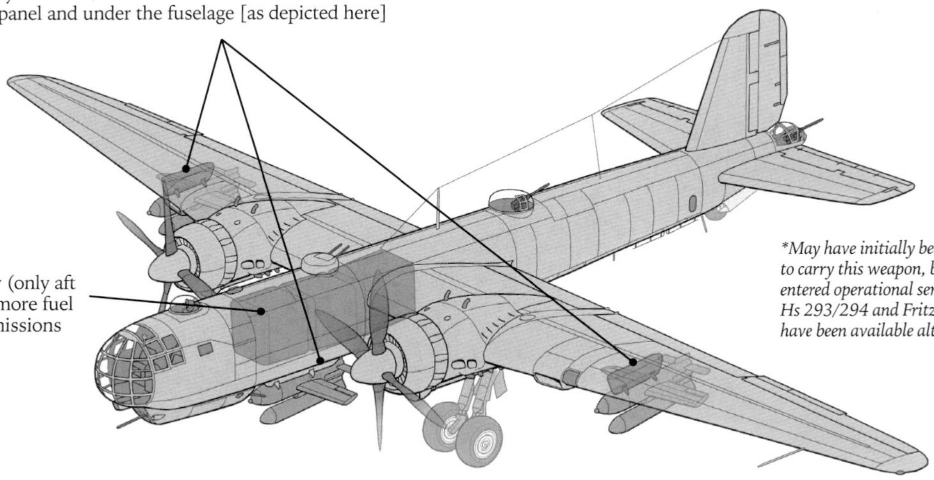

**May have initially been intended to carry this weapon, but as it never entered operational service, the Hs 293/294 and Fritz-X/Peter-X would have been available alternatives*

He 177A-5/R7

Same as He 177A-5 except:

- Experimental heavy bomber with pressurised cockpit similar to the proposed He 177A-4
- Maximum bomb load of 7,300kg; made up of either 48x 70kg bombs on 8/50 bomb racks or 16x 1,000kg bombs or 2x 2,500kg bombs internally. Plus, three Hs 293/Hs 294, or three PC 1400 Fritz-X guided-bombs on fuselage/wing external racks or 2x SC1800 bombs on the wing racks
- Never got beyond drawing-board

He 177A-5 Höhentweil

Same as He 177A-5 except:

A small number of operational (not those involved in trials) He 177A-5s were fitted with FuG 200 Höhentweil anti-shipping radar, with its associated 'toasting fork' radar antennae mounted ahead of the nose

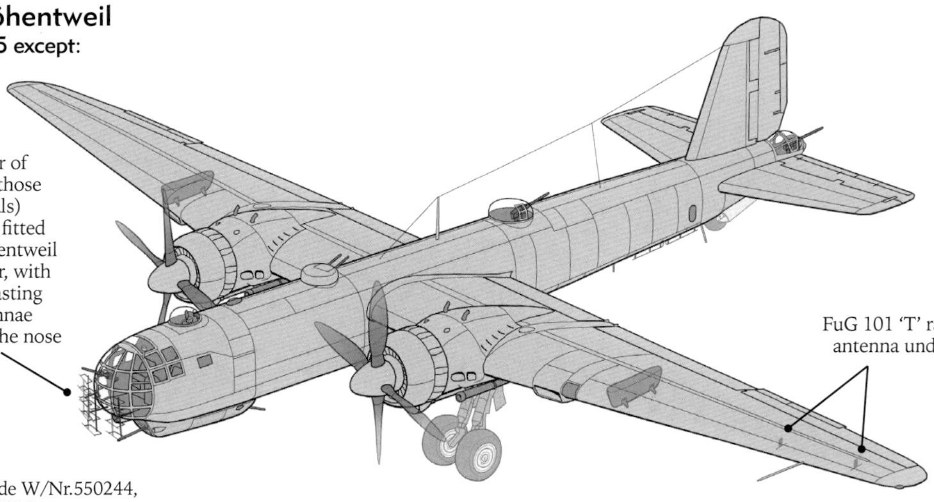

FuG 101 'T' radio altimeter antenna under port wing

Known examples include W/Nr.550244, GP+RN and W/Nr.550316

Note: The following W/Nrs do not fit with any known production batch, but are shown in Luftwaffe loss records?
- 2278 – Shown 100% destroyed 12th June 1944 – possibly He 177A-1 '5278' (W/Nr.15278)?
- 2444, 6N+EP with 6./KG 100, crashed 26th November 1943 – possibly He 177A-3 '5444' (W/Nr.535444)?
- 5794 of I./KG40, which was damaged when it hit an object on take-off from Fassberg on the 25th March 1944 – possibly He 177A-1 '5194' (W/Nr.15194) or He 177A-3 '5694' (W/Nr.535694)?

He 177A-6

Proposed high-altitude bomber

Derived from He 177A-5 except:

Not built – cancelled in favour of the A-7

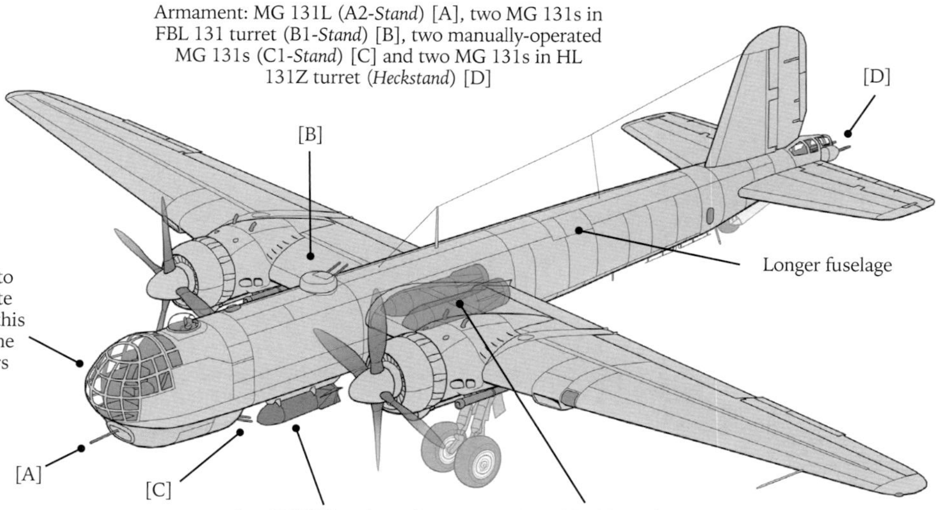

He 177A-6/R1

Same as He 177A-5 except:

Not built

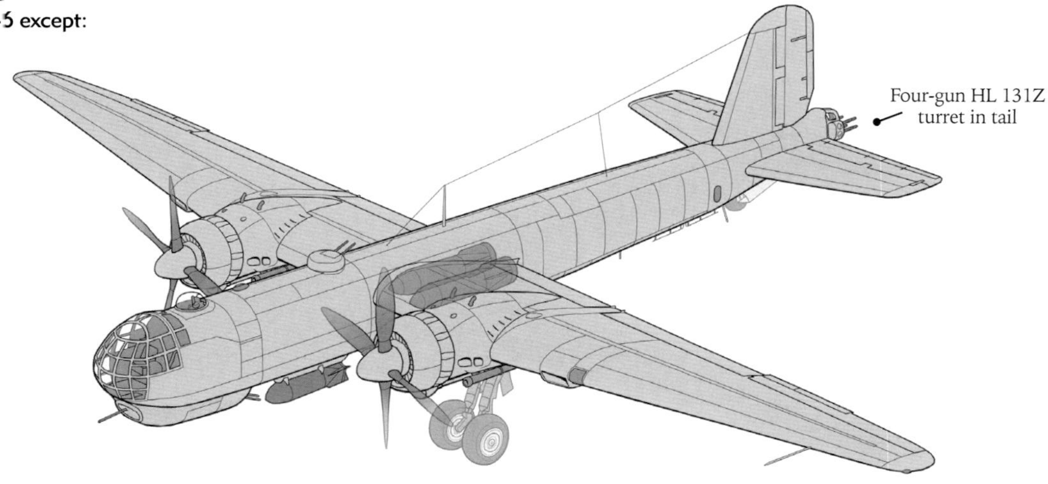

He 177A-6/R2

Same as He 177A-6 except:

Not built

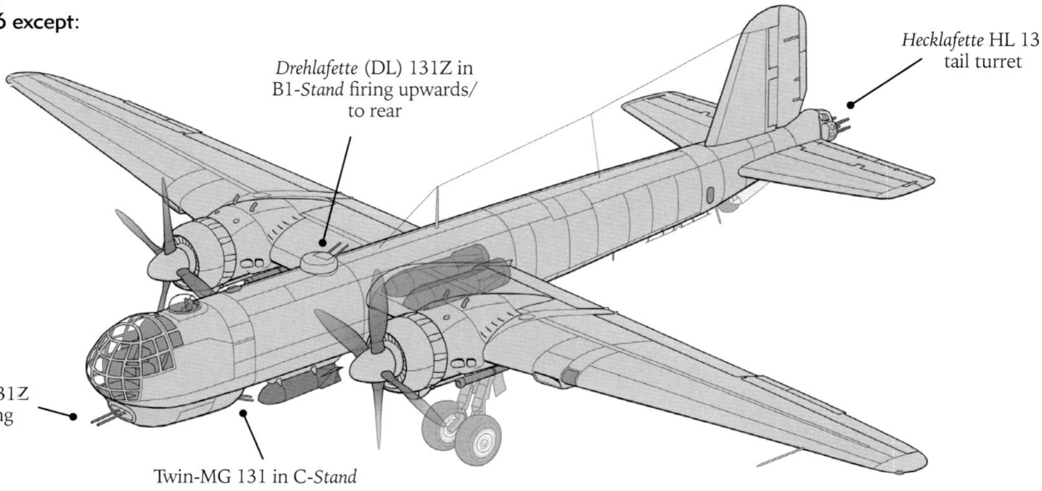

He 177A-7 (Original)

Same as He 177A-5 except:

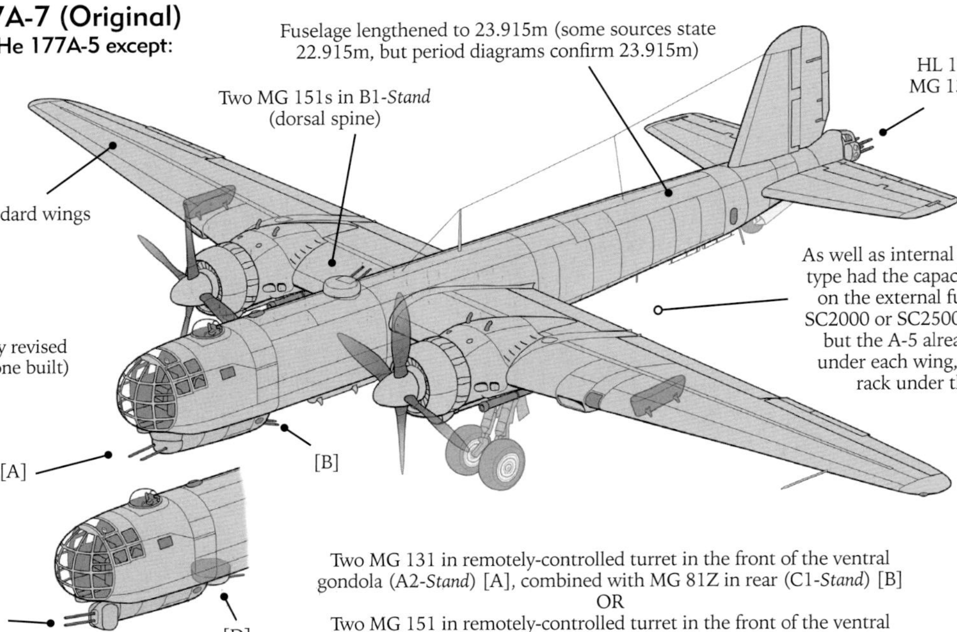

He 177A-7 (Revised)

Same as He 177A-7 (Original) except:

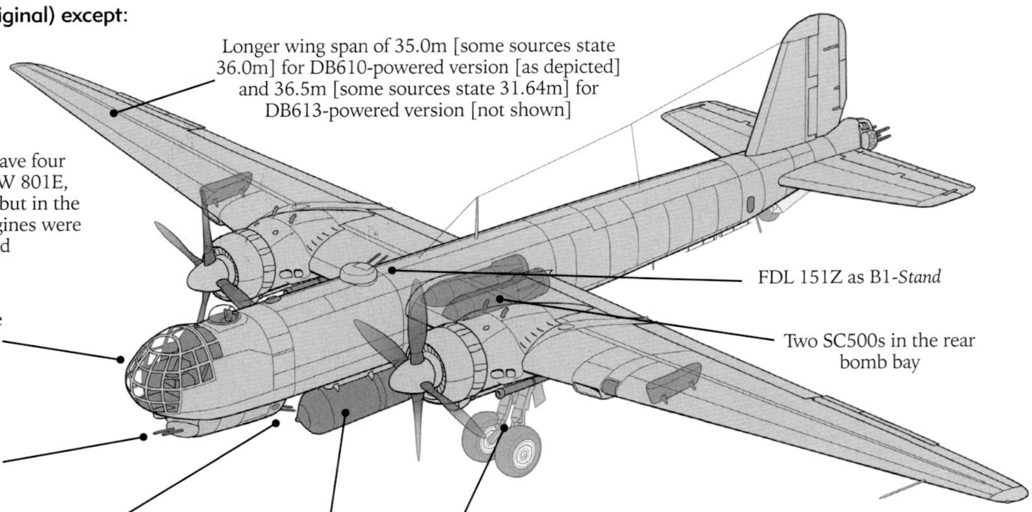

Some sources state that ten (maybe less) were converted from existing airframes, while others state that none were ever completed before the He 177 programme was abandoned in the summer of 1944. The example listed as an A-7 and captured by American forces at the end of the war (W/Nr.550256), was actually an A-5 and period images confirm it retained all the features of the A-5 series, without any of those proposed for the A-7

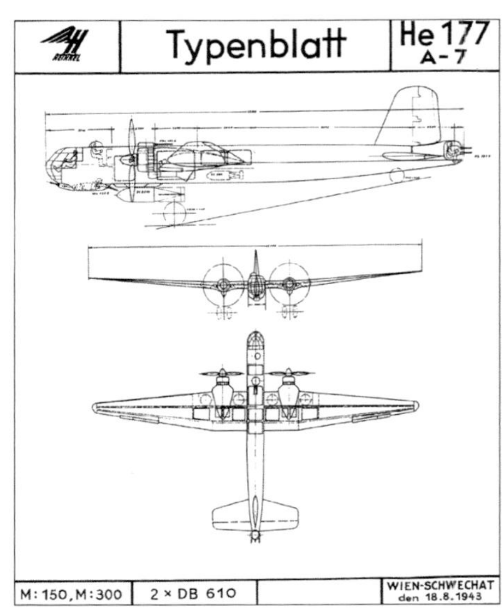

The type sheet of the revised A-7 shows the new forward nose and cockpit area, extended wings etc.

He 177A-8
See He 177B-5

He 177A-9
See He 177B-6

He 177A-10
See He 177B-7

He 177 V101 – Initial Form

W/Nr.525550
Stammkennzeichen: NE+OD
First Flight – 20th December 1943

Same as He 177A-3 (W/Nrs. 535533 to 535570) except:

First prototype of the He 177B-5

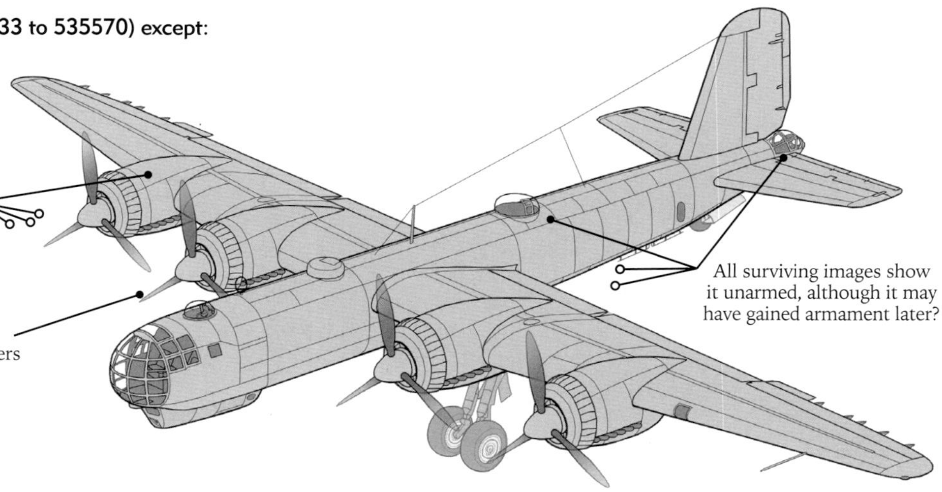

A rather poor, grainly and retouched image that is often listed as the He 277 V1, but this is the V101, NE+OD

He 177 V101 – Final Form

Same as He 177 V101 – Initial Form except:

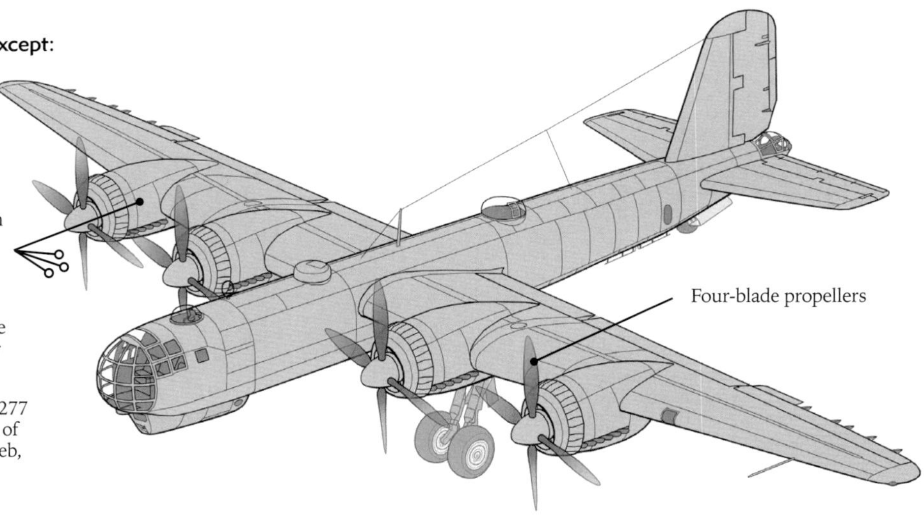

This was probably done in relation to the He 277 development programme, the burnt-out hulk of this aircraft was found at the Eger factory, Cheb, Czechoslovakia at the end of the war

All that was left of the V101, as found at Cheb at the end of the war, note the cowling style which is like the DB 603 installation, rather than the Jumos some claim it was fitted with

He 177 V102

W/Nr. 177 000 0023
Stammkenzeichen: GA+QQ
First Flight – 11th February 1944
Rebuilt from/same as He 177A-08/V9 except:

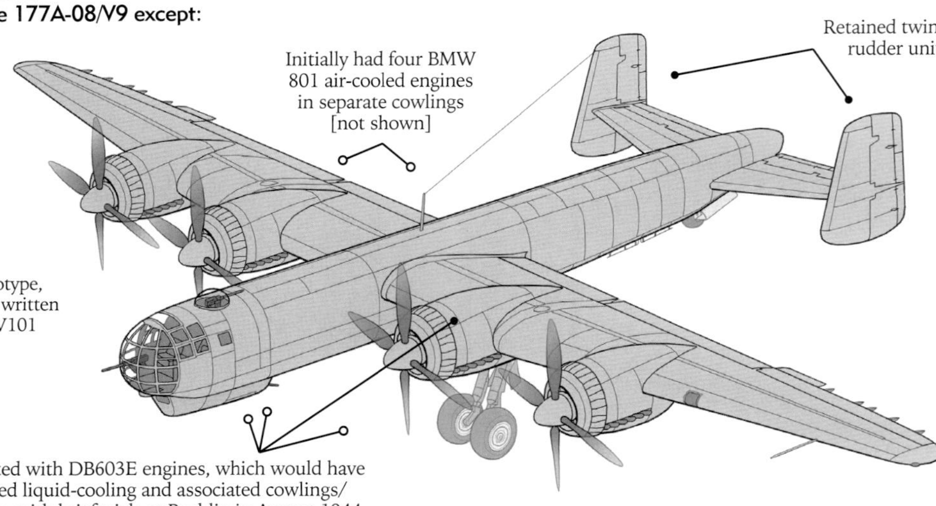

He 177 V103 – Initial Form

W/Nr. 550036
Stammkenzeichen: KM+TL
First Flight – March or April 1944
Same as He 177 V101 – Initial Form except:

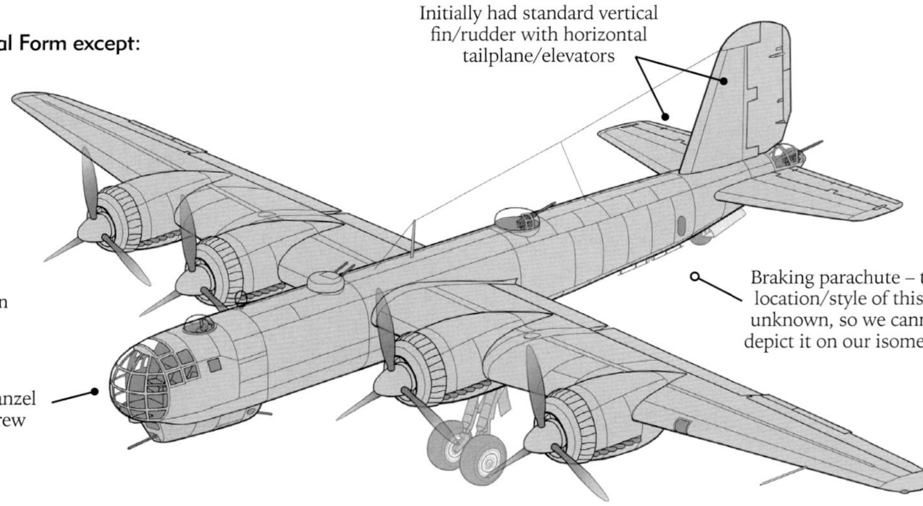

He 177 V103 – Revised Form

Same as He 177 V103 – Initial Form except:

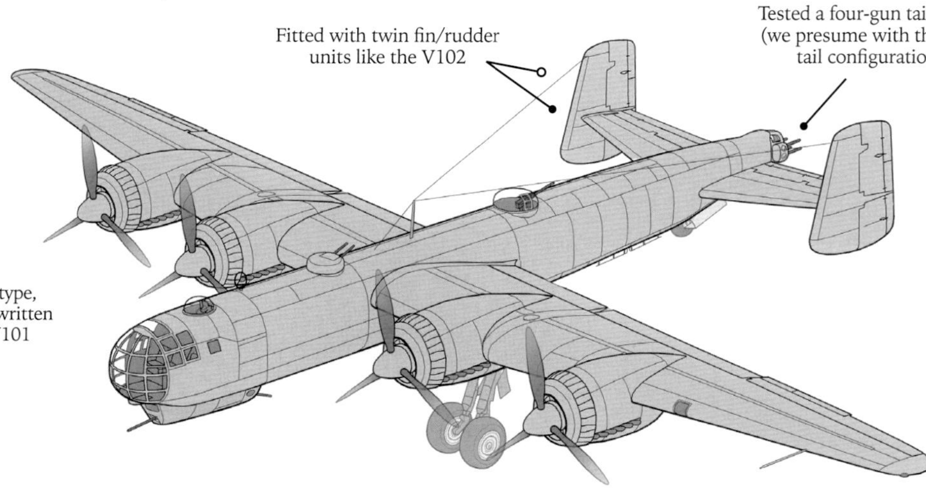

He 177 V104

W/Nr. 550055
Stammkenzeichen: KM+UE
First Flight – 4th May 1944

Same as He 177 V101 – Initial Form except:

Converted from He 177A-5, fourth He 177B-5 prototype

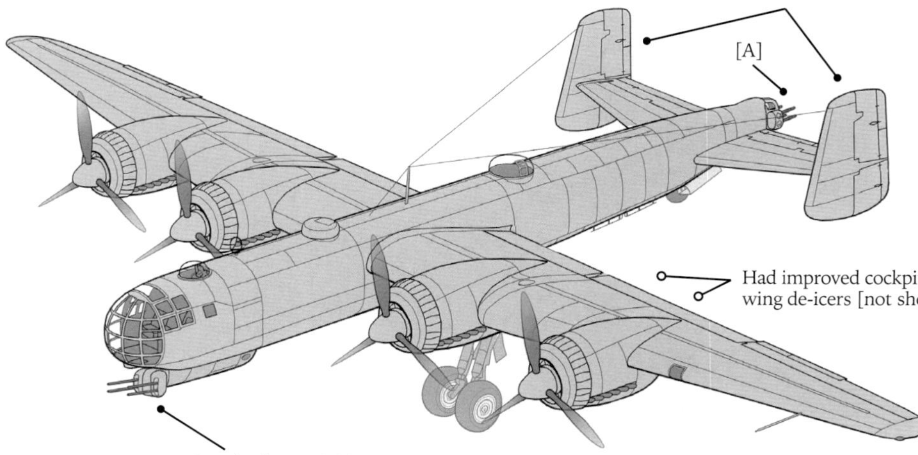

No images exist of this prototype, so our isometric is based on written accounts and images of the V101

Note: The He 177B series would have ultimately led to the He 277, so many sources list them as both He 177 and He 277 variants, we however have done them all as He 177Bs, to reduce confusion

He 177B-0

- Wing span of 32.80m
- Four separate BMW 801E radial engines
- Length of 22.52m
- Never built, as orders were given to cease all work on the He 177 series in April 1944

He 177B-5 (Stage I)

Same as He 177A-5 except:

(see B-5 series Stage I diagram on page 24)

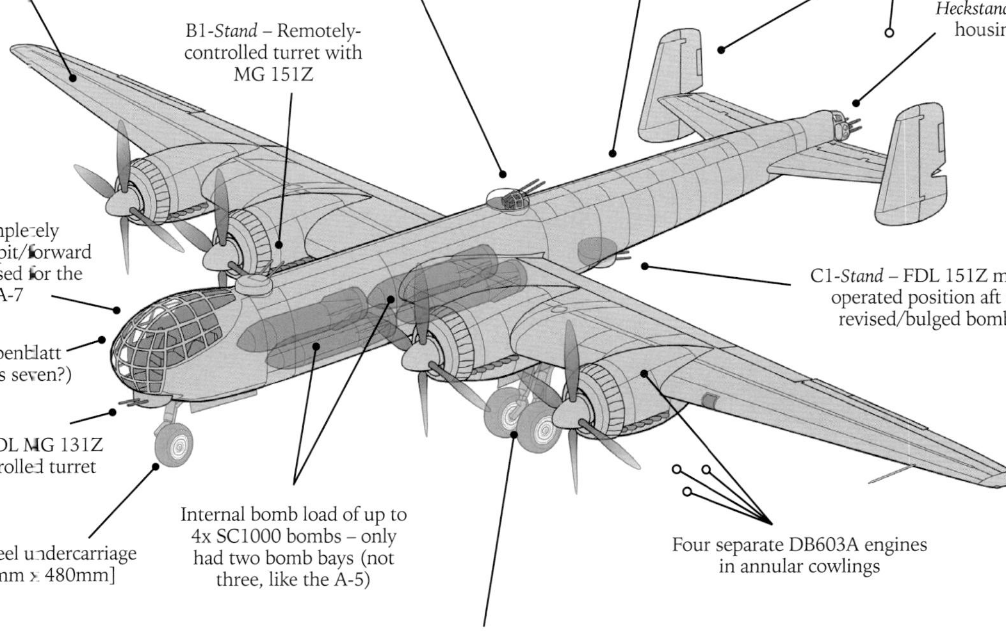

Never built, as orders were given to cease all work on the He 177 series in April 1944

The B-5 sub-variant is also listed in some period documents as the He 177A-8

He 177B-5 (Stage II)

Same as He 177B-5 (Stage I) except:

(see B-5 series Stage II diagram on page 24)

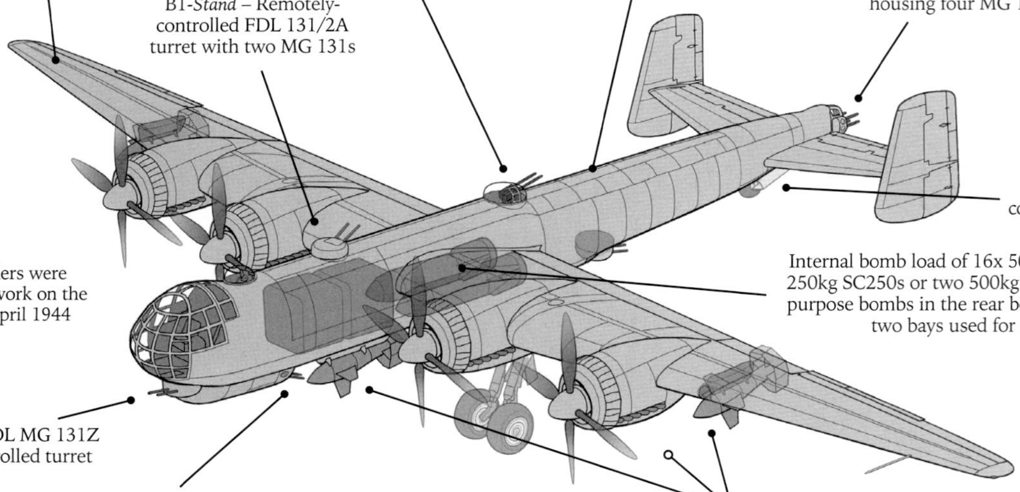

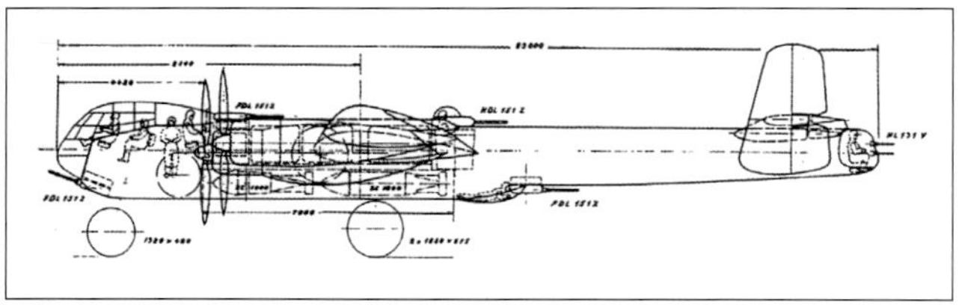

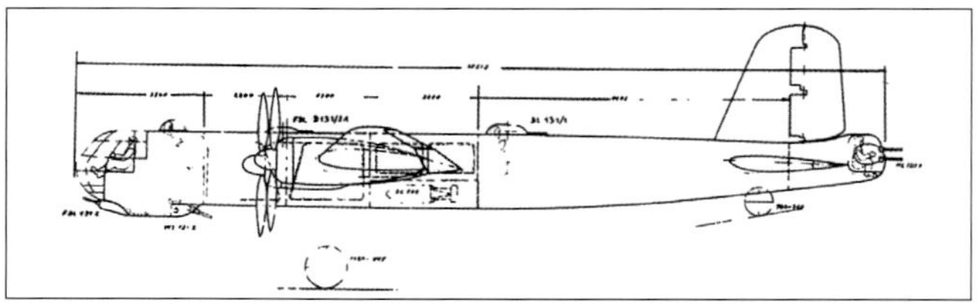

Heinkel diagrams from August 1943 showing the first stage of the B-5 series (left) and second stage (right) – *see page 24 for the full diagrams*

He 177B-6

Same as He 177B-5 (Stage I) except:

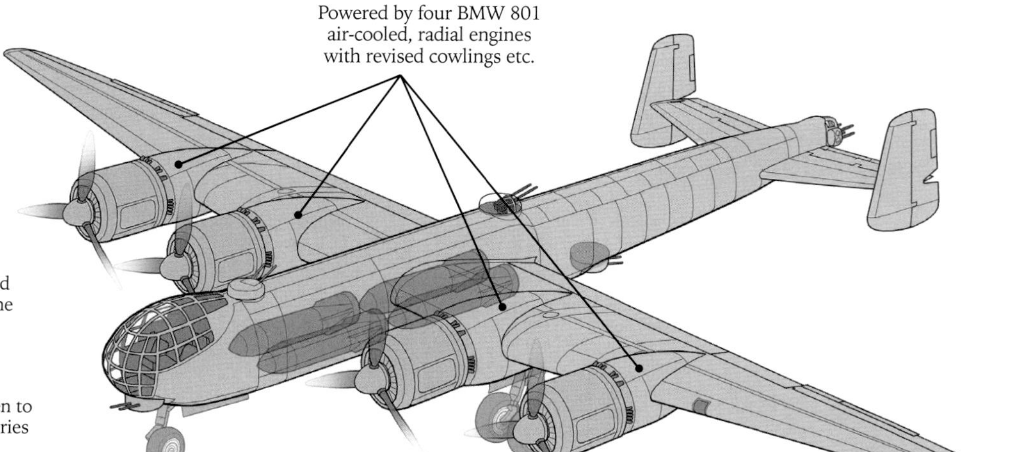

He 177B-6 (Variant 1)

Same as He 177B-5 (Stage I) except:

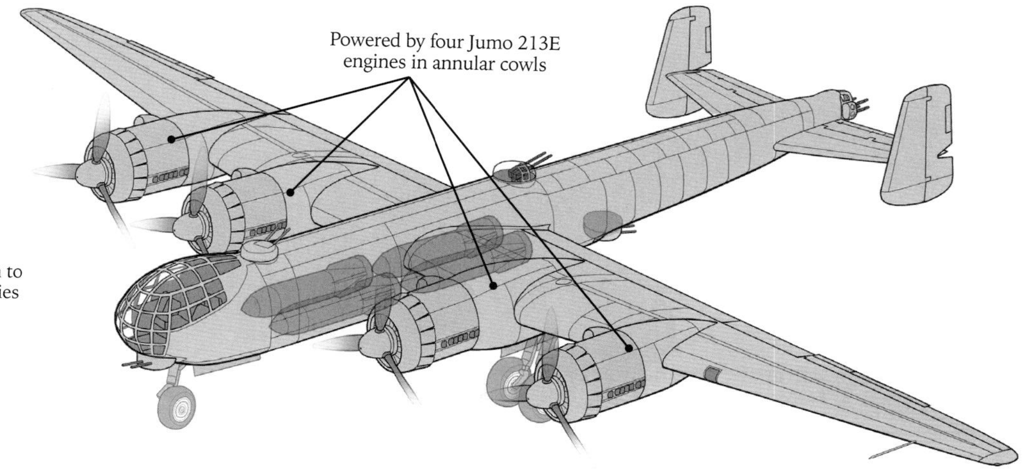

Never built, as orders were given to cease all work on the He 177 series in April 1944

He 177B-6 (Variant 2)

Same as He 177B-5 (Stage I) except:

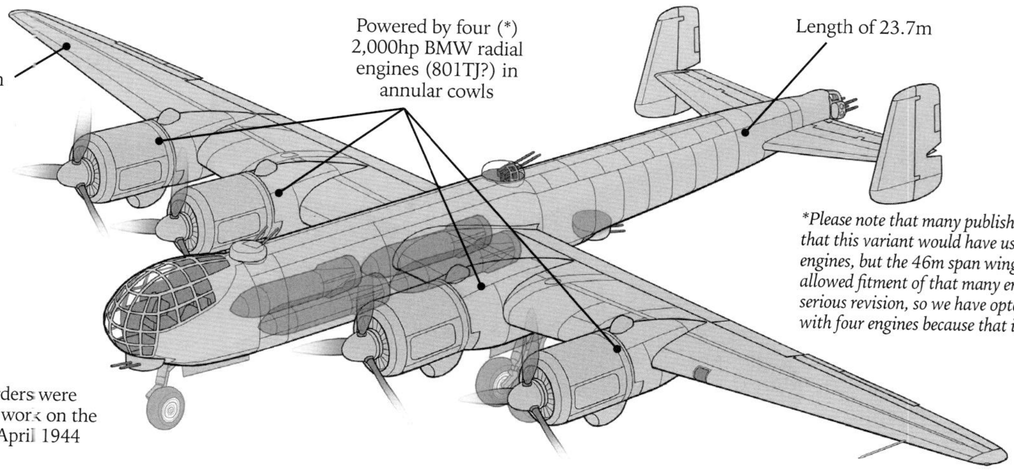

**Please note that many published sources state that this variant would have used six BMW radial engines, but the 46m span wing would not have allowed fitment of that many engines without serious revision, so we have opted to show the type with four engines because that is a more likely layout*

Never built, as orders were given to cease all work on the He 177 series in April 1944

He 177B-6/R1

Same as He 177B-6 (Variant 1) except:

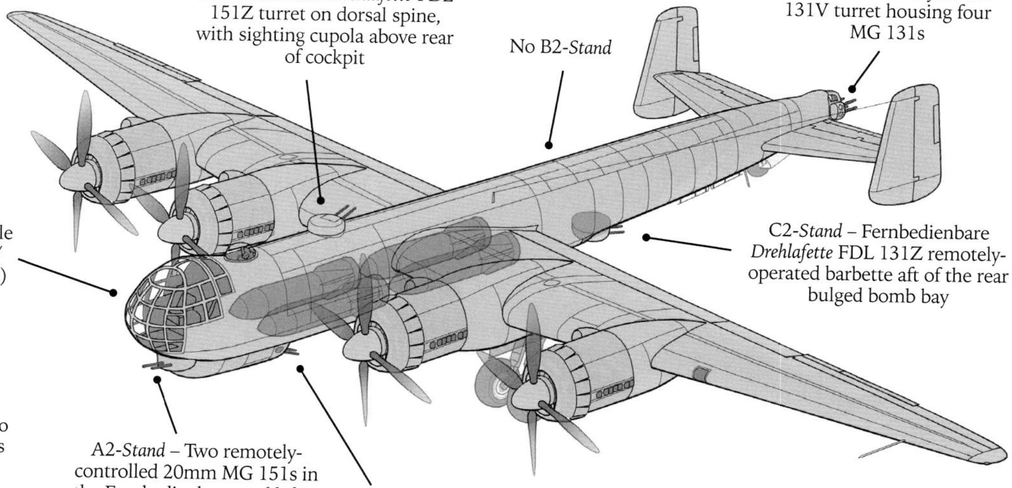

Never built, as orders were given to cease all work on the He 177 series in April 1944

Note: Many sources list this as the He 277B-6/R1

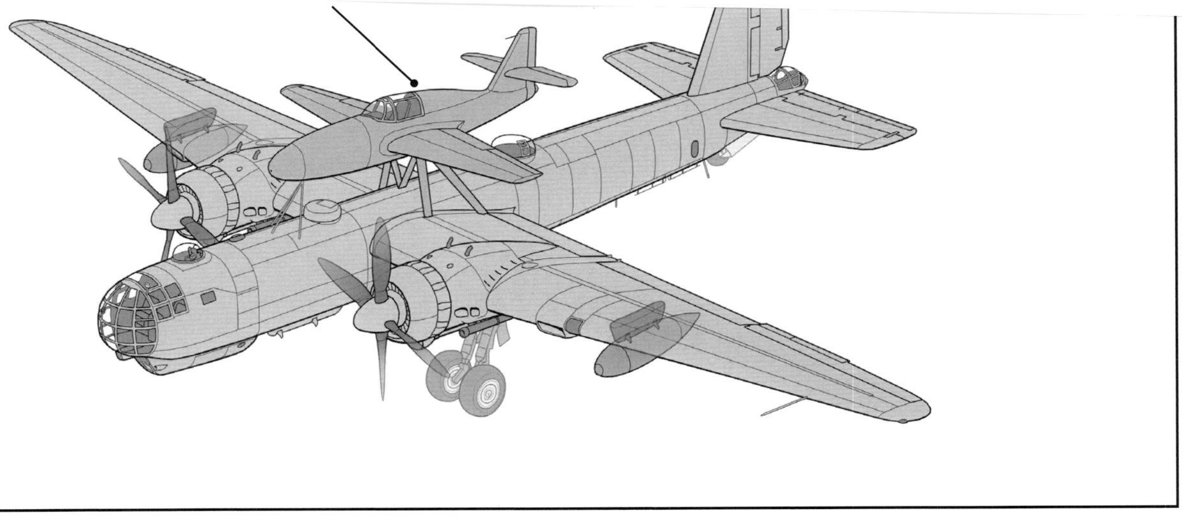

He 177B-6/R2
Same as He 177B-6 (Variant 1) except:

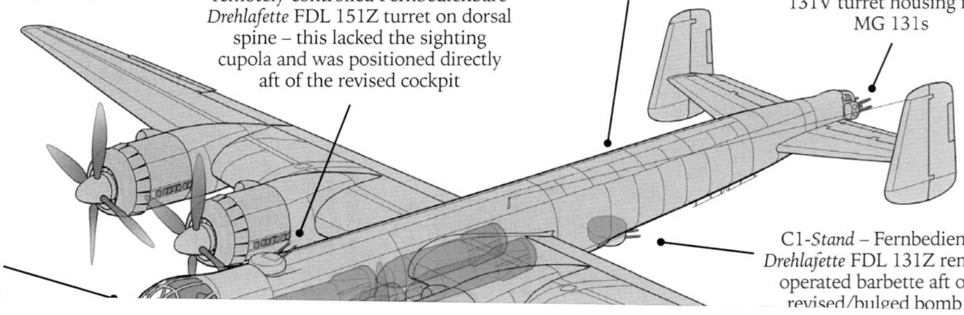

He 177 Mistel Project (3)
Same as the He 177 Mistel Project (1) except:

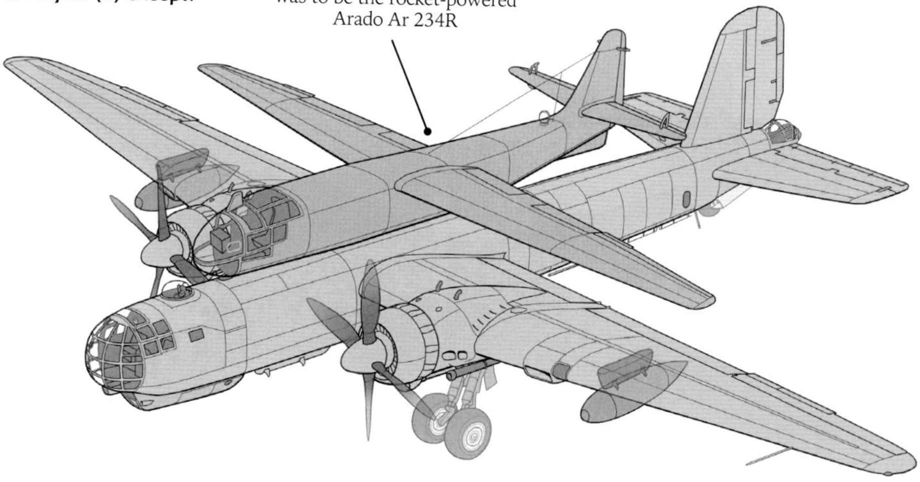

He 177 Production

Built by Heinkel AG at Rostock	
V-Series	8
A-0 (prototype) Series	20
Built by Heinkel-Werke GmbH at Orianienburg	
A-0 (Pre-production) Series	15
A-1 Series	42
A-3 Series	270
A-5 Series	135

Built by Arado Flugzeugwerke GmbH at Brandenburg	
A-0 (Pre-production) Series	5
A-1 Series	150
A-3 Series	185
A-5 Series	85
Total Production	**915**

He 274

Note: Development of the He 274 was handed over to the Société Anonymoe des Usines Farman (SAUF) company, Paris, France in July 1942

He 274 – Original Concept

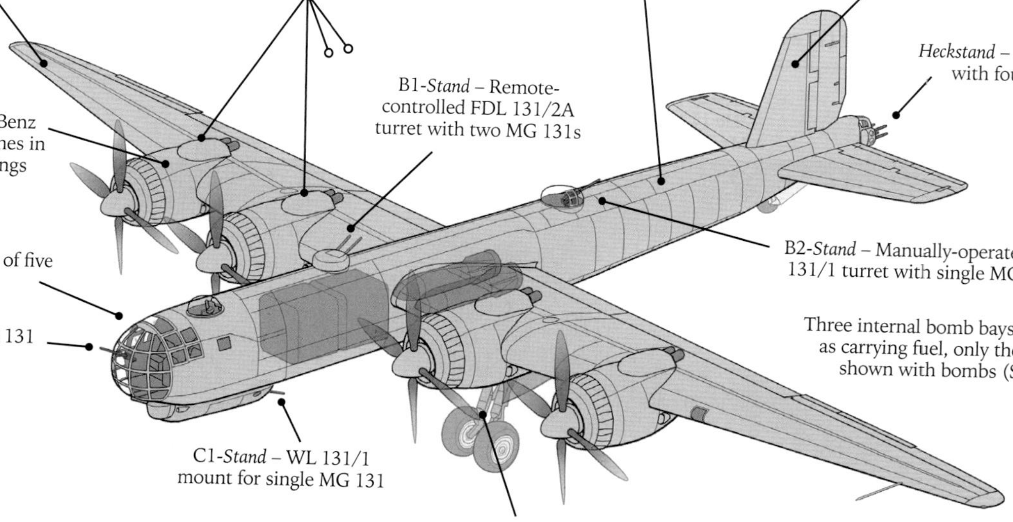

This design was superseded by the version with increased span, fuselage length and twin-tails – *see He 274 V1 elsewhere*

Projects

He 177C Project

Pathfinder version proposed for the Eisenhammer operation

- Nothing more is known of this project and it was never built

He 177H Project

High-level version of He 177A-4:

- Two DB610 engines
- 36.0m span
- Length of 22.0m
- Never built, as the type needed a wing of a much higher aspect ratio than could not be achieved with simple spar extension
- Revised and became the He 274

He 177 Mistel Project (1)

Conversions based on existing A-1, A-3 or A-5 [as depicted here] series airframes:

The project was cancelled on the 27th January 1945 before any conversions were completed

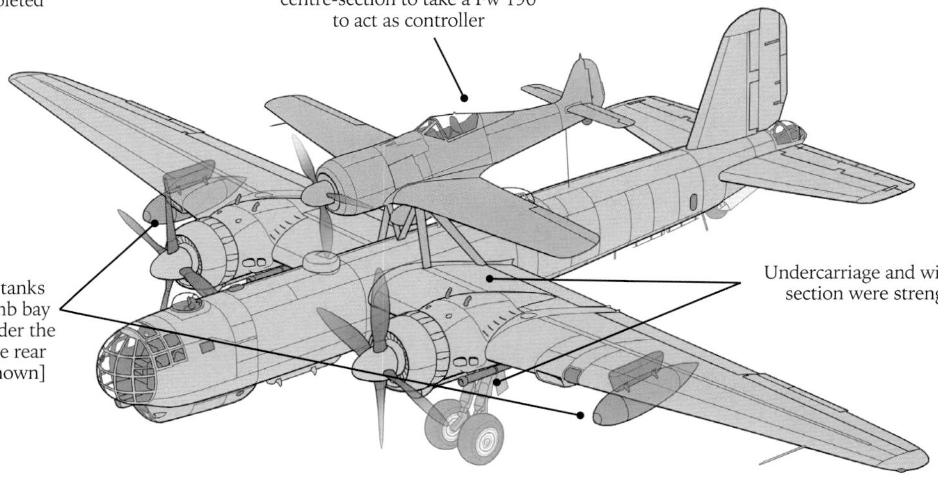

He 177 Mistel Project (2)

Same as the He 177 Mistel Project (1) except:

Never got further than the drawing board

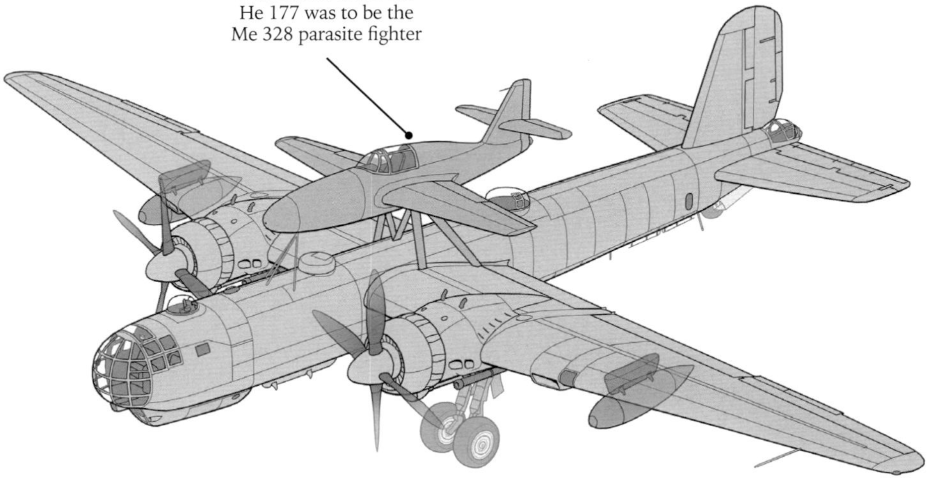

He 177 Mistel Project (3)

Same as the He 177 Mistel Project (1) except:

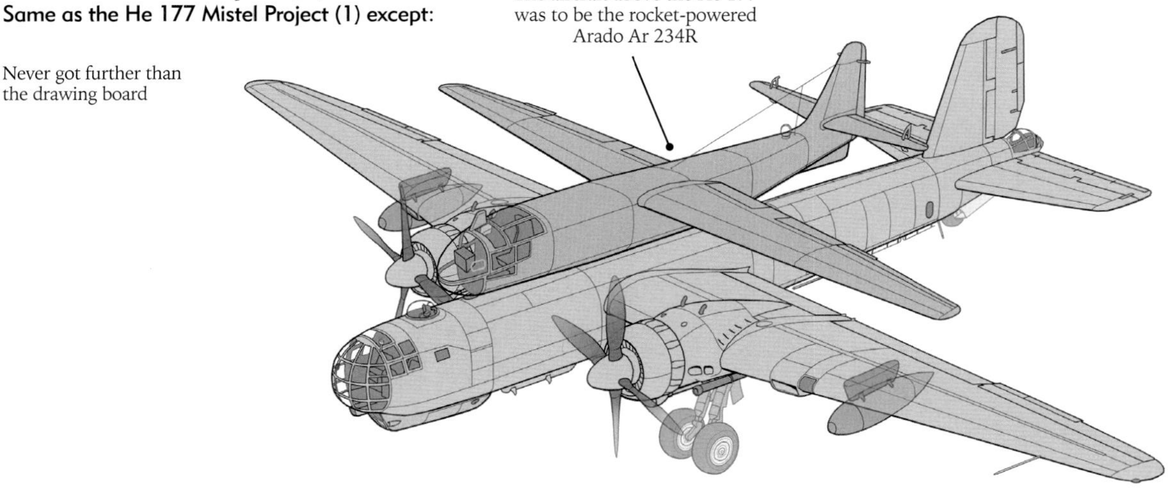

He 177 Production

Built by Heinkel AG at Rostock	
V-Series	8
A-0 (prototype) Series	20
Built by Heinkel-Werke GmbH at Orianienburg	
A-0 (Pre-production) Series	15
A-1 Series	42
A-3 Series	270
A-5 Series	135
Built by Arado Flugzeugwerke GmbH at Brandenburg	
A-0 (Pre-production) Series	5
A-1 Series	150
A-3 Series	185
A-5 Series	85
Total Production	**915**

He 274

Note: Development of the He 274 was handed over to the Société Anonymoe des Usines Farman (SAUF) company, Paris, France in July 1942

He 274 – Original Concept

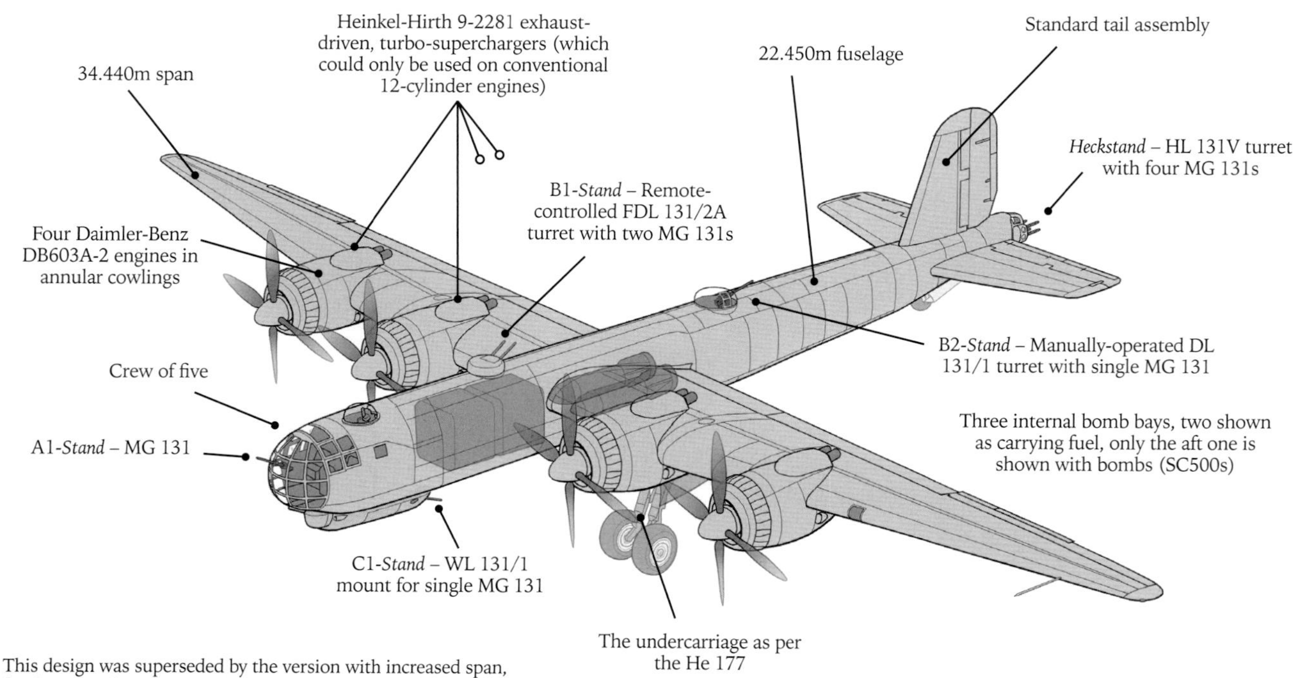

This design was superseded by the version with increased span, fuselage length and twin-tails – *see He 274 V1 elsewhere*

He 274 V1

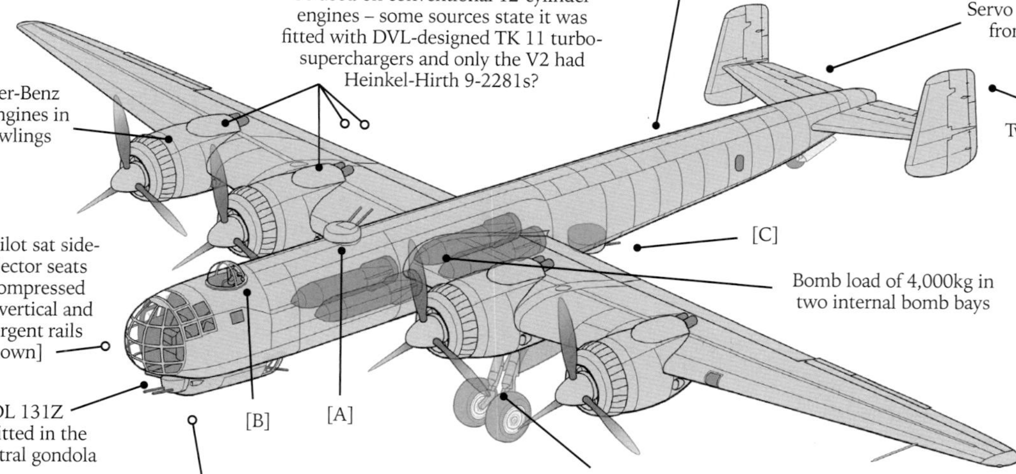

Note: This first prototype was near flight testing when Allied forces liberated Paris in August 1944 – German personnel placed explosive charges in three of the engines.

The He 274 V1 as the AAS 01A being readied for flight at Orléans-Bricy in December 1945

He 274 V1 as AAS.01A

Same as He 274 V1 except:

Note: The damage caused by the explosives planted by Nazi German staff to three of the engines was light (as these were in crates), so development after the liberation was continued by Ateliers Aéronautiques de Suresnes (SAA) [SAUF nationalised], where it became the AAS 01A and first flew (without armament) in December 1945 at Orléans-Bricy.

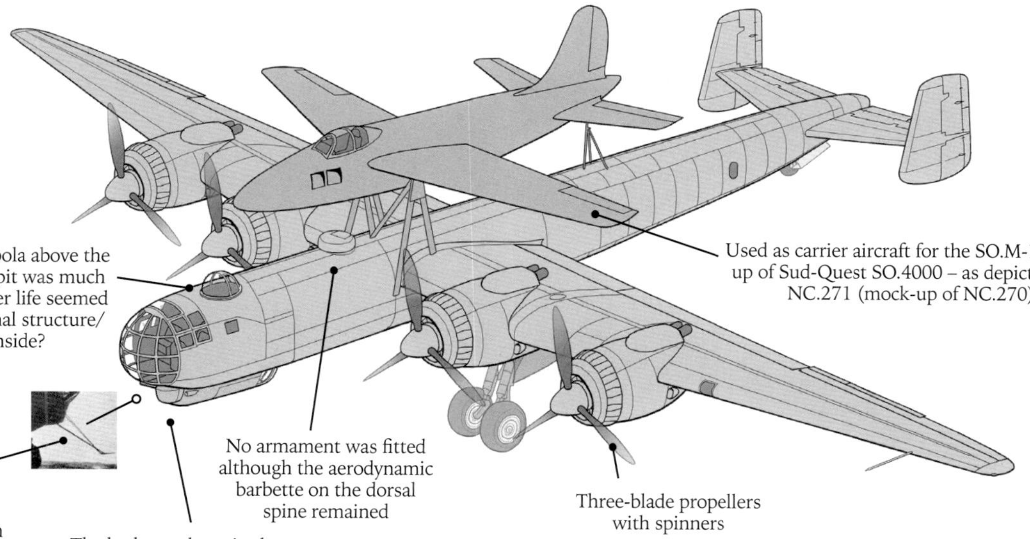

Ceased flying in 1952 and was scrapped at Marseilles-Istres in late 1955

He 274 V2 (AAS.01B)

This was to have been the same as the He 274 V1 and it was completed and first flew on the 27th December 1947. The only difference was:

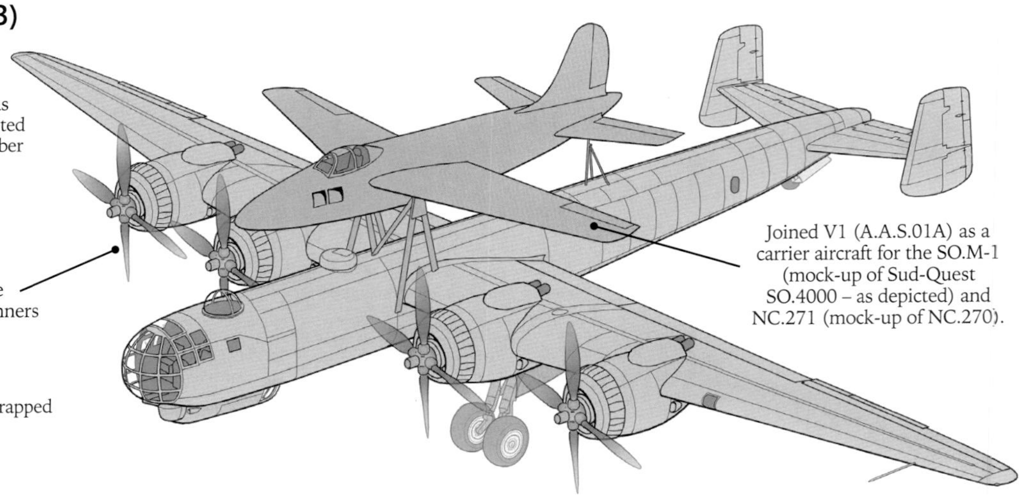

Ceased flying in 1952 and was scrapped at Marseilles-Istres in late 1955

He 277A

Based on the He 177B project except:

Seven-seat heavy bomber project

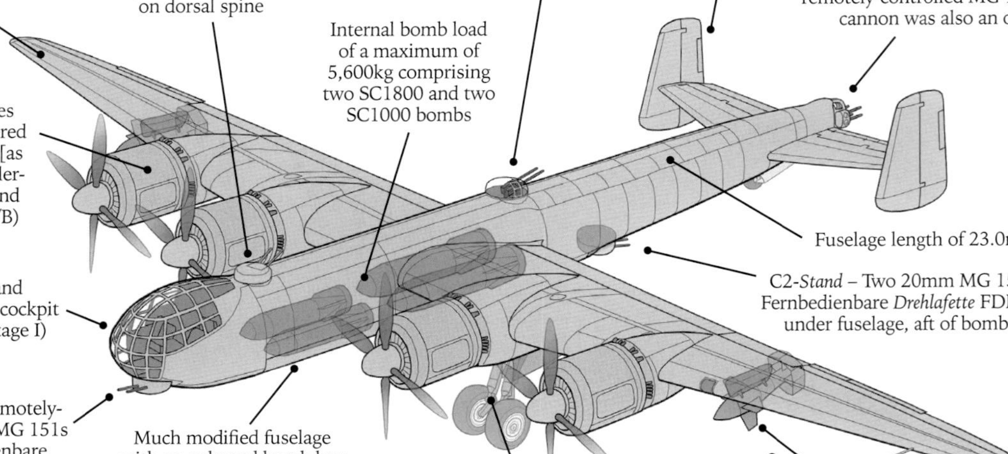

Planned for production at the end of 1946, never built

No true He 277 V-series airframes were ever completed before the war ended the image that many list as the He 277 V1 was the V101, while the He 177 V102 tested the twin fin/rudder units and the He 177 V104 tested the four-gun rear turret in conjunction with the twin fin/rudders

He 277B

Same as the He 277A except:

Planned for production at the end of 1946, never built

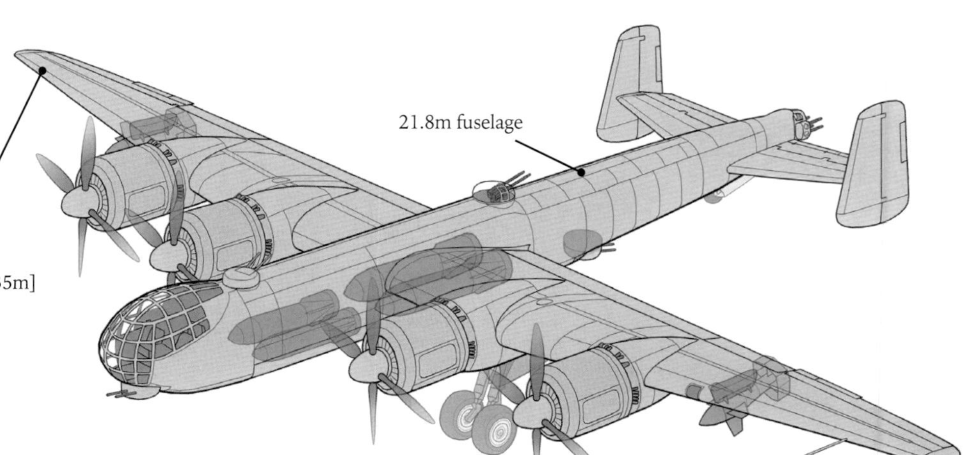

Note: For He 277B-6/R1, R2 and R3, see He 177B-6/R1, R2 and R3 elsewhere

Camouflage & Markings

Heinkel He 177 V1, W/Nr.0000 001, CP+RB, flown by Dipl-Ing Franke for the first time on 19 November 1939 from Rechlin
Believed to be RLM 02 overall with codes in black, repeated 'C+B' below starboard and 'R+P' below port wings. Propeller spinners in RLM 70

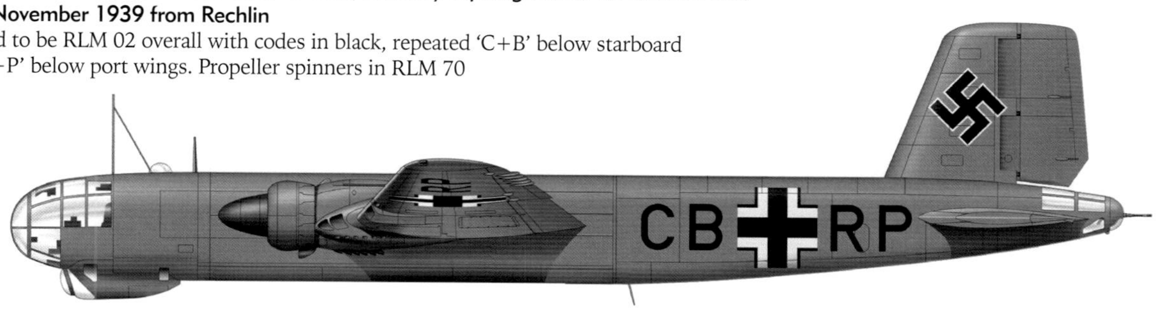

Let us first start by saying that nothing is certain when trying to deduce colours from old black and white photographs. The best you can make is an educated, and with luck intelligent, guess using both photographic and documentary evidence.

He 177 – Prototypes

Nearly all of the true V-series prototypes flew in overall RLM 02 *Grau* with the *Stammkenzeichen* applied in black either side of the fuselage, around the large Type B2 *Balkenkreuz* (cross), with two letters ahead and two aft, always rear from left to right, regardless of the side it was applied to. A Type B2 cross was applied below the wings, with a Type B5 above so that they did not cross onto the aileron/flaps and with the centre of the cross lined up with the inner gap between the aileron and landing (Fowler) flaps; the front edge was inline with the panel line for the wing leading edge. Not all carried the *Stammkenzeichen* under the wings, but if applied this was done in large black characters with the first two outboard of the cross under the starboard wing and the last two, outboard of the cross under the port wing. There are exceptions, the V6 is confirmed as having B+C under the starboard and B+P under the port wing, while the V7 had S+F (starboard) and T+B (port) and the the V8 was S+F (starboard) and T+C (port); the V5 had no codes under the wings and as no images are known to have survived for the V3 and V4, these remain an unknown in this respect. The *Halkenkreuz* (swastika) was applied large on either side of the vertical fin in H2 style with the front and rear arms and thus width of the cross determined by the leading edge of the fin and the hinge line for the rudder, as it did not cross onto the latter.

Later the V6, V7 and V8 are all confirmed as having adopted the operational scheme of RLM 70 *Schwarzgrün* and RLM 71 *Dunkelgrün* in a splinter pattern on the upper surfaces and down each side of the fuselage and across the entire vertical fin/rudder, while the undersides were RLM 65 *Hellblau*. The demarcation between the upper and lower colours was set low down on the fuselage sides, probably at about the 4/5th fuselage depth point. Whilst all the markings remained as before, the swastika slightly overlapped onto the rudder and the *Stammkenzeichen* on the fuselage sides were applied in white, although some modern profiles show them in grey the contrast in period black and white images is such that white is most likely. When the V8 was tested at Rechlin it has a yellow 500mm wide band added around the rear fuselage, with its aft edge in line with the leading edge of the vertical fin and the first (starboard) and last (port) two of the *Stammkenzeichen* were applied on top. The underside of each wing tip, to a point just outboard of the first (starboard) and last (port)

The He 177 V1, CB+RP moments before touch-down, the overall colour of the airframe is obvious as are the overlarge swastika on the tail and crosses on the fuselage and under the wings. You can also just make out the 'CB' element of the identification code letters outboard of the cross under the starboard wing

Heinkel He 177 V7, SF+TB, Rechlin, 1941, for operational trials
RLM 70/71 upper surfaces with RLM 65 undersides. Codes in white, repeated in black below the wings: 'S+F' below starboard and 'T+B' below port

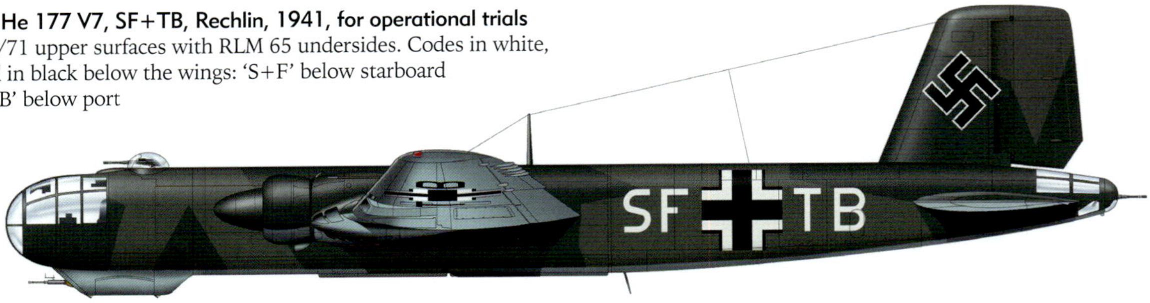

Heinkel He 177 V8, W/Nr.0000 008, SF+TC, '2', Rechlin, 1941
RLM 70/71 upper surfaces with RLM 65 undersides. RLM 04 rear fuselage band and underside of wingtips. Codes in white, repeated in black with 'S+F below starboard and 'T+C below port wings. '2' with an underside dash also in white on rudder

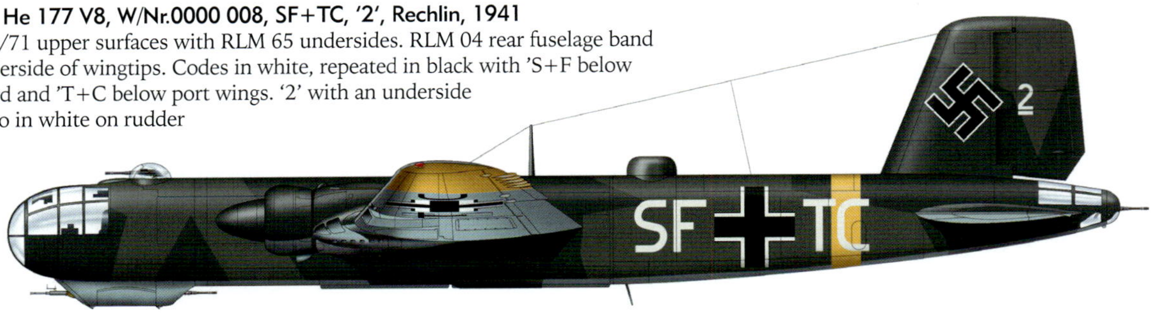

A close-up of the rear fuselage and tail of the He 177 V8, SF+TC, allowing you to see the 500mm wide yellow band around the fuselage with the 'SF' applied on top and the fact that the swastika does overlap onto the rudder on the starboard side (it was contained by the hinge on the port side)

By combining close-ups from these two period images you can see the Stammkenzeichen applied (in white) to the fuselage sides of the A-02 DL+AQ at the top and those applied to the fuselage (in white) and under the wing (as S+F in black, T+C was under the port wing) of the V8 at the bottom

The He 177 V7, SF+TB under cover whilst undergoing trials, the white codes and revised fuselage cross are all visible, as is the fact that with this particular machine the swastika does not go back over the rudder

letter of the *Stammkenzeichen* was also in yellow and it carried the number '2' with a line under it, in white on the port side of the rudder (not on the starboard), in line with the centre of the swastika.

Stammkenzeichen

The primary identification code letters (*Stammkenzeichen*) was applied at the factory prior to delivery, in large black characters either side of the fuselage cross (*Balkenkreuz*) and below the wings. This latter application was done so that the characters could be read from the trailing edge looking forward and the characters were split either side of the cross (*Balkenkreuz*) under each wing, so you would have V+D under the starboard wing and X+S under the port. The *Stammkenzeichen* was usually removed from the fuselage on delivery and replaced with the codes or individual aircraft letter. However, as with all things Luftwaffe, this was not always the case, so check your references

He 177 – Pre-production

The twenty test airframes number A-01 to A-020 were all finished in the same scheme as applied to the last V-series machines, so were RLM 70/71 over 65. Markings comprised Type B2 cross above the wings and Type B5 above, with Type B3 on the fuselage sides and a Type H2 swastika on the vertical fin (not crossing onto the rudder). The *Stammkenzeichen* was applied in white characters on either side of the fuselage (again, always read from left to right) with these repeated under the wings with the first two (e.g. D+L) under the starboard and last two (e.g. A+Q) under the port in smaller black characters. The only other markings you will find on these machines, unless remarked for specific trials, was the identification number in small white characters on either side of the nose, positioned at the halfway point directly below the sighting cupola aft of the cockpit; this was done as just the numbers, so the A-02 was '02', the A-06 was '06' etc. with a horizontal white line underneath.

High contrast in an old image that has been reproduced many times can be useful, as seen here these two images of the He 177A-02, which allows you to see the splinter camouflage of the very dark RLM 70 and 71 upper surfaces, whilst just visible in the top image, under the canopy is the underlined '02' denoting this as the second test airframe in the A-01 to A-020 batch

A nice in-flight of He 177A-1, WNr.5215, VE+UO, that highlights the Stammkenzeichen under the wings and on the fuselage, the low demarcation on the fuselage sides and the thin white elements of the older Type B1 cross on the fuselage in comparison with the much wider bars of the Type B2 under the wings

He 177 – Production

The A-0 pre-production airframes were in the same RLM 70/71 over 65 scheme with Type B2 cross above and Type B5 below the wings and Type B3 on the fuselage sides combined with a Type H2 swastika on either side of the the vertical fin (not crossing onto the rudder). On delivery the *Stammkenzeichen* would have been applied in black characters on either side of the fuselage (again, always read from left to right) with these repeated under the wings. These codes were often retained if the specific airframe was used for trials work, so you will find those used by the test unit, Erprobungsstaffel 177, often retained the *Stammkenzeichen* on either side of the fuselage and under the wings. Once in service most A-0s and A-1s had the *Stammkenzeichen* removed and replaced with unit codes and individual aircraft identification letters.

The expansion of the Luftwaffe led to certain re-organisational changes and in February 1939 the new *Luftflotten* (Air Fleets) were created. These comprised *Luftflotte 1* covering Northern and Eastern Germany plus East Prussia; *Luftflotte 2* covered North-West Germany; *Luftflotte 3* covered South-West Germany; and *Luftflotte 4* (created in March 1939) covered South East Germany, Austria and Czechoslovakia. Within each was a *Luftgau* (Air District) that took over the role previously done by the *Luftkreiskommando* and operational functions were undertaken by the *Fliegerdivision* (Air Divisions – later renamed *Fliegerkorps* (Air Corps)). All this reorganisation led to a new coding system for bombers, dive-bombers and multi-engine aircraft. The new system used four characters, two each side of the fuselage cross, and was introduced in the spring of 1939. This system comprised two characters (either

Heinkel He 177A-1, VF+RP, 6./KG 1, Brandis, 1943
RLM 70/71 upper surfaces with RLM 65 undersides. Codes 'VF' in black, 'RP' in white. Yellow rear fuselage band

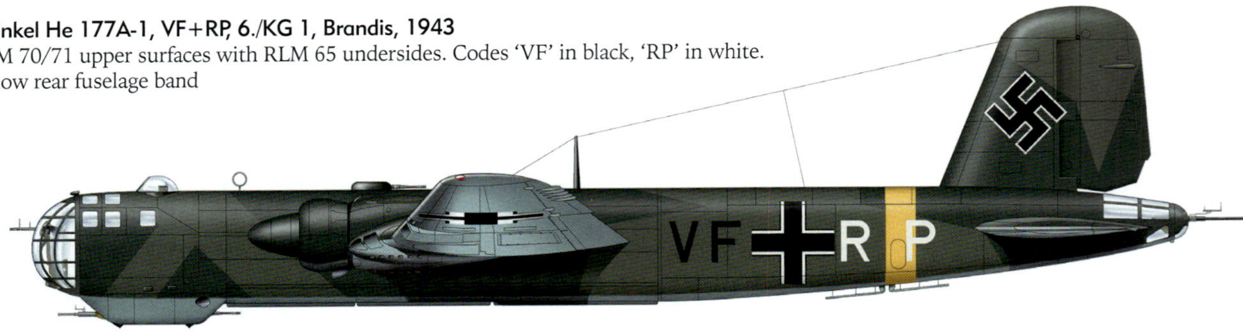

A He 177A-1 of KG 40 at Châteaudun in 1943 lacking codes but with the individual aircraft letter applied as a very large white character on the rudder

a letter/number or number/letter combination) to the left of the cross that identified the unit, usually the *Geschwader* or for smaller units, the *Gruppe*. The first of the two characters to the right of the cross was invariably painted in the *Staffel* or *Stab* (Staff) colour and identified the individual aircraft, whilst the final character identified the *Staffel* within the *Gruppe*. The three *Staffel* within each *Gruppe* were identified by colour; the first was RLM 21 *Weiss* (white), the second was RLM 23 *Rot* (red) and the third was RLM 04 *Gelb* (yellow). Because there were cases when there were more than three *Staffel* in the *Gruppe*, colours such as RLM 24 *Dunkelblau* (dark blue) and RLM 25 Hellgrün (light green) were also used, even though these were basically *Stab* (Staff) colours. The individual aircraft letter was often repeated under each wing, outboard of the cross. Some machines also had the individual aircraft character applied on the upper surfaces of the wings, outboard of the cross on both side and usually in the same manner/colour as they were applied on the fuselage, although there are instances of these being just in white (probably to give contrast with the dark camouflage).

The A-1s of 6./KG 1 were in the RLM 70/71 over 65 scheme with the yellow band around the rear fuselage, but not under the wings. The unit code (VF) was applied in black, while the remainder of the codes (e.g. RP) was applied in white and these codes were not repeated under the wings.

The A-1s used by KG 40 often lacked the unit and individual identification codes, instead they just had a single letter, applied as a large white character on either side of the rudder, set with it on a hypothetical line at the halfway point for the height of the rudder.

The A-1s of 1./FKG 50 operating out of Russia were in the RLM 70/71 over 65 scheme and had a yellow band around the rear fuselage, with yellow on the underside of each wing tip. The crosses were Type B2 under (and B5 above) the wings with the narrow older Type B1 on the fuselage sides. Codes were applied so that the unit element (F8) was in characters about 1/5th the height of the last two. Most usually carried the badge of KG 40 on either side of the nose and this could be applied in black or red.

A He 177A-1 of FKG50 used in the transport role from Zaporozhye in South Russia, note the KG 40 badge on the nose, the demarcation along the lower fuselage and the yellow band around the rear fuselage; not visible are the yellow undersides to each wing tip

Heinkel He 177A-1, E8+HK, 1./FKG 50, Zaporozhye-Süd (Russia), early 1943
RLM 70/71 on upper surfaces with RLM 65 undersides. Codes in black, repeated below the wings. Spinner tips in RLM 23, RLM 04 below wing tips and rear fuselage band. Unit badge on forward fuselage

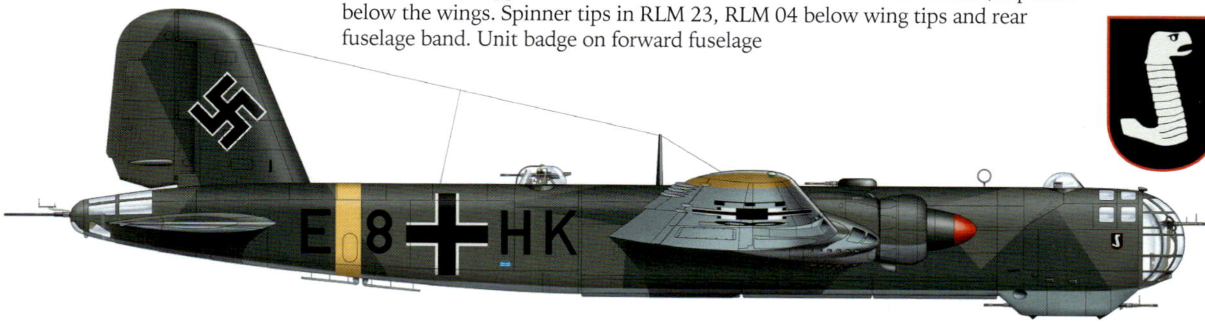

Heinkel He 177A-1, E8+FH, 1./FKG 50, Zaporozhye (Russian Front), winter 1943
RLM 70/71 upper surfaces with RLM 65 undersides. Yellow underside of wing tips and rear fuselage band. Codes in black. Badge on nose belongs to KG 40

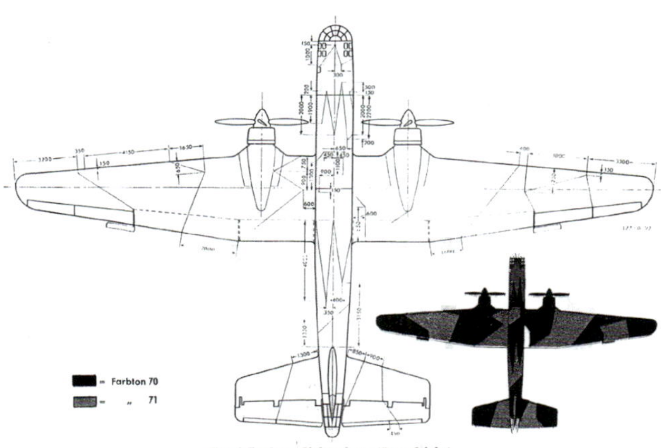

This diagram from the handbook shows the splinter camouflage pattern of RLM 70/71 for the upper surfaces of the A-1 series

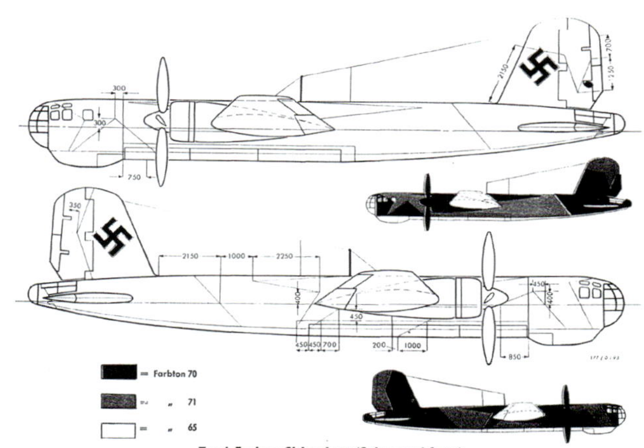

This diagram, also from the handbook, shows the splinter camouflage pattern of RLM 70/71 for the port and starboard sides, as well as the RLM 65 regions of the A-1 series

The A-1s of 5./KG 100 had the unit code '6N' with the individual aircraft letter (e.g. 'A') applied in red with a thin white outline.

Heinkel He 177A-1, 6N+AN, 5./KG 100, Alborg (Denmark), 1944
RLM 70/71 upper surfaces with RLM 65 undersides. Codes in black, with 'A' in RLM 23, outlined in white

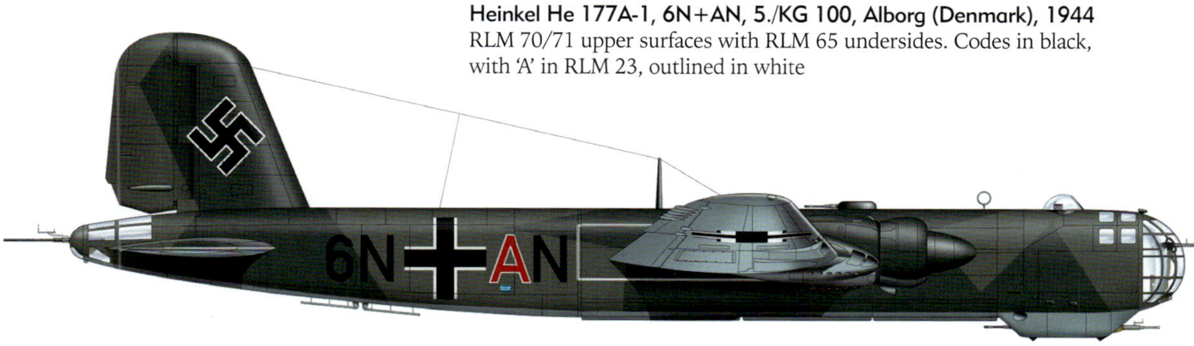

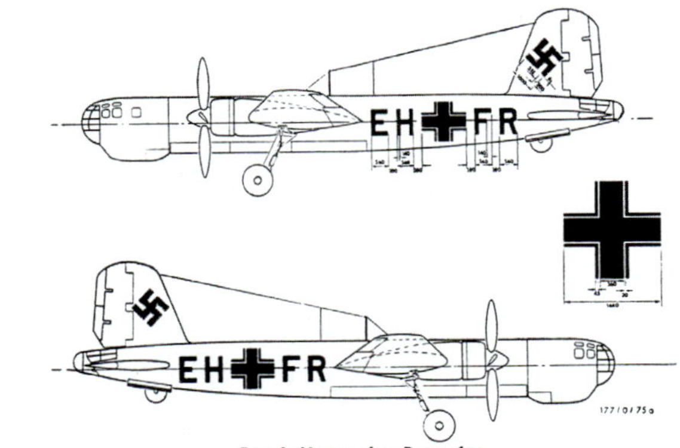

Beschriftung des Rumpfes

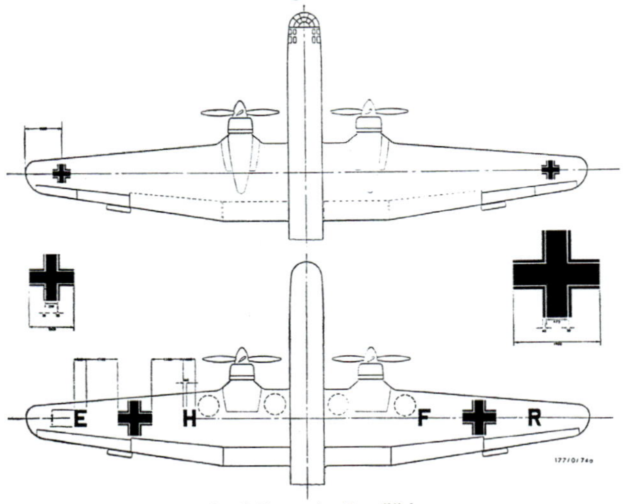

Beschriftung der Tragfläche

These two diagrams from the handbook shows style, size and location of the national insignia and unit markings for the A-1 series

He 177A-1 Test Airframes

A number of A-1s were used for test purposes, too many to cover individually, so we thought we would just offer a couple of colour profiles (see bottom of the page).

He 177A-3

This was the first true series production variant made in any large number and it had a variety of schemes applied throughout its life. The best way to cover all the potential scheme is to look at specific machines based on period images.

Daylight

Those used for daylight bombing operations tended to retain the RLM 70/71 over 65 scheme, but had a high demarcation on the fuselage combined with dense areas of scribbles in RLM 02 Grau on the upper surfaces and extending right down the fuselage sides and undersides as well as under the wings to about mid-chord. Markings remained as Type B1 for the fuselage, Type B2 for underneath the wings and Type B5 above, with a H2 swastika. The unit codes were in black and 1/5th the height of the remaining two, with the individual aircraft letter either in colour or black outlined in colour.

Some machines can be found in period images with a demarcation slightly lower down the fuselage sides, inline with the bottom edge of the side windows aft of the nose cupola. This usually combines with a total lack of any form of mottling on the fuselage sides, but the markings remain Type B1 (fuselage), Type B2 under the wings and Type B5 above.

Later a dense mottle of RLM 70/71 and/or RLM 02 was applied along the fuselage sides, engine cowlings/nacelles and across the vertical fin and rudder, while all other markings remained as before.

Heinkel He 177A-1/U2 (V12), GI+BL, test bed for the twin 30mm Mk 101 cannon, June 1942
RLM 70/71/65 finish with black codes, with 'G+I' repeated below the starboard and 'B+L' repeated below the port wings

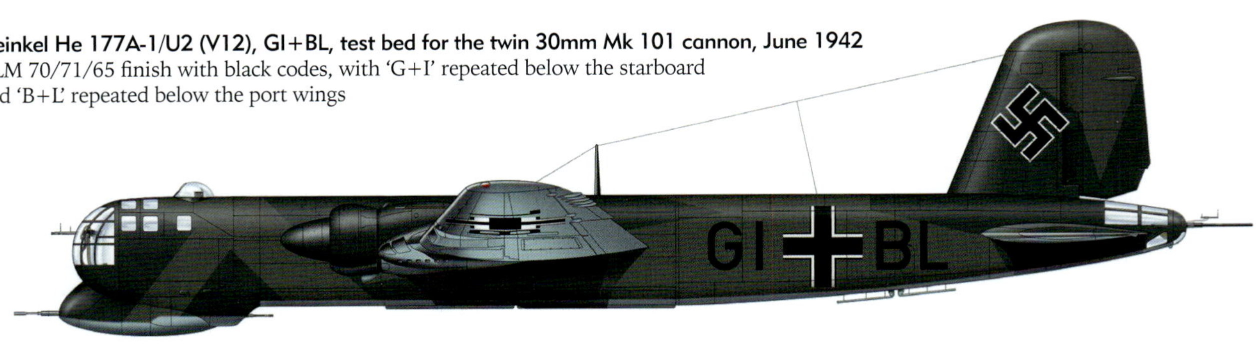

Heinkel He 177 V31 W/Nr.550202, TM+IF, Torpedowaffenplatz, Gotenhafen-Hexengrund (Germany), early 1944
RLM 70/71 upper surfaces with RLM 65 undersides with a high demarcation line on the fuselage sides. RLM 70/71 mottling on fuselage side and vertical tail surfaces. RLM 04 rear fuselage band. Codes in white, repeated in black below the wings. Below the starboard wing only, it is carrying a Blohm und Voss L10 glider torpedo carrier with a LT F5b torpedo; the head is marked in red and white to denote that it was a dummy warhead

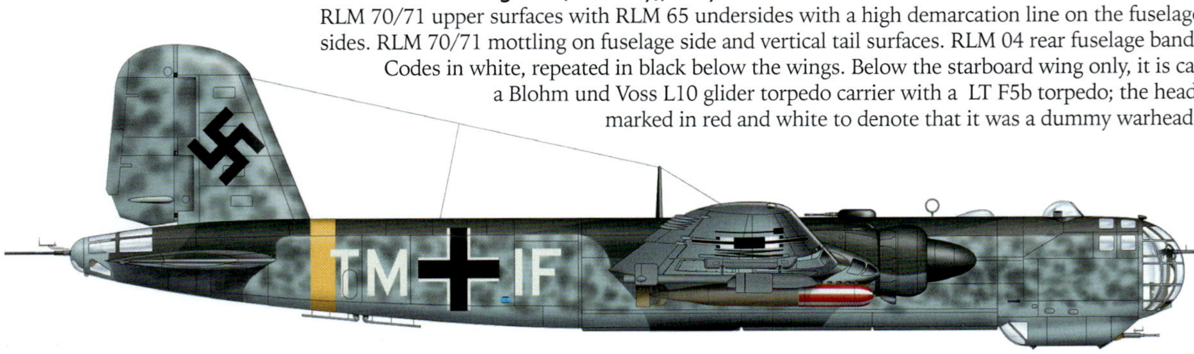

Heinkel He 177A-3, W/Nr.332206, 5J+KK, 1./KG 100 (but carrying the codes of its previous unit, 2./KG 4)
RLM 70/71 upper surfaces with RLM 65 undersides and vertical tail surfaces with high separation line on fuselage sides. RLM 02 *Wellenmunster* (with possible RLM 70 touches; part of bomb bay doors probably from a different machine) on all surfaces Codes in black with the first 'K' having a red outline. RLM 23 sections (on propeller blade roots) over the RLM 70 spinners, with a white vertical band

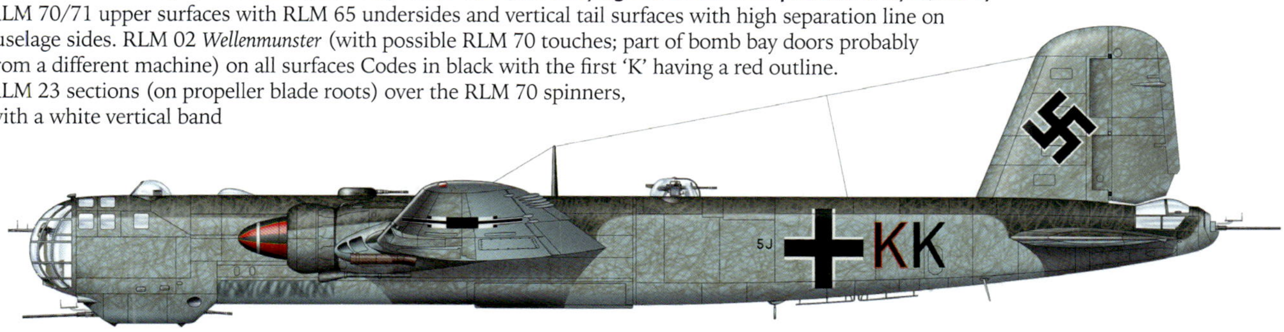

Heinkel He 177A-5, V4+AK, KG 1, 1944
RLM 70/71 upper surfaces with undersides in RLM 65; note lower demarcation fuselage line than standard, in line with wing root at leading edge. Codes in black, with 'A' repeated on nose. White band around propellers

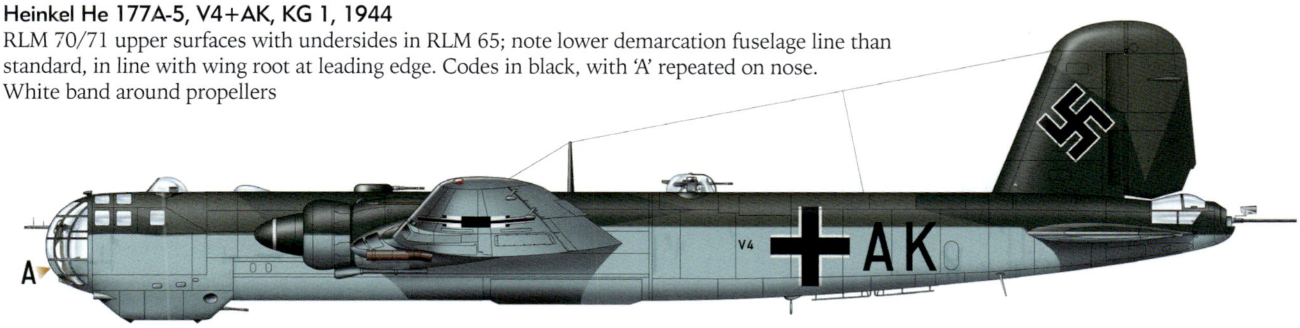

The slightly lower demarcation is very obvious on this He 177A-3, V4-AK, of the KG 1 photographed at Brandis probably during the unit's conversion to the type in 1944

He 177A-3, V4+BL at Brandis while I KG 1 converted to the type in 1944, note the large number applied to the rudder, probably denoting these aircraft were being used for training

Night & Operation Steinbock

Those A-3s used for night bombing operations were RLM 75 on the upper 1/3rd of the fuselage and upper surfaces of the wings and tail, with the remainder including the entire vertical fin/rudder in black (RLM 22). The demarcation between upper and lower colours meant that there were distinct curves down to meet the leading and trailing edge of the wings and leading edge of the horizontal tailplane, whilst the demarcation from the trailing edge of the elevators was a straight line. The exact point of the demarcation does vary though, resulting in more pronounced curves, while on the engine nacelles you will find those that had the demarcation set at the midway point, while others had it set at about 1/3rd; the latter option obviously resulting in black regions that were above the wings as a result. The upper surfaces could be covered with a dense *Wellenmunster* (scribble) of RLM 02 and RLM 70 or in a dense, but not heavy, blotching of RLM 75 *Grauviolett* (some state RLM 74 *Graugrün*). The crosses tended to be simplified, so it was the outline only Type B6 on the fuselage and under the wings. Those on the fuselage and under the wings could be white or grey. Those above the wings would have been black (Type B6a) and the

Heinkel He 177A-3, 6N+HK 'Helga', 2./KG 100, 'Operation Steinbock', early 1944
RLM 22 overall with RLM 75 upper surfaces over which a *Wellenmunster* (scribble) of RLM 02 and 70 has been applied. RLM 76 '6N' of code, fuselage Balkenkreuz and fin Hakenkreuz. Codes 'HK' in RLM 23 outline, Name on nose in white, spinners in RLM 23

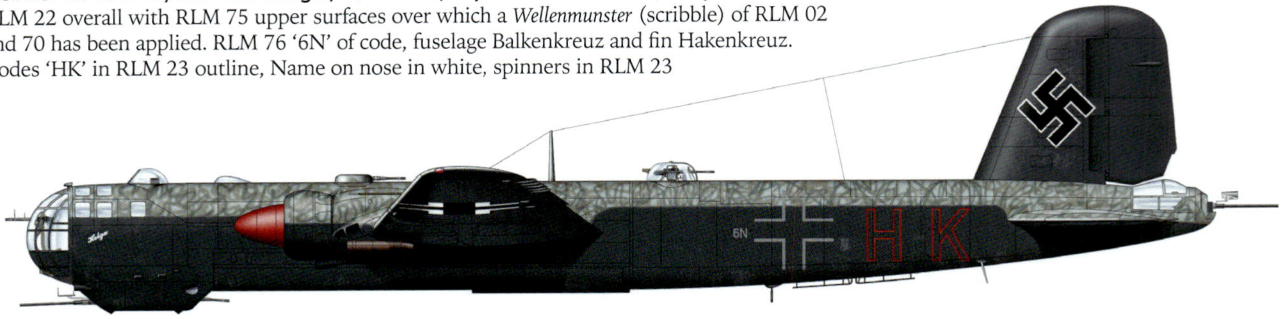

Heinkel He 177A-3, 6N+SK 'Susi', 2./KG 100, spring 1944
RLM 22 overall with upper surfaces in RLM 76 that is covered in RLM 75 mottling. National markings in RLM 74. '6N' of code in white; 'SK' in RLM 23 outlined in white. Spinner and name on nose in RLM 23, the latter outlined in white. ''S' of code repeated on front of nose in white

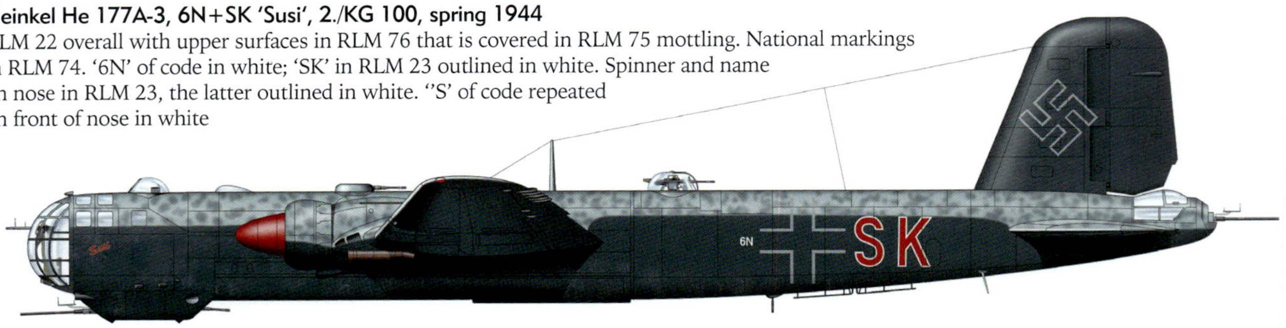

Heinkel He 177A-5, 6N+EK, 'Edith', 2./KG 100, Operation Steinbock, Châteaudun (France), 1944
RLM 22 overall with upper surfaces in RLM 76 with *Wellenmunster* in RLM 75. Fuselage Balkenkreuz and fin Hakenkreuz in RLM 76. Codes '6N' in RLM 76, 'EK' in red outlined in white. 'Edith' in white on nose. Red front of spinners

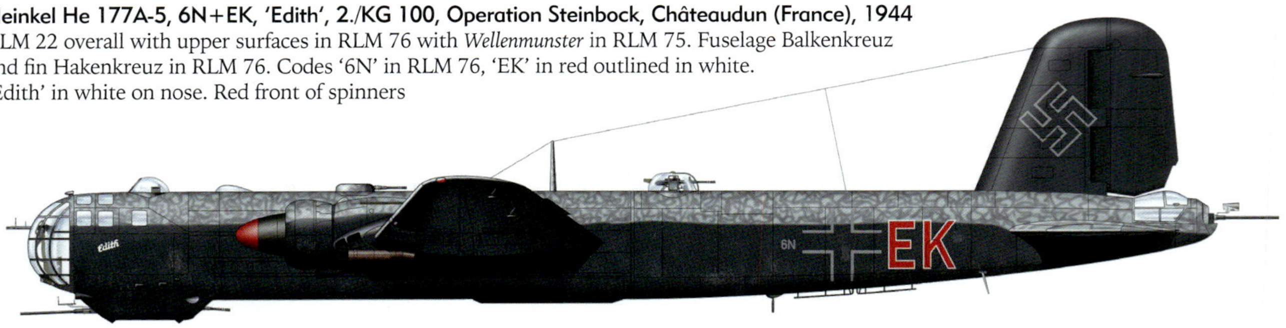

Two views of He 177A-3, 6N+SK, 'Susi' of 2./KG100 at Rheine in the spring of 1944

A He 177A-3 and A-5 of I./KG 100 at Munich-Riem whilst in transit to the Eastern Front, you can just make out the tiny Type B6a cross above the starboard and port wings

He 177A-3 or A-5 with the name 'Edith' on the nose from 2./KG 100 found at Châteaudun in the summer of 1944

swastika was also the simplified Type H4 in white. Those used during Operation Steinbock often had names applied in white script on either side of the forward fuselage, directly below the aft section of cockpit glazing.

KG 1 machines were in the same overall scheme, but the vertical fin/rudder was in the RLM 76 with RLM 74 or 75 mottle and used the H2a style of swastika. The spinners were RLM 70, but some had the tip in yellow. The crosses were applied in a dark grey, as were the codes, although the aft two may have been outlined in white, while some state this was yellow?

It seems that later, some He 177A-3s operated by KG 100 adopted the scheme applied to their A-5s (see KG 100 section from page 171). These machines were in the old RLM 70/71 upper surfaces combined with RLM 76 undersides. The entire upper regions of RLM 70/71 were then covered with large random 'clouds' of RLM 65. The fuselage cross was Type B6, but those under the wings were the older Type B2, with Type B5 above. The swastika was the older Type H2 and the unit code (6N) was applied in black characters that were 1/5th the height of the remaining two, while the individual aircraft identification letter was in colour (e.g. red) outlined thinly in white. In some instances, the spinners were black with a thin white spiral, like that seen on fighters and a two-digit code number was applied in black characters on either side of the ventral gondola (this was most likely the last two of the W/Nr.).

Heinkel He 177A-3, 6N+EM, 4./KG 100, early 1944
Probably, RLM 70/71 upper surfaces with RLM 76 undersides. Large irregular blotches of RLM 65 applied over the upper surfaces. Codes in black, except 'E' which is RLM 23, outlined in white. Black '33' on gondola below front fuselage. Black spinners with white spiral

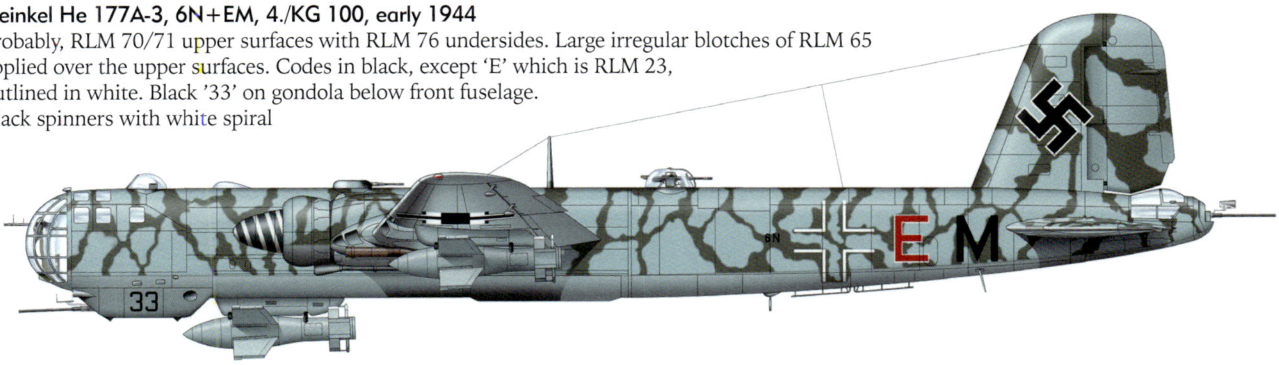

Heinkel He 177A-1, VF+RJ, FFS(C) 16, Burg bei Magdeburg, 1943
RLM 70/71 upper surfaces with RLM 65 undersides. RLM 04 rear fuselage band and underside of wingtips. Codes in black, outline in white. Unit badge on forward fuselage, both sides

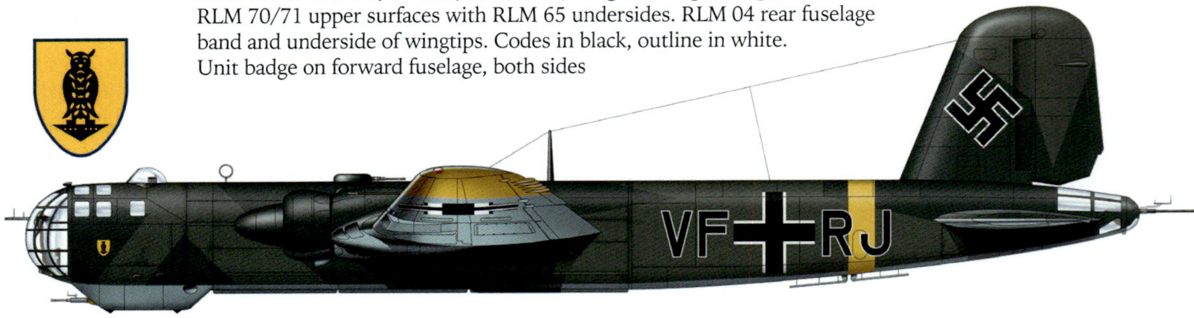

Heinkel He 177A-3, GU+HO, FFS(B) 16, Burg bei Magdeburg, 1943
RLM 70/71 upper surfaces with RLM 65 undersides. RLM 04 underside of wing tips and rear fuselage band. Codes in black, outlined in white. Unit badge on forward fuselage

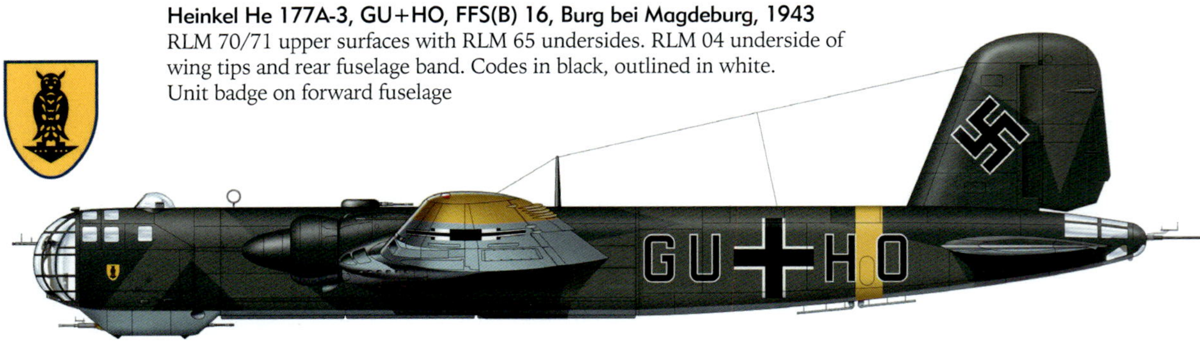

Training

The FFS(B) flight training schools adopted old airframes, so these could have a mix of schemes. Included in a period photo of a line-up of aircraft with FFS(B) at Burg bei Magdeburg was GU+HO in a very faded RLM 70/71 over 65 camouflage. It had the yellow band around the rear fuselage and yellow undersides to each wing tip, whilst the codes were applied only on either side of the fuselage and these were black with a thin white outline. The crosses were Type B2 under the wings (and we suspect also above) with the older thinner Type B1 on either side of the fuselage. The swastika was Type H2 and applied on either side of the vertical fin, without crossing on to the rudder.

Another well photographed examples include VD+XS with FFS(B) 16 at Burg bei Magdeburg, which had the upper 1/3rd of the fuselage and all the upper surfaces of the wings and tail in RLM 76 *Lichtblau* and all the remainder in black (RLM 22). The upper surfaces had also received a tight but not heavy scribble (*Wellenmunster*) of RLM 75 *Grauviolett*. A yellow band was applied around the rear fuselage, aft of the last two of the codes, with the underside of each wing also in yellow, from a point just outboard of the first (starboard) and last (port) characters of the codes. These codes were applied as black with a thin white outline on the fuselage, but as solid white characters under the wings. By this stage the fuselage cross was the simplified Type B6 , probably with the B6a version above. Very little can be seen of the cross under the wing, so it was most likely over-sprayed with black to make it less prominent, but it too seems to be the simplified Type B6. The swastika on the tail is also the simplified Type H4 and is of the big format seen on the earlier A-0/A-1 series and the last three of the

Close-up of the nose of a He 177A-1 from FFS(B) 16 at Burg bei Magdeburg, the very faded nature of the RLM 70/71/65 scheme is evident as is the various retouched areas around where panels have been removed. The badge on the nose was a black owl on a yellow shield and it is interesting to note the outline of what looks like the 'World in a ring' insignia of KG 40 that has been painted out just aft of the FFS(B) 16 badge?

Heinkel He 117A-3, FFS(B) 16, Burg bei Magdeburg, 1943
RLM 22 overall with upper surfaces in RLM 76 that is covered in RLM 75 mottling. RLM 04 undersides of wing tips and rear fuselage band. Codes in white. Unit badge on forward fuselage

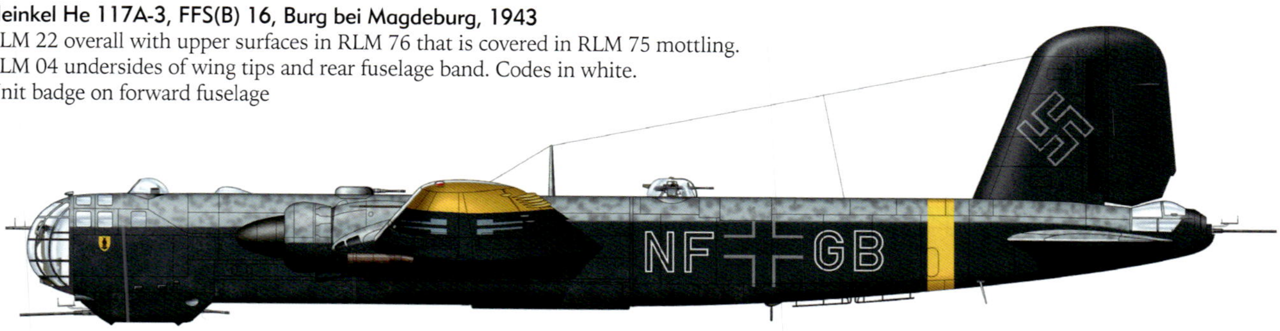

Heinkel He 177A-3, VD+XS, FFS(B) 16, Burg bei Magdeburg, late 1943
RLM 22 overall with RLM 76 upper surfaces which is covered in RLM 75 *Wellenmunster*. RLM 04 underside of wing tips and rear fuselage band. Codes in black with white outline over the original RLM 70/71 background. Codes repeated below the wings. Unit badge on forward fuselage

W/Nr. ('2143') is applied in very small white characters just forward of the swastika.

Another machine used by FFS(B) 16 was in a very weathered and faded RLM 70/71 over 65 camouflage, with irregular *Wellenmunster* (squiggles) of RLM 71 on the forward, mid and aft fuselage, vertical fin/rudder and side of the engine cowlings. The application of the squiggles varies in intensity with it being large and heavy on the fuselage sides, but light and small on the engine cowls. The old unit codes have obviously been covered over with denser areas of RLM 71 and the type had the yellow lower wing tips, but lacked the fuselage band. Crosses comprised the old Type B2 under (and most likely above) the wings with an unusual Type B1a on either side of the fuselage. A Type H2 swastika was applied on either side of the vertical fin and a large '32' was applied in white on either side of the rudder. No codes were carried on the fuselage or under the wings.

Two views of He 177A-3, W/Nr.2143, VD+XS of FFS(B) 16 at Burg bei Magdeburg, the top one gives an overall view, whilst the lower one is interesting due to the 'light' areas visible around the codes on the fuselage? This is actually most likely due to masking that has been applied whilst these codes were first being applied, the photographer obviously not wanting to wait!

Heinkel He 177A-3, 'White 32', FFS(B) 16, Burg bei Magdeburg, 1943
RLM 70/71 upper surfaces with RLM 65 undersides over which a *Wellenmunster* in RLM 71 has been applied. White '32' on rudder. RLM 04 underside of wing tips. The aircraft appears to have a very weathered finish

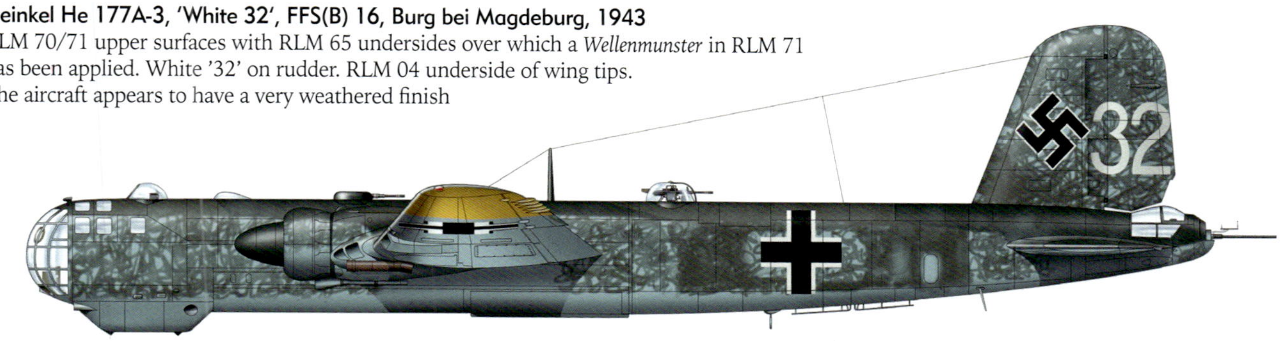

The sighting cupola, B2-Stand and guns for the B1-Stand all in place, as well as thin elastic thread used for the radio antenna

All the engraved surface detail benefitted from an oil wash, just to highlight it

Conclusion

The Revell kit still has a lot to offer despite its age (yes, it is over 20 years old already!), and its construction is relatively easy despite the massive size of the model. Moreover, there is no other viable kit in 1/72nd scale anyway and it doesn't seem that any of the mainstream manufacturers are going to work on this type anytime soon. If you are determined to buy the kit, try to obtain the older release when the moulds were still in good condition and, if possible, check the quality of the transparent parts. It's a little bit of a shame that Revell didn't take full advantage of the kit's potential, after all, with a few new parts they could have brought to the market an equally attractive A-3 version, not to mention possible reissues of the original A-5 but with the Hs 293 bombs from the A-6 edition.

Paints Used
Gunze-Sangyo Mr Color Aqueous acrylic:
Mr Surfacer 1000 (Grey)
H64 RLM 71
H67 RLM 65
H70 RLM 02
GX100 Super Clear 100

The He 177 In Scale

As already stated, there have not been that many kits of the He 177 over the years, but there are injected plastic kits in 1/72nd and 1/48th scales. What follows therefore is a brief look at your options in each scale.

No Scale

• Meng Models Heinkel He 177
#MP-003S – This was in the 'Meng Kids' series and was released in 2015, it was an unscaled caricature of the real aircraft in a similar vein to the Hasegawa Egg Plane series. I built one in 2020 and posted the review up on our website. Visit 'The Stash' element within the Modelling Resource section on www.valiant-wings.co.uk for more details.

Small Scale

• Anigrand Craftworks 1/144th
Heinkel He 274 #AA-4102 (2019) – This manufacturer from Hong-Kong offers a mass of unusual subjects as resin kits and the He 274 was one of them. We have never actually seen one of these kits so cannot comment on its contents

• Sanwa/Tokyo Plamo 1/435th
Heinkel He 274 #522 (1950s-60s) – This Japanese manufacturer made 'scaled to the box' kits back in the 1950s and whilst we have never actually seen one, we suspect they were pretty basic.

Meng Models Heinkel He 177

Airfix #05009-2

1/72nd Scale

• Airfix
Heinkel He 177 #Patt. No.589 (1967) – Renumbered #05009-2 in 1973, #05009 in 1983, #905009 in 1985 and #05009 in 1986 and 1993 – Which Luftwaffe modeller has not made this one? I have certainly made it on more that one occasion over the last 40+ years in both the original pale blue-coloured plastic and the more modern horrible hard light grey-coloured stuff. The kit is complex and my main memory of it was how badly the canopy glazings fitted! The kit had three Hs 293s and all the gimmicks of the era in which it was created, e.g. movable control surfaces and turrets, plus it was covered in raised details. For years this was the only choice for the type in this scale and numerous conversions have been produced or it over the years allowing you to even make it as the He 274 or He 277. Nowadays it is purely for the collector as the Revell kit is easier to build and looks a lot nicer when it is.

Being unique in the scale at the time, it got reissued by a lot of other firms as well including Eidai (#A-106) in the late 1960s, Gunze-Sangyo (#GX-203) in the early 1980s, MPC (#1200, #2-1200, 2-0303 & 2-2502) in 1970, 1972 and 1976 and Plasty Modelle (#9) in the early 1970s.

• Delvac Models
Heinkel He 277A-5/V1 – This firm announced this vac-formed kit in the early 2000s, but it was never actually released

• Revell
Heinkel He 177A-5 & Fritz X (#04616) – It was no real surprise for this German manufacturer to consider the He 177, so in 2000 the A-5 came along. I recall building it at the time, it was very nice, not without some issues in construction and a few people pointed to various details that they felt were wrong, plus going with the last production version meant that back-dating it was not a simple issue; thankfully AIMS gave use the split ailerons as a resin conversion, so that made things easier. It was reissued as part of the 'Historic German Aircraft' set (#057140 in 2011 and was reissued just marked as the He 177A-5 (#03913) but still with the Fritz Xs in 2018, so it is still generally available.

• Revell
Heinkel He 177A-6 with Hs 293 (#04306) – In 2007 Revell updated the basic A-5 moulds to produce the 'what if' A-6 complete with three Hs 293s and the modified Heckstand with twin MG 151s. It was a bit of an odd choice and back-dating the kit to the A-3 would have probably been a better choice, but Luftwaffe 'What If?' has always had a huge following in the modelling community, so it sort of made sense. This version has been out of production for many years, so tends to command quite a high price second-hand nowadays.

• Sanger Engineering
Heinkel He 274 #N/K – This firm, which also traded as Elliott Models & Bristol Models may have produced this vac-

Revell #03913

Special Hobby #SH48062

formed kit, but we have never seen one, so its release is not confirmed.

• **Sanger Engineering [vac]**
Heinkel He 277 #N/K – Once again, this firm may have produced this vac-formed kit, but we have never seen one, so its release is not confirmed.

• **Vami Models/Dujin**
He 177B #N/K – Some sources list this Belgian firm as having produced a resin kit of the He 177B, but there are no other details and we have never seen anything further about it, so its release remains unconfirmed.

• **Vami Models/Dujin**
He 277 #N/K – Again, we have never seen anything further about this resin kit, so its release remains unconfirmed.

1/48th Scale

• **Combat Models**
He 177A-1 Grief #48-019 – This American firm produced this vac-formed kit in 1980, like all of their products you just got the basic main components, there were no detail parts, although Marine Air Products did do a resin and white-metal update set for it in the 1990s.

• **ID Models**
He 177A-1 #N/K – The release of this vac-formed kit from this British manufacturer is unconfirmed, although if it was release it would have just been the basic main components, the builder would have to add the rest from scratch.

• **Karo-As Modellbau**
He 177 Greif #AM-48.29 (1987-1996) – This German manufacturer is supposed to have released this vac-formed and resin kit at some stage in their 1987 to 1996 existence, but we have never seen an example so its release remains unconfirmed.

• **MPM Heinkel**
He 177A-5 Greif #48058 – This Czech manufacturer announced this kit in 2004, but it took until 2006 to actually be released. It was a typical limited-run injected kit with some resin detail parts. Like many, I have an example but have not got around to building it yet. Those who have built it, seem to find it typical of this type of kit and it is therefore very much aimed at the experienced modeller, as you are going to have to do a lot of test-fitting and adjusting before committing to cement. The end result is impressive though and the 'hi-Tech' (#48060) version released in 2007 and reissued in 2011, has additional resin detail parts that make it an even better option. It was also reissued with new decals as He 177A-5 'Captured Markings' (#48062) in 2013, even though it was originally announced back in 2007!

• **MPM Heinkel**
He 177A-3 #48063 – This was also announced in 2007, but was not actually released until 2010. It is based on the A-5 with all the required revisions to back-date it to this earlier version and, as with the A-5, it is intended for the more experienced modellers out there.

• **MPM/HML**
He 177 Greif #HML005 – This 'Hand-Made Limited' range from MPM offered some Luftwaffe types in 1/48th scale that no-one ever expected to be produced in anything other than vac-formed plastic. Each kit was made up of resin, white-metal and vac-formed plastic, the former being offered as glass-fibre mouldings for the main elements and traditional pure resin parts for the detail stuff, while the metal was used for things like the undercarriage and the vac-formed plastic for the clear parts. This kit was first announced in 1997, but not actually released until 1998. It was originally intended for release under the Classic Resin Airframes label in 1997, but that was renamed MPM/HML before this kit was released. Today this is very much a collector's item, as the MPM/Special Hobby version is a far easier option if you actually want to build it.

• **Pend Oreille Models**
He 177A-5 #4834 – This French manufacturer announced this kit first in 1998, but it was continually delayed before finally being scheduled for 2001/2002 release, but in the end, it was never actually produced.

• **R&D Replicas**
He 177 Greif #48.29 – This firm is supposed to have reissued the Karo-AS kit in the mid to late 1990s, but as that kit's release is not confirmed, so is this potential reissue.

• **Schmidt Vacu-Modellbau**
He 177 Greif #4809 (1984-2000) – This was the Combat Models vac-formed, this this firm reissued under the Blue Max label.

• **Special Hobby**
Heinkel He 177A-3 Greif #SH48210 – This was to be a reissue of the MPM (#48063) kit and it was announced in 2020, 2021 and 2022, then was noted as delayed, so still remains unreleased.

1/32nd Scale

• **Combat Models**
He 177 Grief #32-058 – This American firm produced this vac-formed kit in the 1990s, like all of their products you just got the basic main components, there were no detail parts, so the builder had to add these all from scratch.

Airfix #05009-2

Airfix #05009 (1986)

Airfix #05009 (1990)

Meng Models #003

MPM #48058 (2006)

MPM #48058

Revell #03913

Revell #04306

Revell #04616

Special Hobby #SH48062

Below is a list of all static scale construction kits produced to date of the Heinkel He 177, He 274 and He 277. This list is as comprehensive as possible, but if there are amendments or additions, please contact the author via the Valiant Wings Publishing address shown at the front of this title.

All are injection moulded plastic unless otherwise stated.

No Scale

- Meng Models Heinkel He 177 #MP-003S (2015) – *This was in the 'Meng Kids' series and these were unscaled caricatures of the real aircraft in a similar vein to the Hasegawa Egg Plane series*

1/144th or smaller

- Anigrand Craftworks [res] 1/144th Heinkel He 274 #AA-4102 (2019)
- Sanwa/Tokyo Plamo 1/435th Heinkel He 274 #522 (1950s-60s)

1/72nd Scale

- Airfix Heinkel He 177 #Patt. No.589 (1967) – Renumbered #05009-2 in 1973, #05009 in 1983, #905009 in 1985 and #05009 in 1986 and 1993
- Delvac Models [vac] Heinkel He 277A-5/V1 #N/K (2001->) – *Never released*
- Eidai (ex-Airfix) Heinkel He 177 #A-106 (late 1960s)
- Gunze-Sangyo (ex-Airfix) Heinkel He 177 #GX-203 (early 80s)
- MPC (ex-Airfix) Heinkel He 177 #1200 (1965-1985) Also #2-1200, 2-0303 & 2-2502
- Plasty Modelle (ex-Airfix) He 177 #9 (mid-50s – early 70s)
- Revell Heinkel He 177A-5 & Fritz X #04616 (2000) – Reissued as part of the 'Historic German Aircraft' set #05714 in 2011
- Revell Heinkel He 177A-5 #03913 (2018)
- Revell Heinkel He 177A-6 with Hs 293 #04306 (2007)
- Sanger Engineering [vac] Heinkel He 274 #N/K – *Also traded as Elliott Models & Bristol Models*
- Sanger Engineering [vac] Heinkel He 277 #N/K – *Also traded as Elliott Models & Bristol Models*
- Vami Models/Dujin [res] He 177B #N/K – *Release not confirmed*
- Vami Models/Dujin [res] He 277 #N/K – *Release not confirmed*

1/48th Scale

- Combat Models [vac] He 177A-1 Grief #48-019 (1980)
- ID Models [vac] He 177A-1 #N/K
- Karo-As Modellbau [vac/res] He 177 Greif #AM-48.29 (1987-1996) – *Release not confirmed*
- MPM Heinkel He 177A-5 Greif #48058 (Announced 2004, released 2006)
- MPM Heinkel He 177A-5 Greif 'Hi-tech' #48060 (2007) – Reissued, same kit number, 2011
- MPM Heinkel He 177A-5 'Captured Markings' #48062 (Announced 2007, not released, reconfirmed and released in 2013)
- MPM Heinkel He 177A-3 #48063 (Announced 2007, released 2010)
- MPM/HML [res/mtl/vac] He 177 Greif #HML005 (1997, not actually released until 1998) – *Originally intended for released under the Classic Resin Airframes label in 1997, but that was renamed MPM/HML before this kit was released*
- Pend Oreille Models [res] He 177A-5 #4834 – *Announced in 1998 and eventually scheduled for 2001/2002 release but never actually produced*
- R&D Replicas (ex-Karo-As) [vac/res] He 177 Greif #48.29 (1994-1999) – *Not confirmed this was actually released*
- Schmidt Vacu-Modellbau, (ex-Combat Models) [vac] Heinkel He 177 Greif #4809 (1984-2000) – *Issued under their Blue Max label*
- Special Hobby (ex-MPM) Heinkel He 177A-3 Greif #SH48210 (Announced 2020, not released, announced again 2021, not released, announced again 2022, not released to date)

1/32nd Scale

- Combat Models [vac] He 177 Grief #32-058

Notes

inj – Injection moulded plastic
ltd inj – Limited-run injection moulded plastic
pe – Photo-etched metal
res – Resin
vac – Vacuum-formed Plastic
3dpr – 3D Printed Resin
(1999) – Denotes date the kit was released
(1994->) – Dates denote start/finish of firm's activities, the exact date of release of this kit is however unknown
ex- – Denotes the tooling originated with another firm, the original tool maker is noted after the '-'the original tool maker is noted after the '-'

He 177A-1, E8-G? of KG 50 having the starboard propeller changed

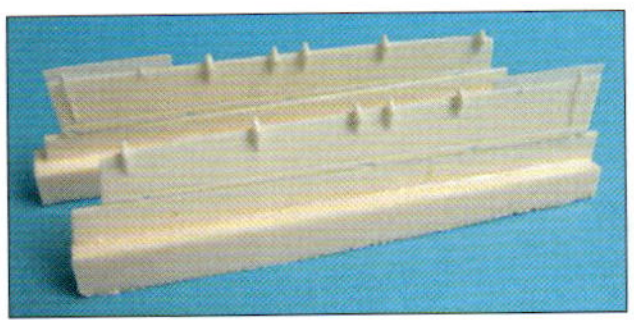

AIMS #72P002

Antares Models #ANT-7209

Brengun #BRL72215

CMK #4174

CMK #4176

Eduard #BIG4881

Eduard #FE365

Eduard #SS288

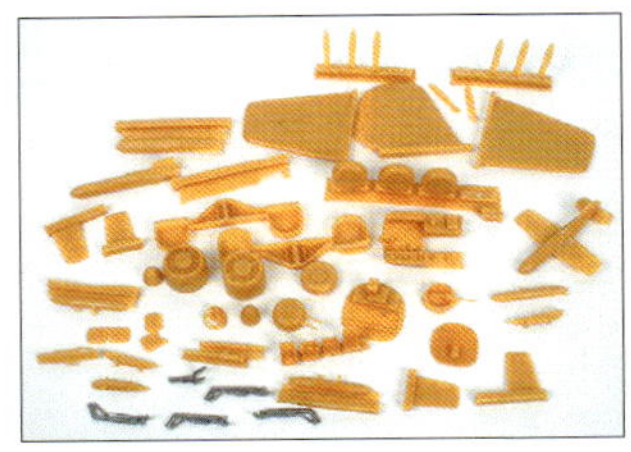

Marine Air Products 48th He 177 update for Combat Models kit

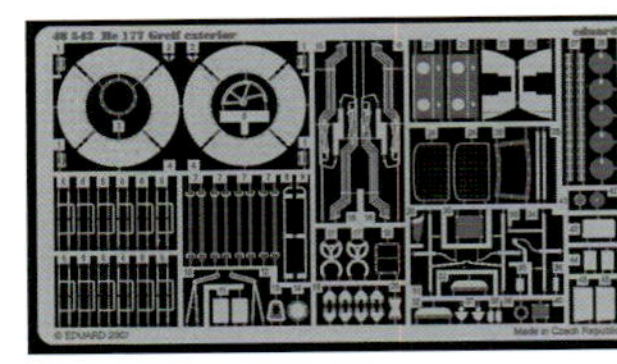

Eduard #48543

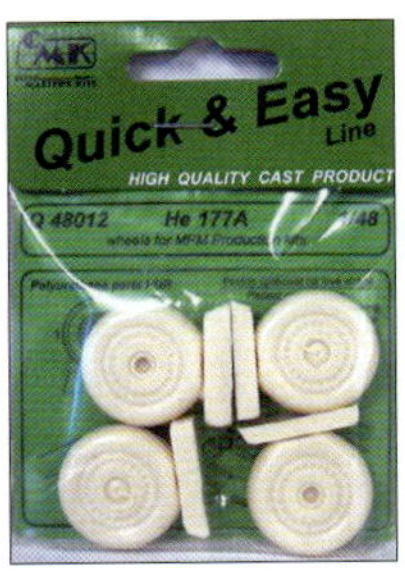

Quick & Easy #Q48012

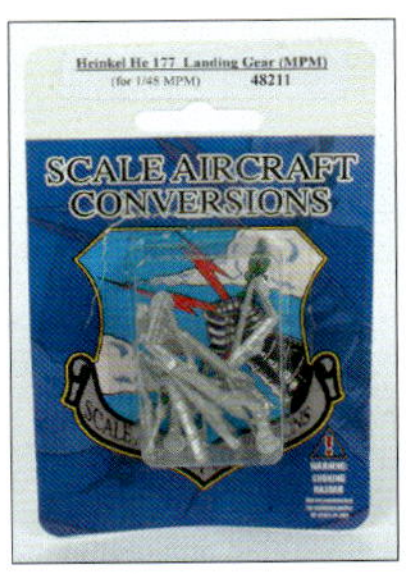

Scale Aircraft Conversions #48211

Squadron #9187

Montex #MM48244 (instructions)

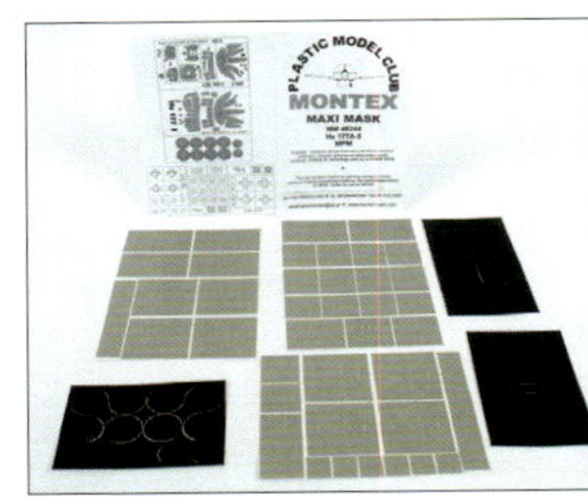

Montex #MM48244

As there are relatively few accessories, decals and masks for the Heinkel He 177, He 274 or He 277 we thought it best to combine these in one Appendix. Below therefore is a list of all accessories, decals and paint masks for static scale construction kits produced to date for the type. This list is as comprehensive as possible, but if there are amendments or additions, please contact the author via the Valiant Wings Publishing address shown at the front of this title.

Accessories

1/72nd

- AIMS [res] He 177A-3 lower ailerons #72P002 {Revell}
- Aerolis [res] Hydraulische Drehlafette HD 151Z #AEC004
- Airwaves [[e] He 177 Detail Set #AC72126 {Airfix}
- Antares [res]} He 277 Conversion #ANT-7209 {Revell He 177A-6}
- Avia Equipage Auto [res/rb] He 177 Wheel Set #72055
- Bird Models [res/mtl] He 177A-1/U2 Zerstörer Conversion #720146 {Revell or Airfix kits}
- Bird Models [res/mtl/vac] He 274A-01 Conversion #720140 {Revell or Airfix He 177A-5 kits}
- Bird Models [res/mtl/vac] He 277 V3 Conversion #720123 {Revell or Airfix kits}
- Bird Models [res/mtl/vac] He 277 V4 Conversion #720112 {Revell or Airfix kits}
- Bird Models [res/mtl/vac] He 277B-6/R2 Conversion #720157 {Revell He 177A kit}
- Bird Models [res/mtl/vac] He 277C-1 mit Daimler-Benz DB604 Conversion #720150 {Revell He 177A-5 kit}
- Brengun [pe] He 177 Detail Set #BRL72215 {Revell}
- CMK [res] He 177 Engine Set (DB610) #7060 {Revell} – *Inc. horizontal stabiliser*
- CMK [res] He 177 Exterior Set #7061 {Revell}
- CMK [res] He 177 Undercarriage Set #7062 {Revell}
- Eduard [pe] He 177 Detail Set #72357 {Revell}
- Eduard [pe] He 177 with HS 293 'Zoom' Detail Set #SS288 {Revell}
- Eduard [pe] He 177 with HS 293 Detail Set #73288 {Revell}
- Extratech [pe] He 177 Detail Set #EX72061 {Airfix}
- Extratech [pe] He 177A-3 Detail Set #EX72122 {Revell}
- Falcon [vac] Luftwaffe Bombers WWII, Clear-Vax Set No.9 – *Included canopy for Airfix kit*
- Falcon [vac] Luftwaffe WWII Part 7, Clear-Vax Set No.42 – *Included canopy for Revell kit*
- Kora Models [res] He 177A Wheels #D7298
- Kora Models [res] PC 1400 Fritz X with ETC racks #DS7217 {Revell He 177A-5}
- Scale Aircraft Conversions [wm] He 177 Landing Gear #72030 {Revell}
- Schatton Modellbau [res/br] He 177 Großzerstörer Conversion #7271{Revell}
- Schatton Modellbau [res/br] He 177A-6/R1 Conversion #7261{Revell}
- Squadron [vac] He 177 Canopy #9187 {Revell}
- Swan Model Engineering [ex-Toad Resin] He 277 Conversion #SME10 {Airfix He 177 kit} – *Announced late 1990s, never released*
- Toad Resin [res/mtl/vac] He 277 Conversion #N/K {Airfix He 177 kit}
- White Cat Models [res/mtl/dec] He 177 Fernmistel Conversion #WCM7204 {Revell}

1/48th

- CMK [res] He 177A Armament Set #4175 {MPM/Special Hobby}
- CMK [res] He 177A Engine Set #4174 {MPM/Special Hobby}
- CMK [res] He 177A Undercarriage Set #4176 {MPM/Special Hobby}
- Eduard [pe/ma] He 177 Big ED Detail & Mask Set #BIG4881 {MPM/Special Hobby}
- Eduard [pe] He 177 Exterior Detail Set #48543 {MPM/Special Hobby}
- Eduard [pe] He 177 Interior Detail Set #49365 {MPM/Special Hobby}
- Eduard [pe] He 177 Interior 'Zoom' Detail Set #FE365 {MPM/Special Hobby}
- Eduard [pe] He 177 Seat Belts #49035 {MPM/Special Hobby}
- Loon Models [res] He 177 External Bomb Racks (3) with open & closed sway braces #LO48222 {MPM/Special Hobby}
- Loon Models [res] He 177 Properly Bulged Rear Bomb Bat & Lower Rear Fuselage #LO48027 {MPM/Special Hobby}
- Nautilus Models ([wn] He 177 Wing Brace #48-803 {MPM/Special Hobby}
- Quick & Easy [res] He 177AWheels #Q48012 {MPM/Special Hobby}
- Scale Aircraft Conversions [wm] He 177 Landing Gear #48211 {Rewvell}

1/32nd

- Master [br/res] 30mm MK 103 Cannon Barrels and Flash Eliminators #AM-32-106

Notes

3dp – 3D Printed
br – Brass
brz – Bronze
fb – Fabric
ma – Die-cut Self-adhesive Paint Masks [tape]
pa – Paper (laser-cut)
pe – Photo-etched Brass
PP – Pre-painted (photo-etched)
res – Resin
SA – Self-adhesive
vac – Vacuum-formed Plastic
vma – Vinyl Self-adhesive Paint Masks
wm – White-metal (including Pewter)
{Academy} – Denotes the kit for which the set is intended

Decals

1/144th

Peddinghaus-Decals
#EP1615 Deutsche Luftwaffe Bombers No.1
Inc.
- He 177A-5, TM+IF. Hexengrund, 1944

1/72nd

AIMS
#72D017 Heinkel He 177A-3 & A-5
- He 177A-3, 6N+SK, 'Susi', 2./KG 100, France, 1944
- He 177A-3, 6N+EK, 'Edith', 2./KG 100, captured at Châteaudun, 1944
- He 177A-3, 6N+HK, 'Helga', 2./KG 100, France, 1944
- He 177A-3, W/Nr.332206, 5J+KK, flown by Lt. Goetze, 2./KG 4, October 1943
- He 177A-3, V4+HP, 6./KG 1 Hindenburg
- He 177A-5, W/Nr.550316, found abandoned 1945
- He 177A-5, W/Nr.550215, F8+FH, 1./KG 40, Bordeaux-Mérignac, France, June 1944
- He 177A-5, W/Nr.550131, 6N+DN, 5./KG 100, flown by Fw. Niederstadt, Aalborg, 1945

#72D031 Heinkel He 177A-3
- He 177A-3, 6N+EK, 'Edith', 2./KG 100, captured at Châteaudun, 1944
- He 177A-3, 6N+HK, 'Helga', 2./KG 100, France, 1944
- He 177A-3, 6N+SK, 'Susi', 2./KG 100, France, 1944
- He 177A-3, W/Nr.332206, 5J+KK, flown by Lt. Goetze, 2./KG 4, October 1943
- He 177A-3, V4+HP, 6./KG 1 Hindenburg

Eagle Strike
#72040 He 177 Greif Part I
- He 177A-3, 6N+SK, 'Susy', 2./KG 1 Hindenburg, Châteaudun, 1944
- He 177A-3, 6N+HK, 2./KG 100, Châteaudun, 1944
- He 177A-3, V4+AS, 5./KG 1 Hindenburg, 1944
- He 177A-5, TM+IU, Niemcy, France, 1944
- He 177A-5, V4+CA, flown by Capt. Otto Edler von Ballasko, 1./KG 1 Hindenburg, Prowehren, 1944
- He 177A-5, V4+AA, 3./KG 1 Hindenburg, 1944

#72041 He 177 Greif Part II
- He 177A-3, 6N+EK, 'Edith', 2./KG 100, Châteaudun, France, 1944
- He 177A-3, 5J+QK, 2./KG 4, Rennes, France, April 1944
- He 177A-3, F8+FM, 2./KG 40, Bordeaux-Mérignac, France, 1944
- He 177A-5, W/Nr.550202, TM+IF, Gotenhaven-Hexengrund, 1944
- He 177A-5, W/Nr.550002, KM+TB, Praha-Kbely, 1945
- He 177A-5, W/Nr.550024, 6N+BN, 5./KG 100, 1944

Esci
#27 He 177 & He 219
Inc.
- He 177A-5, KD+NL
- He 177A-5, 8N+SK
- He 177A-5, V4+AA, KG 1 Hindenburg, Eastern Front

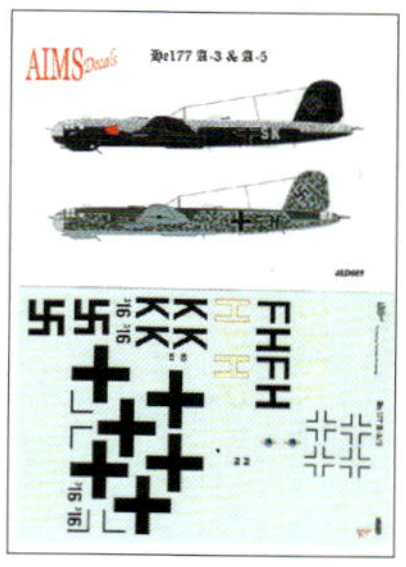
AIMS #48D009

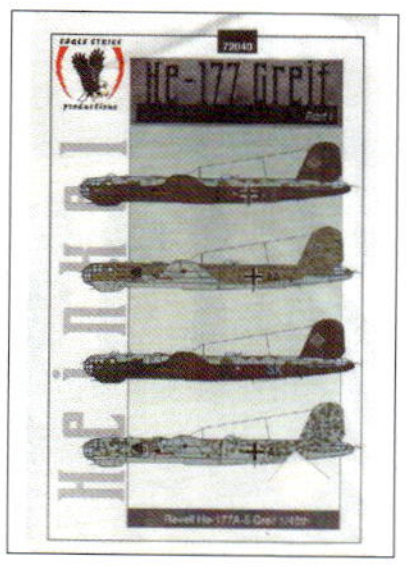
Eagle Strike #72040

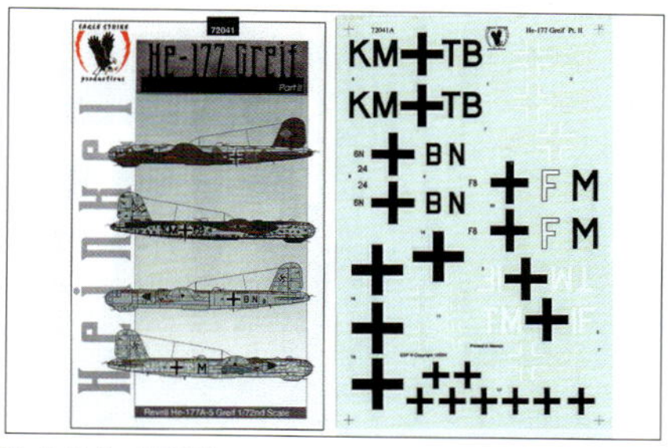
Eagle Strike #72041

AIMS #72D031

Owl Decals
#OWLD72005 Die Nachtbomber W.Nr 001
Inc.
- He 177A-5, W/Nr.550077, F8+AN, flown by Hptm. Stolle, 2./KG 40, August 1944

#OWLDS72102He 177A-5
- He 177A-5, W/Nr.550077, F8+AN, 2./KG 40

Peddinghaus-Decals
#EP940 He 177A-5
- He 177A-5, W/Nr.550202, TM+IF, Gotenhaven-Hexengrund, 1944

#722362 He 177A-5
- He 177A-5, F8+CM, II./KG 40, Bordeaux-Merignac, France

#EP2364 He 177A-5
- He 177A-5, 6N+PP, IKG 100/I/KG 6, Staffel 2, Gruppe 4, Operation Steinbock

#EP2800 He 177A-3
- He 177A-3, 5N+HK, 2./KG 100, Châteaudun, France, 1944

#EP2801 He 177A-5
- He 177A-5, F8+FH, 1./KG 40, Châteaudun, France, January 1944

Tally Ho! (Canada)
#7207 He 177A-5
- He 177A-5, F8+DM, 4./KG 40
- He 177A-5, 6N+HM, 4./KG 100
- He 177A-5, V4+LN, 5./KG 1
- He 177A-5, 6N+SK, 2./KG 100
- He 177A-5, 6N+HL, 3./KG 100

1/48th

AIMS
#48D009 Heinkel He 177A-3 & A-5
- He 177A-3, 6N+EK, 'Edith', 2./KG 100, captured at Châteaudun, 1944

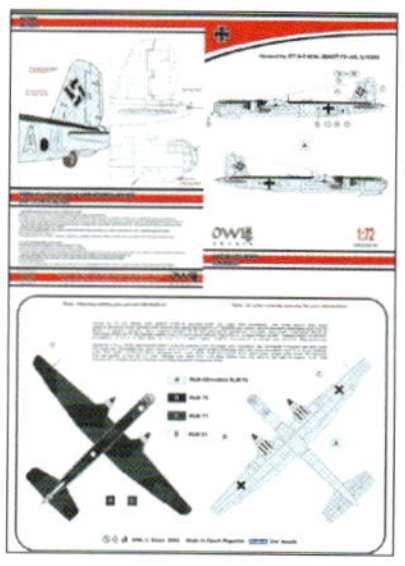
Owl Decals #OWLDS72102

- He 177A-3, 6N+HK, 'Helga', 2./KG 100, France, 1944
- He 177A-3, 6N+SK, 'Susi', 2./KG 100, France, 1944
- He 177A-3, W/Nr.332206, 5J+KK, flown by Lt. Goetze, 2./KG 4, October 1943
- He 177A-3, V4+HP, 6./KG 1 Hindenburg
- He 177A-5, W/Nr.550316
- He 177A-5, W/Nr.550215, F8+FH, 1./KG 40, Bordeaux-Mérignac, France, June 1944

Owl Decals
#OWL 48005 Die Nachtbomber W.Nr 001
Inc.
- He 177A-5, W/Nr.550077, F8+AN, flown by Hptm. Stolle, 2./KG 40, August 1944

Peddinghaus-Decals
#EP2363 He 177A-5
- He 177A-5, F8+CM, II./KG 40, Bordeaux-Merignac

Masks

1/72nd

- Eduard [vma] He 177 Canopy & Wheel Masks #XS0948 {Revell}
- Eduard [ma] He 177 Canopy & Wheel Masks #CX038 {Revell}
- Eduard [vma] He 177 National Insignia Masks #XS538 {Revell}
- LF Models [vma] He 177A-3 Camouflage Pattern Masks #M7292
- LF Models [vma] He 177A-5 Camouflage Pattern Masks #M7293
- Montex [vma] He 177A-5 Canopy & Wheel Masks #SM72022 {Revell}
- Montex [vma] He 177A-5 Canopy, Wheel & Kit Marking Masks #MM72022 {Revell}
- Pmask [vma] He 177A-5 Canopy & Wheel Masks #PK72138 {Revell}

1/48th

- Eduard [ma] He 177 Canopy & Wheel Masks #EX186 {MPM/Special Hobby}
- LF Models [vma] He 177A-3 Camouflage Pattern Masks #M4885 {MPM/Special Hobby}
- LF Models [vma] He 177A-5 Camouflage Pattern Masks #M4886 {MPM/Special Hobby}
- Montex [vma] He 177A-5 Canopy & Wheel Masks #SM48244 {MPM}
- Montex [vma] He 177A-5 Canopy, Wheel & Kit Marking Masks #MM48244 {MPM}

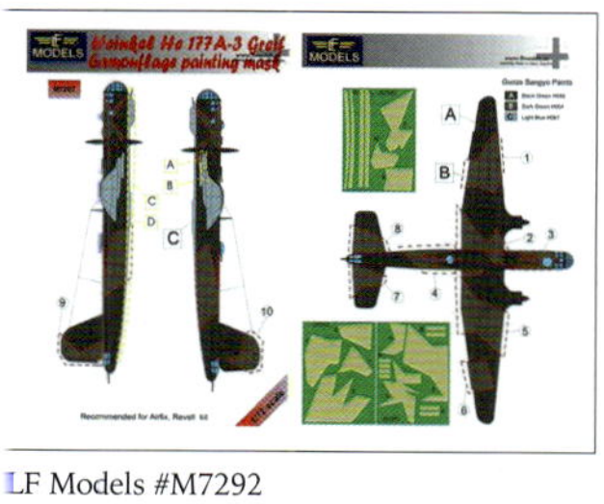
LF Models #M7292

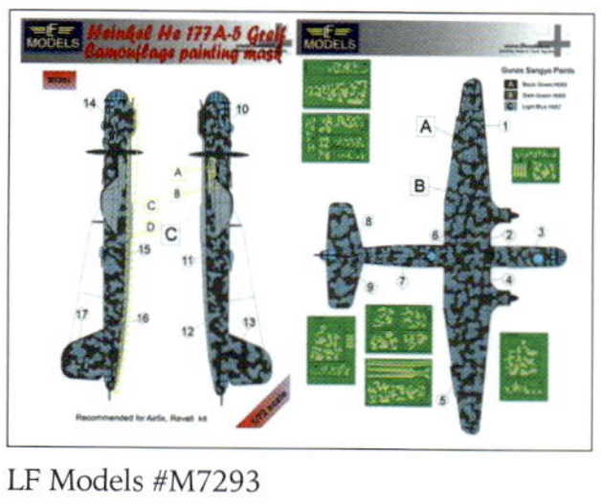
LF Models #M7293

Montex #MM72022

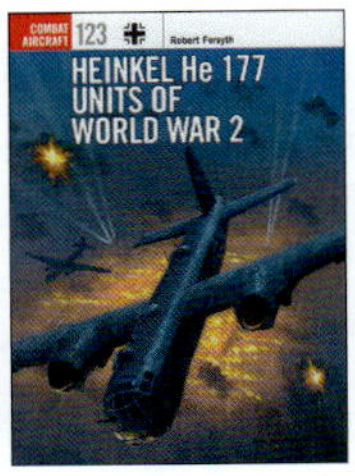

The list of Heinkel He 177, He 274 and He 277 related publications below is as comprehensive as possible, but there are bound to be omissions so if you have amendments or additions, please contact the author via the Valiant Wings Publishing address shown at the front of this title.

Official Documents

- He 177A-0, Flugzeug-Handbuch, 1941
- He 177A-0, Bedienungsvorschrift-Fl, 1941
- He 177A-1, Flugzeug-Handbuch, D(Luft)T 2177 A-1, 1943
- He 177A-1, Exerzierkarte LDvT2177 A/Fl, 1944
- He 177A-3, Flugzeug-Handbuch. 1943
- He 177A-3, Bedienungsvorschrift/Fl, 1943
- He 177A-5, Ersatzteilliste, 1944

Publications

- Aircraft of World War II by C. Chant (Dempsey Parr, 1999)
- Aufklärer: Luftwaffe Reconnaissance Aircraft & Units 1935-1945 by D. Wadman, J. Bradley & B. Ketley (Hikoki Publications1997 ISBN: 0-9519899-8-7)
- Bomber Units of the Luftwaffe 1933-1945 Vol.2 by H.L. de Zeng IV & D.G. Stankey (Classic Publications 2008 ISBN: 978-1-903223-87-1)
- Camouflage & Markings of the Luftwaffe Aircraft Vol.2 Night Fighters, Bombers & Others, Model Art Special No.356 (Model Art Co., Ltd 1990)
- Cockpit Profile No.6 – Deutsche Flugzeugcockpits und Instrumentenbretter by P.W. Cohausz (Flugzeug Publikations GmbH 2000)
- Colours of the Luftwaffe by S.W. Parry & F.L. Martshall (Clifford Frost Ltd 1987 ISBN: 1-8700666-03-0)
- Cutaway Aircraft of World War Two [He 177A-5/R2] (Argus Books 1989, ISBN:0-85242-993-2)
- Das Kampfflugzeug Heinkel He 177 und seine Weiterentwicklungen by Helmut Stubner (Eurodoc.Corporation ©2008 ISBN: 978-3-9502493-0-9)
- Das Kampfflugzeug Heinkel He 177 by Hans-Jürgen Becker, Jet & Prop Typen-Chronik Special Nr.2 (VDM Heinz Nickel Verlag ©2001 ISBN: 978-3-925480-49-2)
- Eagles of the Third Reich: Hitler's Luftwaffe by S.W. Mitcham (Airlife Publishing Ltd 1988/Guild Publishing Ltd 1989)
- German Aircraft of the Second World War by J.R. Smith & A.L. Kay (Putnam, 1972)
- German Air Projects 1935-1945 Vol.3 by M. Rys (Mushroom Model Publications 2007 ISBN: 978-83-89450-30-2)
- German Anti-Tank Aircraft by J. Dressel & M. Griehl (Schiffer ISBN: 0-88740-520-7)
- German Bombers of World War Two Volume Two by Alfred Price
- German Heavy Bombers by M. Griehl & J. Dressel (Schiffer ISBN: 0-88740-670-X)
- He 177 Greif: Design, Production & Operations by T. Dinan (Casemate ©2010 ISBN: 978-91-85657-97-1)
- He 177 Greif: Design, Production & Operations by T. Dinan (Leandoer Förlag ©2016 ISBN: 978-91-85657-97-1)
- He 177 Greif by J. Ledwoch, Militaria No.46 (Wydawnictwo Militaria 1997 ISBN: 83-86209-83-66)
- Heinkel Combat Aircraft by M. Griehl (Arms & Armour Press 1992 ISBN: 1-85409-025-9)
- Heinkel He 177 by R.S. Hirsch & U. Feist, Aero Series No.13 (Aero Publishing Inc 1967)
- Heinkel He 177 by Alfred Price, Profile No.234 (Profile Publications 1972)
- Heinkel He 177 by K. Darling, Warpaint No. 33 (Hall Park Books 2001 ISBN: 9780888-8802-30-4)
- Heinke He 177, Famous Airplanes of the World No.192 (Bunrin-Do ©2019, ISBN: 978-4-89319-297-4)
- Heinkel He 177 Greif by J.R. Smith & E.J. Creek (Classic Publications 2009 ISBN: 978-1-903223-93-2)
- Heinkel He 177 Greif by M. Griehl, WWII Combat Aircraft Photo Archive No.8 (AirDOC Publishing 2009 ISBN: 978-3-935687-47-8)
- Heinkel He 177 Units of World War 2 by Robert Forsyth, Combat Aircraft No.123 (Osprey Publications ©2018 ISBN: 978-1472820396)
- Heinkel He 177, 277 & 274 Eine luftfahrtheschichtliche Dokumenation by Manfred Griehl and Joachim Dressel (Motorbuch-Verlag ©1989 ISBN: 978-3-613-01299-8)
- Heinkel He 177, 277 & 274 by Manfred Griehl and Joachim Dressel (Airlife Publishing Ltd 1998 ISBN: 1-85310-364-0) – This was the English translation of the German-language title
- Heinkel He 274 et Junkers Ju 488 Les bombardiers stratégiques allemands développés en France durant l'occupation by Alain March, Jean-Christophe Carbonel (Artipresse 2011 ISBN: 978-2-919231-02-7)
- International Air Power Review Volume 11 (AIRtime Publishing Inc. 2004 ISBN: 1-880588-61-7/1-880588-60-9)
- Kampfflieger – Bombers of the Luftwaffe Summer 1943 – May 1945 by N. Beale (Classic Publications 2005 ISBN: 1-903223-50-4)
- Luftahrt International No. 3 May-June 1974 [He 177 Exhaust Dampers]
- Luftfahrt International No.13, Jan-Feb 1976 [FDL-B 131/1A & 131/2A Remote Turrets]
- Luftfahrt International No.14, Mar/April 1976 [DFS towed fuel tank]
- Luftwaffe at War, German Elite Pathfinders KG 100 in Action, by Manfred Griehl
- Luftwaffe at War 'German Bombers Over England 1940 – 1944' by Manfred Griehl (PSL Ltd)
- Luftwaffe Bombers In Action (Squadron/Signal Publications)
- Luftwaffe Colours 1935-1945 by M. Ullmann (Hikoki Publications Ltd 2002/Crécy Publishing Ltd 2008 ISBN: 9-781902-109077)
- Luftwaffe in World War II Part 1, Aero Pictorials 1 (Aero Publishers Inc. 1968)
- Luftwaffe in World War II Part 2, Aero Pictorials 5 (Aero Publishers Inc. 1979 ISBN: 8168-0316-1) – V.good armament photos
- Luftwaffe in World War II Part 3, Aero Pictorials 6 (Aero Publishers Inc. 1980 ISBN: 0-8168-0320-X)
- Lufwaffe Warbirds Photo Album Vol.1, Tank Magazine Special Issue (Delta Publishing 1992 ISSN: 05706-6)
- Lufwaffe Warbirds Photo Album Vol.5, Tank Magazine Special Issue (Delta Publishing 1994)
- Lufwaffe Warbirds Photo Album Vol.6, Ground Power Special Issue (Delta Publishing 1994)
- Photo Archive 1 – Luftwaffe Camouflage & Markings 1933-1945 by K.A. Merrick, E.J. Creek & B. Green (Midland Publishing 2007 ISBN: 1-85780-275-6)
- Sea Eagles Volume 2 by C. Goss (Classic Publications 2007 ISBN: 1-903223-56-3)
- Secret German Aircraft Projects of 1945 (Toros Publications 1997) – First published as 'Paper Planes of the Third Reich' by them in 1996
- The Luftwaffe In Camera 1939-1942 by A. Price (Budding Books 2000 ISBN: 1-84015-111-0)
- The Secret Years: Flight Testing at Boscombe Down 1939-1945 by T. Mason (Hikoki Publications 1998 ISBN: 1-951899-9-5)
- The Warplanes of the Third Reich by William Green (Macdonald & Co Ltd, 1970)
- War Prizes: The Album by P. Butler (Midland Publishing 2006 ISBN: 1-85780-244-6)
- Wings of the Black Cross No.3 by M. Proulx (Eagle Editions Ltd 2006 ISBN:0-9761-034-9-4)
- Wings of the Luftwaffe by Capt. Eric Brown (Airlife Publishing Ltd 1987, 1993 & 2000 ISBN: 1-85310-413-2)
- WWII Luftwaffe Heinkel He 177 'Greif by Takao Kunie, Graphic Action Series (Bunrin-Do ©2007 ISBN: 978-4-89319-151-9)

Periodicals & Part-works

- Aeroplane Monthly, July 1996 & September 2006
- Aeroplane Spotter 3rd May 1945
- Air Pictorial November 1959
- Airplane No.162
- Flight 10th May 1945
- IPMS/UK Magazine, March 1970
- Maquettes Plastique Magazine No.112
- Mini Replika No.29 1/2003
- RAF Flying Review, April 1957
- Replic Nos.111 (November 2000), 116 (April 2001) & 210 (February 2009)
- Scale Aircraft Modelling Vol.22 No.12 February 2001
- Scale Models, Vol.5 No.57 June 1974
- Wings, Vol.2 No.4 August 1974
- Wing Masters No.21 March-April 2001